European Drug Policies

The drug control regime established by the international community has not succeeded in curbing either the demand for, or the offer of, narcotics. But, despite a series of developments in the Americas – including the legalisation of cannabis in Uruguay and in several states in the United States of America – there is still little support in Europe for repealing drug prohibition laws. Nevertheless, a gradual policy convergence reveals the emergence of a European model favouring public health strategies over a strictly penal approach to combatting drugs, while growing transnational support for legalisation indicates the persistence of an alternative paradigm for drug policy. This book examines the various influences on drug policies in Europe, as grassroots movements, NGO networks, private foundations and academic research centres increasingly confront the prevailing discourses of drug prohibition. Pursuing an interdisciplinary approach and bringing together legal scholars, social scientists and practitioners, it provides a comprehensive and critical assessment of drug policy reform in Europe.

Renaud Colson is Associate Professor at the Law & Political Science Faculty of the University of Nantes.

Henri Bergeron is Research Fellow at the Centre for Sociology of Organisations, Sciences Po, CNRS, scientific coordinator of the Chair in Health Studies, and director of the Health Research Programme at the LIEPP (LABEX), Sciences Po.

European Drug Policies

The Ways of Reform

Edited by
Renaud Colson and Henri Bergeron

a GlassHouse Book

First published 2017
by Routledge
2 Park Square, Milton Park, Abingdon, Oxon OX14 4RN

and by Routledge
711 Third Avenue, New York, NY 10017

a GlassHouse book

Routledge is an imprint of the Taylor & Francis Group, an informa business

© 2017 selection and editorial matter, Renaud Colson and Henri Bergeron; individual chapters, the contributors

The right of Renaud Colson and Henri Bergeron to be identified as the authors of the editorial material, and of the authors for their individual chapters, has been asserted in accordance with sections 77 and 78 of the Copyright, Designs and Patents Act 1988.

All rights reserved. No part of this book may be reprinted or reproduced or utilised in any form or by any electronic, mechanical, or other means, now known or hereafter invented, including photocopying and recording, or in any information storage or retrieval system, without permission in writing from the publishers.

Trademark notice: Product or corporate names may be trademarks or registered trademarks, and are used only for identification and explanation without intent to infringe.

British Library Cataloguing in Publication Data
A catalogue record for this book is available from the British Library

Library of Congress Cataloging in Publication Data
Names: Colson, Renaud, editor. | Bergeron, Henri, editor.
Title: European drug policies : the ways of reform / edited by Renaud Colson and Henri Bergeron.
Description: New York : Routledge, 2017. | Includes bibliographical references and index.
Identifiers: LCCN 2016030753 | ISBN 9781138915206 (hbk) | ISBN 9781315690384 (ebk)
Subjects: LCSH: Drug control--Europe. | Narcotic laws--Europe. | Drugs of abuse--Europe.
Classification: LCC HV5840.E8 E9394 1996 | DDC 364.1/77094--dc23
LC record available at https://lccn.loc.gov/2016030753

ISBN: 978-1-138-91520-6 (hbk)
ISBN: 978-1-315-69038-4 (ebk)

Typeset in Baskerville
by Taylor & Francis Books

Printed and bound by CPI Group (UK) Ltd, Croydon, CR0 4YY

Contents

List of illustrations	vii
List of contributors	ix
Acknowledgements	xvii
Foreword	xix

European drug policies in context	1
HENRI BERGERON AND RENAUD COLSON	

PART I
Regional dimensions of European drug policies   11

1	The politics of expertise and EU drug policy	13
	MARTIN ELVINS	
2	Pathways to integration of European drug policy	27
	CAROLINE CHATWIN	
3	The soft power of the European Monitoring Centre for Drugs and Drug Addiction	40
	HENRI BERGERON	

PART II
Domestic drug policies in Europe   57

4	Belgian drug policy	59
	CHRISTINE GUILLAIN	
5	Danish drug policy	73
	ESBEN HOUBORG	
6	French drug policy	87
	IVANA OBRADOVIC	

vi Contents

7 German drug policy   100
TILMANN HOLZER

8 Italian drug policy   114
GRAZIA ZUFFA

9 Drug policy in the Netherlands   128
JEAN-PAUL C. GRUND AND JOOST J. BREEKSEMA

10 Polish drug policy   149
KASIA MALINOWSKA

11 Portuguese drug policy   164
CAITLIN HUGHES

12 Spanish drug policy   182
CRISTINA DÍAZ GÓMEZ AND EMILIANO MARTÍN GONZÁLEZ

13 Swedish drug policy   195
JOHAN EDMAN

14 Swiss drug policy   206
FRANK ZOBEL

15 Drug policy in the United Kingdom   217
SUSANNE MACGREGOR

PART III
Trends and prospects in European drug policies   239

16 Changing paradigms in drug policies in EU Member States: from
digression to convergence   241
FRANZ TRAUTMANN

17 The changing face of harm reduction in Europe   254
DAGMAR HEDRICH AND ALESSANDRO PIRONA

18 Legal responses to drug possession in Europe: from crime to
public health   272
BRENDAN HUGHES

19 Cannabis social clubs in Europe: prospects and limits   285
TOM DECORTE AND MAFALDA PARDAL

Index   300

Illustrations

Figures

10.1	Drug possession arrests in Poland, 1999–2007	157
12.1	Prisons providing therapy for drug users	183
17.1	Year of introduction of OST and NSPs in EU countries	257
17.2	Estimated number of clients receiving opioid substitution treatment in the EU (EU15 and EU13)	259
17.3	Number of problem opioid users in opioid substitution treatment as a percentage of the estimated number of problem opioid users, 2013 or most recent year available	262

Tables

9.1	Dutch coffee shop criteria	133
9.2	Outcomes of Dutch drug policy	140
11.1	Timeline of key events leading to the Portuguese decriminalisation of illicit drugs	166
12.1	System of penalties for drug related offences	190
15.1	Timeline of major legislation and policies	218
15.2	Drugs classification system under the MDA	228

Boxes

Main drivers in Spain for the counter-reforms of the 1990s	186
The development of Cannabis Social Clubs (CSC) under the umbrella of 'shared drug use'	191

Contributors

Henri Bergeron is a CNRS Research Fellow at the Centre for Sociology of Organisations (Sciences Po), co-director of the Health Department of the Interdisciplinary Centre for the Evaluation of Public Policies (Centre of Excellence – LABEX), and scientific coordinator of the Chair in Health Studies – Sciences Po. He is also the director of the Master on 'Organisational Behaviour and Human Resources' at Sciences Po and the scientific director of the Global Health Policy track at Sciences Po's School of Public Affairs. He conducts research on public health, healthcare policy and changes in medical practice through the study of various subjects: illegal drugs, alcohol, obesity and cancer. His recent books include *Drugs and Culture. Knowledge, Consumption and Policy* (Ashgate, 2011, with Geoffrey Hunt and Maitena Milhet), *Sociologie politique de la santé* (PUF, 2014, with Patrick Castel), *Les drogues face au droit* (PUF, 2015, with Renaud Colson).

Joost J. Breeksema works as an independent drug policy researcher and is currently working in the harm reduction field for the Mainline Foundation. As president of the Dutch OPEN Foundation he organises academic conferences and promotes scientific research into psychedelic substances in the Netherlands and beyond. Among his recent publications are 'The Beneficial Effects of Psychedelics, with a Special Focus on Addictions' (*Current Drug Abuse Reviews*, 2014, with Rudie Kortekaas) and *Coffee Shops and Compromise: Separated Illicit Drug Markets in the Netherlands* (Open Society Foundations, 2013, with Jean-Paul Grund).

Caroline Chatwin is Senior Lecturer in Criminology at the University of Kent. She has more than 10 years' experience researching European drug policy and has published a research monograph on this subject; *Drug Policy Harmonization and the European Union* (Palgrave Macmillan, 2011). More recently, she has worked as an advisor on European drug policy to the House of Lords and has participated in a special project on 'Improving Global Drug Policy' sponsored by the Brookings Institute. Her latest work examines the contribution that European drug policy can make to recent discussions on global drug policy reform.

Renaud Colson is Associate Professor at the Law and Political Science Faculty of the University of Nantes and Honorary Lecturer at Cardiff University. He

x List of contributors

was previously British Academy Visiting Fellow at Cardiff University and Marie Curie Fellow at the European University Institute (Florence). He has written on a variety of subjects including comparative law, European law, drugs law and criminology. His most recent books are *Les drogues face au droit* (PUF, 2015, with Henri Bergeron) and *EU Criminal Justice and the Challenges of Diversity: Legal Cultures in the Area of Freedom, Security and Justice* (Cambridge University Press, 2016, with Stewart Field).

Tom Decorte is Professor of Criminology at Ghent University (Belgium) where he is the director of the Institute for Social Drug Research (ISD). He has co-founded the *Global Cannabis Cultivation Research Consortium* (GCCRC) and is currently trustee of the Board of the *European Society for Social Drug Research* (ESSD) and of the *International Society for the Study of Drug Policy* (ISSDP). Tom Decorte has published widely on patterns of substance use, on the supply side of cannabis markets, and on the development and implementation of local monitoring systems of drug policies. His recent publications include 'The Globalisation of Cannabis Cultivation: A Growing Challenge' (*International Journal of Drug Policy*, 2015, with Gary Potter), and 'Cannabis Social Clubs in Belgium: Organizational Strengths and Weaknesses, and Threats to the Model' (*International Journal of Drug Policy*, 2014).

Cristina Díaz Gómez is head of the Unit on Public Policy Evaluation within the *Observatoire français des drogues et des toxicomanies*. She holds a Master's degree in Economics from the Universidad de Alcalá and an MSc in Health Economics from the Universidad Nacional de Educación a Distancia (Spain). Her main areas of expertise include public services and expenditure, law enforcement and health programmes' evaluation. She regularly provides expertise on public policy and on evaluation research projects as scientific advisor in the field of drugs and drug addictions. She publishes reviews on a regular basis focusing on drug policy and drug law.

Ruth Dreifuss is one of the founding members and the current chair of the Global Commission on Drug Policy. From 1993 until 2002 she was one of the seven members of the Swiss Federal Council and head of the Swiss Federal Department of Home Affairs, overseeing public health, social security, and scientific research and higher education. Ruth Dreifuss was also the President of the Swiss Confederation in 1999. During the last fourteen years she has been active mainly in the fields of public health and intellectual property, abolition of the death penalty and drug policy. She is also chair of the Advisory Commission on Addiction of the Canton of Geneva and co-chair of the High Level Panel on innovation and access to medical technology, convened by the UN Secretary General.

Johan Edman is Associate Professor in History and deputy director at the Centre for Social Research on Alcohol and Drugs (SoRAD) at Stockholm University. His research focuses on historical analyses of social exclusion,

List of contributors xi

substance misuse treatment, and alcohol and drug policy. His recent publications include 'An Ambiguous Monolith; The Swedish Drug Issue as a Political Battleground 1965–1981 (*International Journal of Drug Policy*, 2013), 'An All-embracing Problem Description; The Swedish Drug Issue as a Political Catalyst 1982–2000' (*International Journal of Drug Policy*, 2013), and 'Temperance and Modernity. Alcohol Consumption as a Collective Problem 1885–1913' (*Journal of Social History*, 2015).

Martin Elvins is Lecturer in Politics and International Relations at the University of Dundee. He is the author of *Anti-Drugs Policies of the European Union. Transnational Decision-Making and the Politics of Expertise* (Palgrave Macmillan, 2003). Following a grant award from the UK Economic and Social Research Council (ESRC) he completed a research project entitled *UK and Dutch Counter-Drugs Policies in the Caribbean: A Comparative Analysis* during 2008 and 2009, including fieldwork in six countries. He has also published on transnational organised crime. More recently he has focused on various aspects of policing with an emphasis on practice in Scotland.

Jean-Paul Grund holds a Master's degree in Clinical and Developmental Psychology and a PhD in Social Science. He is Research Director at the Addiction Research Centre (CVO) in Utrecht and a senior Research Associate in the Department of Addictology, First Faculty of Medicine, Charles University in Prague. He has published extensively on drug culture, drug-related harm, peer-driven harm reduction approaches and how these matters interact with public policies. Recent publications include 'NPS in Europe: Special Issue' (*Adiktologie*, 2016, with Lenka Vavrinčiková and Michal Miovský) and '"Should I Buy or Should I Grow?" How Drug Policy Institutions and Drug Market Transaction Costs Shape the Decision to Self-Supply with Cannabis in the Netherlands and the Czech Republic' (*International Journal of Drug Policy*, 2015, with Vendula Belackova, Nicole Maalsté and Tomas Zabransky).

Christine Guillain is Professor of Law at Université Saint-Louis – Bruxelles and the director of the Groupe de recherche en matière pénale et criminelle (GREPEC). After having practised as a lawyer for several years, she now teaches penal procedure and criminal law. She is the author of *Introduction au droit pénal: Aspects juridiques et criminologiques* (PUSL, 2015, with Françoise Tulkens, Michel van de Kerchove and Yves Cartuyvels) as well as articles on drug policy. Recent publications include 'Vos droits en matière de cannabis' (*Prospective Jeunesse*, 2015) and 'Sortir du champ pénal' (*Politique: Revue de débats*, 2014).

Dagmar Hedrich is a psychologist with postgraduate qualification in the treatment of dependencies. She joined the European Monitoring Centre for Drugs and Drug Addiction in 2001, where she currently heads the Health Consequences and Responses sector. Her field of work covers health-related harms, drug treatment and harm reduction responses. She contributes regularly to EMCDDA publications, and has written book chapters, scientific papers and reviews on

xii List of contributors

harm reduction interventions and policies, on topics such as supervised drug consumption facilities, effectiveness of opioid substitution treatment in prisons, and assessment of infection risks and trends among people who inject drugs in Europe.

Tilmann Holzer has a background in political science and contemporary history. His Master's thesis was on the influence of the protestant ethic on the genesis of the international drug prohibition regime, *Globalisierte Drogenpolitik. Die protestantische Ethik und die Geschichte des Drogenverbotes* (Verlag für Wissenschaft und Bildung, 2002) and his PhD on the history of drug policy in Germany, *Die Geburt der Drogenpolitik aus dem Geist der Rassenhygiene: Deutsche Drogenpolitik von 1933 bis 1972* (Norderstedt: Books on Demand GmbH, 2007) have been published. Tilmann Holzer has worked for the German Federal Drug Commissioner and is now working at the Federal Health Ministry of Germany.

Esben Houborg is Associate Professor at the Centre for Alcohol and Drug Research at Aarhus University (Denmark). His main areas of research are drug policy in a historical and contemporary perspective, criminological research particularly concerning law enforcement and the relationship between science and politics in policy making, policy implementation and urban studies of drug related issues. Recent publications include 'Construction and Handling of Drug Problems in Denmark from the 1870s to the 1980s' (*Nordisk Alkohol- & Narkotikatidskrift*, 2014), 'Drug Consumption Rooms and the Role of Politics and Governance in Policy Processes' (*International Journal of Drug Policy*, 2014, with Vibeke Asmussen Frank), and 'Addiction, Drugs and Experimentation: Methadone Maintenance Treatment Between "In Here" and "Out There"' (*Contemporary Drug Problems*, 2015, with Bjarke Nielsen).

Brendan Hughes has been working as a scientific analyst at the European Monitoring Centre for Drugs and Drug Addiction since 2001 in the field of national drug legislation. He manages the European Legal Database on Drugs (ELDD) which holds various comparative overviews and analyses on different topics relevant to drug laws: not only use, possession and trafficking laws, but also issues such as drug classifications, threshold quantities, alternatives to punishment, drug driving, procedures for classifying new substances as drugs, and regulatory frameworks for substitution treatment. He published the first European quantitative comparison of drug law sentencing and outcome statistics in 2009, and is currently working on a pilot index for comparing drug laws across countries and over time.

Caitlin Hughes is a criminologist and Senior Research Fellow at the National Drug and Alcohol Research Centre, UNSW, Australia. She has spent many years analysing the Portuguese decriminalisation of illicit drugs, studying both the policy process of reform and evaluating the reform outcomes. In 2010 she wrote the first independent academic review on the reform: 'What can we learn from the Portuguese decriminalisation of illicit drugs?' (British Journal of Criminology, with Alex Stevens). Her other research focuses on evaluating Australian drug laws and criminal justice policies (including laws on use/possession, threshold limits for drug trafficking, and alternatives to arrest) and monitoring trends in high-level drug trafficking.

Emiliano Martín González held the position of director of the first agency for drug users in Madrid and supervised, from 1988 to 1996, the planning project and implementation of the Strategy on Drugs for the Spanish capital city. He has been Deputy Director-General for the Spanish National Plan on Drugs from 1996 to 2003 and vice-president of the *Observatorio Español de la Droga y las Toxicomanías* Advisory Committee. As delegate of the Spanish Government, he was a member of the Advisory Committee of the European Monitoring Centre for Drugs and Drug Addiction and has taken part in several European meetings and Latin American summits on drugs. He collaborates as an expert with the Inter-American Drug Abuse Control Commission (CICAD). He has published, among others, *Manual de intervención en drogodependencias (Análisis e intervención social)* (Síntesis, 2004, with Elisardo Becoña Iglesias).

Ivana Obradovic is Deputy Director of the *Observatoire français des drogues et des toxicomanies* and Associate Researcher at *Centre de recherches sociologiques sur le droit et les institutions pénales* (CESDIP). Her main research interests are drug policy analysis and evaluation, cannabis policy issues in France and Europe and, most recently, in Uruguay and the United States. Recent publications include 'La pénalisation de l'usage de stupéfiants en France au miroir des statistiques administratives: Enjeux et controverses' (*Déviance et Société*, 2012), 'Programmes d'échange de seringues en milieu pénitentiaire: Revue internationale des expériences' (*Psychotropes*, 2013) and 'Usages de drogues et société addictogène' (*Adolescence*, 2015).

Susanne MacGregor is Honorary Professor of Social Policy at the London School of Hygiene and Tropical Medicine, at the Centre for History in Public Health (where she held a Leverhulme Emeritus Fellowship), and Professor Emerita at Middlesex University London, attached to the Drug and Alcohol Research Centre. She was programme coordinator for the UK Department of Health Drug Misuse Research Initiative from 2000 to 2009 and edited a collection based on this programme; *Responding to Drug Misuse: Research and Policy Priorities* (Routledge, 2010). With Linda Hantrais and Ashley Thomas Lenihan she recently edited *International and Interdisciplinary Insights into Evidence and Policy* (Routledge, 2016). She has been an associate editor of the *International Journal of Drug Policy* and is on the International Advisory Board of the journal *Drugs: Education, Prevention and Policy*.

Kasia Malinowska is the founder and director of the Global Drug Policy Program (GDDP) at the Open Society Foundations. Before joining Open Society, she worked for the United Nations Development Programme in New

York and Warsaw, where she developed and managed training and programmes on harm reduction, women's health, HIV, and medical ethics. She co-authored Poland's first national AIDS programme and has helped formulate policy at the Global Fund, the WHO, and the Millennium Challenge. She holds an MA in social work from the University of Pennsylvania and a PhD from Columbia University's School of Public Health. She speaks and publishes regularly on drug policy as it relates to women, social justice, health, human rights, civil society, and governance.

Mafalda Pardal is a PhD researcher at the Institute for Social Drug Research at Ghent University, where she is working on a three-year research project examining Cannabis Social Clubs in Belgium. Previously, she was an analyst at RAND Europe. Recent publications include 'Modeling the Structure and Operation of Drug Supply Chains: The Case of Cocaine and Heroin in Italy and Slovenia' (*International Journal of Drug Policy*, 2016, with Jonathan P. Caulkins, Emma Disley, Marina Tzvetkova, Hemali Shah and Xiaoke Zhang) and *Multinational Overview of Cannabis Production Regimes* (RAND, 2013, with Beau Kilmer, Kristy Kruithof, Jonathan P. Caulkins, Jennifer Rubin).

Alessandro Pirona is a psychologist with a PhD in experimental psychology from Sussex University. In 2007 he joined the European Monitoring Centre for Drugs and Drug Addiction where he now works as a principal scientific analyst. He is responsible for the reporting on health and social responses to drug use and harms in the EU, with a particular interest in the functioning of European drug treatment systems. He has published several articles in journals such as the *Journal of Psychopharmacology* and *Neuropsychopharmacology*, as well as a number of key EMCDDA publications on Internet-based treatment, treatment for ageing drug users, and health responses to new psychoactive substances (NPS).

Franz Trautmann served as the head of the Unit of International Affairs at the Trimbos Institute for 15 years. He made substantial contributions in international drug policy as a senior researcher and advisor. Throughout his career, he developed, coordinated and executed an extensive range of international projects focused on drug demand reduction through prevention, treatment and harm reduction approaches. Recent publications include 'The Emergence and Influence of the Concept of Governance in the European Addiction Field' (ALICE RAP, 2014, with Susanne MacGregor and Nicola Singleton) and *A Report on Global Illicit Drugs Markets 1998–2007* (European Communities/RAND/Trimbos Institute, 2009, with Peter Reuter).

Frank Zobel is Deputy Director of Addiction Switzerland and a member of the National Advisory Board on Addiction of Switzerland. His former positions were with the European Monitoring Centre for Drugs and Drug Addiction in Lisbon, as policy analyst and coordinator of the European Drug Report, and with the University Institute of Social and Preventive Medicine in Lausanne, as external evaluator of the Swiss drug strategy. His recent publications include

Nouveaux développements concernant la régulation du marché du cannabis: De A (Anchorage) à Z (Zürich) (Addiction Suisse, 2016, with Marc Marthaler) and *Neue Tendenzen im Drogenbereich (NTD): Methamphetamin in der Schweiz* (Sucht Schweiz, 2015, with Marc Marthaler and Christian Schneider).

Grazia Zuffa is a psychologist and former Professor of Drug Addiction Psychology at the University of Florence (2000–2006). She is now responsible for research activity at Forum Droghe (a leading Italian NGO in the field of drug policies). She has been a member of the Italian National Committee of Bioethics since 2006. From 1987 to 1994, she was a member of the Senate of the Italian Republic. She was also a member of the National Scientific Committee on Drug Addiction (2006–2008). Her books include *I drogati e gli altri* (Sellerio, 2000), *Droghe e riduzione del danno: Un approccio di psicologia di comunità* (Unicopli, 2002, with Patrizia Meringolo) and *Cocaina: Il consumo controllato* (Edizioni Gruppo Abele, 2010).

Acknowledgements

This book has its genesis in a workshop which brought together a group of academics, decision makers and human rights activists working in the field of drug policy at the European University Institute (Florence) in June 2013. The seminar was funded by a grant of the Drug Policy Program of the Open Society Foundations and by a Marie Curie Intra-European Fellowship within the European Commission's 7th Framework Programme. Additional funding in the preparation of the book was provided by the Drug Policy Program of the Open Society Foundations, the research centre *Droit et Changement Social* (UMR CNRS – Université de Nantes), the *Laboratoire interdisciplinaire d'évaluation des politiques publiques* (LIEPP – Labex – Sciences Po) and the *Chaire Santé* (Sciences Po).

The editors are indebted to the European University Institute, and especially Professor Loïc Azoulay, Professor Hans Micklitz and Ms Annick Bulckaen for their academic support and material assistance. They are grateful for the invaluable editorial assistance from Ms Monica Roman. This volume would not exist without her incomparable help.

Finally, heartfelt thanks to all the individual chapter authors who have given their time and energy and who have graciously accepted the comments and suggestions of the editors. One of the contributors, Franz Trautmann, passed away during the preparation of this manuscript. Franz was a charismatic and a dedicated expert, an internationally renowned and respected expert in national and international drug policy. The editors wish to acknowledge his committed support of this project and the value of his contributions, both to the field, and to this volume.

Foreword

The Single Convention on Narcotic Drugs concluded under the aegis of the United Nations (UN) is 55 years old. Widely ratified, the Single Convention gradually, seemingly indelibly, left its mark on national laws and policy. Prohibition gained the upper hand over public health objectives, and a commitment to the reduction of supply and demand drove an escalation of repressive measures against those who, in whatever way, came into contact with substances declared illicit. In this context no reasoned debate was possible and the stratagems of the 'war on drugs' – elevated to public enemy number one – were shielded from scientific scrutiny. Neither the testimony of suffering, the evidence of the risks of prohibition (no less than drug consumption itself), nor research in the humanities, natural and social sciences, could challenge an ideologically driven denial of reality. On the one hand, we had to acknowledge the absence of progress in international debate. On the other hand, the needs of the populations concerned were more and more clearly expressed by social workers, activists and physicians. But beyond calls for pragmatic policies, very few voices pleaded for a change of paradigm. A change which, if not impossible, appeared difficult to foresee.

Today the situation is evolving. The taboo is broken. Reform no longer seems like an unrealisable utopia but a path which should, prudently, be explored. At the Special Session of the United Nations dedicated to drug policy (UNGASS 2016) the benefits and legitimacy of prohibition were thrown into doubt by many speakers. Even if the final declaration, drawn up by the Commission on Narcotic Drugs, reiterates the view that the UN drug control conventions are the cornerstone of international cooperation, it also includes an insistence on the necessity of enacting an efficient health policy and a respect for human rights. It is more than a tremor and less than a quake. It is a step towards an analysis of the effects of more than a half century of drug policies. It is the beginning of a phase based on experiments in healthcare (the expansion of treatment options, risk reduction measures, clinical studies on the use of various substances), on *de jure* or *de facto* decriminalisation of consumption, and on drawing lessons from the financial and human costs of repression which will finally lead the way towards a new consensus. Sooner or later one conclusion will be reached at the international level: prohibition is not the right response to the problems associated with drugs; states, not criminal organisations, have the responsibility to control the production of drugs and the drug market.

Today it is important not only that we share our experiences, but that we evaluate and adapt them to different contexts. Those whose research, reports and books had, in the past, seemed like so many messages in a bottle are now more in demand than ever. Now is the time to expand and share our knowledge. This book, which presents reforms that have been implemented in Europe, is timely. Our continent has been the starting point for innovations that have proven effective, that have saved lives and increased social cohesion and security. However, we must overcome the formidable contradiction which persists between an approach characterised by health and social integration policies and the continuation of prohibition. This book can contribute to this objective.

Ruth Dreifuss

European drug policies in context

Henri Bergeron and Renaud Colson

European drug policies in historical context

For much of human history psychoactive substances were geographically confined products, the use of which was restricted by limited availability and both formal (religious and political rituals) and informal regulation. Some of these mind-altering substances were propelled outside their traditional settings by the development of global commerce in the seventeenth and eighteenth centuries. Tobacco, coffee, opiates, cannabis, alcohol or coca became global commodities thanks to the rise of maritime European empires (Mills and Barton, 2007). Quickly escaping the therapeutic realm, psychoactive substances entered into nonmedical use. Wide popular consumption at times occasioned social alarm and political controversy. Yet official intervention long remained scarce.

Not only did the spread of psychoactive substances appeal to European elites, who sometimes indulged in the new intoxicants and often turned them into fashionable commodities, but it also served the interests of the wealthy and powerful who promoted the use of these products in the colonies and at home as a way to corrupt their opponents, pacify their soldiers and soothe their workers. In an era of *laissez-faire* economics with little control over private enterprise, the world's governments were mainly concerned with how best to tax the traffic, not how to suppress it (Courtwright, 2002, p. 165).

In the course of the nineteenth century, objections to non-medical drug use grew more vocal, invoking individual harm, social costs and moral considerations which generated increased regulatory pressure. Gradual medico-technological advances and the progressive 'medicalisation of political power' (Withington, 2014, p. 20) gave rise to the framing of drugs as a regulatory concept (Seddon, 2016). The association of particular substances with deviant groups or ethnic minorities fuelled social anxieties harnessed by moral entrepreneurs. By the beginning of the twentieth century the movement to restrict the production, the trade and the use of psychoactive substances gained momentum, both at national and international levels. European drug policies were born out of this great historical about-face which precipitated the shift in priorities of Western political elites from the promotion of intoxicants to their partial prohibition. International activism to form a

2   Henri Bergeron and Renaud Colson

global response to drug abuse actually preceded, and heavily influenced, the development of comprehensive domestic regulation of psychoactive substances in European states.

European powers in international drug policy

The negotiation of the 1912 Hague Opium Convention – the first treaty which set the trajectory of a century of drug control efforts – showed the lack of enthusiasm of European powers for an American drug control initiative which could endanger their economic interests. While colonial powers such as France and the United Kingdom defended their government monopolies of opium in their colonies, Portugal pledged to protect the Macao opium trade, and Germany, Switzerland and the Netherlands, which possessed pharmaceutical industries, objected to limitations on manufactured drugs (McAllister, 2000, pp. 31–32). Eventually, the 1912 Convention preamble stated that the international community was 'determined to bring about the gradual suppression of the abuse of opium, morphine and cocaine', but the treaty was a non-binding document with no implementation mechanisms.

Other conventions were negotiated in the following decades leading to the creation of a functional bureaucratic structure in order to implement this treaty framework, first organised under the banner of the League of Nations and then transferred to the United Nations in 1946. International law formalised a distinction between global licit markets controlled by oversight bodies and the illicit markets against which, initially, no enforcement response was designed at the global level. The configuration of this international drug control system owes much to the competition between states advocating an absolutist prohibitionist approach, led by the United States, and those promoting international regulation in order to manage commodity flows and encourage better domestic management of the issue. The majority of European states, which followed that second strand, led the opposition to strong supervisory bodies in the organisation of the licit market. European states also resisted American plans to secure an international agreement over an end to 'all non-medical and scientific drug use'.

The Second World War changed the balance of power in international drug control. Before the end of the conflict, the US extracted commitments from Britain, France and the Netherlands to end opium monopolies, and new American predominance strengthened the position of control advocates.[1] The aim of drug supply minimisation which characterised the first drug control treaties was consequently reinforced with plans of bringing synthetic narcotics under control

---

1   In the following years, influential prohibitionist figures such as Henri Anslinger, the American representative to the Commission on Narcotic Drugs from 1945 to 1970 and possibly the most prominent actor in international drug control circles in the twentieth century, and Charles Vaille, a French civil servant singleminded in his focus on supply control, set the tone for the future of the regime (McAllister, 2000, pp. 89–90 and 168).

European drug policies in context 3

(1948 Synthetic Narcotics Protocol) and limiting agricultural production (1953 Opium Protocol). Yet the negotiation of the 1961 Single Convention on Narcotic Drugs shows that under the leadership of British officials, the majority of European states adopted the cause of 'regulatory moderation' in defeat of the American hard line (McAllister, 2000, p. 195). This development turned out to be temporary as the 1971 Convention on Psychotropic Substances and the 1988 Convention against Illicit Traffic in Narcotic Drugs and Psychotropic Substances revealed a renewed resolve for international drug control, with the promotion of an ambitious target of eradication of non-scientific and non-medical use and the encouragement of states to pursue more aggressive domestic policies in the implementation of this objective. Here again, most European powers (with the exception of France and then Italy) defended a minimalist approach to the further development of the global drug prohibition regime as a whole (Friedrichs, 2008, pp. 113–133). But this did not prevent a strongly punitive interpretation of the drug control regime coming to dominate in the international arena in the last decades of the twentieth century.

European Union drug policy

Though framed as an international necessity from the early twentieth century, drug control was hardly a subject of regional cooperation in Europe before the 1970s. It was only when the threat of a 'drug epidemic' developed in the late 1960s that concern over this issue grew and an intergovernmental 'co-operation group to combat drug abuse and illicit trafficking in drugs' was set up in 1971, at the initiative of the French President Georges Pompidou, as France was going through a moral panic about drug abuse. The Pompidou group, which originally consisted of seven European countries – France, Belgium, Germany, Italy, Luxembourg, Netherlands, United Kingdom – was created to allow states to share their experience and knowledge in the field of drug abuse and drug trafficking. This informal group was incorporated by the Council of Europe in 1980, a time when the then European Communities (EC) had no stake in drug policies. Although still active, the Pompidou group, which has extended to new countries and now includes 38 states, has suffered from competition with the European Union.

The 1980s saw the development of transnational political interest in the drug issue in the European public sphere as demonstrated by a variety of resolutions and reports of the European Parliament. The creation, in 1989, of the European Committee to Combat Drugs (CELAD), an *ad hoc* political committee established by the European Council to coordinate drug-related activities within the EC, gave drugs a more prominent place on the European political agenda (Estievenart, 1995). With drug-related matters formally added to the area of competence of the European Union in 1991 (Maastricht Treaty), an EU drug policy slowly came into being (on this issue, see the chapter in this volume by Martin Elvins). The dynamics of European decision-making on drugs are complex. Beyond the

4 Henri Bergeron and Renaud Colson

objective of tackling drug trafficking – a criminal activity which might benefit from the abolition of internal borders within an integrated union – the need to respond to European public opinion anxious about drug-related crime and addiction motivated European politicians to take action (Boekhout van Solinge, 2002, pp. 80–90). Once set in motion by the European Council, the Council and the Commission have produced a number of policy documents promoting harmonisation between Member States (discussed by Caroline Chatwin in her chapter).

The development of an EU drug policy is in line with a general constitutional evolution transforming the EU into a guarantor of the security and health of the nationals of the Member States. The Treaty on the functioning of the European Union explicitly provides regulatory powers to fight 'illicit drug trafficking' (Art. 83(1) TFEU) and reduce 'drugs-related health damage' (Art. 168 (1) TFEU). With a view to promoting research and facilitating evidence-based decision making, the institutionalisation of an EU drug policy included the establishment of a European Monitoring Centre for Drugs and Drug Addiction (EMCDDA) (for the origins and development of this institution see the chapter by Henri Bergeron). Three 'strategies' were successively adopted by the European Council[2] presenting a comprehensive approach linking drug supply reduction, drug demand reduction, European coordination and international cooperation. Notwithstanding the Europeanisation of drug policy, national specificities still prevail in institutional responses to the drug issue in Europe.

Diversity of European domestic drug policies

In spite of their obligation to abide by the global prohibition regime and their shared commitment to EU policies, each European state has developed their own way of dealing with drug use and drug trafficking (Boekhout van Solinge, 2004). Within the international drug control framework, textual ambiguity allows states some leeway in the implementation of global prohibition. EU action, meanwhile, remains limited in scope and power. On the one hand, illicit drugs remain an area where subsidiarity reigns supreme and the autonomy of Member States prioritised, except when the objectives of the proposed action are not sufficiently achievable at the national level. On the other hand, when specific measures are eventually adopted by the Union, they either bring limited added value compared to international law (Kert and Lehner, 2013), or belong to the realm of soft law and appear toothless. No wonder, then, that at first sight plurality seems to prevail in European domestic drug policies.

The range of drug policy models is often highlighted by reference to the Swedish and the Dutch examples, two countries at either ends of a continuum from a very punitive form of drug prohibition to the most tolerant (see the chapters on Sweden by Johan Edman, and on the Netherlands by Jean-Paul C. Grund and

---

2   The last one was issued in 2012: European Council (2012) *EU Drugs Strategy (2013–20)*. Official Journal of the European Union C 402/1, 29.12.2012, pp. 1–10.

Joost J. Breeksema). But there is more to European diversity than coffee shops in the Netherlands and a Swedish policy of zero tolerance. And any attempt to describe European drug policies by reference to a scale of punitiveness falls short of conveying the complexity of the matter. The drugs issue cuts across a spectrum of controversial topics ranging from basic rights and freedoms, through public health policies including HIV prevention, to criminal justice responses. And each of these areas is influenced by national traditions and depends on the domestic politico-cultural environment.

When it comes to developing policy responses, the extent of the drugs problem itself seems to have less of an influence than institutional and political determinants among which are: political values, a particular notion of citizenship, the organisation of a given political system, specific legal and administrative traditions and institutional power balances, the role of expertise and the weight of science in shaping/framing public policy, degrees of independence and involvement of the medical profession and pharmacists, the access of social movements to the locus of public power and the legitimacy of these actions (compare the chapters on Denmark by Esben Houborg, and on Italy by Grazia Zuffa).

Many studies claim that the particularities of national public policies are due primarily to such singularities, which reflect cultural habitus. Berridge (1996) points out that common historical patterns can be discerned in the policies and policy instruments used in European countries (e.g., the laws passed against drug use and sale in the 1920s, then again in the 1970s, and those passed in the 1980s and 1990s in response to the HIV/AIDS epidemic), but most existing studies have drawn attention instead to the formal diversity of these relatively synchronous policy responses (compare the chapters on France by Ivana Obradovic, and on the United Kingdom by Susanne MacGregor). What should be emphasised here is that beyond their diversity, European drug policies are very much in a state of flux: most of them were subject to many reforms in recent decades and they now display a certain level of convergence.

Convergence of European drug policies

Starting in the mid-1980s in some European countries (see the chapter on Switzerland by Frank Zobel), and in the remainder from the following decade, the drug policies of European countries were reformulated through the beefing up of health and social provisions and by the design and extensive implementation of so-called 'risk reduction' instruments which most Member States had until then resisted (Bergeron, 2009). It gradually became clear in European countries that the strategic requirement that treatment *cure* drug addiction and, in some countries, the hysterical attempt to require abstinence, was not compatible with the risks implied by the growing HIV/AIDS epidemic. It is true that the implementation level of these policies (i.e., degree to which user populations are covered) and the accessibility of their programmes still differ considerably by country and 'setting' (e.g., prison, treatment centres). Some measures are still subjects of controversy, such as the controlled distribution of heroin or medically supervised injection centres. Still, it can be said that a number of important harm and risk-reduction instruments (distribution of sterile injection equipment, extensive distribution of substitution substances, 'low threshold' treatment centres, targeted prevention campaigns, and so on) have now become part of the 'legitimate' strategy of most European states (see the chapter by Dagmar Hedrich and Alessandro Pirona). The European Union, meanwhile, officially recognised the importance of harm reduction measures by way of a Council recommendation adopted in 2003.[3] This overall policy approach signifies that Member States have recognised – and (to varying degrees) are willing to assume the political consequences of that recognition – that drug use is not, as was thought in the 1970s and 1980s, a disease but, indeed, a lasting anthropological fact of Western societies, and that not only its causes but also its risk-heavy consequences have to addressed.

Another example of convergence in European drug policies is the legal status granted to the use of drugs (without any aggravating circumstances) or to possession of drugs for personal use. In terms of both legislation and policies, European countries were deeply divided only 20 years ago as to appropriate responses for discouraging the use or possession of controlled substances for personal use. Rooted in history and tradition, penal justice emerges within a national context which overwhelmingly determines its character (Colson and Field, 2016, pp. 1–10), and we can observe an array of very different regimes when it comes to criminal justice systems in Europe. Nonetheless, recent developments within those systems reflect a tendency in which drug use offences are no longer punishable by prison sentences, with the complementary understanding that treatment and reintegration measures are to be preferred (see the chapter by Brendan Hughes). In a growing number of countries, drug use is no longer considered an offence (in this volume see the chapters on Germany by Tilmann Holzer, and on Spain by Cristina Díaz Gómez and Emiliano Martín González) thus allowing the development of grassroots drug users social clubs (see the chapter by Tom Decorte and Mafalda Pardal). Even in countries where it is heavily policed, personal use repression policy can be said to have undergone relative *de facto* (as opposed to *de jure*) depenalisation (see the chapter on Belgium by Christine Guillain), a process rendering unlikely the punishment with a court sentence of legally punishable behaviour.

The rise of harm reduction and partial and uneven decriminalisation of drug use in Europe followed such a multiplicity of paths that one may be tempted to emphasise differences over similarities. While some European governments have been early active proponents of a public health oriented approach in drug policy (see the chapter on Portugal by Caitlin Hughes), others still defend a morally inspired approach at the expense of harm reduction policies and continue

---

3   Council Recommendation of 18 June 2003 on the prevention and reduction of health-related harm associated with drug dependence, Official Journal of the European Union L 165, 3.7.2003, pp. 31–33.

European drug policies in context **7**

prosecuting drug users (see the chapter on Poland by Kasia Malinowska). And the links between drug policy and other public policies, such as criminal, social or public health policy, vary between different countries. But in this landscape characterised by heterogeneity, commonalities have increased (see the chapter by Franz Trautmann) and in most European jurisdictions there has been a drift towards a more common approach to drug policy which includes the political recognition of a common experience of the drug phenomenon and a growing commitment to give the policy debate a scientific and rational foundation (as exemplified by the common European position during the last Special Session of the General Assembly of the United Nations on the world drug problem).[4] In this respect, the existence of shared elements of expertise has contributed to increasing the similarities between European drug policies.

Purpose and structure of the book

Dutch tolerance towards cannabis and Swiss emphasis on harm reduction, once considered European exceptions to a punitive orthodoxy maintained by UN bureaucracy, are no longer a regional singularity. And the EU is no longer the only constituted intergovernmental structure to promote a move towards more pragmatic approaches.[5] Signs of soft defection and systemic breaches now come from outside Europe and official calls to establish alternative regulatory regimes for drug control are now heard in other regions of the world (Bewley-Taylor, 2012; Boister, 2016). The long dominant punitive interpretation of the treaty system promoted by UN bodies under the influence of the United States has lost its appeal: the Special Session of the United Nations General Assembly on the world drug problem held in April 2016 may well have reaffirmed the commitment of the international community to a traditional prohibitionist approach,[6] but it hardly conceals the growing tensions within the drug control regime.

New ways of governing addiction are gathering momentum and this is the time to take stock of European experiences. While the ideological context, bureaucratic politics and the policymaking process often seem to impede any deviation from the path initially set by public policy entrepreneurs, other historical phases offer examples of windows of opportunity for a policy change. After a long period

---

4   United Nations, Special Session of the General Assembly UNGASS 2016, European Union common position on UNGASS 2016. Available from: https://www.unodc.org/docum ents/ungass2016/Contributions/IO/EU_COMMON_POSITION_ON_UNGASS.pdf [Accessed: 22 June 2016].

5   See e.g. the Report on the Drug Problem in the Americas issued by the Organization of American States (OAS) in 2013, available from: www.oas.org/documents/eng/press/ Introduction_and_Analytical_Report.pdf [Accessed: 22 June 2016]

6   Resolution adopted by the General Assembly of the United Nations. Our joint commitment to effectively addressing and countering the world drug problem, A/RES/S-30/1 (19 April 2016), Available from: undocs.org/ A/RES/S-30/1 [Accessed: 22 June 2016].

8   Henri Bergeron and Renaud Colson

during which they were shaped by a grammar of public order, moral decline and medical treatment, two decades ago European drug policies entered a new phase.

The purpose of this book is to describe the origins and the outcomes of the slow transformation by which new priorities have emerged in European drug policy. The contributions to this volume reflect the various contexts and different outcomes which characterise domestic policies in Europe, and trace a gradual convergence in the emergence of a model favouring public-health strategies over a strictly penal approach to combating drugs.

Reflecting the diversity of functions generally assigned to comparative research, the book has two distinct, although related, goals. In terms of analytical purpose, it aims at describing drug policies in a variety of settings. From a more evaluative perspective, it also critically assesses these policies in order to increase knowledge about various national approaches and provide tools to reformers in search of successful models. Whereas a substantial proportion of social science research strives to develop indicators to measure the success of drug policies, this collection does not rely on a single evaluative approach. On the contrary, it highlights the weight of cultural tradition in policy-making and the impossibility of promoting a one-size-fits-all policy. The development of new metrics to measure drug policies is fundamental to continuous improvement in addiction governance (Ritter, 2009). But one should remember that policy transfers and legal transplants cannot be successfully undertaken without paying attention to local environment. The politico-cultural contexts from which policies, ideas and practices emerge have a significant impact on their potential for adaptation (Newburn and Sparks, 2004).

In the light of increasing evidence of the complexity of 'policy convergence', this book analyses the social and institutional conditions of drug policy reform in Europe from a variety of perspectives. It provides a transnational perspective as well as national case studies and offers a broad-stroke comparative analysis of European trends. The first part investigates the genealogy and the framework of European Union drug policy; it also offers a critical account of the governing tools used to promote European harmonisation (Part 1: Regional dimensions of European drug policies). The second part is devoted to case studies on twelve European Member States (Part 2: Domestic drug policies in Europe). These chapters describe the diverse evolutionary patterns followed by national drug policies in Europe starting with their origins and development from the early twentieth century onward in relation to the specific national history of drug use. Each of these chapters outlines the legal regime in force and delineates the drivers of change and conservative forces in current policy (including national, international and transnational institutions and advocacy groups...). The third part of the book provides an insight on contemporary trends in European drug policies (Part 3: Trends and prospects in European drug policies).

The contributions to this volume leave no doubt as to the importance of the ongoing shift in European drug policies. Policy makers in European countries increasingly share a common understanding of the drug phenomenon and even if they may differ on the most appropriate responses, there is a growing commitment, in what is a highly ideological area, to give drug policy a rational foundation.

From a public policy perspective, the development of harm reduction and the slow decriminalisation of drug use have mostly been the result of gradual and non-coordinated institutional transformation rather than major change as a result of explicit political choice. This incremental process of 'layering', adding new rules alongside existing institutions, has been cumulatively transformative but has left the prohibitionist framework almost intact. The question remains: how can the law confer legal status to harm reduction measures and drug users be fully included in the political community when drugs remain illegal? The legal paradox is often ignored, all the more as it can be circumvented in everyday politics. But the contradiction remains and will not be resolved unless we advance the reasoned debate on alternative options including *de jure* decriminalisation and regulated legalisation.

References

BERGERON, H. (2009) *Sociologie de la drogue*, Paris: La Découverte.
BERGERON, H. and COLSON, R. (eds.) (2015) *Les drogues face au droit*. Paris: Presses universitaires de France.
BERGERON, H. and GRIFFITHS, P. (2006) Drifting Towards a More Common Approach to a More Common Problem: Epidemiology and the Evolution of a European Drug Policy. In Hughes, R., Lart, R. and Higate, P. (eds.). *Drugs: Policy and Politics*. London: Open University Press.
BERRIDGE, V. (1996) European Drug Policy: The Need for Historical Perspectives, *European Addiction Research*. 2(4). pp. 219–225.
BEWLEY-TAYLOR, D. R. (1999) *The United States and International Drug Control: 1909–1997*. London/New York: Continuum.
BEWLEY-TAYLOR, D. R. (2012) *International Drug Control: Consensus Fractured*. Cambridge: Cambridge University Press.
BOEKHOUT VAN SOLINGE, T. (2002) *Drugs and Decision-Making in the European Union*. Amsterdam: CEDRO/Mets en Schilt.
BOEKHOUT VAN SOLINGE, T. (2004) *Dealing with Drugs in Europe. An Investigation of European Drug Control Experiences: France, the Netherlands and Sweden*. The Hague: BJu Legal Publishers.
BOISTER, N. (2001) *Penal Aspects of the UN Drug Conventions*. The Hague / London / Boston: Kluwer Law International.
BOISTER, N. (2016) Waltzing on the Vienna Consensus on Drug Control? Tensions in the International System for the Control of Drugs. *Leiden Journal of International Law*. 29. pp. 389–409.
CHATWIN, C. (2011) *Drug Policy Harmonization and the European Union*. Basingstoke: Palgrave Macmillan.
COLSON, R. (ed.) (2005), *La prohibition: Regards croisés sur un interdit juridique*, Rennes: Presses universitaires de Rennes.
COLSON, R. and FIELD, S. (2016) *EU Criminal Justice and the Challenges of Diversity: Legal Cultures in the Area of Freedom, Security and Justice*. Cambridge: Cambridge University Press.
COURTWRIGHT, D. T. (2002) *Forces of Habit: Drugs and the Making of the Modern World*. Cambridge/London: Harvard University Press.

ELVINS, M. (2003) *Anti-Drugs Policies of the European Union.* Basingstoke: Palgrave Macmillan.

ESTIEVENART, G. (1995) The European Community and the Global Drug Phenomenon: Current Situation and Outlook. In Estievenart, G. (ed.). *Policies and Strategies to Combat Drugs in Europe. The Treaty on European Union: Framework for a New European Strategy to Combat Drugs?* Dordrecht: Martinus Nijhoff Publishers. pp. 50–93.

FRIEDRICHS, J. (2008) *Fighting Terrorism and Drugs: Europe and International Police Cooperation.* London: Routledge.

HUNT, G., MILHET, M. and BERGERON, H. (eds.) (2011) *Drugs and Culture: Knowledge, Consumption and Policy.* Farnham/Burlington: Ashgate.

KERT, R. and LEHNER, A. (2013) Content and Impact of Approximation: The Case of Drug Trafficking. In Galli, F. and Weyembergh, A. (eds.). *Approximation of Substantive Criminal Law in the EU: The Way Forward.* Brussels: Editions de l'Université de Bruxelles.

NEWBURN, T. and SPARKS, R. (2004) Criminal Justice and Political Cultures. In Newburn, T. and Sparks, R. (eds.). *Criminal Justice and Political Cultures: National and International Dimension of Crime Control.* Cullompton: Willan Publishing. pp. 1–15.

MCALLISTER, W. B. (2000) *Drug Diplomacy in the Twentieth Century: An International History.* London: Routledge.

MILLS, J. H. and BARTON, P. (2007) *Drugs and Empires: Essays in Modern Imperialism and Intoxication.* Basingstoke: Palgrave MacMillan.

RITTER, A. (2009) Methods for Comparing Drug Policies: The Utility of Composite Drug Harm Indexes. *International Journal of Drug Policy.* 20. pp. 475–479.

SEDDON, T. (2016) Inventing Drugs: A Genealogy of a Regulatory Concept. *Journal of Law and Society* (forthcoming 43/3).

WITHINGTON, P. (2014) Introduction: Cultures of Intoxication. *Past and Present.* 222 (suppl. 9). pp. 9–33.

YSA, T., COLOM, J., ALBAREDA, A., RAMON, A., CARRIÓN, M. and SEGURA, L. (2014) *Governance of Addictions: European Public Policies.* Oxford: Oxford University Press.

Part I

Regional dimensions of European drug policies

Chapter 1

The politics of expertise and EU drug policy

Martin Elvins

> Another challenge that I would like to highlight is the waning political attention on the drugs phenomenon in Europe.
>
> Wolfgang Götz, 27 January 2015

The above remarks by Wolfgang Götz, the then Director of the European Monitoring Centre for Drugs and Drug Addiction (EMCDDA), were made in the course of a speech at the European Parliament in January 2015, and there are two broad factors that may offer initial explanation as to why he expressed these sentiments at this time. The first, as he acknowledged later in his speech, is that the policy maker's priorities are more sharply focused on other issues of public concern, such as terrorism and immigration. The second, on which he did not offer comment, is that the high degree of autonomy over the content of national drug policy preserved under the European Union (EU) treaties has made substantive political dialogue on the topic progressively less important for individual member states, especially as the main contours of the problem have shown some degree of stabilisation in recent years.

One way of conceptualising EU policy actions around illegal drugs is to see them as a distillation of a well-established normative political consensus around the causal dynamics of the problem. In which case, with little incentive for a wider policy debate the emphasis then shifts to programmes rather than ideas. The sense that EU policy on drugs is now in a mature phase is well supported by the fact that since the Treaty on European Union (TEU) entered into force there have now been three iterations of an *EU Drugs Strategy* (2000–2004, 2005–2012, and 2013–2020) and five iterations of an *EU Action Plan on Drugs* (the first covering 1995–1999 and the most recent covering 2013–2016), each drafted by the European Commission. The latter are the main instrument of EU drug policy, utilised to help Member States reach common positions and as a basis upon which to operationalise the overall *Drugs Strategy* (Diamandourous, 2005). Individual instruments have also had a significant impact. In particular, Hedrich, Pirona and Wiessing (2008, pp. 504–505) highlight the significance of a Recommendation on the prevention and reduction of health-related harm associated with drug dependence approved by the European Council in 2003 (European Council,

2003). A further important, and in this case binding, legal instrument was the Council Decision 2005/387/JHA of 10 May 2005 on the information exchange and risk assessment for the control of new psychoactive substances (NPS).

With this context in mind, this chapter offers a commentary on the possible consequences of waning political attention for drug policy outcomes, informed by analysis of the role of expertise in generating and preserving normative consensus at the EU level.

The EU and drugs: policy, but not as we know it

The first thing to say about EU drug policy is that it 'has a very narrow legal basis in the EU treaties' (Edwards and Galla, 2014, p. 943) and 'competencies for drugs policy (including its public health, criminal justice, enforcement and customs components) remain primarily at member state level' (Culley et al., 2012, xiii). Babor et al. (2010, p. 5) define drug policy as a set of administrative actions:

1   programmes to prevent the initiation of drug use by non-users;
2   health and social service programmes intended to help heavy drug users change their behaviour or reduce the consequences of their drug use; and
3   laws, regulations, and initiatives to control the supply of illegal drugs (as well as the supply of diverted prescription drugs used for non-medical purposes).

Analytically, in all three cases primacy of decision-making over law, policy design and implementation rests firmly at the national level, albeit the latter is heavily coloured by public international law, so further enquiry is needed to truly understand the purpose and outcomes of EU activity in the field of illegal drug policy.

An EU citizen motivated to understand the current role played by the EU in the field of illegal drugs policy would find that a search engine query would almost certainly direct them to the website of the Directorate General (DG) Migration and Home Affairs (European Commission, 2016) within the European Commission, from which they would learn that the EU's current response is set out in the *EU Drugs Strategy 2013–2020*. The website states that the 'important coordination and support role' of the European Commission encompasses the following functions:

- monitor and evaluate actions taken by EU countries to reduce drug use and prevent drugs-related crime and trafficking;
- propose EU-wide control measures for new drugs when necessary after carefully analysing risk assessments;
- enforce the EU law to control and prevent the use of chemical substances for the manufacture of illicit drugs;
- foster European cooperation by providing financial assistance in the field of illicit drugs;

- ensure the overall coherence of the EU drugs policy framework and coordinate EU positions in international forums;
- support cross-border projects in the illicit drugs field.

On closer inspection the internal organisation of DG Home shows that this policy field is administered via the Anti-Drugs Unit (D. 4), which comes under the remit of sub-Directorate D: Security. This unit was transferred from DG Justice in September 2014 under the administration of new EU President Jean-Claude Juncker (European Commission, 2014), after more than a decade under the justice framework. A link from the DG Home website to the *EU Drugs Strategy 2013–2020* yields a 10-page document first published in the Official Journal in December 2012 (OJ C 402/1–10, 29.12.2012).

A close look at the role of DG Home elicits the following point from its website: 'Drugs policy is largely the responsibility of the EU national authorities, which are best placed to make those choices that suit the local culture and socio-economic conditions. But drugs are a transnational threat, and therefore EU countries cannot tackle it effectively on their own.'

'EU drug policy' is a misnomer; the EU supports rather than leads on this matter.[1] The *EU Drugs Strategy* is formally approved at the level of head of state, that is, at the European Council. For such agreement to occur, what is the process that underpins this?

In a highly insightful 2014 article, Carel Edwards (the ex-head of the European Commission's Anti-Drug Policy Unit 2003–2010) and Maurice Galla – who have direct knowledge of the inner workings of EU drug policy – make a strong case that EU advocacy of a balanced approach to drug policy (mixing demand- and harm-reduction policies on the one hand, and law enforcement and international cooperation on the other) has made a positive contribution in a world where many states regard illegal drugs as a pretext for the use of strongly repressive measures. With virtually all states in the world now party to the three UN Drug Conventions (1961, 1971 and 1988) it is clear that the prohibition principle enshrined within them affords very wide scope in the form of its implementation within national boundaries, and in accommodating differences it may well, somewhat paradoxically, serve to sustain the continuity of the conventions (Bewley-Taylor, 2012, p. 97). Whilst harm reduction has become synonymous with a *European* approach to drug policy, and is widely adopted by Member States, it does not, by definition, claim to be an overall solution to the drug problem. In fact, precisely because policies under the rubric of harm reduction

---

1 The DG Home webpage makes no specific reference to it but another DG, the Directorate General Health and Food Safety, has responsibility for EU policy concerning HIV/AIDS. Given that injecting drug use is identified as its second most significant transmission mode there is clear overlap with both EU and national drug policies in its work. Under Article 6 of the Treaty of Lisbon, public health is a policy area where the Union supports, complements or supplements the actions of the Member States.

intrinsically recognise the likely continuity of the problem (that is, that the demand for, and use of, psychoactive substances will persist), they do not tend to invoke deeper questioning of its causal dynamics and the systemic role played by policies aimed at supply.

Despite claims of gradual convergence in drug policies across Member States (MacGregor and Whiting, 2010; Culley et al., 2012), Edwards and Galla note that 'it is difficult to establish a causal link between EU policy on the one hand and changes in national drug policies on the other' (2014, p. 943). MacGregor and Whiting support a conclusion that 'progressive although limited convergence in European drug policies' has occurred, with harm reduction both an element and an indicator of this convergence (2010, p. 75). Culley et al. (2012, xix) concluded that the *EU Drugs Strategy 2005–2012* and its *Action Plans* had contributed to a convergence in the way individual Member States formulate and adopt their own national drugs policies and strategies. Whilst embracing harm reduction has come to symbolise a form of distinctively European progress there may be a danger that asking more radical questions thus becomes tantamount to heresy due to the strength of collective agreement on this overarching principle, with the result that deeper normative understanding of the drugs problem and how to address it reflects a longer term consensus. As a result 'new' approaches are inherently more likely to be incremental versions of past consensus. It is therefore important to assess the underlying nature and basis of that consensus.

Experts, drugs and European policy: a long view

The role of expertise in framing and shaping drug policy is a phenomenon that has received relatively little attention. In practice the credentials of designated drug experts are not placed under any real scrutiny and the impact of their role is routinely seen as uncontroversial, benign and essential to ensure policymaking is qualitatively efficient. It is rare – certainly in drug policy – to see direct attention given to questions such as what is the precise nature and content of expert knowledge? To what extent does expert input shape normative outcomes, and via what mechanisms? Whilst there will generally be some form of entry qualification threshold to an expert group, the processes and criteria are opaque regarding how such qualifications are validated, defined and potentially disclosed for scrutiny. However, this is not unique to drug policy, as many readers will be aware.

This chapter examines a series of interrelated questions: how have drug experts influenced the evolution of EU drug policy at key stages? Why did their ideas gain saliency? What analytical tools are available to direct analysis of the ongoing role and influence of experts? The chapter takes the position that expertise on supply reduction has achieved a normative pre-eminence in framing the causal dynamics of the drugs issue at the EU level. To understand normative aspects of European drug policy it is necessary to take a longer view. After the signing of the Single European Act (SEA) in 1986, collective anti-drug trafficking policies became part of a broader normative policy framework, based on the idea that 'removing' internal borders would causally increase crime and that the most effective way to address this was through 'compensatory' law enforcement measures. At this time, law enforcement professionals were thus placed at the forefront of political change in Europe; it was imperative that the new political and economic system should operate without problems. This process significantly enhanced the professional competence and authoritative claim to policy-relevant knowledge of law enforcement experts. The precedent for bringing law enforcement experts together in specialist European forums had been set as early as 1972, when the formation of a Customs Mutual Assistance Group (MAG) under European Economic Community (EEC) auspices established the principle that direct dialogue between experts (specialist officials and practitioners) was the best way for strategic thinking and practical ideas regarding European law enforcement cooperation to be formulated. The significant point here is that national actors were given authority to develop a basis for *international* cooperation, and to propose specific activities around this, before submitting them for political approval. This blueprint for policy-making has subsequently proved remarkably influential in relation to the course of law enforcement policy development in Europe, especially in relation to anti-drugs actions.

Around 1985, drug trafficking and related 'serious crime' became a central concern of the Trevi Group. Trevi was an intergovernmental mechanism for dialogue between senior law enforcement officials and practitioners from Member States. Policy ideas were developed within small specialist groups or 'working parties'. Within the confines of secretive transnational policy-making forums, a rationale was generated for increased law enforcement measures to combat projected rising levels of drug trafficking. A transnational law enforcement policy network began to emerge, facilitated via the Trevi framework, as well as a growing interaction between interior ministries in this burgeoning area of policy development. In short, the basis for a common policy enterprise had been founded, bringing together experts from the home affairs ministries of national administrations and senior law enforcement officers from national policing, customs and security agencies.

On 3 October 1989 President François Mitterrand of France sent a letter calling for more coordination between the then twelve EC members to counter the growing evidence of an 'escalation' in the drugs problem. The Strasbourg European Council of 8–9 December 1989 formally agreed to the proposals and to the setting up of a European Committee to Combat Drugs (better known by its French acronym CELAD). CELAD did generate several tangible outputs, the most notable being the first two European plans to combat drugs of 1990 and 1992, which pre-dated the post-TEU plans and strategies listed earlier in this chapter. Elsen (1995, pp. 362–366) questions whether CELAD ever really took on the mission of 'essential coordination' within its original remit: 'CELAD, by its origins and activities could not confine itself to areas to do with home affairs and justice: the greatest of its achievements (the European Plan to fight drugs, the Monitoring Centre, the European Prevention Week) are either entirely outside this framework or go considerably beyond it.'

It is clear from analysis of documents relating to the Dublin European Council of 25–26 June 1990 that in drafting the 1990 plan to combat drugs, CELAD simply incorporated the recommendations of Trevi and the MAG on a wholesale basis without any debate, highlighting the rigidly demarcated nature of policy ideas from these 'supply-side' expert sources (Elvins, 2003).

The entry into force of the TEU on 1 November 1993 brought with it a new institutional framework, resulting in the formal disbanding of both CELAD and Trevi. However, the TEU marked the political legitimisation of the Trevi era and all of the decisions and agreements made at that time. It also formalised and institutionalised the Trevi decision-making framework, without introducing a new system of transparency or accountability for the highly secretive form of policy-making characteristic of the Trevi era. The 1985 Schengen agreement had the aim of creating free movement of persons, goods and services between its original five members through the abolition of internal borders. The agreement (revised in 1990) further consolidated the use of and need for compensatory measures to improve coordination between police and judicial authorities, including the Schengen Information System (SIS) database. Schengen furthered the logic that the main driver of the expansion of drug use was supply related, and following the 1997 Treaty of Amsterdam it became fully incorporated into the EU framework. This complex accumulation of precedents, preferences and political validation has shown a consistent pattern whereby expert knowledge has been used to validate particular courses of action, and in the process elevate certain causal under-standings over others. Evidence supporting the Trevi claims was never placed in the public domain; hence there was no possibility of public debate. Before assessing current policy structures in comparative terms it is important to consider what analytical tools may inform our understanding.

Epistemic communities: a brief outline

The concept of epistemic communities focuses on the role played by networks of 'knowledge-based experts' in articulating the cause-and-effect relationships of complex problems, helping states identify their interests, framing the issues for collective debate, proposing specific policies, and identifying salient points for negotiation. The concept firmly directs attention to how knowledge and ideas influence the course of international policy development through examining the role of 'knowledge based networks' of experts. The fullest development of the concept is found in the work of Peter Haas, seeking to examine the role of such experts 'in articulating the cause-and-effect relationships of complex problems, helping states identify their interests, framing the issues for collective debate, proposing specific policies, and identifying salient points for negotiation' (Haas, 1992, p. 2).

Critical to the definition of an epistemic community is its possession of an authoritative claim to policy-relevant knowledge (Haas 1992, p. 3). Members of an epistemic community generally share (1) normative and principled beliefs;

(2) causal beliefs; (3) internally defined criteria for weighing and validating knowledge in the domain of their expertise; and (4) a common policy enterprise. The definition is founded on the much deeper premise that *control over knowledge and information is an important dimension of power*, and that the diffusion of new ideas and information can generate 'new' patterns of behaviour, and thereby determine the course of international policy co-ordination. The suggestion here is that an epistemic community is capable of developing – in some sense autonomously – some form of 'vision' concerning a particular issue before introducing it into the political policy arena.

Of course, an 'epistemic community' is entirely free to suggest any 'causal' ideas that it wishes. However, at some point, its members must be cognisant of *pre-existing* social and political conditions in framing those ideas. This is particularly true for policy areas that do not involve what we might call 'pure' science, but draw upon technical experts from specific professions. In evaluating the epistemic communities model and its depiction of causation, it is important to consider the effects of cognitive processes that essentially treat social phenomena as if they were natural objects; that is to say, that they are broadly unchanging both in terms of a causal chain of events and the relationship between causal factors. If the influence of an epistemic community is based upon its effective association of a set of causal beliefs then it is important that the underlying basis of those beliefs is questioned. Why are the beliefs held? An epistemic community *could* be successful precisely because its causal analysis does not challenge certain social or political values; that is, its success is based not upon the radical 'newness' of its 'causal' ideas but on their conservatism (in taking social relations as emerging out of an established and 'given' pattern of causal factors). This contrasts with the image of an epistemic community working from some kind of 'neutral' epistemological position. Professional training, prestige, and reputation for expertise in an 'area highly valued by society or elite decision makers' affords members of an epistemic community 'access to the political system and legitimise[s] or authorise[s] their activities' (Haas, 1992, p. 17).

The Trevi Group performed the kind of uncertainty-reducing role claimed by Haas to be typical of an epistemic community when the idea of free movement within a common European space became a serious possibility, driven by powerful political and economic forces. In the process, a set of causal ideas about drug problems were propagated, based on the notion of expanded threat arising from the removal of internal border controls, and became politically elevated over other causal explanations (and hence policy alternatives) at this time.

The Trevi working methods were seamlessly adopted and formalised once the TEU entered force, but from this point national ministries took a much closer interest in the broadening agenda of EU Justice and Home Affairs (JHA) and the process became more bureaucratic in nature. Nonetheless, by retaining the emphasis on developing drug policy within the JHA policy arena, law enforcement expertise retained the highest status in the development of policy ideas. A more mature phase, in which epistemic influence retained its saliency but ideological

20 Martin Elvins

argument became increasingly replaced by a more technocratic style of policy development was apparent by the mid-1990s. The preparedness of Member States to support a balanced approach at EU level relies in part on the fact that it preserves the ability of national politicians to retain the option of exercising tougher enforcement when they sense the public mood requires evidence of action. National drug policy is more closely dependent on electoral cycles within Member States but, with some irony, Edwards and Galla suggest that 'it was partly the very reluctance of national politicians to get involved in this high risk issue that produced an unusually consensual climate among the Member States' (2014, p. 943). In this view the EU policy offered little challenge to national prerogative, allowing quite wide variations in national approach to co-exist, with Portugal adopting its distinctive decriminalisation of drug use policy in 2001 whilst other states sought to give the impression of retaining a tough stance on all aspects of the drug issue in the following decade or so. This lack of conflict has largely preserved the Trevi era understanding of a causal relationship between open borders and increased drug problems in Europe, allowing law enforcement activities in drug policy to continue seemingly without any EU debate around their efficacy conflated as they are within a broader security agenda.

When it entered force in 1999 the Treaty of Amsterdam had the objective of providing EU citizens with a high level of safety within an area of freedom, security and justice (AFSJ), for which 'The fight against drugs is an inseparable objective' (European Commission, 1999, p. 2). It is therefore interesting to consider how expert discourse articulates the rationale for such a fight in the AFSJ era, and mobilises ideas in support of it, and whether some form of epistemic community can be defined. The cohering principle of the 1992 project and Trevi's central ideas and causal logic around drugs is much harder to discern amidst ostensibly more mature multidisciplinary thinking on drug policy, yet the seemingly unshakeable desire for 'action' by way of 'fighting' drugs persists unabated.

Contemporary patterns: back to the future?

Edwards and Galla suggest drug policy in the EU was focused on drug supply reduction in the early 1990s – rooted in police and judicial cooperation – before moving to a post-Lisbon Treaty (Treaty on the Functioning of the European Union – TFEU) phase of shared competence (2014, p. 943). It is in the most recent part of this phase where there seems to be evidence of a shift away from policy-making in the round to a more separate, discrete set of policy actions, with security issues re-emerging as a dominant theme.[2]

Wider EU competence encompasses aspects such as controlling the trade in drug precursors, preventing money laundering, establishing minimum penalties for illicit drug trafficking in Member States' criminal law, as well as information

---

2 For an overview of the impact of the TFEU on the EU approach to drugs see Culley et al., 2012, pp. 16–17.

exchange, risk assessment and control of new psychoactive substances (NPS), hence the obvious need, not least administratively, to coordinate policy initiatives. The Horizontal Working Party on Drugs, more usually termed the Horizontal Drugs Group (HDG), formed in 1997, performs this role. It reports to the Committee of Permanent Representatives to the European Union (COREPER) and is chaired by whichever country holds the rotating EU presidency. Delegates from each member state attend along with staff from the relevant part of the European Commission (now DG Home, and before that various incarnations of DG Justice), EMCDDA, Europol, and – post-Lisbon – the European External Action Service (EEAS). Around 80 civil servants from a variety of backgrounds (health, justice and foreign affairs) from all Member States, and the Commission and the Council Secretariat attend (Edwards and Galla, 2014, p. 943).[3]

The Member State holding the presidency prepares working documents for discussion, with the aim of ultimate approval by the Council of the European Union (or as with the Drugs Strategy, the European Council). In cases where legislation is proposed the European Parliament has the right of co-decision. The lead DG within the Commission (now DG Home) is instrumental in preparing most documents, but Member States can also take non-legislative initiatives (Edwards and Galla, 2014, p. 943). The HDG is not the only forum for drug policy discussion as matters regarding precursor control also fall under the ambit of the Customs Working Party and, since its formation in 2010, the Standing Committee on Operational Cooperation on Internal Security (COSI), which has a mandate concerning operational actions relating to internal security. On the matter of cross-border supply and organised group activity this body has a direct interest in illegal drugs, albeit in a more narrowly conceived sense.

The TFEU contained no specific clauses relating to drug issues but did introduce a number of changes in both the AFSJ and public health, each with implications for drugs policy. For example, in addition to changes in legislative instruments and procedures, the European Court of Justice (ECJ) was given full jurisdiction in the areas of judicial cooperation in criminal matters and police cooperation. The EU can now also adopt measures regarding the way in which Member States conduct evaluations in the policy areas relevant to DG Home (and previously DG Justice), which include drugs (Article 70 TFEU). More overtly, under Lisbon drug trafficking is defined as one of several 'Eurocrimes' within the EU, allowing for the establishment of minimum rules concerning the definition of criminal offences in the areas of particularly serious crime with a cross-border dimension, which includes illicit drug trafficking (Article 83(1) TFEU). On the face of it, the TFEU ushered in a strong emphasis toward strengthening the enforcement aspect of drug policy, which might be expected to have subsequently elevated the prominence and status of ideas and claims to policy knowledge in that domain.

---

3   For more details on the evolution and mechanisms inherent to this process see Boekhout van Solinge, 2002; Elvins, 2003.

Edwards and Galla explain how the EU drug strategy and action plans provide a working agenda for the HDG (which meets monthly) and point out the distinctive – and in some ways remarkable – feature of this system whereby 'policy in an extremely sensitive area is left to a large extent to civil servants. As much of drug policy in the EU is prepared and implemented at national level, the discussions at EU level concentrate on cross-border and international aspects, common approaches to specific issues such as the challenges posed by new psychoactive substances etc.' (Edwards and Galla, 2014, p. 943).

Informed by regular Commission evaluations of how the Strategies and Action Plans are being implemented gives the impression of a rigorous, scientific process, but in practice Edwards and Galla suggest this is undermined because 'political pressure' is such that a presidency country in the year an action plan is up for renewal 'has hardly ever accepted a pause for analysis and reflection' (*ibid.*).

Unlike the HDG, COSI has an operational focus, aiming to support actions by Member States in the field of internal security. The decision to shift Commission responsibility for drugs from DG Justice to DG Home in 2014 appears to suggest that this dimension has been strengthened. This suggests a return to the model in which supply reduction becomes an end in itself, more detached from the wider 'balanced approach' in practice. Whilst there is no doubt that the EU and its Member States favour a balanced approach, the effect of seeing supply reduction as a self-regulating end in itself highlights the reality that decision-making is locked into what Edwards and Galla term 'accommodation' of the problem. The reason this is problematic is not because under the UN framework there is any serious possibility of abandoning prohibition in the near future, but a longstanding causal logic is perpetuated: that drug demand is causally related to supply. This is in spite of the fact that the 2012 RAND evaluation of the *EU Drugs Strategy 2005–2012* found 'few visible indicators that trends on the supply side are moving in a desirable direction' (Culley et al., 2012, xv). However, it also recorded the critical point that implementation of supply reduction objectives is to a great extent a matter of national legislation.

Herein lies an apparent paradox. The *EU Drugs Strategy*, and the policy-making machinery at EU level are in place to 'add value' to national actions, yet in reinforcing what might be ineffective strategies we must ask, what sustains this? Politically, it is clear that supply reduction measures continue to hold a seductive charm. The creation of COSI has introduced a body not focused on wider drug policy as such, but with a remit to promote operational actions in the field of internal security. This is seen as a challenge to the multidisciplinary coordination of drug policy to some extent (Edwards and Galla, 2014, p. 943). As Culley et al. (2012, xvii) observe: 'Law enforcement activities in drugs policy have gained importance in the EU internal security agenda. This may have caused the HDG to begin to reduce or lose some of its coordinating role in the area of supply reduction, posing a threat to the balanced approach'.

Not only that, the operational aspect of COSI's work also impinges on the EU's external relations in the field of drugs. There is little doubt that illegal drugs have recently become more deeply embedded in a much wider EU security agenda, and within this politicised environment it is more difficult to extricate the separate causal dynamics that underpin, say, the use of drugs from factors that stimulate human trafficking. Merely acting against both is an end in itself. COSI 'has increasingly gained prominence and traction, in part for its perceived "action-oriented approach" in the field of supply reduction' (Culley et al., 2012, p. 99). The sense that drug policy is embedded without question in actions against transnational organised crime more generally is reinforced by the 2015 European Agenda on Security. The agenda sets three priority areas for European security, two of which – serious and organised cross-border crime, and cybercrime – merely list drugs alongside other forms of threat without any kind of distinction as to their underlying causes (European Commission, 2015).

Conclusion

Speaking in June 2015 to the Civil Liberties, Justice and Home Affairs (LIBE) Committee of the European Parliament on the subject of the 2015 EMCDDA Annual Report on Europe's drug problem – its twentieth such report – the aforementioned Wolfgang Götz made a choice of words that exemplifies the sense of accommodation of the problem, present in the recent EU drug policy narrative identified by Edwards and Galla. In reflecting on how a heroin epidemic and related HIV-transmission issues characterised an EU of 15 states back in 1995 when the first EMCDDA report was published, he said: 'Although these problems persist today, the responses needed are largely in place and other emerging issues now demand our attention': Götz noted that more than 6,000 overdose deaths were reported in the EU in 2013, but again 'widespread responses to the problem are now being implemented' (Götz, 2015b). The same speech also drew on the detailed analysis in the main report (EMCDDA, 2015) highlighting increases in drug purity, the acceleration of new psychoactive substances (the EU was then monitoring over 480), and the fact that both new and established drugs are increasingly available online. These factors suggest a problem with dimensions that are not being well served by historical approaches, yet Europe's 'record' on drugs and its 'balanced' approach are often presented as an exemplar for the world – indeed Mr Götz' closing remarks in the speech make precisely such a claim.

This chapter has attempted to locate the source of the apparent inertia in EU drugs policy identified by Edwards and Galla, and places it in a longer established pattern of expert-driven EU policy development in which supply-side expertise is pre-eminent. Member States have shown clear diversity in the ways they have re-thought drug policy approaches in their own societies (as other chapters in this volume demonstrate). Yet, at the collective, EU level the broad consensus on a 'balanced approach' has produced a parallel trend of hiving off drug law enforcement activities to an area of policy development that is more action- than ideas-oriented, while being deeply embedded in institutionalised approaches to security. This marks something of a return to a previous era when authoritative claims to policy-relevant knowledge rested primarily with those representing a security perspective focused on drug-supply-side objectives. The consequences of this situation can be examined through the lens of epistemic communities: pointing to the way in which a dominant causal understanding of a problem effectively ensures continuity for certain approaches over others, largely on the basis that they do not challenge wider political interests. The emergence of EU-level discourse supporting an enforcement-led approach to a largely undifferentiated series of security threats (viz. the European Agenda on Security) may well indicate a return to the implicit, unchallenged assumption that the drug problem is predominantly a supply side problem amenable to intervention by a combination of national and EU law enforcement measures and bodies. In the process, the likelihood of clear analysis of the specific features of the drugs problem and the artificial black markets that are the corollary of prohibition is effectively sidelined. A striking absence of reliable metrics and underdeveloped indicators persists in relation to supply reduction – an absence identified in the RAND review of the 2005–2012 Drugs Strategy (Culley et al., 2012, p. 92), perhaps revealing a latent unwillingness to homogenise indicators by ministries of interior and justice. It is not, perhaps, waning attention to the drug phenomenon that underpins these issues after all, but simply an offsetting, sharper interest in propagating the existence of a more generic-threat agenda on which a range of security actions can be rationalised. In consequence any search for a new approach to managing drugs that goes beyond accommodation of the problem is deprioritised.

The dizzying array of opinion, evidence, law and data on drug issues in the 28 Member States of the EU somewhat works against clarity at times. As Roberts (2014, p. 955) astutely observes: 'many of the key issues for drug policy are not in principle amenable to purely evidential solutions because they have a normative aspect. There is often an implicit assumption that rational governance processes should produce a reasoned consensus on a policy solution … [B]ut many of the key issues in drug policy are inherently contestable.'

Viewed through this lens, and with the perspective outlined in this chapter that validated expert knowledge serves primarily to satisfy a results-focused political process, then for all the intimations of progress, the possibility of more radical debate on drug policy in, and via, the auspices of the EU appears remote at present. For 'balanced approach' read no desire to change the political expediency of pursuing action-oriented supply policies, despite a dearth of evidence as to their efficacy.

References

BABOR, T. F., CAULKINS, J. P., EDWARDS, G., FISCHER, B., FOXCROFT, D. R., HUMPHREYS, K., OBOT, I. S., REHM, J., REUTER, P., ROOM, R., ROSSOW, I. and STRANG, J. (2010) *Drug Policy and the Public Good*. Oxford: Oxford University Press.

BENNETT, T. and HOLLOWAY, K. (2010) Is UK Drug Policy Evidence Based? *International Journal of Drug Policy*. 21. pp. 411–417.

BEWLEY-TAYLOR, D. (2012) *International Drug Control. Consensus Fractured.* Cambridge: Cambridge University Press.

BOEKHOUT VAN SOLINGE, T. (2002) *Drugs and Decision-Making in the European Union.* Amsterdam: DRO/Met and Schilt.

CULLEY, D. M., TAYLOR, J., RUBIN, J., HOORENS, S., DISLEY, E. and RABINOVICH, D. (2012) *Assessment of the Implementation of the EU Drugs Strategy 2005–2012 and its Action Plans.* Cambridge: Rand Europe.

DIAMANDOUROS, N. (2005) The European Ombudsman and EU Drugs Policy. Presentation by the European Ombudsman, Professor P. Nikiforos Diamandouros, to the 10th European Conference on Rehabilitation and Drug Policy – Drug Addiction, Treatment and Prevention in a United Europe: Diversity and Equality, Heraklion, Greece, 14 May 2005. Available from: http://ombudsman.europa.eu/speeches/en/2005-05-14.htm [Accessed: 29 April 2016].

EDWARDS, C. and GALLA, M. (2014) Governance in EU Illicit Drugs Policy. *International Journal of Drug Policy*. 25. pp. 942–947.

ELSEN, C. (1995) Drugs as a Priority in Cooperation in the Fields of Justice and Home Affairs. In Estievenart, G. (ed.). *Policies and Strategies to Combat Drugs in Europe. The Treaty on European Union: Framework for a New European Strategy to Combat Drugs?* Dordrecht: Martinus Nijhoff, pp. 360–368.

ELVINS, M. (2003) *Anti-drugs Policies of the European Union.* Basingstoke: Palgrave Macmillan.

EUROPEAN COMMISSION (1999) *Communication from the Commission to the Council and the European Parliament on a European Action Plan to combat drugs (2000–2004).* Brussels: 26 May 1999, COM (1999) 239. Available from: http://eeas.europa.eu/drugs/docs/ap00_04_en.pdf [Accessed 29 April 2016].

EUROPEAN COMMISSION (2014) The Juncker Commission: A Strong and Experienced Team Standing for Change. *Press Release IP/14/984*, 10 September 2014. Available: http://europa.eu/rapid/press-release_IP-14-984_en.htm

EUROPEAN COMMISSION (2015) The European Agenda on Security. *Communication from the Commission to the European Parliament, the Council, the European Economic and Social Committee and the Committee of the Regions*, Strasbourg, 28. 4. 2015 COM (2015) 185 final. Available from: http://ec.europa.eu/dgs/home-affairs/e-library/documents/basic-do cuments/docs/eu_agenda_on_security_en.pdf [Accessed: 29 April 2016].

EUROPEAN COMMISSION (2016), *EU's response to drugs* webpage. Available from: http://ec.europa.eu/dgs/home-affairs/what-we-do/policies/organized-crime-and-human-trafficking/drug-control/eu-response-to-drugs/index_en.htm [Accessed: 29 April 2016].

EUROPEAN COUNCIL (2003) Council Recommendation of 18 June 2003 on the prevention and reduction of health-related harm associated with drug dependence *(2003/488/EC)*, OJ L 165, 03. 07. 2003, pp. 31–33.

EUROPEAN COUNCIL (2012) *EU Drugs Strategy (2013–20).* OJ C 402, 29. 12. 2012, pp. 1–10.

EMCDDA (2015) *European Drug Report 2015.* Luxembourg: Publications Office of the European Union.

GÖTZ, W. (2015a) Drug policies in the perspective of the United Nations General Assembly Special Session (UNGASS 2016) – Views of the EMCDDA Director. *Speech to European Members of the Global Commission on Drug Policy at the European Parliament, Brussels,*

27 January 2015. Available from: http://www.emcdda.europa.eu/news/speeches [Accessed: 29 April 2016].

GÖTZ, W. (2015b) European Drug Report 2015. *Speech to the Committee for Civil Liberties, Justice and Home Affairs (LIBE) of the European Parliament*, 17 June 2015. Available from: http://www.emcdda.europa.eu/news/speeches [Accessed: 29 April 2016].

HAAS, P. M. (1992) Introduction: Epistemic Communities and International Policy Coordination. *International Organization*. 46. pp. 1–35.

HEDRICH, D., PIRONA, A. and WIESSING, L. (2008) From Margin to Mainstream: The Evolution of Harm Reduction Responses to Problem Drug Use in Europe. *Drugs: Education, Prevention and Policy*. 15(6). pp. 503–517.

MACGREGOR, S. and WHITING, M. (2010) The Development of European Drug Policy and the Place of Harm Reduction Within This. In Rhodes, T. and Hedrich, D. (eds.). *Harm Reduction: Evidence, Impacts and Challenges*. EMCDDA Monographs 10. Luxembourg: Publications Office of the European Union.

ROBERTS, M. (2014) Making Drug Policy Together: Reflections on Evidence, Engagement and Participation. *International Journal of Drug Policy*. 25. pp. 952–956.

Chapter 2

Pathways to integration of European drug policy

Caroline Chatwin

Introduction

A brief examination of national drug policies in operation within the European Union (EU) demonstrates considerable variety in approach. The drug policies of the Netherlands and Sweden offer good examples of the two different extremes of drug policy operating within Europe and thus deserve a brief exploration here. In Sweden drug policy is strictly control-oriented and moralistic, operating as a cross political party issue where policy is endorsed by wider society in its entirety (Boekhout van Solinge, 1997; Lenke and Olsson, 2002; Goldberg, 2004). The ultimate aim is to achieve a drug free society, which has resulted in a policy that is stricter than that of many other European countries. Policies disallow the consumption of drugs (as compared to many European countries which only criminalise their possession), recognise no difference between soft and hard drugs, ensure that users are targeted with as much vigour as dealers and invest primarily in abstention-based or coercive-treatment programmes. Tham (1995) describes the Swedish drug problem as having become entwined with national identity; the life of the drug abuser is held up as the antithesis of the life of the good citizen. Drugs are seen as a problem that has come from outside Sweden and, as such, constitute a threat to the Swedish lifestyle (Gould, 1994). It is therefore an issue that supersedes party political interest and requires the participation of all if it is to be overcome.

In the Netherlands, meanwhile, drug policy has been based on the principle of normalising the drug problem as much as possible (van Vliet, 1990). Rather than seeking to stigmatise and marginalise drug users, pushing them to the outskirts of society, policy seeks to normalise their experience and include them within society as far as possible. Where they are treated as 'different' is as patients in need of cure rather than as criminals in need of punishment. Pragmatic policy initiatives such as the 'separation of the markets' have been implemented whereby, in an effort to keep cannabis users away from potentially more damaging drugs, semi-legal environments (coffee shops) have been established where cannabis can be bought and consumed under some form of regulation. The overall aim, which has become as important a part of national identity to the Dutch as the pursuit of a drug free society is to the Swedes, is to minimise the harm done to society by the use of drugs and, therefore, the principle of harm reduction has gained much ground here.

Other European Member States differ along the continuum between the Netherlands and Sweden, and there are many innovative drug policy practices in operation in Europe. One example is provided by the 'cannabis clubs' emerging across Europe that exploit national legislative loopholes tolerating the growth of one or two cannabis plants for personal consumption, to allow the collective production of much larger amounts of cannabis (Decorte, 2014). Another example is decriminalisation (the removal or partial removal of criminal penalties in relation to certain drug offences), popularised in Portugal with national legislation in 2001 that removed the possibility of criminal penalty for possession of small quantities of all illegal substances. Indeed, Vasconi (2013, p. 2) has described Europe as 'the region with the most diverse experience, expertise and evidence around drug policy'. Based on this evidence, it would be easy to imagine that there has been very little in the way of harmonisation of European drug policy. On the contrary, this chapter aims to outline a brief history of the considerable developments in European drug policy within the EU, and to explore the different pathways to harmonisation that have been conceptualised in relation to policy in this area.

Policy integration and the European Union

Since its cautious inception in 1950, born out of a desire to inextricably link policy making between countries after the Second World War, the European Union (EU) has burgeoned into the most powerful supranational institution in the world (McCormick, 1999; Dinan, 2005). During this time, the harmonisation of national policies has clearly been a defining policy concept, as demonstrated by the overarching aim of providing an 'ever closer union' between Member States. Most European commentators would agree that economic harmonisation has been increasing: in 1988 a customs union was formed, followed by a single market in 1993 and a single currency in 1999. Integration theorists have since observed that the single market and monetary union operated in Europe is the most advanced form of economic integration between sovereign states (Dinan, 2005).

Integration has not, however, been consistently applied across policy areas, and social policy in particular has been described as a 'poor relation' to economic integration (McCormick, 1999, p. 66). As economic integration has advanced, it has been increasingly necessary to introduce and develop some social integration (Ross, 1995), but developments have lacked the motivation born out of a drive to create an influential and powerful trading entity, as in the economic policy arena. Originally envisaged as a 'handmaiden to economic objectives' (Hantrais, 2007, p. 18), the complexities of national social policy (other than those areas deemed essential for continued economic integration such as policies surrounding migrant workers) were judged too formidable to submit to the kind of European Union control of economic policy. Policy implementations in this area have, therefore, not tended to be of as concrete and well-structured a nature as those relating to economic matters.

Nevertheless, some progress has been made in the integration of social policy, where integration has been interpreted, not as leading to uniformity, but as being built on 'co-operation and co-ordination based on recognition and tolerance of diversity' (Hantrais, 2007, p. 29). This falls in line with the application of the principle of subsidiarity, which dictates that decisions should be taken as closely as possible to the citizen and that the EU should only intervene where action cannot satisfactorily be left to Member States (Duff, 1993). European social policy has not, therefore, developed towards the creation of EU institutions and legislation as the replacement for national governments' social policy regimes. Rather, its limited promotion has allowed the EU to obtain a regulatory role overseeing, and making small adjustments to, national policies. It has been described as 'a multi-leveled, highly fragmented system in which policy "develops" but is beyond the firm control of any single political authority' (Pierson and Liebfried, 1995, p. 433). Geyer (2000, p. 212) has further suggested that 'instead of harmonising national-level social policy regimes, EU social policy may actually encourage them to diversify'.

Integration and drug policy

Drug policy has long been an area subject to international as well as national control. Until the early 1900s, few European countries had any form of national drug legislation, but this situation was to radically change from the date of the first Opium Convention held in Shanghai in 1909. Thirteen powers met at this convention (although it is generally recognised that America provided the main driving force behind the meeting) and formed an aim to make international drug policy subject to stricter control measures. Progress towards this aim was made via a series of international meetings and treaties that culminated in the 1961 Single Convention on Narcotic Drugs, which committed signatories to the recognition that 'addiction to narcotic drugs constitutes a serious evil for the individual and is fraught with social and economic danger'. This convention bound its signatories to a prohibitive approach in controlling illicit substances and had them acknowledge the need for international cooperation in combating them. International cooperation has continued under the 1971 Convention on Psychotropic Substances and the 1988 Convention against Illicit Traffic in Narcotics and Psychotropic Substances. Today, all EU Member States are committed to formulating their national drug policies within the boundaries of these conventions and commitment to them is a prerequisite for countries seeking to join the EU.

In fact, the European Union has been slow and cautious in its attempts to impact on the national drug policies of its members over and above what is required as a signatory of the UN conventions. Two European Parliamentary commissions were charged with investigating the best approach for drug policy in the late 1980s and early 1990s (Blom and van Mastrigt, 1994). After being unable to come to a majority agreement on this issue, the principle of subsidiarity was applied in the field of drug policy, as in many other areas of social policy, and, as a result, the national governments of individual Member States remained ultimately in control of their national drug policies. European level interventions are restricted to providing a framework within which national drug policy can operate, collecting and disseminating data in an effort to achieve a better understanding of the nature of the drug problem throughout Europe, and directly intervening only in the finer details of drug policy where it can be demonstrated that so doing can offer both 'clear added value' and results that are 'measurable and realistic' (Council of the European Union, 2004a, p. 7).

Despite these restrictions, over the intervening years, there has been considerable activity in the field of European drug policy. In 1980 a European coordination group on the drugs issue was set up (CELAD) which was responsible for proposing the first European Action Plan to Combat Drugs as part of an 'Anti-Drugs Strategy' adopted at the Rome European Council in 1990. It was also responsible for creating REITOX, a European information network on drugs and drug addiction, in 1993, which later led to the development of its coordinating and governing body, the European Monitoring Centre for Drugs and Drug Addiction (EMCDDA) in 1995. Many other drug policy related working bodies and groups have also been created to monitor drug policy developments including: the Horizontal Drugs Group (HDG), the Common Foreign and Security Policy Council Working Group on Drugs (CODRO), and the K4 or Article 36 group. Furthermore, in 1994, a specialised European Drugs Unit (EDU) was created which, in 1999, became part of Europol. Today these institutions are thriving and continue to be engaged in the development of drug policy at the European level. Similarly, since the adoption of the first Action Plan in 1990, updates have been made at four-year intervals and the 'European Drug Strategy' is now used by the EU to state their aims and guide individual Member States without compromising rights to national subsidiarity. Finally, in what has been described as a 'major step' (Council of the European Union, 2004a) towards drug policy integration, two legally binding Framework Decisions have been implemented to guide and shape national policy in the areas of minimum-maximum penalties for drug traffickers (Council of the European Union, 2004b) and the control of new psychoactive substances (Council of the European Union, 2005).

Furthermore, each European Treaty has added to the complexity and depth of policy making regarding illicit substances. For example, the Maastricht Treaty specifically mentioned drugs as an area of European concern, the Amsterdam Treaty gives special attention to the fight against drugs, and the Lisbon Treaty specifically makes provisions for reducing drug-related health damage and implements minimum rules surrounding the definition of crimes and their punishment. Drug policy can, therefore, be seen to have been a steadily increasing concern for the EU. This has led some commentators to suggest that the integration of European drug policy remains a realistic goal at the European level. For example, Boekhout van Solinge (2002) suggests that there has been so much activity in this field that European citizens could be forgiven for thinking that the decision to fully integrate has already been taken. Furthermore, Estievenart (1995), in his role as director of the EMCDDA (1994–2005), stated that the foundations had been laid for an EU drug policy, ready for when European policy makers and citizens desired harmonisation to occur.

Pathways to integration

The previous EU drug strategy defined integration or coordination of policy as 'key' to its success (Council of the European Union, 2004a, p. 8), but, as described above, policy integration in the EU can be conceptualised in a variety of ways. In the early days, the 'hard harmonisation' of national policies was attempted by using binding EU legal instruments (such as Directives) to *force* Member States to standardise their national policies. This type of integration has been described by Standring (2012, p. 12) as 'synonymous with a hard, top down, hierarchical approach'. Majone (1997, p. 268) suggests that, under this system, 'decision-making is slow and cumbersome because of the ever-growing complexity of the subjects covered and of the need for consensus'. Instead, over time, European powers have increasingly invested in the process of 'soft convergence' whereby national policies organically become more similar over time, largely by *encouraging* them to do so through the development of 'soft law' practices such as the formulation of resolutions, memoranda and guidelines, and the bringing together of networks of experts (Radaelli, 1999). Convergence can either be achieved via top-down political efforts or bottom-up national initiatives. Elements of both 'hard harmonisation' and 'soft convergence' can be seen in current EU drug policy practices and the success of each will be evaluated in the remainder of this chapter.

'Hard harmonisation'

The most advanced example of this type of policy integration in practice is provided by the Framework Decisions outlined in the previous section. A discussion based around evaluating the effectiveness of the Framework Decisions will thus serve to draw out the effectiveness of policies aimed at bringing about integration through 'hard harmonisation' in general. One area of broad consensus in European drug policy making has been the control of drug trafficking and drug traffickers. Even those countries that practise relatively liberal policies towards the users of illicit drugs generally agree that stricter sanctions should be applied to drug traffickers. Unsurprisingly, then, this was an area earmarked at the EU level for the advanced development of policy integration strategies. In 2004 a Framework Decision (Council of the European Union, 2004b) was adopted which set out minimum rules surrounding offences related to illicit drug trafficking. Specifically, it defines the acts constituting criminal offences and sets the lowest level of maximum penalties that Member States must provide as sanctions for them. Similarly, Europe has been at the forefront of New Psychoactive Substances (NPS) policy development since a 1997 Joint Action (Council of the European Union, 1997) on the control of new synthetic drugs established a mechanism for information exchange, risk assessment, and ultimately, control via an EU-wide ban. Following on from the 2004 drug trafficking framework decision, these NPS-related processes were solidified in a 2005 Framework Decision (Council of the European Union, 2005).

Taken together, the Framework Decisions represent the clearest and most advanced form of 'hard harmonisation' of drug policy in existence in Europe. It does not necessarily follow, however, that they represent the most successful form of drug policy integration in operation in Europe. The Commission's own evaluation of the Framework Decision on drug trafficking (European Commission, 2009, p. 10) recognises that the majority of Member States have not felt it necessary to adapt the wording of their national strategies to reflect European legislation in this area, and that national penalties are actually usually much higher than those demanded by European legislation – in the case of 12 Member States, their national penalties are more than twice the range of those dictated at the EU level. Furthermore, deep divisions remain around which drugs should be prioritised under the legislation, what amounts of drug seized constitute a serious offence, and how to apply aggravating and mitigating factors (Chatwin, 2013).

Similarly, in an evaluation of the NPS Framework Decision (European Commission, 2011b), attention was drawn to the slow and cumbersome nature of imposing legislation at the European level. At the time of the evaluation, despite 115 new substances having been reported between 2005 and 2010, only two of these substances had been banned throughout Europe. In the case of mephedrone, by the time the EU had taken one and a half years to conduct a risk assessment and issue a ban, 15 Member States had already taken action themselves (Chatwin, 2013). While there has been a significant increase in the number of NPS being subject to control in recent years, it remains difficult for the bureaucratic processes involved in the formulation of 'hard harmonisation' to keep pace with the rapid development of new substances. So, while attempts to impose 'hard harmonisation' do still exist, it is not clear that those attempts are bringing 'added value' to national policies, as they must under the terms of subsidiarity. Instead, as cautioned by Majore (1997), the evidence suggests that they have achieved little more than an approximation or average of national legislation at the European level; that ultimately represents the bare minimum of policy already practised across Europe.

Recent developments suggest that, despite the lack of success outlined above, the plans for top-down 'hard harmonisation' of drug policy within the European Union will continue. On 25 October 2011, the Commission published a Communication 'Towards a Stronger European Response to Drugs' (European Commission, 2011a), which pledged to produce a raft of stronger legislation in various areas of drug policy making, including drug trafficking penalties and the control of NPS. In 2013, based on the arguments outlined in 'Towards a Stronger European Response to Drugs' (European Commission, 2011a), new proposals for regulation and a Directive on the control of NPS in Europe (considerably increasing and extending powers at the European level and allowing a faster response to emerging NPS) were presented (European Commission, 2013). In

April 2014 the European Parliament indicated its strong support for these proposals, but, since then, discussions have been put on hold while some Member States challenge their legal basis (House of Commons European Scrutiny Committee, 2016). These developments indicate both a continued desire for 'hard harmonisation' in the drugs arena, as well as a continued failure to implement this type of policy integration effectively.

'Soft convergence'

This type of 'hard harmonisation', however, is only one route that European drug policy integration may follow. Standring (2012, p. 14) proposes that 'convergence, a gradual process whereby policies and practices become increasingly similar [including] policy emulation and elite networking, both of which are considered part of the EU's 'soft' approach to governance may more accurately reflect the development of an integrated European drug policy. There are many examples of drug policy integration within Europe that fall into this category of 'soft convergence'. For example, the EMCDDA is charged with collecting and disseminating data on the nature and changing patterns of the European drug situation. The quality of their work represents a gold standard in work of this type and could, in some respects, be viewed as engendering a convergence of national drug policy (Bergeron and Griffiths, 2006). This might be achieved, for example, through policy emulation whereby Member States are readily able to access a variety of incidences of best practice and national drug-strategy evaluations, or through elite networking where those working with drug users, as drug policy advisors and analysts are brought together to discuss national experiences and issues of common interest.

Furthermore, the EU Drug Strategies and Action plans, in combination with the encouragement of national drug policy evaluations by the EMCDDA, have been useful in prompting those Member States without such documents in existence at the national level, to adopt them. Many of the newer Member States, for example, have adopted the framework and objectives of the European-level versions in their entirety, presumably leading to policies that are rather similar on the ground. Finally, one further example of the 'soft convergence' of drug policy is the important emphasis that the EU has given to the promotion of harm reduction, resulting in the mandated adoption of measures such as needle exchange and substitution treatment programmes in all EU Member States and applicant countries (Hedrich et al., 2008; MacGregor and Whiting, 2010).

A close examination of these examples, however, suggests that there has also been some limitation to the 'soft convergence' pathway to policy coordination. For example, as anticipated by Standring (2012), national drug policies do not appear to be becoming more similar. In recent years some countries have relaxed their policies towards cannabis (Portugal, Belgium, the Czech Republic), while others have toughened them (UK, Denmark). Despite some small cosmetic changes, neither Sweden nor the Netherlands (representing paradigmatic opposites in terms of drug policy application) have committed to any change in their respective underlying principles of drug control (Chatwin, 2010). This is a somewhat surprising turn of events, particularly if we consider what has happened in similar policy areas at the European level. For example, in the area of alcohol policy, increasing similarity between national policies can more clearly be seen. Prior to entry into the EU, Nordic countries had uniquely control orientated alcohol policies in comparison with the rest of Europe. Since Sweden and Finland joined the EU, changes have been swift and have encompassed abolishing restrictions on travellers' allowances and the monopolies on import, export and wholesale; lowering taxes on alcohol; and generally liberalising their restrictive anti-drinking measures (Andreasson et al., 2006; Cisneros Ornberg, 2008).

This argument is further borne out by examining those countries that have adopted the EU Drug Strategy and Action Plan wholesale in the formulation of their national drug policies. Because the EU versions are themselves rather vague, counter-intuitively, it has been possible for countries that have adopted these documents at the national level to display rather different interpretations of them. For example, both Portugal and Turkey (adopting European drug policy standards as a candidate for EU membership) have based their national drug policy on the European documents (EMCDDA, 2011), yet Portugal has decriminalised the possession of all drugs for personal use, while in Turkey it is possible to punish drug users with two years of prison. Turning to look at the 'soft convergence' around harm reduction policies, while these do represent an important and valuable step forward, there also remains a wide variety of commitment to harm reduction measures in Europe. Only 2% of the substitution treatment delivered in Europe, for example, occurs in the 12 Member States which joined the EU in 2004 and 2007 (EMCDDA, 2010). Furthermore, despite the European Parliament's recommendation to accept the Catania Report (ENCOD, 2004) – announcing the failure of previous European drug strategies and recommending the adoption of a new one based on the protection of public health – the EU has continued to endorse strategies focused on supply and demand reduction without including reference to harm reduction measures in the overarching aims and objectives (Council of the European Union, 2004a). These types of policy integration, while on the surface appearing more advanced than those brought about under 'hard harmonisation', are therefore also limited.

Multi-level governance

Although the EU drug strategies and action plans advocate for the desirability of increasing the alignment of national policies' finer legislative details, a case can also be made for the desirability of diversity within European drug policy. Given that, to date, no strategy of drug control employed anywhere across the globe has been successful in eradicating the drug problem (or even in significantly reducing the use and/or supply of drugs), in many ways it makes sense to encourage a diversity of innovative drug policy strategies in the effort to find effective ways to reduce the harm caused by both drug use and the policies employed to control drugs. Rather than seeking to close down the available drug policy options, international drug policy regimes ought, therefore, to be concerning themselves with opening 'up the possibility of policy experimentation at the national level (...) or subnational levels' (Room and Mackay, 2012, p. 8). In other words, it is only through experimentation with innovative policy options that we will discover effective and appropriate drug policy solutions. The variety of drug policy innovations in operation within the EU, rather than being seen as a barrier to policy integration, could therefore be viewed as constructive, especially underpinned as they are by the work of the EMCDDA.

These ideas, far from being unique to the field of drug policy, are in line with the suggestion presented earlier in this chapter, that integration in social policy does not have to lead to uniformity and conformity, but instead may actually encourage policy diversification (Pierson and Liebfried, 1995; Geyer, 2000). The theory of multi-level governance (Marks, 1992) has been invoked to describe this kind of integration and provides an illuminating way to view the complexities of integration in the field of European illicit drug policy. Garcia (2006, p. 745) describes how the principle of subsidiarity has led to a subtle shift from government by those in power to governance which seeks the 'involvement of stakeholders and civil society organisations besides government bodies and experts'. Marks' (1992) conceptualisation of governance has been termed 'multi-level governance' because of its inclusion of actors at the civil, subnational, national and transnational level (Hooghe and Marks, 2001; Armstrong, 2002). Piattoni (2010, p. 255) suggests that multi-level governance offers 'the best single description and explanation of how the EU actually functions', and should thus be viewed, not as a prediction of the way that integration could develop in the future, but rather as a lens for viewing the way that integration is actually developing now.

It follows that, to a certain extent, drug policy in Europe is already operating in accordance with multi-level governance, or multi-level participation (Bache, 1998). At the European level, minimum penalties have been adopted in the areas of drug trafficking and the control of NPS, and the development of the European Action Plan on Drugs and the European Anti-Drugs Strategy have gone some way towards implementing a set of guidelines or a framework for national drug policy, particularly since these documents have been so influential in the development of national drug policy in the newer Member States. At the national level governments have remained free to implement strategies that are either broadly liberal or broadly restrictive in their treatment of drug use and drug users. Though less well developed, at the local level there is some evidence of commitment to citizen participation which has been championed by ENCOD, a non-governmental organisation campaigning for a more humane European drug policy (ENCOD, 2004), and there is evidence to suggest that cities are working together on issues of drug policy implementation through the creation of networks such as 'European Cities Against Drugs' and 'European Cities on Drug Policy' (Kaplan and Leuw, 1996).

A further principle of multi-level governance is the development of integration in the form of exchange of best practices (Roberts and Springer, 2001). In recent years, the EMCDDA has expanded its role to deal not just with statistics, but also with the collation of instances of 'best practice' in relation to drug policy. The EMCDDA now collects and makes available information on the evaluation of individual strategies in the areas of prevention, treatment, harm reduction, prevention of drug-related crime, drug supply reduction and data collection tools. Furthermore, it uses this information to develop guidelines and frameworks with which EU Member States are encouraged to construct their drug policies. Nor is this a practice that is confined to the institutions of the EU itself. The radical new policy adopted in Portugal in 2001, placing harm reduction at the heart of policy making and decriminalising the possession of all drugs for personal use, has been the focus of much international attention and has attracted visits from the governments of Norway and Britain, amongst others, in the search for answers as to which direction the future drug policies of their own countries should take.

Conclusion

It is clear that, in order to bring true 'added value' to policy that is constructed at the national level, the integration of European Drug Policy must not be overly focused on the kind of top-down, hierarchical harmonisation that is achieved by Framework Decisions and imposed by European institutions. The analysis presented here, based on a discussion of the Framework Decisions as the most advanced form of this type of integration, suggests that the value of this legislation is significantly limited. This chapter has sought to draw attention to the important role that 'soft convergence' (in the provision of drug policy guidelines and frameworks, through the work of the EMCDDA, and by bringing together networks of experts) has to play in the integration of drug policy within the EU. It is a mistake, therefore, to prioritise only the 'hard harmonisation' of drug policy at the expense of initiatives designed to bring about 'soft convergence'.

The analysis presented here, however, seeks to go further and to suggest that there is also a limit to the value of 'soft convergence', at least in its aim to bring about increasing similarity between national policies. In line with the work of Pierson and Liebfried (1995) and Geyer (2000) which conceptualises social policy developments in the EU as likely to result in policy diversity, the theory of multi-level governance has been used to explain drug policy developments. The application of multi-level governance suggests that to see real success we may need to apply a conceptualisation of integration that encourages the development of innovative national and local level responses, within international guidelines and frameworks, subject to rigorous evaluations that are shared widely. Viewed through this lens, it is unlikely that national drug policies will become more similar. But the evidence presented here provides reason to remain optimistic that Europe can be at the forefront of innovative drug policy, and of evidence building and sharing, because of the diversity of policy that already exists, underpinned by the valuable role fulfilled by the EMCDDA.

References

ANDREASSON, S., HOLDER, H., NORSTROM, T., OSTERBERG, E. and ROSSOW, I. (2006) Estimates of Harm Associated with Changes in Swedish Alcohol Policy: Results From Past and Present Estimates. *Addiction*. 101. pp. 1096–1105.

ARMSTRONG, K. (2002) Rediscovering Civil Society: the European Union and the White Paper on Governance. *European Law Journal*. 8. pp. 102–132.

BACHE, I. (1998) *The Politics of European Union Regional Policy: Multi-level Governance or Flexible Gate-keeping?* Sheffield: Sheffield Academic Press.

BERGERON, H. and GRIFFITHS, P. (2006), Drifting Towards a More Common Approach to a More Common Problem: Epidemiology and the Evolution of a European Drug Policy. In Hughes, R., Lart, R. and Higate, P. (eds.). *Drugs: Policy and Politics*. London: Open University Press.

BLOM, T. and VAN MASTRIGT, H. (1994) The Future of the Dutch Model in the Context of the War on Drugs. In Leuw, E. and Haen Marshall, I. (eds.). *Between Prohibition and Legalisation: the Dutch Experiment*. Amsterdam and New York: Kugler Publications.

BOEKHOUT VAN SOLINGE, T. (1997) *The Swedish Drug Control System: An In-Depth Review and Analysis*. Amsterdam: Uitgevenj Jan Mets, Cedro.

BOEKHAUT VAN SOLINGE, T. (2002) *Drugs and Decision-Making in the European Union*. Amsterdam: CEDRO/Mets en Schilt.

CHATWIN, C. (2010) Have Recent Evolutions in European Governance Brought Harmonisation in the Field of Illicit Drugs any Closer? *Drugs and Alcohol Today*. 10. pp. 26–32.

CHATWIN, C. (2013) A Critical Evaluation of the European Drug Strategy. *The International Journal of Drug Policy*. 24(3). pp. 251–256.

CISNEROS ORNBERG, J. (2008) The Europeanization of Swedish Alcohol Policy: The Case of ECAS. *Journal of European Social Policy*. 18. pp. 380–392.

COUNCIL OF THE EUROPEAN UNION (1997) *Joint action of 16 June 1997 adopted by the Council on the basis of article K.2 of the Treaty on European Union, concerning the information exchange, risk assessment and the control of new synthetic drugs*. 97/39/JHA.

COUNCIL OF THE EUROPEAN UNION (2004a) *EU Drugs Strategy 2005–2012*. Available from: http://www.emcdda.europa.eu/html.cfm/index6790EN.html [Accessed: 8 June 2016].

COUNCIL OF THE EUROPEAN UNION (2004b) *Framework Decision 2004/757/JHA of 25 October 2004, laying down minimum provisions on the constituent elements of criminal acts and penalties in the field of illicit drug trafficking*. Brussels: OJ L355.

COUNCIL OF THE EUROPEAN UNION (2005) *Council Decision 2005/387/JHA of 10 May 2005 on the information exchange, risk-assessment and control of new psychoactive substances*. Brussels: OJ L127.

DECORTE, T. (2014) Cannabis Social Clubs in Belgium: Organisational Strengths and Weaknesses, and Threats to the Model. *International Journal of Drug Policy*. 26(2). pp. 122–130.

DINAN, D. (2005) *Origins and Evolution of the European Union*. Oxford: Oxford University Press.

DUFF, A. (1993) Towards a Definition of Subsidiarity. In Duff, A. (ed.). *Subsidiarity within the European Community*. London: Federal Trust for Education and Research.

EMCDDA (2010) *2010 Annual Report on the State of the Drug Problem in Europe*. Luxembourg: Publications Office of the European Union.

EMCDDA (2011) *2011 Annual Report on the state of the drug problem in Europe*. Luxembourg: Publications Office of the European Union.

ENCOD (2004) *Catania Report: European Parliament Recommendation to the Council and the European Council on the Drugs Strategy 2005–2012*. Available from: http://www.encod.org/info/catania-report-european-parliament.html [Accessed: 8 June 2016].

ESTIEVENART, G. (1995) The European Community and the Global Drug Phenomenon. Current Situation and Outlook. In Estievenart, G. (ed.). *Policies and Strategies to Combat Drugs in Europe. The Treaty on European Union: Framework for a New European Strategy to Combat Drugs*. Dordrecht: Martinus Nijhof Publishers.

EUROPEAN COMMISSION (2009) *Report from the Commission on the implementation of Framework Decision 2004/757/JHA laying down minimum provisions on the constituent elements of criminal acts and penalties in the field of illicit drug trafficking*. Brussels: COM(2009)669 final.

EUROPEAN COMMISSION (2011a) *Towards a Stronger European Drug Policy*. Brussels: COM (2011) 689 final.

EUROPEAN COMMISSION (2011b) *Report from the Commission on the assessment of the functioning of Council Decision 2005/387/JHA on the information exchange, risk assessment and control of new psychoactive substances*. Brussels: COM(2011) 430 final.

EUROPEAN COMMISSION (2013) *Proposal for a regulation of the European Parliament and of the Council on new psychoactive substances*. Brussels: COM (2013) 619/2.

GARCIA, M. (2006) Citizen Practices and Urban Governance in European Cities. *Urban Studies*. 43. pp. 745–765.

GEYER, R. (2000) *Exploring European Social Policy*. Cambridge: Polity Press.

GOLDBERG, T. (2004) The Evolution of Swedish Drug Policy. *Journal of Drug Issues*. 34. pp. 551–576.

GOULD, A. (1994) Pollution Rituals in Sweden: The Pursuit of a Drug-Free Society. *Scandinavian Journal of Social Welfare*. 3. pp. 85–93.

HANTRAIS, L. (2007) *Social Policy in the European Union*. Third Edition Basingstoke: Palgrave Macmillan.

HEDRICH, D., PIRONA, A. and WIESSING, L. (2008) From Margin to Mainstream: The Evolution of Harm Reduction Responses to Problem Drug Use in Europe. *Drugs: Education, Prevention and Policy*. 15. pp. 503–517.

HOOGHE, L. and MARKS, G. (2001) *Multi-Level Governance and European Integration*. Oxford: Rowland & Littlefield Publishers.

HOUSE OF COMMONS EUROPEAN SCRUTINY COMMITTEE (2016) *Twenty-fifth Report of Session 2015–16. Documents considered by the Committee on 9 March 2016*. Available from: http://www.publications.parliament.uk/pa/cm201516/cmselect/cmeuleg/342-xxiv/34212.htm [Accessed: 8 June 2016].

KAPLAN, C. and LEUW, E. (1996) A Tale of Two Cities: Drug Policy Instruments and City Networks in the European Union. *European Journal on Criminal Policy and Research*. 4. pp. 74–89.

LENKE, L. and OLSSON, B. (2002) Swedish Drug Policy in the Twenty-First Century: A Policy Model Going Astray. *Annals of the American Academy of Political and Social Science*. 582. pp. 64–79.

MACGREGOR, S. and WHITING, M. (2010) The Development of European Drug Policy and the Place of Harm Reduction Within This. In Rhodes, T. and Hedrich, D. (eds.). *EMCDDA Monographs. Harm Reduction: Evidence, Impacts and Challenges*. Available from: http://www.emcdda.europa.eu/publications/monographs/harm-reduction [Accessed: 8 June 2016].

MAJONE, G. (1997) The New European Agencies: Regulation by Information. *Journal of European Public Policy*. 4(2). pp. 267–275.

MARKS, G. (1992) Structural Policy in the European Community. In Sbragia, A. (ed.). *Europolitics: Institutions and Policymaking in the 'New' European Community*. Washington: The Brookings Institute.

MCCORMICK, J. (1999) *Understanding the European Union: A Concise Introduction*. Basingstoke: Palgrave Macmillan.

PIATTONI, S. (2010) *The Theory of Multi-level Governance: Conceptual, Empirical and Normative Challenges*. Oxford: Oxford University Press.

PIERSON, P. and LEIBFRIED, S. (1995) The Dynamics of Social Policy Integration. In Leibfried, S. and Pierson, P. (eds.). *European Social Policy: Between Fragmentation and Integration*. Washington: The Brookings Institute.

RADAELLI, C. M. (1999) The Public Policy of the European Union: Wither Politics of Expertise? *Journal of European Public Policy*. 6(5). pp. 757–774.

ROBERTS, I. and SPRINGER, B. (2001) *Social Policy in the European Union: Between Harmonisation and National Autonomy*. London: Lynne Reiner Publishers.

ROOM, R. and MACKAY, S. (2012) *Roadmaps to Reforming the UN Drug Conventions*. A Beckley Foundation Report: Available from: https://www.tni.org/files/publication-downloads/roadmaps_to_reform.pdf [Accessed: 8 June 2016].

ROSS, G. (1995) Assessing the Delors Era and Social Policy. In Liebfried, S. and Pierson, P. (eds.) *European Social Policy: Between Fragmentation and Integration*. Washington: The Brookings Institute.

STANDRING, A. (2012) 'An Ever Closer Union' – Towards the 'Soft' Convergence of European Drug Policies. *Drugs and Alcohol Today*. 12(1). pp. 12–20.

THAM, H. (1995) Drug Control as a National Project: The Case of Sweden. *The Journal of Drug Issues*. 25. pp. 113–128.

VASCONI, C. (2013) Where Next for Europe on Drug Policy Reform? *Expert seminar, Lisbon, Portugal, 20th–21st 2013. Transnational Institute*. Available from: https://www.tni.org/en/briefing/expert-seminar-where-next-europe-drug-policy-reform [Accessed: 8 June 2016].

VAN VLIET, H-J. (1990) Separation of Drug Markets and the Normalization of Drug Problems in The Netherlands: An Example for Other Nations? *Journal of Drug Issues*. 20. pp. 463–471.

Chapter 3

The soft power of the European Monitoring Centre for Drugs and Drug Addiction[1]

Henri Bergeron

Introduction

Numerous studies have attempted to identify the institutional and political conditions and the motives behind the recent creation of a superabundance of independent European agencies. Although the literature can be mapped in more than one way, two principal types of explanations can be distinguished. Firstly, there are those which give decisive importance to the contingent occurrence of one-off events. Secondly, we might distinguish another set of studies, according to which the creation of European agencies is more often a manifestation of the recent appearance of a 'post-regulatory' principle or set of practices (Guigner, 2008). The creation of agencies is thus seen as an institutional response to contradictory tensions: an acknowledgement of the need for convergence coupled with the political impossibility of delegating direct administrative powers to community institutions (i.e. centralisation) (Dehousse, 1997).

Whether responding to 'external' events[2] or the product of hesitant internal moves towards change, agencies, positioned as stabilised European centres linking (national) networks (Dehousse, 1997), are nevertheless thought of as promoting the coordination and, it is hoped, the convergence of national policies, consequent upon the transfer of good practice and policies from one country to another. In this context the role of agencies is crucial in that the information they produce is thought to make it possible to compare national policies measured against common cognitive categories, as well as to identify the national responses and solutions considered the most effective (Chiti, 2000). Some authors (Majone, 1996, 1997) thus postulate knowledge and information as the essential attributes and principal resources for European policies, which are essentially regulatory, and see agencies as mechanisms and 'cognitive technologies' (Desrosières, 1997)

---

1   This chapter is a revised and shortened version of the 2010 article 'La force d'une institution faible: Le cas d'une agence européenne d'information'. *Politique européenne.* 32. pp. 39–76.

2   Again, a crisis is not completely independent from the institutional field within which it is expressed: it does not strike a sector, an institution or a policy in the same way as an asteroid might strike another celestial body (Mahoney and Thelen, 2009).

The soft power of the EMCDDA 41

thought to inspire the socio-political processes (Radaelli, 1999) of national and European policymaking. In any case, the role of knowledge and information is supposed to be even more important when the policy object manifests a high degree of technical and scientific complexity.

If the information produced by agencies is decisive for the formation of a movement whereby national policies converge, it seems crucial to understand how these productions exercise their power of persuasion (Majone, 1997; Hall, 1997, pp. 185–186), and even, paradoxically, of coercion (Guigner, 2008). If there is indeed a process of 'cognitive Europeanization' (ibid.), it seems from a sociological point of view essential to understand:

1 how this set of information, knowledge and ideas comes to be considered true, right, trustworthy or legitimate by the actors populating these coordinated networks and institutions;
2 by which precise mechanisms they are disseminated within an institutional field or in a public policy sector; and finally
3 how they are a key factor for actions contributing towards policy convergence.

In order to answer these questions, the first two especially, there have been numerous studies of the arenas and forums within which this set of information, knowledge and ideas is thought to be marshalled. In particular, these study the modes of socialisation (Radaelli, 2002 on framing mechanisms; Quaglia et al., 2008; Robert, 2010), experts, interest groups, members of 'civil society', civil servants (national and European) or public decision-makers (national and European), and the horizontal circulation and dissemination (Dehousse, 1997) of this set of information, knowledge, ideas and the way in which social learning phenomena finally take place there (for health policy, see in particular Steffen, 2005; for the notion of learning, see Heclo, 1974; Hall, 1993, 1997; Haas, 1989 or Radaelli, 2002). It seems fundamental, in order to shape a satisfactory causal explanation, to precisely explicate what these processes of dissemination, circulation, socialisation and social learning consist of (Checkel, 2005; de Maillard and Robert, 2008) and identify the elementary mechanisms from which they are made.

Few research studies have examined the *practical* work of producing this information, regulation, knowledge and skill, all described as 'expert', and the socio-political dynamics and specific institutional constraints influencing their production. While agencies, and more broadly those institutions producing the knowledge and information for policies (monitoring centres, statistical, institutes, etc.), have recently multiplied, studies of their actual 'concrete' work (Robert, 2010) and the genesis of their productions remain rare (Hauray, 2006; Robert, 2010). Now this kind of study seems to be exactly that which is needed to contribute towards our understanding of the processes of socialisation and social learning which flourish within the confines of European institutional spaces. Exploring the conditions and dynamics by which this expertise is produced makes it possible for us to identify

42 Henri Bergeron

the nature of, and the particular properties acquired by, this knowledge and information in the course of being formed; by doing so, it helps us to grasp why these productions are considered to be (more or less) true, objective or legitimate, why actors within these national and European social formations take ownership of them and use them as a reference, and why, finally, they come to be shared, in other words circulated and disseminated, within these social spaces. In short, this type of study makes possible a fuller understanding of one of the links in the causal chain underpinning the (cognitive) Europeanisation argument: that which involves the political efficacy of its productions, an efficacy understood as their capacity to engage, convince and affect (Majone, 1997) the behaviour of those who are its main targets.

We propose exploring these production processes on the basis of one particular case, that of the European Monitoring Centre for Drugs and Drug Addiction (EMCDDA), an independent agency of the European Union created in 1993. Its key missions are to collect, process and provide, to all sorts of agents[3] 'factual, objective, reliable and comparable information' (EC Regulation 1920/2006 on the EMCDDA, Article 1.2) on all dimensions of the drugs phenomenon within the European Union. This chapter thus intends to study the work of this institution's experts, and that of their collaborators throughout Europe, situating it in the context of the historical dynamics driving the development of the agency. The chapter has three objectives:

1   We shall attempt to show how this agency, whose programme of work and productions is subject to tight political control (by Member States and the Commission), has nevertheless succeeded in producing knowledge and information considered to be reliable and legitimate, and how this provides cognitive and normative support for reflection on, and debate about, drugs undertaken by numerous actors in European arenas and forums.
2   However, we shall also show that the indicators produced by the EMCDDA do not merely generate information providing food for thought and official documents circulating within the policy world. We shall see that these expert productions and these indicators comprise an effective cognitive matrix, in that they have managed to constitute themselves as the elementary building blocks of an a priori cognitive framework through which public problems linked to drugs are now perceived. This cognitive, and therefore normative, framework (since it also indicates what is to be done) is revealed as an institution driven, in a non-reflexive manner, by numerous actors in all sorts of situations, in order to think through all sorts of questions, problems and solutions.
3   This offers an additional and perhaps original opportunity to reflect on the links between politics, expertise and science.

3   Public decision-makers, researchers, professionals and European citizens.

EMCDDA: independence under control

Europe and drugs

It is hardly possible here to trace back the full set of political and institutional conditions which made possible the creation of an agency specialising in what turns out to be a political subject of medium importance (although an ambiguous one) regarding which the status quo has long seemed a better option than a dangerous debate and the vilification of any alternative policy. The outbreak of the AIDS epidemic in the mid-1980s, the fears to which it gave rise and the 'public health scandals' which it occasioned in a number of Member States would, however, open a new window of political opportunity. Until then gripped by a grammar of security, threats to public order, moral decline and pathological lack of willpower, drug use, especially the intravenous use of opiates, was redefined as a major risk to public health in national political arenas (Bergeron, 1999).

It was in this particular context, in October 1989, that François Mitterrand decided to send a letter to his eleven counterparts and to the President of the European Commission inviting them to consider, as the Single European Market got under way, whether the drugs problems required a more extensive policy of coordination on a European scale. Although political action on drugs at the European level does not date from this initiative[4] it had remained timid for a long time (Martel, 2003). While the first tentative moves to initiate coordination on a European scale emanated from the European Parliament,[5] it is not unreasonable to consider François Mitterrand's letter the decisive stage in more substantial European engagement with these questions.

Information by default

President Mitterrand's letter also invited Member States and the Commission to precisely measure the extent of drug use and its consequences in Europe, and to consider, for this purpose, the appropriateness of creating a European observatory or monitoring agency. While the Commission played a role in structuring European networks and promoted exchanges of good practice, a number of its officials were mistrustful of the autonomous role which an agency of this sort might play in this context. The 'agency' solution, while it had become a legitimate administrative category within the Commission, did not enthuse all those within it dealing with the drugs problem. It was hardly ever conceived of during this period, by most of the officials in the General Secretariat responsible for the question, as something which could or should become the armed branch of a controlled and thought-through

---

4 These paragraphs on the history of European institutions' gradual involvement in the area of 'drugs' owe a great deal to the exhaustive work of Aline Grange (2005).

5 In 1988 the European Parliament created an EEC budget line intended to fund projects (often pilot projects) not only in the areas of health and prevention operations, but also for the development of epidemiological tools (Grange, 2005).

strategy of 'cognitive Europeanization' which would promote a gentle convergence of national policies resistant to direct, binding intervention at the European level. Its creation was more the result of a complex encounter between the activism of the official (and his team) responsible for the drugs issue at the Secretariat, who would become its first Director, and the political need to respond quickly to the invitation in President Mitterrand's letter.

For a number of European officials forced to react to President Mitterrand's proposals, and for the Member States which had timidly conceded the political importance of greater European coordination on the subject, creating a European monitoring agency tasked with collecting and producing reliable, objective and comparable information was in the end considered to be a low-cost piece of window dressing, provided that its missions were properly supervised. Political agreement on the projected Council Regulation creating the EMCDDA was obtained in June 1992 and the Regulation was finally adopted on 8 February 1993.[6] The EMCDDA was set up on the legal basis of Article 235 (308) of the Treaty of Rome and was entrusted with carrying out strictly defined missions, as is the case for many other agencies (Demortain, 2006). In addition to its role as a producer of information, it was to constitute itself at the centre of a network of experts, link the action of existing networks, act as their 'permanent secretariat' (Grange, 2005), and thus play a part in disseminating common interpretation frameworks (Dehousse, 1997).

The EMCDDA Regulation defined five priority areas for the collection of information. However, it also stipulated that the EMCDDA should, at least during the first three years of its existence, concentrate on the first of these areas: 'demand and demand reduction', which mainly concerned the social and health aspects of the drugs phenomenon.[7] The development of activities primarily monitoring aspects of demand and demand reduction should not be seen as the product of a Commission strategy supporting the new policy turn whereby Member States considered the drugs problem as more of a health-related problem, or the encouragement of this in States which had not yet reached this point. Neither was focusing the EMCDDA's attention, at least at the outset of its activities, on these epidemiological dimensions a community strategy aimed at encouraging a process of framing (Snow et al., 1986) the drugs problem in particular terms – 'sanitising' or reducing the public object 'drugs' to a matter of health, in Didier Fassin's term (1998). This selective framing of the EMCDDA's brief to inform was more the result of a compromise negotiated within the Council at the time the founding Regulation was adopted. It was thought at the time that this would make the information it had to collect inoffensive: within the Council epidemiological

6 Council Regulation (EEC) No 302/93 of 8 February 1993 on the establishment of a European Monitoring Centre for Drugs and Drug Addiction.
7 Prevalence of use in the general population, among young people, etc.; associated morbidity and mortality; the existence, types and coverage of health and prevention responses, etc.

knowledge and language had a benevolently neutral image, while other dimensions of the problem were judged to be too political by some Member States.[8]

The Council of Europe had already undertaken pioneering work (since the early 1980s) into the formulation of economic indicators which might be used in different countries in a practical way, i.e. taking account of the specific technicalities associated with the various existing (or future) systems of information collection in Member States. As the first significant act in support of his science strategy, the new Director recruited the official responsible for this pioneering epidemiological work at the Council of Europe. The latter then unceasingly asserted the EMCDDA as the new and true European centre for epidemiology, thus beginning a long, continuous process of weakening the role, and thus the legitimacy, of the Pompidou Group of the Council of Europe.[9] However this may be, this initial focus, which was to have been provisional, was maintained for some time, especially because of the regular resistance of some Member State representatives on its Management Board to the development of activities monitoring areas other than those pertaining to demand reduction.

An independent agency?

The EMCDDA's Regulation provides for specialised centres (focal points) to be set up in each Member State, responsible for collecting national information and transmitting it to the EMCDDA. But the designation of these specialised centres, which were supposed to form a network named REITOX, was not to be made by the EMCDDA: Member States mistrustfully stipulated that selection of these centres should be their prerogative. These regulatory arrangements thus provided for political control of the information transmitted by each of the Member States. In order to collect reliable and, above all, comparable information, the EMCDDA's teams of epidemiologists put in place an original working method: on the basis of the work done at the Council of Europe, they identified five types of health areas to be monitored annually. These 'five key indicators' quickly formed the heart of EMCDDA's professional practice.[10] As the agency grew, other areas

---

8 In particular France and the Netherlands, but for different reasons.

9 This process of weakening the legitimacy of Council of Europe activities would gather momentum in pace with the admission of new Member States to the EU, in particular at the time of the enlargement of the European Union in May 2004. Similar community strategies aimed at capturing Council of Europe resources were identified by Sébastien Guigner (2006) in the area of public health policies. The 'death' or weakening of an international institution thus appears to be linked to the creation of, and competition offered by, new structures, as Paul-André Rosental (2008) has shown in the case of the International Labour Office, quickly relegated to a 'diplomatic role' by the European Coal and Steel Community.

10 The five groups of indicators today are: (1) prevalence of use in the general population; (2) 'Problematic' drugs use; (3) Indicators describing the characteristics of populations following courses of treatment; (4) Mortality (including overdoses); and (5) Infectious diseases linked to drugs use. The value of these indicators would be recognised politically by the Council as part of a Resolution adopted in 2001 (CORDROGUE 67 of 15 November 2001).

were soon identified and explored: prevention campaigns, types of treatment, rehabilitation activities, etc. Beginning in the 2000s, following a great deal of negotiation with, and persuasion of, the Management Board, information was finally collected on overall policies, laws, the number of arrests, and from the mid-2000s, more overtly, on the enforcement measures operative within Member States. It thus took more than ten years for the EMCDDA to cover, if in a very unequal way, most dimensions of the drugs phenomenon. However, the health aspect, seen inside and outside the agency as being the domain with the greatest amount of scientific content, remained central to the EMCDDA's expertise.

EMCDDA experts produce numerous documents and deliverables (reports, online databases, internet sites, information letters, scientific studies, guides to good practice, etc.). They also draw up the EMCDDA's annual report 'The State of the Drugs Problem in Europe', the only production mentioned, and thus made compulsory, in the founding Regulation. Once this report has been written, it is passed to the Management Board. This body does not merely approve the EMCDDA's annual programme of work – approval which has often given rise to tensions with and between Member States, as well as with the Commission – it also has the mission of monitoring the EMCDDA's key report, and may contest any information which does not suit it. The report is also sent to the Scientific Committee: until the EMCDDA's Founding Regulation was revised in 2006, this body was made up of one expert appointed by each Member State. Once it has been reworked to meet some of the demands for changes inevitably made – by some Member States, as well as the Commission which may be dissatisfied by the information or by developments concerning their country or institutions – the report is finally disseminated. This tedious, if schematic, description of the formal procedures and processes of producing the EMCDDA's assessments is merely intended to stress to what extent the publications and deliverables produced by the agency, which is often described as independent, are, in reality, subject to tight control by Member States and the Commission. In these conditions, how is it possible to view this agency as being able to produce information and expertise which most experts and scientists outside the EMCDDA – as well as Member States and European institutions – consider (relatively) reliable, comparable and legitimate? In order to try to answer this question, we need to study the ways in which the EMCDDA's experts, and those with whom they are networked, carry out their work which, although under control, has acquired a certain degree of scientific autonomy.

Providing expertise: between political constraints and the demands of science

From weaknesses, strength

It appears contrary to any method of expert investigation, as defined by international (Demortain, 2006) as well as national standards (Benamouzig and Besançon,

The soft power of the EMCDDA 47

2005), to set up a so-called independent agency – one supposed to produce reliable and objective information – and at the same time to make its expert publications and deliverables subject to control methods and procedures exercised by those whom it is expected to observe. But out of two weaknesses, the EMCDDA was to find its strength. The first apparent weakness is in fact linked to the limited informational jurisdiction of the EMCDDA in its initial stages. What was 'a birth defect' in the eyes of its founding director would reveal itself to be a godsend: since epidemiological monitoring was not initially considered by the members of the Board of Management to be liable to generate information and expertise which might erode the reputation of Member States, the work of standardising methodological tools for collecting information could begin without meeting too much resistance on the part of Member States.

The second weakness lay in the substantial structure of institutional control bearing down on the information gathered and produced by the EMCDDA. Here again, what may appear on first sight to have been a potential factor in a predetermined failure nevertheless turned out to become an asset: precisely because the information had been validated by these procedures and authorities it could legitimately circulate within the circle of European institutions and national decision-makers. We should, in fact, recall that at the time that the EMCDDA was set up that there was a clash between profoundly-contrasting axiological positions on the subject of drugs. The information and expertise produced by all sorts of social institutions (States, research institutes, NGOs, etc.) was often considered in public debate at the time to be unrepresentative and was frequently disqualified for this reason. For their part, ministerial statistics (from the Ministries of Justice, the Interior and Health) were often considered to more obviously reflect particular institutional principles and practices[11] unlikely to foster diagnoses representative of the overall situation. Finally, numerous reports and studies produced by non-governmental organisations did not achieve political standing, because they were thought to be produced by organisations with political aims described as extreme. This was true both for anti-prohibitionist positions and perspectives defending the 'virtues' of highly repressive policies (as was the case with work carried out by Swedish activists). The EMCDDA was thus able to occupy a vacant position on the drug expertise market, offering information that was European, supra-national and officially recognised.

Collecting reliable and comparable information: the formation of methodological tools for the collection of information

But how, more exactly, was this reliable and legitimate information disseminated, in spite of the numerous control procedures bearing down on the collection and

11 On the imprint left by professional and institutional principles and practices on the nature of the information collected by administrations with responsibility for drugs, see Setbon (1995), Bergeron (1999) and Mouhanna and Matelly (2007).

production process? As we suggested above, the turn to epidemiology made it possible to draw up indicators seen as less contentious and the EMCDDA's scientific activity began to gain confidence and respect within political and scientific circles by this means.[12] The work of drawing up methodological guidelines was undertaken by EMCDDA experts recruited for their epidemiological skills and knowledge. These would soon form expert groups around each indicator, groups tasked with achieving the difficult compromise between the need to define indicators capable of significantly reflecting the reality which they were supposed to capture and the requirement that they be capable of implementation throughout Europe. While a large proportion of the experts called upon to take part in the European epidemiological enterprise were sympathisers with, or even ardent defenders of, the doctrine of risk reduction, the EMCDDA always took care to maintain a suitable public distance from members of networks perceived as too obviously anti-prohibitionist, such as the George Soros' Open Society Foundation, the Transnational Institute, the Drug Policy Alliance, or later, the Senlis Council. The discussions which developed in these methodology work groups took on an essentially technical and scientific aspect and it was not possible to reduce the representation of specialised centres and/or national experts within the EMCDDA's expert groups to a mere defence of individual Member States' political interests (policies for or against more enforcement, policies for or against more risk reduction, etc.).

Several conditions favoured the development of a deliberative, essentially scientific and technical dynamic. We should, first of all, note that these experts rarely had any role in the political decision-making process affecting drugs, as much at the national as at the European level, which was a factor favouring emancipation from national affiliations (De Maillard and Robert, 2008). Regular meetings of 'officially recognised' experts, most often unassociated with policy decision-making processes, thus fostered a collective learning dynamic of collaboration (Robert, 2003). A consensus culture, the importance attached to the register in which discussion took place (De Maillard and Robert, 2008), together with (often tacit) collective commitments within what soon became a stable network of expertise, all incentivised and constrained individuals (Majone, 1997) to concentrate on 'credible' technical and scientific arguments and reject any less secure assertions (Sabatier, 1988). These networks thus functioned as institutions, in the sense that shared norms structuring interactions and exchanges developed within them (Chiti, 2000). If feelings of loyalty to the EMCDDA and its missions to standardise epidemiological observations developed within these networks, this was also, and often primarily, because for a number of specialised centres, the EMCDDA's success set the seal on their success at national level. Set up at the same time as the EMCDDA, they owed part of their national credibility and thus their continued institutional existence to the success of European-level expertise.

---

12 The more so because the EMCDDA's working programme on the social and health-related dimensions of the phenomenon was defined and initiated before Sweden's accession to the EU.

Producing information and expertise: internalising political constraints

On the basis of the information collected thanks to these methodological tools, EMCDDA experts began to produce comparisons which quickly gave rise to more strictly political forms of resistance.[13] In order to understand how these debates and forms of resistance were gradually (and in part)[14] left behind, we need to look more closely at how expertise was produced within the EMCDDA itself. EMCDDA experts operated within a European institution, and they were aware that it did not offer the same conditions of freedom of speech and scientific production which could be had, for example, in a research institute. Within the EMCDDA there was thus, whether people liked it or not, a lot of patient work carried out to strike a balance between political demands and the desire to 'do science'. Adjustments were made so that reliable information which might rub political masters the wrong way would be presented in such a way as to avoid censure from members of the Management Board.

The compromise responded to the constraints of contradictory normative and utilitarian demands: the information which they produced remained scientifically credible, was not transformed or distorted, while numerous possibilities opened up when it came to presenting it. It was in fact possible to avoid presenting data from all countries within the same table, avoid using certain adjectives or avoid highlighting some dimensions of a national situation. The expert epidemiologists at the EMCDDA thus became virtuosos at presenting information that, when it seemed necessary, could draw the sting from announcements which might otherwise be spectacular about the situation in certain countries. This particularly concerned countries which had influence with the Management Board, to whit 'major countries' singled out as targets for a clearly precautionary political strategy.

At the same time, these drafts never emerged untouched from the expert circles within the EMCDDA's scientific organisational structure: the EMCDDA Scientific Coordination Unit, the Heads of Scientific Departments and those overseeing communications, all had a hand in editing the principal outputs of EMCDDA experts, and also adopted a posture intended to forestall the potential consequences of certain types of information and their accompanying analyses. They kept an eye on their project managers and scientific analysts as presentations were drafted. Internalisation of political constraints was thus not just an individual process: the need for it marked the EMCDDA's whole internal production chain.

A gradual process of cognitive autonomisation

It would, however, be a mistake to see these practices and arrangements imbued with political foresight as necessarily leading to the production of scientifically

---

13 Such as the number of overdose cases in different countries, or the greater or lesser prevalence of drug use in certain sections of the population (amongst young people for example).

14 In reality this was a continuous process which, even today, is far from being completed.

meaningless outputs by the EMCDDA. This is for two main reasons: the first, which has already been mentioned, concerns the fact that most of the statistics and information produced were not transformed, distorted or dressed up; and those items which were problematic were not distorted but presented in a way which would make them more inoffensive.[15] When conflicts of a political nature have occurred between the EMCDDA and some Member States or the Commission, EMCDDA experts change their drafts, adjust their presentations, thus demonstrating their good will. But these conflicts of interpretation do not merely result from a (specific) failure of internal mechanisms for forestalling political clashes. They are also the consequence, often expected, of a strategy which EMCDDA experts tried out from time to time, over the years and depending on the scientific material, in the monitoring areas where they felt most assured. The EMCDDA does not passively undergo political constraint, but advances stealthily in sensitive areas, patiently taking up a more favourable position. For, and this is the second reason, as increasingly reliable and comparable information has been produced from an ever-growing number of countries (in particular, 'major countries'), the requirements for political foresight could be gradually relaxed. While EMCDDA experts have to demonstrate goodwill, the same goes for Member States, who cannot avoid complying with the missions assigned to the agency which they have helped to set up and over which they have oversight.

Thus, over the course of a history which we have partially described, there has been a gradual affirmation of a dynamic of cognitive autonomisation: dependence has gradually given way to an assertion of autonomy. This gradual autonomisation has come about by the successive conquest of specialised areas: firstly, of epidemiology indicators, and then, although undoubtedly in a less complete way from a scientific point of view,[16] of data on health-related and social intervention and, more recently, on other subjects (enforcement and interventions by States, public spending, etc.). A dual, cumulative process has driven this sector-by-sector autonomisation: (1) The autonomy won by some experts in certain areas (especially epidemiological ones) has worked to the advantage of that which others have attempted to achieve in other domains; while (2) The success of epidemiological indicators has also been based on a strategy of institutional absorption of monitoring studies originally devised in primarily scientific spaces, and thus enjoys strong academic credibility.[17] The cognitive autonomisation which we describe here

---

15 Occasionally, some statistics are suppressed. But this is in borderline cases and while they are suppressed in a given case C, they will often be publicised in case C + 1, following a process of cognitive automonisation which we will describe below.

16 A good proportion of the qualitative and quantitative information produced on these subjects remains 'quite soft', as many experts have remarked, and the EMCDDA is often criticised for collecting a mass of information which is of little scientific (and political) significance or relevance.

17 This is the case for the ESPAD (European School Survey Project on Alcohol and other Drugs) study into drug use among young people where the EMCDDA has recently taken responsibility for its scientific coordination.

The soft power of the EMCDDA 51

does not, in the strict sense of the term, mean the end of control or of its acuteness, but its gradual focus on more specific aspects or themes newly addressed by the EMCDDA.[18] The links between political demands and the wish to do science thus remains, now as before, at the heart of the daily activities of EMCDDA experts. The requirement for political foresight in some of the subjects covered by the EMCDDA has however been gradually eroded and/or displaced towards other domains.

Finally, we should stress the fact that the EMCDDA has succeeded in establishing itself at the centre of a vast network of information providers, over which it now has a near-monopoly of comparative data processing: in the same way as the activities of the International Labour Office studied by Rosental (2008), it has benefited from the increasing gains it makes from its unique centralisation of European know-how about drugs. One of the factors behind the EMCDDA's capacity for political impact is thus related to its exclusive control of know-how, which it has (partly) been able to emancipate from its original political dependence and often make more conflictual, while at the same time benefiting from the symbolic and political assets associated with being an official informant of the European Union. The work of producing expertise also aims at forming alliances and supporting coalitions, at interesting a large number of institutional actors (Robert, 2003), not only within the Commission but also within other institutions (in particular, the European Parliament's Committee on Civil Liberties, Justice and Home Affairs). Illustrative of this is the way in which the EMCDDA has patiently negotiated a seat as an observer within the Horizontal Working Party on Drugs (HDG) of the European Council. Accepting a seat initially conceded without conviction, those representing the EMCDDA within this key forum for European decision-making on drugs have had the wit to maintain this position by skilfully informing its discussions, by responding to information requests and by presenting the EMCDDA as a significant, though low-key, resource servicing the sessions and programmes initiated under various EU presidencies. The particular (epidemiological) cognitive prism which the EMCDDA has been able to patiently build up and which has established itself as a key source of information for grasping the drugs situation in Europe owes a great deal to these linking and articulating activities. This has been one of the many strengths of this 'weak' institution.

Conclusion

We would like to start by reviewing the heuristic benefits which may be provided by a study of the conditions and dynamics behind the production of expertise and

18 Political control does not exercise comparable constraints over all substantive dimensions of EMCDDA monitoring. In addition, on any one subject, the aspects which it monitors may be transformed over time. While, for example, in the mid-1990s the general subject of risk reduction was scrupulously monitored by the Board of Management, in the mid-2000s political oversight concentrated more on a number of specific aspects of this area.

52 Henri Bergeron

expert assessments. We have shown how the EMCDDA, despite the gagging effect of clearly-delimited missions, and numerous control bodies and procedures, has succeeded in producing (relatively) autonomous expertise: a series of indicators, information and expert deliverables which have slowly proven their reliability, objectivity[19] and comparability (at least some them). The performative dynamics of comparison, stimulated by the production of indexes, of dashboards, key statistics, even league tables, has of course contributed towards their success (Guigner, 2008; Bruno, 2008) in that Member States doing well in these tests tend to make use of them and in so doing legitimise them (on a similar dynamic at national level, see amongst others Le Galès and Scott, 2008). But it will be recalled that if these dynamics of comparison have been able to develop, and have the political effects which they have had, this is because they are based on the deployment of knowledge and information considered to be (more or less) reliable and legitimate. This is why we think that a study of this sort makes for a greater understanding of one of the links in the causal chain on which cognitive Europeanisation is based: it helps us to grasp some of the mechanisms of the political effectiveness of ideas. Here, their effectiveness is understood as their capacity to be used, to convince and finally to affect the behaviour of actors in these arenas. We thus see how a sociology of production can enrich a sociology of reception.

We would like to go deeper into this argument by highlighting a second point. Our study shows that these indicators do not merely generate information providing food for thought and official documents circulating within the policy world. These expert productions and indicators, especially those on epidemiology, all interlinked, also form an effective cognitive frame. While more often the teleonomic consequence of the meeting of partially independent causal chains than the teleological result of a voluntary action,[20] they constitute the basic components of an a priori cognitive frame (bearing on health) through which problems of European (and often national) public policy are now perceived. One may, at the conclusion of this study, acknowledge that these indicators have not left unaffected the subject which they set out to capture objectively. They have, at the very least, tinged the drugs phenomenon with their own particular colouring, objectivising and selectively drawing attention to some of its dimensions, with the

---

19 The author of this chapter is not in a position to rule on the objective nature of these productions. The objectivity of such is freely acknowledged today by the actors who take part in the processes we are studying: they consider the assessments, knowledge and information to be objective in that they are hardly ever (if at all) thought to reflect the interests or individual beliefs of any particular group.

20 Teleonomic rather than teleological, in that the process of drawing up each of these indicators has been coordinated and carried out by various EMCDDA officials, having involved specific groups of external experts and been developed according to their own timescales. It is thus difficult to identify any actor or group of actors who might be said to have completely and knowingly steered the formation of what can now, at the end of the process, be seen as a cognitive frame.

The soft power of the EMCDDA 53

social and health-related dimensions, long neglected, now well to the fore. Indicators have turned out to be institutions, used in a taken-for-granted way (in the sense of neo-institutionalist sociologists) by a great number of professionals, officials, experts or political decision-makers who gravitate around and reflect upon the problems linked to drugs in Europe. And it is because a number of them have become institutions, in the sense that hardly anyone thinks about what they are, while they are deployed by a large number of actors in all sorts of situations to work on all sorts of questions, that they have helped to produce diagnoses and assessments organised around the same numerical values and features. This provides additional justification for studying the processes whereby expertise is produced: it enables identification of the mechanisms by which knowledge and information are endowed with a nature and with properties which help make them, in the eyes of those manipulating them, reliable and legitimate.[21] This study therefore enables us to grasp how this information, reasoning and knowledge comes to be internalised, and sets itself up as a cognitive framework (Boudon, 1986, 1990, 1995),[22] thus, finally, becoming even more effective. It would, however, be singularly reductive, even naive, to attribute the convergence of domestic policies, as evidenced by a number of works (Bergeron, 2005; Grange, 2005, MacGregor and Whiting, 2010) to this one single cause, itself of a cognitive nature.

We would like to conclude by making some other remarks. The EMCDDA's expert productions – which have succeeded in inducing the relegation to distant memory of the work of articulation which in part helped to generate them – constitute 'silent' cognitive resources (Bowker and Star, 1997, 1999) impacting on the reflections, interactions and negotiations driven by other categories of 'experts', themselves situated in other, more political positions, within European institutions, and more transparently defending the interests of the States which they represent. The availability of a great deal of legitimate information and expertise has not, however, blunted the acute power dynamics permeating these European arenas: it has displaced them. Neither has it helped to shape uncertain political preferences: it has played a part in redefining them. The EMCDDA has worked to shift the framework of political exchanges,[23] until then mainly oriented towards questions linked with enforcement, towards a taking account of the social and health-related dimensions of the phenomenon.[24] These ideas would be worth

21 We would once again stress this essential point: the effectiveness of these productions cannot of course be entirely explained by their own nature and characteristics. For there to be a satisfying, if not full, explanation we also need to understand the determinants of their appropriation and thus engage in a sociology of their reception.

22 By reconstructing the heterogeneous complex of 'good reasons', which actors have for believing what they believe, one is able, as Boudon asserts, to show that internalisation is more obviously a consequence of holding certain ideas than one of the causes of holding them.

23 Castel (2009) has made similar observations, at a more local level, about the political effects of the dissemination of medical expertise and guides to good practice.

24 Which rather capped it all for an agency which significantly was 'attached', as soon as it was set up, to the Justice and Home Affairs Directorate (*Justice et affaires intérieures*, JAI).

developing in a more thorough and detailed fashion, but we might in conclusion hazard the idea that information does not enable learning by erasing power relationships. Instead, it shifts the frame within which power relationships flourish, affects their structure by providing a resource for some and a constraint for others, and transforms the rhetorical registers and the hierarchy of operational methods deployed in these circles. The use of information and evidence has become a necessity. But information is also persuasive, and the EMCDDA has worked hard to promote 'the power of knowledge'. This study can thus be thought of as helping to shed light on the socialisation and learning dynamics which take place in these spaces, (the importance of which has been stressed by a number of authors) as well as the difficulty of defining them precisely (De Maillard and Robert, 2008), thus achieving a more subtle understanding of what motivates them.

References

BENAMOUZIG, D. and BESANÇON, J. (2005) Administrer un monde incertain: les nouvelles bureaucraties techniques. Le cas des agences sanitaires en France. *Sociologie du travail*. *47*. pp. 301–322.

BERGERON, H. (1999) *L'État et la toxicomanie. Histoire d'une singularité française*. Paris: PUF.

BERGERON, H. (2005) Europeanization of Drug Policies: from Objective Convergence to Mutual Agreement. In Steffen, M. (ed.). *Health Governance in Europe: Issues, Challenges, and Theories*. London: Routledge. pp. 174–187.

BOUDON, R. (1986) *L'Idéologie ou l'origine des idées reçues*. Paris: Le Seuil.

BOUDON, R. (1990) *L'Art de se persuader*. Paris: Fayard.

BOUDON, R. (1995) *Le Juste et le vrai, Études sur l'objectivité des valeurs et de la connaissance*. Paris: Fayard.

BOWKER, G. and STAR, S. L. (1997), Problèmes de classification et de codage dans la gestion internationale de l'information. In Conein, B. and Thévenot, L.(eds.), *Cognition et information en société*. Paris: Éditions de l'EHESS. pp. 283–309.

BOWKER, G. and STAR, S. L. (1999) *Sorting Things Out. Classification and its Consequences*. Paris, Cambridge and London: MIT Press.

BRUNO, I. (2008) Y a t-il un pilote dans l'Union? Tableaux de bord, indicateurs, cibles chiffrés : les balises de la décision. *Politix*. 2(82). pp. 95–118.

CASTEL, P. (2009) What's Behind a Guideline? Authority, Competition and Collaboration in the French Oncology Sector. *Social Studies of Science*. 39(5). pp. 743–764.

CHECKEL, J. T. (2005) International Institutions and Socialization in Europe: Introduction and Framework. *International Organization*. 59(4). pp. 801–826.

CHITI, E. (2000) The Emergence of a Community Administration: The Case of European Agencies. *Common Market Law Review*. 37. pp. 309–343.

DEHOUSSE, R. (1997) Regulation by Network in the EC: The Role of European Agencies. *Journal of European Public Policy*. 4(2). pp. 246–261.

DEMORTAIN, D. (2006) Mettre les risques sous surveillance. L'outillage de la sécurité sanitaire des médicaments et des aliments en Europe. Doctorat en sciences politiques. École normale supérieure de Cachan. Unpublished.

DESROSIÈRES, A. (1997) Du singulier au général. L'argument statistique entre la science et l'Etat. In Conein, B. and Thévenot, L. (eds.) *Cognition et information en société*. Paris: Editions de l'EHESS. pp. 267–282.

FASSIN, D. (ed.) (1998) *Les Figures urbaines de la santé publique. Enquête sur des expériences locales*. Paris: La Découverte.

GRANGE, A. (2005) *L'Europe des drogues. L'apprentissage de la réduction des risques aux Pays-Bas, en France et en Italie*. Paris: L'Harmattan.

GUIGNER, S. (2006) The EU's Role(s) in European Public Health: The Interdependence of Roles within a Saturated Space of International Organizations. In Elgström, O. and Smith, M. (eds.) *New Roles for the European Union in International Politics*. London, New York: Routledge. pp. 225–244.

GUIGNER, S. (2008) L'Institutionnalisation d'un espace européen de la santé. Entre intégration et européanisation. Doctorat de l'Université de Rennes I. Unpublished.

HAAS, P. M. (1989) Do Regimes Matter? Epistemic Communities and Mediterranean Pollution Control. *International Organization*. 43(3). pp. 377–403.

HALL, P. A. (1993) Policy Paradigms, Social Learning, and the State. The Case of Economic Policymaking in Britain. *Comparative Politics*. 25(3). pp. 275–296.

HALL, P. A. (1997) The Role of Interests, Institutions, and Ideas in the Comparative Political Economy of the Industrialized Nations. In Lichbach, M. and Zuckerman, A. (eds.). *Comparative Politics*. Cambridge: Cambridge University Press. pp. 174–207.

HAURAY, B. (2006) *L'Europe du médicament*. Paris: Presses de Sciences Po.

HECLO, H. (1974) *Modern Social Politics in Britain and Sweden*. New Haven: Yale University Press.

LE GALÈS, P. and SCOTT, A. (2008) Une révolution bureaucratique? Autonomie sans contrôle ou 'freer markets, more rules'? *Revue française de sociologie*. 49(2). pp. 301–330.

MACGREGOR, S. and WHITING, M. (2010) The Development of European Drug Policy and the Place of Harm Reduction Within This. In Rhodes, T. and Hedrich, D. (eds.). *Harm Reduction: Evidence, Impacts and Challenges. EMCDDA Monographs 10*. Luxembourg: Publication Office of the European Union. pp. 59–77.

MAHONEY, J. and THELEN, K. (2009) A Theory of Gradual Institutional Change. In Mahoney, J. and Thelen, K. (eds.). *Explaining Institutional Change. Ambiguity, Agency and Power*. New York: Cambridge University Press. pp. 1–37.

MAILLARD de, J. and ROBERT, C. (2008) Les comités dans l'Union européenne: conflits d'interprétation et pistes de recherche. In Belot, C., Magnette, P. and Saurruger, S. (eds.). *Traités d'études européennes*. Paris: Economica.

MAJONE, G. (1996) *La Communauté européenne: un État régulateur*. Paris: Montchrestien.

MAJONE, G. (1997) The New European Agencies: Regulation by Information. *Journal of European Public Policy*. 4(2). pp. 267–275.

MARTEL, C. (2003) Eléments de réflexion sur l'enjeu de l'adhésion de la Turquie à l'Union européenne. Aspects de lutte contre le phénomène des drogues. In Flaesch-Mougin, C. and Lebullenger, J. (eds.). *Les Défis de l'adhésion de la Turquie à l'Union européenne*. Brussels: Éditions Bruylant.

MOUHANNA, C. and MATELLY, J. H. (2007) *Police, des chiffres et des doutes*. Paris: Michalon.

QUAGLIA, L., DE FRANCESCO, F. and RADAELLI, C. M. (2008) Committee Governance and Socialization in the European Union. *Journal of European Public Policy*. 15(1). pp. 155–166.

RADAELLI, C. M. (1999) The Public Policy of the European Union: Whither Politics of Expertise? *Journal of European Public Policy*. 6(5). pp. 757–774.

RADAELLI, C. M. (2002) The Domestic Impact of European Union public Policy: Notes on Concepts, Methods, and the Challenge of Empirical Research. *Politique européenne*. 5. pp. 105–136.

ROBERT, C. (2003) L'expertise comme mode d'administration communautaire: entre logiques technocratiques et stratégies d'alliance. *Politique européenne*. 11. pp. 57–78.

ROBERT, C. (2010) Etre socialisé à ou par l'Europe? Dispositions sociales et sens du jeu institutionnel des experts de la Commission européenne. In Michel, H. and Robert, C. (eds.). *La Fabrique des Européens. Construction européenne et processus de socialisation*. Strasbourg: PUS. pp. 313–346.

ROSENTAL, P. A. (2008) La silicose comme maladie professionnelle transnationale. *Revue française des affaires sociales*. 2–3. pp. 255–277.

SABATIER, P. A. (1988) An Advocacy Coalition Framework of Policy Change and the Role of Policy-Oriented Learning Therein. *Policy Sciences*. 21. pp. 129–169.

SETBON, M. (1995) Drogue, facteur de délinquance? D'une image à son usage. *Revue française de sciences politiques*. 45(5). pp. 747–774.

SNOW, D. A., BURKE, R.E., WORDEN, S. K. and BENFORD, R. D. (1986) Frame Alignment Processes, Micromobilization, and Movement Participation. *American Sociological Review*. 51. pp. 464–481.

STEFFEN, M. (ed.). (2005) *Health Governance in Europe: Issues, Challenges, and Theories*. London: Routledge.

Part II

Domestic drug policies in Europe

Chapter 4

Belgian drug policy

Christine Guillain

Introduction

This contribution deals with the criminal policy pursued in relation to the consumption and possession of illicit drugs in Belgium. Its aim is to trace, from a socio-historical perspective, the genealogy of Belgian criminal law on drugs. This will provide an opportunity to examine the political and social reasoning that underpin the criminalisation of drugs and attempts to decriminalise the behaviours surrounding the consumption of drugs, and will serve to highlight the impasse of those rationales.

Belgian drug regulation at the beginning of the twentieth century: A course clearly dictated by international law

The criminalisation of drugs appears to be an artificial construct that reflects the logic of interests entirely separated from social realities. Under the influence of external factors, the process of the criminalisation of drugs plainly preceded the existence of a problem related to their consumption. The adoption of the criminal Act in this case is of an essentially symbolic and only slightly instrumental nature (van de Kerchove, 1985). This explains its weak application by the courts before the 1960s.

A public health approach to drugs

Until the late 19th century, the consumption of drugs – then confined to the medical world – does not appear to have been a problem for Belgian society. The main objective of the regulations relating to it was to protect the consumer from illegal medical practices, and to ensure the delivery and selling of medication by health professionals (Tisseyre, 1977, p. 3). Contrary to France or the Netherlands which had colonies in Asia, Belgium was only slightly familiar with opium consumption and dens. Belgium was not, incidentally, represented at the International Opium Conference held at The Hague in 1911. Belgium did, nevertheless, ratify the International Opium Convention of 23 January 1912 resulting from the

60 Christine Guillain

Conference, because of the moral value represented by international engagement and the importance for Belgium of association with the Convention after the end of the First World War. Drugs had become a global problem calling for universal reaction to which Belgium could not remain indifferent.

The 24 February 1921 Act: a repressive turn

The ratification of the International Opium Convention of 1912 resulted in a Belgian counterpart, the 24 February 1921 Act regarding the trafficking of poisonous, narcotic, disinfectant or antiseptic substances. Despite the fact that the consumption of drugs was not a problem in Belgium, the report outlining the reasons for the Act was impassioned. The report spoke of the 'ravages caused in all the classes of our population by the dire abuses of narcotics' which necessitate the taking of drastic measures to 'combat the dreadful curse that is threatening our country' (Commission de l'Intérieur, 1921, p. 1). The over-dramatisation and exaggeration of parliamentary speeches enabled the adoption of measures that appear to be especially ill-adapted to the Belgian situation. This is seen in the criminalisation of group consumption of such substances – or the act of facilitating their consumption – measures borrowed in their entirety from the French Act of 12 July 1916 targeting opium dens.

The need to fight against this 'new social peril', in the name of international solidarity explains the enactment of an emergency measure completely at odds with social reality. The adoption of the 24 February 1921 Act and of its implementation marks a real turning point in the Belgian approach to the phenomenon of drugs, which is no longer limited to regulations concerning the art of healing, but henceforth aims to suppress drug trafficking through the criminalisation of certain behaviours.

Drugs consumers shielded from the legal system

Despite Belgium having enacted an impressive repressive arsenal, it was sparingly used by police and judicial authorities. And despite the proliferation of texts gradually criminalising drug possession, until the 1960s[1] the application of the law to drug users remained marginal and principally targeted doctors and pharmacists.

Two reasons seem to explain this gap between the process of primary and secondary criminalisation. Firstly, Belgium appeared to be more concerned with the social and political unrest that shook Belgian society during the late nineteenth century. Secondly, alcoholism was seen as *the* major problem needing to be addressed, while drugs were not associated, in the political and social discourse, with issues of security or delinquency. The handful of drugs users detained in mental

---

1   Act of August 14, 1927; Royal decree of December 31, 1930; Act of May 1, 1933 and Act of March 11, 1958.

health hospitals illustrate the medicalisation, at the time, of behaviours deemed to be deviant.

The gradual construction of a social *problématique* related to drug consumption

After a period during which the legal problem of drugs was eclipsed, the issue appeared anew in the political agenda of the 1960s and 1970s, at which time repressive measures towards drugs, across almost all of Europe, were reinforced and gradually applied against drugs users.

A socio-political context favouring the reinforcement of repressive measures

The rise in drug consumption, associated with the rise of a protest counter-culture in Europe, stimulated the interest of the political class in a practice – drug use – that emerged as the distinctive trait of a certain social marginality. Like alcohol in the pre-war period, drugs were, in a relation of causality, associated with other social ills such as juvenile delinquency, prostitution and criminality. The symbolic figure of the drug user became the pretext for the legitimation of a new form of social control with regard to certain marginal social groups. The setting up of specific infrastructures within the police force, particularly proactive in the fight against drugs, had repercussions on the activity of police, judicial and penitential authorities: there are increasingly important seizures of drugs, a rise in the number of convictions for drug use and trafficking and a rise in incarceration rates. The surge in such figures, supposed to reflect the rise in drug use, worried the political class which took fright and called for stepping up the clampdown.

Politicians, attentive to public opinion but with little knowledge about the phenomenon of drugs, tailored their public statements to the tabloid press which terrorised public opinion with dubious data. One read about the ravages caused by drug use, seen as leading to the worst kinds of moral and physical degeneration. As noted by Toro (1998, p. 22), 'an understanding without scientific foundations was substituted to a reality that was observable and not in the least threatening'. Belgium, like other European countries, reinforced its repressive apparatus in a move that it perceived as the best guarantee of the preservation of the social order and the restoration of values. Despite the questions, criticisms and alternative proposals that began to flourish in scientific debate, repression was established as the natural path to follow, as mapped out in the International Conventions.

The 9 July 1975 Act: the reinforcement of repressive measures

The United Nations Convention on Narcotic Drugs of 30 March 1961 served once again as a springboard for the reinforcement of repressive measures

62 Christine Guillain

targeting drugs. It provided the legitimation for the adoption of the 9 July 1975 Act, which largely modified that of 24 February 1921, by stepping up repression in order to 'reach with greater efficiency the new modalities of delinquency in this domain'.[2] Among the 1975 Act's defining features one can note: the extension of the scope of the Act's application to psychotropic substances likely to generate a dependence; the considerable harshening of punishments,[3] including those for minor offences which go beyond the prescriptions of the 1961 International Convention; and the establishment of new crimes, such as incitement to consume. In addition, the Act introduced aggravating circumstances; a series of ancillary punishments; the introduction of exorbitant measures in relation to common law; and the creation of an excuse clause, designed to encourage denunciation with a view to helping the legal authorities dismantle trafficking networks.

At the same time, with the influence of the anti-prohibition movement in criminology, there appeared the first questions about the usefulness of criminalising drug use, and the first reflections on alternatives to penal repression as a way of responding to the expression of a social unease. The Belgian legislator chose, as a result, to widen the probation conditions so as to promote the treatment of drug users within the criminal justice space. This decision illustrates an ambiguity that is also perceptible in the International Conventions. Authorities wavered between the figure of the 'culpable' drug user, justifying the reinforcement of repressive measures, and that of the 'sick' drug user, in need of medical care. A paternalist and protectionist outlook on the issue meant that politicians designated the drug user both victim and perpetrator of the drugs epidemic. A similar trend appears in most European legislation[4] which, while they set up various types of therapeutic injunctions for drug users, did not hesitate to incriminate drug consumption – directly or indirectly, through the criminalisation of possession – in some cases, for the first time.[5]

This tension continued influencing public policy throughout the century, resulting in a hybrid logic that is, nevertheless, dominated by the penal approach.

---

2   Projet de loi modifiant la loi du 24 février 1921 concernant le trafic des substances vénéneuses, soporifiques, stupéfiantes, désinfectantes ou antiseptiques. *Sénat*, 1970–1971 (290). 2 mars 1971. Bruxelles: Documents Parlementaires. p. 2. Available from: http://senaat.be/www/?MIval=/index_senate&MENUID=22103&LANG=fr [Accessed: 28 August 2015].

3   The previous maximums of two years' imprisonment and a fine of 10,000 Belgian francs was raised to five years' imprisonment and 100,000 Belgian francs (now in euros).

4   For a presentation of European legislation: European Monitoring Centre for Drugs and Drug Addiction (EMCDDA). European legal database on drugs. Available from: http://eldd.emcdda.europa.eu/html.cfm/index5029EN.html [Accessed: 28 August 2015]. For a comparative analysis, see Cesoni (2000).

5   Thus, while the French Act of 12 July 1916 did not prohibit individual drug consumption, the Act of 31 December 1970 henceforth suppressed the personal consumption of illicit substances or plants classified as narcotic with a punishment of two months to one year in prison (art. L. 628).

Indeed, any alternative approaches are very quickly deployed from within, or in the shadow of, the criminal justice system. While it is true that the setting up of social or public health policies has softened the strict application of criminal law, these policies have above all legitimated the intervention of the criminal justice system in relation to behaviours deemed to be deviant or immoral.

Criminalising consumption through possession? The law's ambiguity and its interpretation by the courts

Just like in 1921, the 1975 Belgian Act does not criminalise the consumption of drugs. While a certain hesitation on the part of the legislator to punish possession with a view to consumption can be observed, as is the case at the international level, many drug users are convicted for punishable acts preceding the act of consumption, such as the purchase or the possession of drugs. The result of this is a *de facto* criminalisation of drug consumption. The evolution of case law, coupled later with a massive application of special inquiry techniques, confirms the excessive nature of the Drugs Act (Guillain, 2003): adopted in order to suppress drug trafficking, it was nonetheless used in large part against users.

Security as a factor of criminalisation and as resistance to the decriminalisation of behaviours surrounding drug use

Despite the numerous pleas in favour of the decriminalisation[6] of behaviours related to drug use, since the 1990s a safety and security discourse has heavily determined drug policy. In spite of a softening of the punishments applicable and the introduction of harm reduction measures, the repressive approach seems to be galvanised.

The repression of drug consumption as an instrument in the fight against social decline

At the beginning of the 1990s, there was a clear increase in government directives, plans, statements and announcements aimed at addressing the security issues that penetrate Belgian society. Security is at the centre of every debate and is the main concern of public policy. The reading of these political documents quickly shows, however, that these policies do not target the delinquency phenomenon in its entirety but only one aspect of it: repetitive petty urban delinquency, presented as the main vector of urban degeneration. Political discourse points to the drug user

---

6   By decriminalisation we mean the elimination from the criminal field. While the behaviour will no longer be the object of a penal punishment within the framework of decriminalisation, it can, however, still be punished administratively. For more on this, see van de Kerchove (1987), and also Comité européen pour les problèmes criminels (1980).

as the representative figure of prevailing fears about urban decline and places this figure at the centre of various public policies.

Focusing on the drug user as a locus of social vulnerability has led the political class to attempt to set boundaries with the public prosecutor which, to the extent that it has the prerogative to decide whether or not to press charges, occupies a central position within the criminal justice system. Thus, in 1993, the first criminal policy directive[7] was enacted which influenced the choice of whether to press charges as part of the fight against drug use, and also, prosecutorial methods, suggesting that a systematic application of the norm be carried out. The 1993 directive prohibits the immediate abandonment of cases that involve drug use. The political reaction was intended to be directed at a group of the population that is deemed to be at the root of social decline problems.

Although the political attempt to set guidelines for police actions and the public prosecutor have not been successful, it has nonetheless led to the resurgence of prosecutions and punishments regarding drugs. Various studies confirm the growth of narcotics cases during the nineties (De Pauw, 1996). A Brussels study has shown that from 1993 to 1996, the number of drugs cases handled by the Brussels judicial district grew by 60% (Guillain and Scohier, 2000). These studies have also shown that the youth and immigrants are the privileged target of Belgian police and judicial authorities.

The adjustment of the prosecution policy as an alternative to decriminalisation

The increased attention paid by the judicial apparatus to drugs cases led, in the second half of the nineties, to numerous political reactions that lie at the root of the creation, in 1996, of a parliamentary working group tasked with studying the drugs issue. This working group requested the adoption of a global approach to the drugs phenomenon by focusing on social-health measures and recommended a more moderate application of criminal law for drug users, stating that 'drug addiction does not in itself constitute a motive justifying a repressive approach' (Chambre des Représentants, 1997).

The parliamentary recommendations did not, however, give rise to normative instruments and the adoption of the second criminal policy directive, in 1998,[8] symbolised the government's refusal to venture down the path of decriminalisation. Although the directive recommends the attenuation of criminal sanctions for

---

7 Directive générale du Collège des procureurs généraux réunis sous la présidence du ministre de la Justice relative à la politique criminelle commune en matière de toxicomanie du 26 mai 1993, published in the *Journal du droit des Jeunes*, 1994, 138, pp. 19–23.

8 Directive commune relative à la politique des poursuites commune en matière de détention et de vente au détail de drogues illicites, approuvée le 8 mai 1998 après concertation entre le ministre de la Justice et le Collège des procureurs généraux. Available from: http://homeusers.brutele.be/cdc/justice/col9805f.pdf [Accessed: 28 August 2015].

cannabis consumers, by asking the public prosecutor to rank it last in its list of priorities, drugs possession still constitutes an offence. And although the directive purports to decriminalise the possession of cannabis with a view to consumption, this actual decriminalisation is immediately dulled since the public prosecutor can, in order to press charges, take into consideration such material circumstances as 'indications of trafficking', 'information relating to the interested party's personality', a 'problematic consumption' or other additional information, such as 'public nuisance or a real risk of public nuisance'.

An evaluation of the directive highlights the arbitrariness and the distinct treatment that drug users receive from the criminal justice system (Service de la politique criminelle, 1999; Deltenre and Lebrun, 2000). Although the evaluation highlights the divergences among judicial practices, it nevertheless observes that prosecution remains a privileged means in the penal treatment of drug users. Finally, it notes that public prosecutors place much importance on the personal and situational factors of the interested parties. These factors increase the risk of escalation in the scale of penal punishments, and the most restrictive measures are imposed on the most marginalised consumers.

The repression of drug use as an instrument in the fight against public nuisance

The highly critical evaluation of the criminal policy caused the Belgian government, in the wake of the 1999 federal elections, to propose the development of a 'coherent drugs policy'. The drugs question, for a long time confined exclusively to the field of criminal justice, was approached from the point of view of human rights. In this way, it appeared to initiate a new 'approach that breaks with past practices'.[9]

Two years later, a political document concerning the drugs issue was approved by the Council of Ministers (Gouvernement fédéral, 2001). Considering that drug abuse is a public health issue that needs to be integrated into the framework of a policy of normalisation aimed at the rational management of risks, the government's drugs policy is based on three pillars: 1) prevention for non users and non problematic users; 2) assistance, risk reduction and rehabilitation for problematic users; 3) repression for producers and traffickers. A process of reform was in progress, in the beginning of the third millennium, and it translated into the adoption of two new Acts in 2003.[10]

Briefly, these new regulations introduce the decriminalisation of group consumption of substances – no longer an offence – and reduces the applicable punishments for the possession of cannabis for personal consumption. In this way,

9   Déclaration gouvernementale. 14 juillet 1999. Available from: http://www.dekamer. be/FLWB/PDF/50/0020/50K0020001.pdf [Accessed: 28 August 2015].
10 Acts of 4 April 2003 and of 3 May 2003. *Moniteur belge.* 2 juin 2003. Available from: http://www.ejustice.just.fgov.be/loi/loi.htm [Accessed: 28 August 2015].

the simple possession of cannabis by an adult for personal consumption – that is, when this consumption is not accompanied by public nuisance or when it does not appear to be problematic – is now punishable with police sanctions whereas in the past it was subject to correctional punishment.[11] Moreover, the police are requested to no longer produce a typical official report but to settle for an anonymous recording of the facts. Without a registered official report, prosecution is no longer possible, leading the way, in practice, to the *de facto* decriminalisation of simple cannabis possession for personal consumption.

An attentive reading of the legal texts reveals a gap between reality and the government's aims in wishing to grasp drugs policy from the point of view of public health in the framework of 'a policy of normalisation aimed at the rational management of risks' (Gouvernement fédéral, 2001, p. 7). Simple possession of cannabis for personal consumption remains an offence in the eyes of criminal law and the lack of an official report does not constitute a credible alternative to decriminalisation, all the more so as its impact is diminished with the criminalisation of the problematic consumption of cannabis or when accompanied by public nuisance. In short, the decriminalisation of the simple possession of cannabis, which was to have become the norm, became the exception instead, whereas prosecution in case of problematic possession is still the rule. Other than the decriminalisation of group consumption of all substances, the 3 May 2003 Act contains only slight modifications regarding drugs other than cannabis. Possessing them, even for personal consumption, is still an offence and punishments become harsher 'given the unacceptable health risk'.[12]

The message thus conveyed is not of the greatest clarity, to the point that doubts were raised about the effective application of the new regulations. Nor is there greater tolerance in regard to drugs consumption; on the contrary, there is increasing aversion towards uses associated with behaviours deemed asocial or unacceptable.

The new text is not met with indifference. Having triggered strong reactions in various quarters, as much among NGOs as in judicial circles, it did not make it past the Constitutional Court which, in 2004, partially cancelled the 3 May 2003 Act on the basis of its incompatibility with the principle of legality.[13] As the gap created by the decision of the Constitutional Court was not bridged by legislative means, the government settled for an adjustment of the prosecution policy

---

11 Punishments have in this way gone from a three-month to a five-year prison sentence and/or from a fine of €1,000 to €100,000 to a fine of €15 to €25 in the case of a first offence.

12 Directive ministérielle du 16 mai 2003 relative à la politique des poursuites en matière de détention et de vente au détail de drogues illicites. *Moniteur belge*. 2 juin 2003. Available from: http://www.ejustice.just.fgov.be/loi/loi.htm [Accessed: 28 August 2015].

13 Cour Constitutionnelle. 20 octobre 2004, 158/2004. *Moniteur belge*. 28 octobre 2004. Available from: http://www.ejustice.just.fgov.be/loi/loi.htm [Accessed: 28 August 2015].

through the drafting of a new criminal policy directive in 2005.[14] This text, modelled on the 1998 directive, does not fundamentally modify the prior policy course since it meets neither the wish of formulating a coherent policy in regard to drugs nor addresses the criticisms relating to the legality aspect. The new directive stipulates that possession by an adult of a given quantity of cannabis for personal consumption (three grams maximum or a grown plant) falls within 'the lowest level of priority of prosecution policy', while also specifying that possession of cannabis accompanied by public disorder implies different treatment altogether by the judicial authorities.[15]

The limits of a very partial decriminalisation

Since the early 1990s, most of the modifications introduced in drugs litigation are part of the framework of the law but in criminal policy instruments, through directives adopted by the Ministry of Justice. For various reasons, among which is the desire not to be exposed to the criticisms of international organisations, Belgium chooses, like other states, to steer clear from modifying legal actions by contenting itself with an adjustment in its prosecution policy. The possession of drugs is still a criminal offence but no longer leads to prosecution.

In practice this decriminalisation, even if only partial, displaces the burden of responsibility onto the shoulders of police officers and the public prosecutor for the application of policies with regard to drug users. This delegation of responsibility creates a certain arbitrarily applied regulatory scheme, for public servants who might, *a priori*, favour an actual decriminalisation. It should, however, be noted that the members of the public prosecutor's department, for the most part, use their discretion in a less tolerant way than the texts would have them do using the criminalising logic of controlling drug users with a view to public safety.

Thus, the 1993 directive lies at the root of a resurgence in prosecutions and convictions regarding drugs. Although such prosecutions became scarcer after 1996, the public prosecutor demonstrated a desire to increase the degree of social control over some consumers, especially by lengthening the time span of investigations in cases involving drug use. The evaluation of the 1998 directive highlights, in turn, the fact that the residual categories of problematic consumption

---

14 Directive du 25 janvier 2005 relative à la constatation, l'enregistrement et la poursuite des infractions en matière de détention de cannabis. *Moniteur belge*. 31 janvier 2005. Available from: http://www.ejustice.just.fgov.be/loi/loi.htm [Accessed: 28 August 2015].

15 Since the completion of this article, a new circular relative 'to the constatation, registration and prosecution policy in the detention and retail sale of illicit drugs' was adopted on 21 December 2015 by the Minister of Justice and the College of General Prosecutors. This instrument aims to clarify the legal framework while maintaining the prosecution policy previously set in matters of drugs: 'it is not a matter of revising the general philosophy of drug policy'. The circular, which has been classified as confidential, was not published in the *Moniteur belge*.

and public nuisance have become the rule instead of the exception: prosecutions remain frequent and the actors on the field place great importance on the personal and situational factors relating to drug users (Service de la politique criminelle, 1999). This observation was repeated in 2000; the vaguely defined criteria used by the directive, when it translates into significant discretionary power of police officers and public prosecutor, leads to frequent prosecutions and imprisonment sentences, despite the numerous political recommendations aimed at avoiding the incarceration of drug users (De Ruyver and Casselman, 2000, p. 38). More recently, police statistics on criminality show an increase in the number of drug-related incidents recorded by the police between 2005 and 2009 – mostly in regard to the possession of cannabis – whereas penitential statistics reveal a proliferation in preventive incarceration on the sole basis of drugs-related offences (Deltenre and Guillain, 2012).

The omnipresence of the security discourse

The handful of Acts adopted following the 2003 Act and the 2005 directive[16] only bear witness to the difficulty that the government faces in attempting to extricate itself from the legal imbroglio engendered by the adoption of semi-reforms and also highlights the security logic that continues to characterise drugs policy. This is illustrated by the adoption of the 20 July 2006 Act which authorises administrative arrest, for a maximum duration of six hours, of persons manifestly under the influence of soporific or psychotropic substances in a publicly accessible place, if their presence causes disorder, scandal, or puts others or themselves in danger. The preparatory work underlines once more the desire to stigmatise drug users, as well as the public nuisance concerns that underpin the bill. The presence of 'junkies roaming under the influence of narcotics' who 'contribute greatly to the feeling of lack of safety' is mentioned. One reads of 'entire neighbourhoods' in jeopardy where the 'freedom to come and go' is hindered 'because people are afraid to go out' (Commission de la Justice, 2006, pp. 9–10 and 26).

The fight against public nuisance becomes everyone's business: 'attending to a safe society is a shared responsibility that can only be duly exercised through everyone's participation in the common effort'. The fight against drug use is now a priority of an 'integral and integrated nuisance policy' (Conseil des ministres, 2008, pp. 7 and 27). Under the increasing influence of European policy instruments there is the desire to reinforce the fight against the growing of cannabis plants and drug tourism, especially in transborder regions. This fight does not, however, aim to check the supply or demand for cannabis, but appears to be motivated by public nuisance and concerns for tranquillity.

---

16 And more recently, the new circular relative 'to the constatation, registration and prosecution policy in the detention and retail sale of illicit drugs' of 21 December 2015.

Health policies, from a security perspective, in the shadow of the criminal justice system

The repressive discourse regarding drug consumption is regularly in competition with a public health approach, especially following the spread of the HIV virus among drug users. The political document issued by the federal government of 19 January 2001 regarding drugs considers drug abuse a 'public health issue' that needs to be grasped in the framework 'of a policy of normalisation aimed at the rational management of risks (Gouvernement fédéral, 2001, p. 7). Whereas the repressive approach is still privileged in the fight against drug production, trade and trafficking, a health approach seems to prevail when it comes to drugs consumption: 'it is preferable to approach the issue of problematic consumption via an offer of assistance centred on rehabilitation rather than punishing the interested party and imposing on them additional suffering in this way' (Gouvernement fédéral, 2001, p. 7). The Justice minister announced, in 2008, an 'integrated and integral policy regarding drugs, centred on the effective dissuasion through prevention, assistance and repression' (Ministre de la Justice, 2008, p. 58). The Joint Declaration signed during the Interministerial Conference on Drugs on 25 January 2010 proclaims that drug abuse must be treated in priority as a public health issue to be grasped in the framework of a 'global and integrated policy' centred on prevention, assistance and repression. The declaration emphasises the importance of adopting an alternative approach to drug use by privileging the theory of imprisonment as the ultimate resort and by orienting users 'as much as possible' towards assistance services (Cellule Générale de Politique Drogues, 2010).

At the instigation of various NGOs active in the field of prevention and assistance to drug users, awareness is being raised among the political class about the risks to which drug users expose themselves in illicit consumption. Belgium adopted two Acts, in 1998 and 2002, in order to permit needle distribution and exchange schemes outside the pharmaceutical network, and create a legal framework to facilitate and render safe substitution treatment. Moreover, the introduction of new measures, starting in the 2000s, illustrates a desire to stimulate alliances between the health and justice sectors, and to encourage the supply of therapeutic treatment at the various stages of the criminal procedure. Evidence of this is the various initiatives in the judicial district of Ghent, aimed at reactivating therapeutic treatment starting in 2005.

The deployment of these risk reduction policies is rather underwhelming. It only seems possible to envisage risk reduction as an integrated part of a broader repressive approach, and not as an alternative to it: as if each timid advance at the health-risk level had to correspond with a significant reinforcement of the repressive measures. Thus, while the 17 November 1998 Act legally enshrines measures for needle exchanges, it also includes a repressive aspect by expanding application of punishment: the shutdown of establishments in which drugs are consumed or exchanged. These policies give an indication of the security concerns as well as the suspicions raised by the introduction of assistance measures for drug users.

70 Christine Guillain

The consumer of drugs remains, in large part, associated with delinquency and public nuisance, as can be seen in the federal document relating to the issue of drugs of 19 January 2001 which states that drug consumption 'generates far too often either a derived criminality or public nuisance', so that it has to be the object 'of particular attention on the part of the public prosecutor' (Gouvernement fédéral, 2001, p. 51). The national security plan of 2008–2011 emphasises the fight against public nuisance incidents linked to drugs use and no longer speaks of a global, integrated policy but of an 'integral and integrated public nuisance policy' (Conseil des ministres, 2008, p. 24). The Joint Declaration of 25 January 2010 speaks of an 'absolute priority of any criminal policy aiming to limit drugs consumption and drugs-related delinquency' (Cellule Générale de Politique Drogues, 2010). Kaminski (1996) highlights in this respect that 'global and integrated measures, such as those recently adopted by the Belgian federal government, have effectively integrated an approach in terms of risk reduction to an unchanged penal framework, by giving a security and no longer sanitary connotation to the phrase "risk reduction"'.

Conclusion

The history of drugs in modern societies is concurrent with their criminalisation. It is, indeed, a criminalisation model that characterises the management of drugs throughout the twentieth century. Beginning in the 1960s, however, a challenge to the criminalisation of drugs – and more specifically of their consumption and the behaviours surrounding consumption – asserts itself. This challenge is, depending on the period, taken up with more or less intensity by the scientific community and by politicians. Criticisms abound which denounce the inadequacy of the criminal justice approach, of the incarceration of drug users, the aggressive nature of criminal drug laws, the excessive stigmatisation of drug users, and the congestion of judicial and penitential infrastructure.

In Belgium, despite the numerous recommendations and proposals to decriminalise drugs consumption, the criminal status quo is preserved and while its legitimacy is questioned at various times, there has not been enough to shake it. Interest in a public health type of approach, linked to the rise of the ideal of reducing health risks related to drug use, should not deceive us: the few such policies that have been adopted, at the federal level, underline the security approach privileged by the Belgian government. These policies tend, in fact, less to minimise the risks of users than to control the risks to which they expose society. These policies integrate the issue of care for drug users into the orbit of the criminal justice system rather than making treatment an alternative to it. Likewise, although the delegation of responsibility to the public prosecutor for deciding whether to press charges has led to certain forms of tolerance, it only permits a very limited decriminalisation trend in exchange for a reinforcement of the penal control of various types of consumption deemed problematic or threatening in public spaces. The priority of the public nuisance context thus seems to be a factor of great importance in the preservation of the criminalisation and is the main obstacle to the decriminalisation of behaviours that surround the consumption of drugs (Guillain, 2009).

References

CELLULE GENERALE DE POLITIQUE DROGUES (2010), *Une politique globale et intégrée en matière de drogues pour la Belgique. Déclaration Conjointe de la Conférence Interministérielle Drogues.* 25/01/2010. Available from: http://www.belspo.be/belspo/organisation/Call/ forms/drug2011/IMC%20drugs-déclaration%20conjointe%2025%20janvier%202010.pdf [Accessed: 28 August 2015].

CESONI, M. L. (2000). *L'incrimination de l'usage de stupéfiants dans sept législations européennes.* Paris: Documents du Groupement de recherche Psychotropes, politique et société, 4.

COMMISSION DE L'INTERIEUR (1921) *Rapport sur le projet de loi concernant le trafic des substances vénéneuses, soporifiques, stupéfiantes, désinfectantes ou antiseptiques.* Sénat, 1920–1921(44). 10/2/1921. Bruxelles: Documents Parlementaires. Available from: http://senaat.be/ www/?MIval=/index_senate&MENUID=22103&LANG=fr [Accessed: 28 August 2015].

CHAMBRE DES REPRESENTANTS (1997) *Rapport du groupe de travail chargé d'étudier la problématique de la drogue.* Chambre des représentants. 1996–1997(1062) 5/6/1997. Bruxelles: Documents Parlementaires. Available from: http://www.lachambre.be/FLWB/PDF/49/ 1062/49K1062001.pdf [Accessed: 28 August 2015].

COMMISSION DE LA JUSTICE (2006) *Rapport sur le projet de loi portant des dispositions diverses.* Chambre des représentants. 2005–2006(2518/21) 20/6/2006. Bruxelles: Documents Parlementaires. Available from: http://www.lachambre.be/FLWB/PDF/51/ 2518/51K2518021.pdf [Accessed: 28 August 2015].

COMITE EUROPEEN POUR LES PROBLEMES CRIMINELS (1980) *Rapport sur la décriminalisation.* Strasbourg: Conseil de l'Europe. Available from: https://wcd.coe.int/ com.instranet.InstraServlet?command=com.instranet.CmdBlobGet&InstranetImage= 2653006&SecMode=1&DocId=1592804&Usage=2 [Accessed: 28 August 2015].

CONSEIL DES MINISTRES (2008) *Plan national de sécurité 2008–2011.* Available from: https://www.besafe.be/sites/besafe.localhost/files/publicaties/Janec/PlanNationaldeSe curite2008–2011.pdf [Accessed: 28 August 2015].

DE PAUW, W. (1996) Le traitement pénal des affaires de drogues à Bruxelles en 1993 et 1994. *Dossier BRES.* 31, Brussels: Iris.

DE RUYVER, B. and CASSELMAN, J. (2000) *La politique belge en matière de drogue en l'an 2000: le point de la situation.* Ghent: Universiteit Ghent.

DELTENRE, S. and GUILLAIN, C. (2012) Les filières pénales en matière de drogues: les priorités dévoilées par les chiffres. *Revue de droit pénal et de criminologie.* 12. pp. 1268–1295.

DELTENRE, S. and LEBRUN, V. (2000) La nouvelle directive à l'égard des usagers de drogue : changement de politiques ? Entre pénalisation de l'usage et usages de la pénalisation. *Revue de droit pénal et de criminologie.* 5. pp. 534–570.

GOUVERNEMENT FEDERAL (2001) *Note politique relative à la problématique de la drogue.* Chambre des Représentants. 2000–2001(1059/1) and Sénat. 2000–2001/2 (635/1) 19/ 01/2001. Bruxelles: Documents parlementaires. Available from: http://www.senate.be/ www/webdriver?MItabObj=pdf&MIcolObj=pdf&MInamObj=pdfid&MItypeObj=app lication/pdf&MIvalObj=33576073 [Accessed: 28 August 2015].

GUILLAIN, C. and SCOHIER, C. (2000) La gestion pénale d'une cohorte de dossiers stupéfiants. Les résultats disparates d'une justice dite alternative. In Van Campenhout, L.,

Cartuyvels, Y., Digneffe, F., Kaminski, D., Mary, P. and Rea, A. (eds.). *Réponses à l'insécurité. Des discours aux pratiques.* Bruxelles: Labor, pp. 271–320.

GUILLAIN, C. (2003) Le régime dérogatoire du traitement pénal des infractions à la législation sur les stupéfiants. In Kaminski, D. (ed.). *L'usage pénal des drogues.* Bruxelles: De Boeck. Perspectives criminologiques, pp. 83–105.

GUILLAIN, C. (2009) Les facteurs de criminalisation et les résistances à la décriminalisation de l'usage des drogues en Belgique. Du contrôle international aux préoccupations sécuritaires. *Revue interdisciplinaire d'études juridiques.* 63. pp. 119–132.

KAMINSKI, D. (1996) Approche globale et intégrée: de l'usage politique des drogues. In De Ruyver, B., Vermeulen, G., De Leenheer, A. and Marchandise, T. (eds.). *Approches sécuritaire et socio-sanitaire: complémentaires ou contradictoire?* Antwerpen/Bruxelles: Maklu/Bruylant.

MINISTRE DE LA JUSTICE (2008) *Note de politique générale.* Chambre des Représentants. 2008–2009(1529/016) 5/11/2008. Bruxelles: Documents parlementaires. Available from: http://www.lachambre.be/FLWB/PDF/52/1529/52K1529016.pdf [Accessed: 28 August 2015].

SERVICE DE LA POLITIQUE CRIMINELLE (1999) *Évaluation de la directive du 8 mai 1998 relative à la politique des poursuites en matière de détention et de vente au détail de drogues illicites.* Note pour le ministre de la Justice, 23 novembre 1999. Bruxelles: Ministère de la Justice.

TISSEYRE, C. (1977). *La drogue en Belgique.* Bruxelles: Cahiers J.E.B.

TORO, F. 1998. L'évacuation du plaisir : une question de rentabilité? *Les Cahiers de Prospective Jeunesse.* 3(4). pp. 19–23.

VAN DE KERCHOVE, M. (1985) Les lois pénales sont-elles faites pour être appliquées ? Réflexions sur les phénomènes de dissociation entre la validité formelle et l'effectivité des normes juridiques. *Journal des Tribunaux.* 5339. pp. 329–334.

VAN DE KERCHOVE, M. (1987) *Le droit sans peines. Aspects de la dépénalisation en Belgique et aux Etats-Unis.* Bruxelles: Facultés universitaires Saint-Louis.

Chapter 5

Danish drug policy

Esben Houborg

Danish drug policy before the welfare state

During the 1870s and 1880s, 'drug problems' were for the first time articulated in Denmark as an area for regulation (Houborg, 2014). During this period, concerns about misuse of morphine injections were identified as a problem within the medical community, and 1883 saw the first Danish scientific publication concerning drug problems ('chronic morphinism') (Pontoppidan, 1883). In Denmark as in other countries (Berridge, 1979; Hickman, 2004), the development of 'chronic morphinism' was closely related to the new medical technology of hypodermic morphine. Two concerns were specified in medical practice discourse. The first was that patients had too easy an access to hypodermic morphine due to the lack of efficient prescription rules, and the second was that doctors were too liberal in their use of the new medical technology. Two kinds of regulations were developed. First, prescription regulation was made stricter (e.g. by only allowing prescriptions to be renewed after consultation with a doctor). Second, appeals were made to doctors to be more aware of the risks of hypodermic morphine and to demonstrate higher ethical standards. Pontoppidan and other doctors called attention to particular traits in patients which would predispose them to addiction, of which mental illness and mental deficiency were the most significant. The 'drug problem' was therefore constituted, and for many years mainly regulated, as a medical problem concerning the relationship between predisposed individuals and an addictive drug, mediated through medical practice. This issue was handled by the medico-administrative system, initially the Royal Health College, which became the National Board of Health in 1909. During the 1920s and 1930s Denmark ratified the first three Opium Conventions mainly for reasons of international politics. Denmark did not ratify the fourth Opium Convention of 1936 because drug abuse was a minor problem (Kruse et al., 1989).

During the 1930s and 1940s, statistics from the League of Nations showed that Denmark had the world's highest rate of morphine use (Møller, 1945).[1] This

---

1   Even today, Denmark is one of the countries in the world with the highest consumptions of morphine per capita, surpassed only by the USA and Canada in 2012.

sparked debate within the medical community about quantitative and qualitative misuse of medicine in Denmark (Backer, 1938). The drug problem no longer simply concerned access to addictive medicines by psychopathological individuals but also over-medication at a population level. During the 1940s a few doctors were convicted for irresponsible prescription practices and lost their medical licences (Indenrigsministeriet, 1953; Jepsen, 2008). The need to better control medical practice in relation to addictive substances ultimately led to new medical legislation in the 1950s, making it administratively easier to control doctors and revoke their licences to prescribe addictive substances.

Drug misuse as a social and criminological problem

During the 1940s a new drug problem emerged in some of Copenhagen's bar and vice districts, where patrons began using various kinds of drugs (amphetamine, morphine, and synthetic opiates) for intoxication and to alleviate the negative effects of alcohol intoxication and withdrawal symptoms (Indenrigsministeriet, 1953; Nimb, 1972). This developed into a drug scene in which a group of primarily marginalised individuals were involved in acquiring, exchanging and using drugs. Drugs were acquired mainly through criminal activities, such as prescription fraud and burglaries, and were distributed on a black market and through relationships between drug users. This means that the drug problem no longer simply concerned the relationship between the doctor and the predisposed patient in the clinic, but also activities and interactions within a particular social group, in a particular urban environment. The *social* nature of the new drug problem was emphasised by the fact that the scene was seen to constitute a contagious and criminogenic environment inasmuch as there was a continuous need to recruit new 'euphomaniacs' to gain access to drugs by committing prescription fraud against general practitioners (Nimb, 1972; Jepsen, 2008). Drug policy came to include control of deviant groups in an urban environment characterised by anonymity and vice. The Copenhagen health police ended up taking the role of vice squad and took responsibility for managing this aspect of the drug problem because they encountered new drug users and already oversaw this urban environment, including prostitution. In 1943 the vice police thus began registering members of the drug scene and systematically mapping the relationships between them in an effort to control and contain the problem, mainly by disrupting the recruitment of new members. However, the police complained that they lacked the legal instruments to adequately control the drug scene, particularly in their capacity to reach professional drug dealers. Drug distributers would claim that their drugs were for personal use and for this reason it was proposed that possession of illicit drugs for personal use be criminalised. These considerations came to play an important role in a white paper published in 1953 by a committee set by the government to evaluate Danish drug policy and propose a new drug police. The chief of the health/vice police had a seat on this committee. In 1955 the Law on

Euphoriant Substances was enacted. This law, which remains the basis for Danish drug policy, for the first time criminalised possession of illicit drugs for personal use in Denmark. In the 1950s the law was used a few times against professional drug sellers, but the main strategy for controlling the urban drug scene were skid row patrols in which the vice police would monitor the drug scene and control it by issuing fines and probationary sentences. This aspect of the drug problem was treated as a moral problem like other problems in the city, such as prostitution, by the 'moral' policing of the vice police. It is thus illustrative that, in 1951, a special division was established in the Copenhagen police department with responsibility for drugs, prostitution, and homosexuality (Edelberg, 2010, p. 174). It was part of a more general effort to control and contain the immoral aspects of city life.

The entry of the criminal justice system into Danish drug policy led to a bifurcation of Danish drug policy. On the one hand, individual medicine misusers, who had been known and handled within the healthcare system since the 1880s, remained a medical problem and a responsibility of the healthcare system. These *patients*, who were registered by the National Board of Health, were ordinary citizens who had developed dependency in connection with medical treatment. On the other hand, members of the drug scene (mostly in Copenhagen) became a social and criminal problem and mainly the responsibility of the criminal justice system. Treatment of this group would usually take the form of conditions set by court decisions. These *criminals* were registered by the police in the euphomaniac register. This regime existed until the 1960s when a new drug phenomenon emerged, challenging Danish drug policy.

In 1961 Denmark ratified the Single Convention. Following this, the Home Office issued a circular in 1963 that completely banned cannabis and heroin in Denmark. The prohibition of cannabis was mainly a matter of complying with international conventions, not because cannabis use was a problem in Denmark. Cannabis use at that time was minimal.

Youth drugs and the welfare state: a normal social problem

From the early 1960s cannabis (and later also LSD) appeared among young people in Denmark. Initially associated with the avant-garde of the youth rebellion, within a few years cannabis experimentation had spread among more mainstream youth (Ulff-Møller, 1969, 1971; Holstein, 1972; Ulff-Møller and Jørgensen, 1972). The new drug phenomenon received considerable attention in the media where there was a degree of confusion regarding its nature and proportions (Winsløw, 1984; Houborg and Vammen, 2012). A public committee was established to investigate the problem and recommend solutions alongside university scholars carrying out research into the issue. The investigations showed that drug experimentation and drug use spread through ordinary social interactions between young people in their everyday environments and not within

76 Esben Houborg

more-or-less deviant or marginalised subcultures (Ulff-Møller, 1969; Ulff-Møller, 1971; Ulff-Møller and Jørgensen, 1971; Brydensholt, 1972; Ulff-Møller and Jørgensen, 1972). The results also showed that, while the young people who initially developed drug problems came from the middle classes (like the original drug experimenters), within a few years most of the young people with drug problems were coming from socially disadvantaged backgrounds (Jepsen, 1969; Haastrup, 1970; Voss and Ziirsen, 1971; Haastrup, 1973). This group was quite similar to the group of young people who had other difficulties in their social backgrounds. 'Drug abuse' came to be seen as 'a normal social problem' and a symptom of more fundamental social problems in Danish society (Jørgensen, 1969; Voss and Ziirsen, 1971). This was a source of concern and bewilderment because the young people with drug problems represented a huge challenge to the existing institutions handling drug problems (psychiatry), social maladaptation (the childcare and youth care system), and youth crime (youth prisons) (Winsløw, 1984; Houborg, 2008). The existing theories and conceptions proved inadequate, as did existing methods and practices for management. And the anti-authoritarian youth presented the institutions with a significant cultural challenge. It was, furthermore, feared that the great demand for illicit drugs would lead to the introduction of organised crime at a level to which Denmark was unaccustomed.

Policy responses to the new drug problem

From the mid-1960s to the mid-1970s new drug policies were developed with the aim of addressing both criminological and social concerns raised by drug misuse. These policies came to form the basis for Danish drug policy until the 2000s (Storgaard, 2000; Jepsen, 2008; Houborg, 2010). The police and prosecution services advocated for a bill that was presented in parliament in 1969 which sought to modify the Law on Euphoriant Substances. This took the form of a new section of the penal code providing for up to six years' imprisonment for drug dealing and drug trafficking of a professional nature. The bill, which was passed by parliament, sought to address the concern that a professional illegal drug market would develop, but it was also a response to similar policies in the other Nordic countries. In 1968 Norway and Sweden had introduced increased penalties for drug trafficking and requested that Denmark did the same in order to have legal harmonisation among the Nordic countries. Danish authorities also feared that having large differences in penalties between Denmark and the other Nordic countries would attract drug trafficking to Denmark (Laursen, 1996a; Jepsen, 2000). The Nordic Council and Nordic Council of Ministers has been an important venue for drug policy discussions in the Nordic countries. It has also been a venue in which Nordic countries with more repressive drug policies than Denmark's have put pressure on Denmark to have a more repressive policy (Jepsen, 2000, 2008; Laursen, 1996a, 1996b). The increased criminalisation of drug offences was, however, coupled with concern about the negative consequences of criminalising young drug users in general and young people with drug problems in particular. A majority of parliamentary members, therefore, made it a condition of passing the Bill that the state attorney would instruct police and prosecutors that young drug users should not generally be charged for violating the Law on Euphoriant Substances, if they were only in possession of drugs for personal use, particularly cannabis. Such cases should instead be settled with an administrative or court caution. The result was a *de facto* decriminalisation of possession of illicit drugs for personal use. Articulating the prevailing social reform discourse that informed both welfare and criminal justice policy at the time, the majority of Danish politicians wished to reduce drug demand through prevention, treatment, and, more generally, the removal of the social conditions that drove young people to use and misuse drugs. A dual drug control policy was thus developed: welfare policy sought to reduce drug demand and criminal justice policy sought to reduce drug supply, leading to a distinction between drug users and drug distributors (Storgaard, 2000; Jepsen, 2008; Houborg, 2010). The policy also included a distinction between cannabis and other drugs with a more lenient criminal justice policy for cannabis. This policy was strengthened and confirmed by parliament in the following years (Storgaard, 2000), laying the ideological foundations for Danish drug policy until 2004.

The difficulties that the existing institutions faced with regard to handling young drug abusers led to experiments in treatment, often involving public institutions within the social welfare system, NGOs and activists. Many of these experiments were publicly funded and were based on sociological theories that drug abuse resulted from deviancy: young people were attracted to subcultures in which it was normal to use excessive amounts of drugs, making it meaningful for them to use drugs excessively as well (Berntsen, 1971; Jørgensen, 1971; Houborg, 2008). Treatment involved resocialisation that would make it meaningful to live without drugs and to attach oneself to non-drug using environments. Due to this theory of the meaningfulness of excessive drug use, voluntary treatment became a fundamental principle of Danish drug treatment. Within a few years these experiments crystallised into a specialised treatment system for young drug users under the Ministry of Social Welfare. While treatment of older medicine misusers continued to be part of the medical system, it was now the social welfare system that was held primarily responsibility for drug treatment in Denmark. Social workers (social pedagogues) became the specialists in drug treatment and came to dominate the drug treatment system.

The development of a 'social' drug policy in Denmark must be viewed in its wider political context. In 1964 a social reform commission had been given the task of preparing the decentralisation of social and healthcare from the state to regions and municipalities. The commission's work was influenced by reform optimism, a belief in social expertise and the critique of total institutions. The critique of total institutions led to many experiments with new forms of treatment in Denmark in which traditional hierarchical relations between patients

78 Esben Houborg

and treatment professionals were challenged and integration into society played an important role. One of the first institutions to experiment with treating young drug abusers was 'The Youth Clinic' which was originally an outpatient clinic for treatment and provided help to juvenile delinquents (Berntsen, 1971). As the clinic began encountering young drug abusers, it started experimenting with drug treatment, and the work of the clinic came to form a blueprint for much drug treatment in Denmark. Because of the difficulties that the established institutions faced in handling young drug abusers and because an environment existed for new forms of treatment, drug treatment came to the forefront of treatment experimentation in Denmark, attracting social workers and activists who believed in the need for such changes. This also means that drug treatment came to be associated with a particular strand of reform thinking or ideology.

Methadone, the 'old drug abuser', and the introduction of harm reduction in Denmark

According to the treatment policy developed during the 1960s and 1970s, drug abuse was a social problem, and the aim for drug treatment was to make it possible for clients to live meaningful lives without drugs. Methadone maintenance treatment was rejected as counterproductive. This would simply medicalise what was basically a social problem, diverting attention from reducing these problems. It would also confirm the clients in their misconception that they needed drugs (Kontaktudvalget, 1973; Houborg, 2013). However, as time passed, it became clear that the treatment system was unable to help all of its clients attain meaningful lives without drugs. During the 1970s and 1980s, the population of drug users aged and no longer fit into a treatment system designed for younger drug users. These 'old' drug users were excluded, or excluded themselves, from the drug treatment system but they were also excluded from other forms of treatment and services. As a result, the old drug users came to constitute a group with increasingly serious health, mental and social problems. Some general practitioners used their medical authorisation to prescribe methadone to such drug users despite being strongly advised not to do so. The result was the development of a parallel informal treatment system alongside the official drug-free treatment system, with no relationship whatsoever between the two. In the early 1980s the advisory committee on drug issues in Denmark (*Alkohol- og Narkotikarådet*) conducted investigations into the living conditions and various problems of drug users, and on this basis it issued a report in 1984 proposing a radical shift in the Danish drug treatment policy and treatment system (Narkotikarådet, 1984). The report stated that it was necessary to accommodate the many drug users who received no help, or inadequate help, from the existing system. This meant the acceptance that treatment would no longer just mean helping drug users attain meaningful lives without drugs, but would also involve helping them live less damaging lives, even if they continued using drugs. This represented the introduction of harm reduction thinking in Danish drug policy. This policy was articulated in terms of working with 'graduated goals', from the most basic improvement of health, living conditions, etc., to cessation of drug use. This proposed policy change highlighted a new problem and a new field of governance for Danish drug policy. The problem was social exclusion, the discourse of which came to dominate Danish drug policy a few years later. The new policy opened up the daily life of the active drug user as a new governable space for drug policy, not for moral regulation as in the 1950s, but for various forms of outpatient social and health intervention. As part of making the life of the drug user less damaging, the committee stated that it could be necessary to accept methadone maintenance treatment. As a result, harm reduction was introduced into Danish drug policy, not as a public health issue but primarily as a social exclusion issue. This means that harm reduction was introduced as policy in Denmark unrelated to HIV/AIDS. In practice, however, it was public health that served as the driving force behind the implementation of harm reduction in Denmark. The re-articulation of Danish drug policy by the advisory committee on drug issues was ignored by much of the treatment system, and it was only with the advent of the HIV/AIDS problem that the system was compelled to change (Houborg, 2006).

Medicalisation of drug treatment

In the early 1990s Denmark witnessed a major increase in drug-related deaths. In 1990 there were 115 drug-related deaths; in 1991 there were 188; and in 1995 there were 274, after which the number has remained around or above 250 in most years (Schmidt, 1997). Different explanations were put forward to explain this rise in drug-related deaths. One was increasingly poor health among drug users, another was a growth in the population of drug users. Cheaper and stronger drugs, particularly an increased supply of heroin with higher purity, were also put forward as explanations (Schmidt, 1997). This gave rise to a public and political debate concerning Danish drug treatment, involving proposals for the introduction of heroin-assisted treatment and drug consumption rooms in Denmark. In 1994 the government presented a white paper on drug policy, stating its commitment to harm reduction, committing itself to allocating more resources to drug treatment, and making no changes with regard to drug control, including the zero-tolerance strategy in Copenhagen. It is on these grounds that Danish scholars have labelled the white paper 'an ambivalent balance between control and welfare' (Laursen and Jepsen, 2002; Jepsen, 2008). The commitment to harm reduction did not include heroin-assisted treatment and drug consumption rooms. The government did not reject such new measures, but it desired more evidence before introducing them in Denmark (Houborg, 2012). The most significant changes to Danish drug policy in the 1990s took the form of a renewed focus on drug treatment, involving the introduction of twelve-step treatment in Denmark, and a public monopoly on methadone treatment, because methadone prescriptions for drug treatment had to be authorised by a doctor from a public treatment institution. The latter was a consequence of the fact that, since the 1970s, general practitioners had been prescribing methadone to drug users. The monopolisation meant that public drug treatment institutions came to hold sole responsibility for medical drug treatment in Denmark, which can be seen as the first step toward an increasing *medicalisation* of Danish drug treatment. Several reviews of the implementation of the new policy showed major differences in how medical drug treatment was implemented across the country (Houborg, 2006). This led to increased focus on how to ensure quality and equal standards for all citizens in drug treatment, which in turn led to the development of treatment guidelines, quality standards, and quality insurance policies as well as screening tools and diagnostics (Frank et al., 2013). The effort to set standards and guidelines resulted in the establishment of a society for addiction medicine in the early 2000s. This society promoted medical drug treatment as a medical specialty and as an independent part of the drug treatment system. The general discourse on evidence-based treatment in the drug treatment system likewise contributed to more focus on the medical aspects of drug treatment. The introduction of new substitution drugs, particularly buprenorphine, and the debate concerning heroin-assisted treatment also resulted in a tendency to conceive of drug abuse and drug treatment in medical terms. Finally, the 2000s saw an increased focus on co-morbidity among drug users, which led to more psychiatric conceptions of drug abuse. The result was that over the course of the 2000s drug problems were increasingly regarded, and treated, like illnesses.

Criminalisation of drug users

Danish drug policy in the 1980s and 1990s focused on people with drug problems and the supply side of the illegal drug economy. The latter was the object of increasingly stricter criminalisation since the 1970s, with longer prison sentences and new legal instruments for the police (Storgaard, 2000; Laursen and Jepsen, 2002; Jepsen, 2008). In 1990 the Copenhagen police department introduced a zero-tolerance policy against the open drug scene in the neighbourhood of Vesterbro, which attracted considerable media and political attention (Frantzsen, 2005). Among the consequences of this policy was that the Minister of Justice reprimanded the police department and confirmed that 1969's *de facto* depenalisation remained in effect. Nevertheless, the zero-tolerance policy continued, justified by police statements that they were targeting drug dealers.

In 2003 a new government produced the first Danish drug policy white paper since 1994 (Regeringen, 2003). This white paper confirmed the commitment to a drug policy consisting of four 'pillars': control, prevention, treatment and harm reduction. Unlike the 1994 white paper, the 2003 white paper made a clear statement about the balance between these different policy areas and the political ideas upon which the policy was founded. The white paper thus unequivocally stated that the basis for Danish drug policy was the prohibition against non-medical and scientific use of controlled substances. It was recognised that drug policy is complex and may in some instances be contradictory, for example when there is conflict between prohibition and harm reduction. In such instances, the government prioritises prohibition over harm reduction, even if this meant acting contrary to evidence that the rejected measures would reduce harm. On these grounds, the white paper dismissed both heroin-assisted treatment and drug consumption rooms as part of Danish drug policy.

The government's commitment to prohibition was not just a matter of prioritising prohibition over harm reduction. It also involved a break with the depenalisation of possession of illicit drugs for personal use and the dual drug policy of the 1960s in which social policy was designed to reduce drug demand and criminal justice policy was designed to reduce drug supply. From now on, drug demand should also be reduced through criminal sanctions against users. The white paper therefore proposed a repeal of depenalisation, instead making it a general rule that possession of any amount of an illicit drug should be punished. This proposal was voted through parliament by a large majority in 2004.

The re-criminalisation of possession of illicit drugs for personal use occurred against the backdrop of concerns and debate regarding young people's increasing consumption of illicit drugs throughout the late 1990s and early 2000s. Various studies and reports provided evidence of extensive drug use among young Danes and indicated that a new culture of intoxication was developing in which use of illicit drugs was gaining acceptance, even among those who did not use drugs. The context for the normalisation of drug use was, in particular, the night-time leisure economy. Young drug users were described as 'rational' consumers of intoxicating substances, who were not guided by ethical considerations about breaking the law but only by maximising their own pleasure. This view was particularly pronounced in a report by the Union of the Danish Chiefs of Police from 2002, to which the government referred when proposing the introduction of zero-tolerance: 'Today, children and young people are anomic, unlike previously when children and young people typically refrained from committing crimes for ethical reasons. Today, criminal preventive barriers are founded on personal (egoistic) conceptions, e.g. the risk of getting caught and "it may damage my career"' (*Politimesterforeningen* [the Union of Chiefs of Police] 2002, p. 35).

This can be seen as an articulation of what has been put forward as the dominant criminological discourses (discourses) since the 1970s (Garland, 2001). These discourses do not present offenders as necessarily deviant and pathological, but as normal subjects who base their actions on rational choices and, in the case of criminal offences, subjects who calculate the risks and benefits of committing the offence. Such an anomic form of behaviour was considered problematic by authorities and politicians alike. Whereas drug use among young people was constructed as a social problem in the 1960s, it was conceived as a moral problem in the 2000s. In the 1960s it was seen as a collective phenomenon that developed within a particular social and cultural conjuncture, which was amenable to change through social reform and helping young people avoid drugs, or at least preventing drug experimentation from developing into drug problems. In the 2000s drug use was constructed as an individual and rational choice not guided by ethical considerations about breaking the law. This could be seen as 'the death of the social' (Rose, 1996) in the conception of the drug user in Danish drug policy or at least as a de-emphasis of the social understanding of drug demand and the drug user. Now the means of reducing drug demand were to reduce the incentives to use illicit drugs by punishing drug use with significant fines and by promoting a moral order in which the use of illicit drugs was unacceptable. When the government put forward the new legislation, it was communicating that the new policy should not just be seen as a reversal of an inconsistent policy in which crime was not punished – something that was at odds with the government's general tough-on-crime policy – but it was also an attempt to change attitudes towards illicit drugs in Danish society: 'The government is serious when it says that the fight against drugs is to be intensified and that changing the opinion of the population is necessary, so we as citizens all become more attentive and do what we can, particularly to avoid young people becoming part of the [drug] scene' (*Folketingstidende* [The Office of the Folketing Hansard] 2003–2004, p. 7659).

The 2000s thus saw a 're-moralisation' of Danish drug policy in which drug use was constituted as morally offensive behaviour. The criminalisation of drug use was an attempt to influence drug *consumers* (fines were significantly increased in 2007), but criminalisation was also part of the more general reconstruction of the drug problem as a moral problem and an instrument for promoting a particular moral order.

The zero-tolerance policy has one important exception. People who use drugs because they have developed a dependency and who have few economic means can continue to receive cautions when violating the legislation. The background for this is twofold. First, dependent drug users cannot be considered the same kind of consumer as the rational young drug consumer participating in the night-time leisure economy. Second, dependent drug users of few economic means would rarely be able to pay fines and would therefore accumulate a large debt which would be administratively troublesome and expensive to process.

Harm reduction

In 2003, the government prioritised prohibition over harm reduction and rejected the introduction of heroin-assisted treatment and drug consumption facilities. Drug consumption facilities and heroin-assisted treatment were seen as contrary to the prohibition against non-medical and scientific use of controlled substances. In 2007, as part of the campaign to get re-elected, the same government reluctantly accepted the introduction of heroin-assisted treatment in Denmark. The background for this was that, during the campaign, the political party that secured the government its majority in parliament was convinced that heroin-assisted treatment should be part of Danish drug policy. This meant that there was a majority for heroin-assisted treatment because the centre-left also supported it. As a consequence, the government was forced to accept heroin-assisted treatment as part of

Danish drug policy, and when it was re-elected, it made this part of its legislative agenda. In 2008 an amendment to the Law on Euphoriant Substances made it possible for the Minister of Health to reclassify prohibited drugs, so they could be used for drug treatment. Heroin-assisted treatment was introduced without any prior trial because it was assessed that, by 2008, there existed sufficient evidence of the treatment's effectiveness.

With regard to drug consumption facilities, the Narcotics Council that advised parliament on drug policy in the 1990s recommended the introduction of such facilities in Denmark. In 1998 the Minister of Health from the Social Democratic Party asked the International Narcotics Control Board for its opinion on the legality of drug consumption facilities in relation to the international drug control conventions (Jepsen, 2000). The INCB responded that such facilities were a violation of the conventions and on this basis the government, and the centre-right government that followed, declined to introduce drug consumption facilities in Denmark. In 2011 Denmark got a new centre-left government, which had committed itself to introducing drug consumption facilities in Denmark. The Social Democratic party that led the government had changed its position on drug consumption facilities during the 2000s, and in the summer of 2012 an amendment was made to the Law on Euphoriant Substances allowing for the establishment of drug consumption facilities. The part of the drug legislation that permitted the exemption of dependent drug users from punishment was used for this policy. The law stated that local police and municipalities could be lenient regarding dependent drug users' possession of illicit drugs in the vicinity of a drug consumption facility. This was quickly followed by the opening of public drug consumption facilities in Copenhagen and later in two other cities as well.

Sick and deviant drug users

Heroin-assisted treatment and drug consumption facilities have been discussed in Denmark since the early 1990s and have been significant steps in the development of Danish harm reduction policy. The introduction of these measures has moved Danish drug policy away from the prioritisation of prohibition over harm reduction. The contradictions between upholding prohibition and reducing harm have been resolved in favour of reducing harm, at least with regard to these two measures. The measures, however, still exist as part of a zero-tolerance drug policy with regard to possession of illicit drugs. Danish drug policy today can thus be said to have introduced a new distinction between deviant and sick drug users, which differs significantly from that of the 1940s and 1950s. Today it is the mainstream citizen using illicit drugs who is defined as immoral and is the target of the law, whereas in the 1940s and 1950s it was members of a particular marginalised subculture who were defined as deviant. While the sick drug users of the 1940s and 1950s were mainstream citizens who had developed addictions, today it is members of a marginalised subculture who are defined as sick and receive care and treatment instead of punishment.

The introduction of zero-tolerance during the 2000s meant a partial end to the conception of drug use as a normal social problem that should be reduced through social policy and the dual-track social policy. Drug use has instead been articulated as a moral problem involving deliberate violations of the legislation. Here it would be relevant to bear in mind that one-third of the Danish population has experience with illicit drugs and that around 10% have used illicit drugs in the past year.

Conclusion

When significant changes of Danish drug policy have taken place this has in most cases been in periods when new drug related issues have occurred that challenged existing conceptions and practices. In these situations different actors engaged in trying to comprehend the new issues and devised ways of responding to them. In these processes, new areas of government have been established. This, in turn, has affected the ways in which drug users have been constructed as objects of government. The three major constructions of drug users and people with drug problems have been: the person with drug problems as sick, the person with drug problems as mal-adapted to society because of social problems and the drug user as immoral. These constructions have existed and been re-configured in different combinations over time.

References

BACKER, K. H. (1938) Brug og misbrug af medicin. *Maanedsskrift for praktisk lægegerning og social medicin.* 16(6). pp. 201–216.

BERNTSEN, K. (1971) *Tilbud til stofmisbrugere.* Ungdomsklinikkens behandlingseksperiment. København: Christian Ejlers' Forlag.

BERRIDGE, V. (1979) Morality and Medical Science: Concepts of Narcotic Addiction in Britain, 1820–1926. *Annals of Science.* 36. pp. 67–85.

BRYDENSHOLT, H. H. (1972) *Narkotika og straf.* København: Juristforbundets Forlag.

EDELBERG, P. (2010) Den grimme lovs genealogi. *Historisk Tidsskrift.* 110(1). pp. 166–209.

FOLKETINGSTIDNDE [The office of the Folketing Hansard] (2003–2004). p. 7659.

FRANK, V. A., BJERGE, B. and HOUBORG, E. (2013) Shifts in Opioid Substitution Treatment Policy in Denmark from 2000–2011. *Substance Use & Misuse.* 48. pp. 997–1009.

FRANTZSEN, E. (2005) *Narkojakt på gateplan. Om politikontrol av narkotika på Vesterbro.* Det juridiske fakultet. København: Københavns Universitet.

GARLAND, D. (2001) *The Culture of Control: Crime and Social Order in Contemporary Society.* Oxford: Oxford University Press.

HICKMAN, T. (2004) 'Mania America': Narcotic Addiction and Modernity in the United States, 1870–1920. *Journal of American History.* 90(4). pp. 1269–1294.

HOLSTEIN, B. E. (1972) *Spredning af stoffer. Ungdom og stofbrug.* J. Winsløw (ed.). København: Jørgen Paludans Forlag.

HOUBORG, E. (2006) *Stofmisbrug, metadon, subjektivering. Historiske og aktuelle fremstillinger af stofmisbrug.* København: Sociologisk Institut.

HOUBORG, E. (2008) Youth, Drugs and the Welfare State. In Asmussen, V., Bagga, B. and Houborg, E. (eds.). *Drug Policy: History, Theory and Consequences*. Aarhus: Aarhus University Press.

HOUBORG, E. (2010) Control and Welfare in Danish Drug Policy. *Journal of Drug Issues*. 40(4). pp. 783–804.

HOUBORG, E. (2012) The Political Pharmacology of Methadone and Heroin in Danish Drug Policy. *Contemporary Drug Problems*. 39(Spring). pp. 155–192.

HOUBORG, E. (2013) Methadone, a Contested Substance: Danish methadone policy in the 1970s. *International Journal of Drug Policy*. 24(6). e73–e80.

HOUBORG, E. (2014) Constructing and Handling of Drug Problems in Denmark from the 1870s to the 1980s. *Nordic Studies on Alcohol and Drugs*. 31(5–6). pp. 527–550.

HOUBORG, E. and VAMMEN, K. S. (2012) Hashbekymringer 1965–1969. In Dahl, H. and Frank, V. A. (eds.) *Cannabis. Forbrug, interventioner og marked i Danmark*. Aarhus: Aarhus University Press. pp. 23–49.

HAASTRUP, S. (1970) Hospitalsindlagte unge med medicinmisbrug. *Ugeskrift for læger*. 132 (28). pp. 1327–1331.

HAASTRUP, S. (1973) *Young Drug Abusers. 350 Patients Interviewed at Admission and Followed Up Three Years Later*. København: Munksgaard.

INDENRIGSMINISTERIET (1953) *Betænkning om misbrug af euforiserende stoffer*. København: Indenrigsministeriet.

JEPSEN, J. (1969) Stofmisbrug og social isolation. *Mentalhygiejne*. 1. pp. 8–12.

JEPSEN, J. (2000) Internationale indflydelser på dansk narkotikapolitik – solidaritet ctr. responsiv ret. In Henrichsen, C., Storgaard, A. and Vedsted-Hansen, J. (eds.), *Lovens Liv: Festskrift for Jørgen Dalberg-larsen*. København: Djøf/Jurist- og Økonomforbundet, pp. 235–254.

JEPSEN, J. (2008) Danish Drug Control Policy 1945–2007. In Asmussen, V., Bagga, B. and Houborg, E. (eds.). *Drug Policy: History, Theory and Consequences*. Aarhus: Aarhus University Press. pp. 151–180.

JØRGENSEN, A. (1969) Narkotikamisbrug – et nyt symptom. *Socialpædagogen*. 26(1). pp. 4–8.

JØRGENSEN, F. (1971) Principielle synspunkter på behandling af stofmisbrugere. *Ugeskrift for læger*. 133(50). pp. 2524–2526.

KONTAKTUDVALGET (1973) *Metadon i behandlingen af unge stofmisbrugere*. København: Kontaktudvalget vedrørende ungdomsnarkomanien.

KRUSE, S. V., WINSLØW, J. and STORGAARD, A. (1989) *Narkotikakontrol i Danmark*. København: Alkohol- og Narkotikarådet.

LAURSEN, L. and JEPSEN, J. (2002) Danish Drug Policy: An Ambivalent Balance Between Repression and Welfare. *The Annals of the American Academy of Political and Social Science*. 582(20). pp. 20–36.

LAURSEN, L. S. (1996a) Denmark and the Nordic Union. Regional Pressures in Policy Development. In Dorn, N., Jepsen, J. and Savona, E. (eds.). *European Drug Policies and Enforcement*. London: Macmillan. pp. 131–150.

LAURSEN, L. S. (1996b) Scandinavia's Tug of War on Drugs. In Hakkarainen, P., Laursen, L. S. and Tigersted, C. (eds.). *Discussing Drugs and Control Policy. Contemporary Studies in Four Nordic countries*. NAD Publications No. 31. Helsinki: Nordiska nämned för alkohol- och drogforskning. pp. 33–82.

MØLLER, K. O. (1945) *Stimulanser*. København: Gyldendal.

86   Esben Houborg

NARKOTIKARÅDET, A.-O. (1984) *At møde mennesket hvor det er*. København: Alkohol- og narkotkarådet.

NIMB, M. (1972) *Misbrug af euforiserende stoffer i Danmark i 1950erne med efterundersøgelse i 1972*. Aarhus: Aarhus Universitet.

POLITIMESTERFORENINGEN (2002) *Ecstasy-rapport*. Politimesterforeningen.

PONTOPPIDAN, K. (1883) *Den kroniske morfinisme*. København: Th. Linds Boghandel.

REGERINGEN (2003) *Kampen mod narko – handlingsplan mod narkotikamisbrug*. København: Indenrigs- og Sundhedsministeriet.

ROSE, N. (1996) The Death of the Social? Re-figuring the Territory of Government. *Economy & Society*. 25(3). pp. 327–356.

SCHMIDT, D. (1997) Narkotikasituationen i Danmark. In Olsson, B., Rosenquist, P. and Stymne, A. *Narkotikasituationen i Norden. Utveklingen 1990–1996*. Helsinki: NAD. pp. 39–68.

STORGAARD, L. L. (2000) *Konstruktionen af dansk narkotikakontrolpolitik siden 1965*. København: Jurist- og økonomforlagets Forlag.

ULFF-MØLLER, B. (1969) Forbruget af euforiserende stoffer blandt unge i foråret 1968. *Socialt Tidsskrift*. 45. pp. 87–112.

ULFF-MØLLER, B. (1971) *Udbredelse af stofbrug blandt danske skoleelever*. København: Kontaktudvalget vedrørende ungdomsnarkomanien.

ULFF-MØLLER, B. and JØRGENSEN, F. (1971) To modeller for udvikling af stobrug blandt skoleelever i Danmark. *Socialt Tidsskrift*. 47(1–2). pp. 427–438.

ULFF-MØLLER, B. and JØRGENSEN, F. (1972) Spredning af stobrug blandt danske skoleelever fra1968 til 1970. In Winsløw, J. (ed.). *Ungdom og Stofbrug*. København: Jørgen Paludans Forlag.

VOSS, T. and ZIIRSEN, M. (1971) *Stofmisbrug – en samfundssygdom*. København: Thanning and Appels Forlag.

WINSLØW, J. H. (1984) *Narreskibet. En rejse i stofmisbrugerens landskab*. København: Forlaget SOCPOL.

Chapter 6

French drug policy

Ivana Obradovic

Introduction

Despite the long-standing political salience of the problem, coordinated strategies and substantial investment, France remains one of the top countries for drug use and dependence, with the highest levels of cannabis use in Europe, especially among young people. The cannabis issue steadily worsened over the last decades. Currently, 1.4 million regular cannabis smokers are reported (versus 600,000 in 2002) in a 43 million population aged 15 to 64 (Beck et al., 2015). About one half of the generation born in the 1990s have used cannabis at least once in their lifetimes. According to the most recent youth surveys, the highest rate of past-30-days cannabis use at age 16 is found in France (24%), followed by the Czech Republic and Spain (15% each), high above the European average (7%) (Hibell et al., 2012). Despite notably severe law requirements, French adolescents, along with their Canadian, Czech, Swiss, American, and Spanish homologues, are among the highest consumers of cannabis in the world (Hibell et al., 2012). This French paradox may be explained by various factors such as country wealth, high levels of tobacco smoking among youths, high perceived availability of cannabis,[1] advantageous price and purity rates at retail level[2] and estimations of risks associated with use. Unlike France, many European countries have reported a decline in overall cannabis use over the last few years (Spilka et al., 2015; EMCDDA, 2015).

Although a minority of cannabis users use intensively, the number of problematic users seems to be on the rise. It is estimated that 2.2% of French adults are positive on CAST criteria (Cannabis Abuse Screening Test, designed to screen for cannabis use disorders) (Beck et al., 2015). Around three quarters of these are aged between 18 and 25 years and most are male. Cannabis is the second most frequently reported drug among all treatment entrants: the proportion of cannabis-related treatment demands has risen from 22 to 32% in a decade (2000–2011). An important number of those entering treatment in France

---

1 High proportions of adolescents perceive cannabis to be easily obtained (43%).
2 Analysis shows a large increase in the potency level of tetrahydrocannabinol (THC) of both herbal cannabis and resin cannabis, which have doubled in ten years, now exceeding 15% (OCRTIS, 2015).

for primary cannabis use are referred by the criminal justice system, especially among young adults (Obradovic, 2015b).

Use of other illicit drugs that have been associated with youth cultures in the last few decades has also been increasing, even though the rates remain lower than in several European countries. Experimentation with amphetamines, MDMA/ecstasy, hallucinogenic mushrooms, LSD, cocaine, or heroin appear in late adolescence, in proportions decreasing from 4% for magic mushrooms and ecstasy/MDMA to 1% for heroin (Spilka et al., 2015), with rates for cocaine and amphetamine stimulant use in between. Most recent estimates of lifetime prevalence of ecstasy/MDMA use in France are 4.3%, which is higher than the European average (3.2%). The rates of amphetamine and cocaine use have been increasing over the last fifteen years, especially for cocaine, which rate of experimentation for 17-year-olds went from 0.9% in 2000 to 3.2% in 2014 (Beck et al., 2015). This increase has been facilitated by cocaine's declining cost and wider availability (Pousset, 2012).

It is the intention of this paper to provide a broad-based assessment of the drug policy context in France and the country's strategy for drug policy reform. By policy, we mean the pattern of legislation and government action that aims to affect the use of drugs and the related problems. It describes the evolution of the drug legislation, the general population patterns of illicit drug use and the trends over time as well as the legal issues and the effectiveness of French policy. Finally, a picture of the hot topics will be assembled, pointing out the divisions in public opinion over what can be regarded as an example of persistent status quo.

History of drug law and national policy framework

Background and legal issues related to drugs

The first national legal framework, set up in 1916 in response to the recommendations of the International Opium Convention of 1912, criminalised drug use in public. Until the end of the 1960s, no other legislation was passed on illicit drugs, nor was the topic addressed in political debate. The 'outbreak' of drug usage became increasingly visible through the 1960s and became a high-profile public issue after the May 1968 Events (Zafiropoulos and Pinell, 1982; Boekhout van Solinge, 1997; Beck et al., 2010), conspicuously after the press frenzy in summer 1969 following the death by heroin overdose of a young girl. This general context of moral panic, which took on major proportions, led to the passing of a new drug law in 1970, built on both prevention and criminal justice purposes.

Legislation drawn up by the French parliament in 1970 criminalised drug use (both private and public) as well as the glorification of drugs. While drug possession was not a crime until then, the law passed on 31 December 1970 explicitly outlawed all forms of use and appeared extremely stringent in relation to the 'death merchants'. Much of the legal framework created by the 1970 Drug Law was tailored in reference to heroin and operated on the premise of a balance between public health and public order concerns. Sentences for trafficking were increased from five to twenty years of imprisonment, up to forty years for repeat offenders.

After the presidential election of 1974, the political focus shifted away from the drug problem until the mid-1980s, when France experienced severe HIV epidemics among drug injectors. At the time, the only legal provision applicable to drug users in addition to penal sanctions was enforced withdrawal and psychiatric or psychological supervision. Whereas France was among the European countries supporting the highest burden of HIV/AIDS through injecting drug use, it was one of the slowest to embrace targeted prevention programmes. In response to the urgent health threat that AIDS posed to injecting drug users, a significant treatment-focused 'harm reduction alliance' emerged, consisting of various medical practitioners lobbying for a more pragmatic drug policy capable of reducing the health and social damage associated with illegal drug use (Bergeron, 1999). In the context of the HIV/AIDS epidemics and under the pressure of this social movement, drug use started to be viewed as a public health problem rather than a social problem intrinsically linked to criminality. In order to reduce drug-related harms and undermine the spread of the HIV/AIDS epidemics, the French strategy was forced to adapt its enforcement strategies to prioritise treatment of drug-related harms over punishment.

This led to a shift in drug policy in the mid-1990s. Harm reduction policies, based on containing rather than eradicating the problems associated with certain drugs, were introduced in France. This policy involved prioritised access to needle and syringe exchange programmes in low-threshold services, making health education more available, supplying free condoms and introducing opioid substitution treatments (OST) and flexible prescribing of methadone. The long-term picture shows clear improvement in service provision levels and illustrates the impact that provision of appropriate services can have, in terms of HIV and hepatitis C infection rates and drug-related harms (including overdose deaths). Implementation of harm reduction policies in France has been followed by a rapid and substantial reduction in injection practices, HIV prevalence and deaths from overdoses among injecting drug users.

National drug strategies

Starting in the late 1970s, the government launched two commissions to investigate the effectiveness of the approach toward illicit drugs. The results of these commissions emphasised the need for a better integrated and comprehensive approach to drugs (Pelletier, 1978; Trautmann, 1990; Henrion, 1995; Cour des comptes, 1998). Some institutional structures and plans were created but it is only since the end of the 1990s that a particular attention has been dedicated to the coordination system. The turning point came in 1998 with the appointment of Nicole Maestracci as head of a new national anti-drug coordination body, the Interdepartmental Mission for the Fight Against Drugs and Drug Addiction

(*Mission interministérielle de lutte contre la drogue et la toxicomanie*, henceforth MILDT), with a specific mandate: assess the current situation and propose new measures. The presence of a dedicated institutional leadership and the introduction of multi-year national drug strategies were the key elements of promoting new concepts and principles for co-operation and collaboration among professionals and public administrations. Before the first wide-ranging, integrated national drug strategy emerged in 1999 (Three-year Plan against Drugs and for the Prevention of Dependencies 1999–2001, *Plan triennal de lutte contre la drogue et de prévention des dépendances 1999–2001*), the French drug policy relied on the individual strategies of the various government departments (*ministères*) involved in this topic. The 1999 MILDT laid the foundation for a new overall approach tackling all drugs regardless of their legal status, with the ambition to build up and spread common knowledge on drugs to professionals and the population as a whole. One of the core ambitions of the Action Plan was to increase the numbers of problematic drug users entering treatment as well as the proportion successfully sustaining treatment, with a special attention paid to the co-operation between justice and health authorities. Within an overall annual MILDT budget of €46 million, the funding of this programme of co-operation between justice and health authorities was raised from €4.9 million in 1999 to €9.5 million in 2001 (20% of the annual MILDT budget).

Since 1999, successive strategies have included a wide range of efforts mirroring the full spectrum of responses to illicit substances, from drug education and training activities to harm reduction interventions. The 1999 Drug Strategy was followed by three national action plans taking the legal issues into account. The 2004–2008 Action Plan as well as the 2008–2011 Strategy called for drug national policies increasing the numbers of drug users entering treatment in a bid to drive down crime rates. In line with this challenge, the current Government Plan for Combating Drugs and Addictive Behaviour 2013–2017 (*Plan gouvernemental de lutte contre les drogues et les conduites addictives 2013–2017*) calls for a comprehensive and global approach towards illicit and licit drugs (MILDT, 2013).

The French legal regime

The 31 December 1970 Law constitutes the legal cornerstone of French drug policy. This piece of legislation, which ensures compliance with the UN drug conventions ratified by France, amended the Code of Public Health and the Penal Code in order to articulate the repressive and health-related concerns of the legislator. This law pursues a threefold objective: first, to severely repress trafficking; second, prohibit the use of illicit drugs with the possibility of avoiding prosecution through health care; third, ensure free and anonymous care for users who seek treatment. The law does not distinguish between possession for personal use and for dealing, nor does it make any formal legal distinction between sub-stances and quantities (as a possible threshold between serious offences and other less serious offences). The penalty for illicit drug use, public or private, is up to one year in prison and a fine of €3,750 or diversion to a court-ordered treatment programme (*injonction thérapeutique*). Since the 5 March 2007 Law, a new instrument has been introduced to address the growing issue of drug use arrests. The 'drug awareness training course' (*stage de sensibilisation aux dangers de l'usage de produits stupéfiants*) increases the possibility of waiving prosecution in case of minor offences, particularly if related to mere drug use. The successive recommendations of the Ministry of Justice since 1999 have been to apply to the largest possible extent therapeutic alternatives to prison where problematic drug use is reported, while the imprisonment of drug users involved in other related offences should be the last resort. In practice, mere drug users are mainly dealt with by legal warnings (cautioning) or diversion to treatment programmes (therapeutic alternatives to prison). A substantial body of justice directives has been issued to harmonise law enforcement and better articulate the criminal justice system with health provision.

Since the 31 March 2003 Law, France has also prohibited driving under the influence of any illicit substance. Driving a car after having used drugs is an offence punishable by up to two years of imprisonment and a fine of up to €4,500. Penalties may be aggravated in case of a simultaneous use of alcohol (up to three years' imprisonment and a €9,000 fine). Roadside drug testing has been implemented by the 18 June 1999 Law and drug testing is mandatory after every fatal road accident. Drug testing including regular and random screening on potential and suspicious abusers also has a legal basis whenever there are one or several plausible reasons to suspect a driver for using narcotics.

On the drug trafficking side, the 31 December 1970 Law has been modified on several occasions, creating new offences such as selling or supplying drugs for personal use (17 January 1986 Law) and drug-related money laundering (31 December 1987 Law), or enacting new procedures such as the confiscation of drug trafficking profits (14 November 1990 Law) to comply with Article 5 of the 1988 UN Convention against Illicit Trafficking of Narcotics and of Psychotropics. Currently, trafficking offences include selling or supplying drugs for personal use with a penalty of up to five years and a fine and a more serious offence for transportation, possession of, supply, sale and illicit purchase of narcotics with a penalty of up to ten years and a fine of up to €7.5 million (article 222–37). Illicit imports and exports of narcotics are also punishable by ten years of imprisonment and a fine of up to €7.5 million but when the offence is committed by a criminal organisation, the penalty increases to 30 years' imprisonment.

Therefore, the legal framework on drug use has remained relatively stable since 1970, whereas it has been modified several times on the drug trafficking side, with the creation of new offences and a general increase in the severity of punishment.

France among European countries

Along with Sweden, France can be considered as one of the most repressive countries of the European Union as far as drug policy is concerned. The 1970 Drug Law certainly constitutes the current French legal framework but the actual

92 Ivana Obradovic

policy of repressing consumption and possession is more or less effective across the country. In the past twenty years, use of cannabis has become much more popular in France than in other European countries, as well as cocaine use, which has been increasing remarkably.

Drug law enforcement: facts and figures

This section sets out the context of existing diversionary approaches, looking at the range of alternatives to prosecution currently available in French jurisdictions, principally aimed at individuals with little or no previous offending history who have committed relatively minor offences which they do not intend to deny in court.

The reality of law enforcement is flexible. Although French law makes no difference either between illicit substances or between drug use and possession for personal use, in practice, judicial authorities may take into consideration the nature of the substance, the quantity and any prior criminal records in their decision to prosecute, reduce the charges or not prosecute an offender. In most cases involving small amounts of drugs, the French courts can decide simply to issue a warning or impose a compulsory therapy order instead of prosecution. Drug possession, acquisition and/or trafficking is a criminal offence punishable with two to ten years in prison, as the law makes no distinction between small and large quantities. However, when the courts find a person possessing drugs for personal use, it is rare that the person is prosecuted under these offences and the charge is usually reduced to simple drug use. Since a 1978 Ministry of Justice circular, intending to provide guidance for the management of drug use cases, legal action has been focused on restrictive measures such as warnings and diversion to psychological or educative support centres for cannabis users. Some even accused the circular of *de facto* decriminalising the use of cannabis in France.

Even though drug use is a criminal offence, many prosecutors opt for a charge relating to use or trafficking that is based on the quantity of the drug found and the context of the case. Based on the principle of discretionary prosecution, the prosecutor may decide to take legal action against the offender, to simply close the case, or to propose other measures as an alternative to prosecution. In 2013, nearly 200,000 drug law offences were reported, 83% of which were drug use-related and most involved cannabis. The much lower numbers of penalties (56,700 in 2013) suggest large proportions of drug offenders are diverted out of the official criminal justice system with or without special conditions (Obradovic, 2015a). Government statistics show that small-time drug users are mainly dealt with by therapeutic alternatives or a request to contact social or health services, thereby avoiding criminal prosecution. However, the recent legislation provides a range of diversion measures for minor offences, particularly related to mere drug use, including drug awareness training courses, voluntary fine payment, settlement, treatment approaches or community service instead of criminal prosecution.

Available government statistics suggest that the criminalisation of drug use has grown steadily in France, refuting the current statement that the

French drug policy 93

December 1970 Law is decreasingly applied. Drug prohibition remains the rule, but sanctions for use infrequently fall within the framework of criminal law. First-time offenders are warned and can be detained by the police for up to 48 hours, while repeat offenders may be put in prison. A first cannabis offence usually leads to a warning or a drug awareness training course if drug use is occasional and the user socially integrated. Medical and social care is offered to heavy cannabis users and acceptance of treatment is increasingly used as an alternative to penalties. New data also show the growing importance of cannabis within drug treatment systems in Europe, with an increase in the treatment demands for cannabis-related problems resulting from the criminal justice system referrals (Obradovic, 2015b). Depending on the definition given to 'criminalisation', the understanding of the trends is subject to contrasting analyses. If criminalisation of drug use is typified as the ratio between arrested and convicted drug users, it is assuredly on the decline; if, on the other hand, criminalisation is defined as responding to drug use offences with the instruments of criminal law, including pre-trial procedures, the criminalisation of such offences has become more systematic and increasingly diversified for the last two decades (Obradovic, 2012). Despite significant attempts to achieve balance, the dominant policy regarding illicit drugs has remained focused on criminal prohibition. Law enforcement seems to expand the net of prohibition further still.

Policy discussions and drug reform initiatives

The criminalisation of drug use under the law of 1970 has been generating a lively debate since its adoption. Since the mid-1980s, there has been growing acknowledgment of the serious limitations of law enforcement and education in reducing the demand for drugs. As illicit drug policy meant a criminal record for hundreds of thousands of people who had been convicted of illicit drug possession, the problem gained political salience, even though the changes were scarce and remained ineffective. This section provides an overview of the main topics in domestic policy discussions and a review of the main policy reform initiatives.

Hot topics in domestic policy discussions

Since the 1970s substance use has been regarded in France as both a criminal justice issue and a public health issue. The 1970 Law itself was immediately criticised for introducing ambiguities and contradictions in the definition of the drug user, regarded as an offender as well as a potential treatment client. Several objections to the 1970 Law are repeatedly made. Firstly, the ambiguity of the concept of voluntary treatment within the criminal justice system: drug users enter treatment in order to avoid prosecution more than they are motivated to receive treatment but since treatment entails much more than detoxification to be successful it also requires motivation. Secondly, any treatment of drug dependence should be individually designed and a penal constraint is considered by practitioners as the least suitable to this individualisation.

Some argue that, unlike legal drugs, illegal drugs, especially cannabis, have been viewed through a law enforcement lens from the start. They stress that the current policy approach to cannabis is fundamentally different from current approaches to alcohol, where a public health strategy instead focuses on high-risk users, risky use practices and settings, and especially on modifiable risk factors, to reduce harms to individuals and society. Given that the majority of harms related to cannabis use appear to occur in selected high-risk users or in conjunction with high-risk use practices, a similar public health-oriented approach to cannabis use could possibly be considered. Such an approach would rely on targeted and health-oriented interventions mainly aimed at those users at high risk for harms, and not criminalisation of use – and its limited effectiveness and undesirable side effects – as the main intervention paradigm, therefore increasing benefits for society. This standpoint is dominant in the arguments of a civil society and the community of professionals. For example, one main French association of professional workers from specialised addiction centres (*Fédération Addiction*) regularly issues press releases requesting changes in the French policy. The most recent one (20 November 2014) was issued after the publication of a parliamentary report proposing minor changes: it was entitled 'Criminalisation of use has failed, we must be pragmatic and evolve from prohibition to control'.

While initiatives have been undertaken in the Americas on the regulated sale of cannabis, generating international interest and debate, in France as more broadly in Europe, discussion on cannabis remains largely focused on the potential health risks associated with this drug and the major role played by cannabis in drug-related crime statistics. The debate also considers the social costs of the struggle against cannabis users. Economist Pierre Kopp has recently found that the State could save about €300 million on spending arising out of [cannabis] arrests, or perhaps even more including the cost of custody, the running of courts and the enforcement of sentences. The state would also receive duty worth about €1 billion. These figures have raised public attention but no specific political reactions were recorded.

Drivers of change versus conservative forces: review of the policy reform initiatives

The French situation shows a low-profile public mobilisation on drug legal issues. There are neither strong advocacy groups on that topic nor any well-structured 'policy entrepreneurs' or lobbies advocating for drug policy reform. Unlike other European countries, there is not one umbrella non-governmental organisation or institution leading debate on cannabis but several small groups (associations and collective actions from motivated cannabis smokers mostly).

Sporadically there have been demonstrations requesting changes in cannabis legislation, such as the annual Cannabis Day March (*l'Appel du 18 Joint*), organised every year on 18 June since 1993 by a French association (*Collectif d'information et de recherche cannabique*, henceforth CIRC). There have also been collections of signatures, or votes of citizens requesting changes in cannabis legislation. Lately, the CIRC has opened an online petition for the decriminalisation of cannabis, which has been signed by some 20,000 persons without raising much public attention. Similarly, the European petition called 'Weed like to talk' for the establishment of a common policy of regulation and control of the production, sale and consumption of cannabis found no echo in France and was little publicised outside the activist network. Since 2013 France has been following the international initiative 'Support. Don't Punish' of the International Drug Policy Consortium (IDPC). In 2015 it mobilised eight big towns with the support of the *Fédération Addiction*. The number of participating cities has doubled since 2015.

There have been a few civil society initiatives and regulation attempts at local or regional level on cannabis use, growing or selling besides national legislation. By creating Cannabis Social Clubs, associations of French cannabis smokers were hoping to stir public opinion and raise awareness among political parties. Some of the estimated 200,000 cannabis growers started organising Cannabis Social Clubs (henceforth CSC) in 2009, with the intention of encouraging members to grow the herb for their own use and avoid illegal dealers. In their best years, the number of clubs was estimated between 150 to 425 with 2,500–7,500 members according to non-academic sources. There has been an attempt to have CSCs recognised as non-profit organisations but in June 2013, a Tours court decided on the dissolution of the club's federative structure and banned its members from meeting. As of today, nothing really came out of this initiative.

As far as public opinion is concerned, it appears divided, with rather negative attitudes towards drug users and a tendency to attribute the relatively high levels of drug use to the need for a more restrictive drug policy. Meanwhile, the general attitude of French media and the public seems to be slightly shifting in favour of changing drug laws. According to opinion polls, 33% of the French population agrees on the proposal to legalise cannabis (Tovar et al., 2013), while most of public opinion generally agrees that drug traffickers should be treated relatively severely.

The existing body of research on public attitudes to sentencing has shown that the majority of the population thinks that court sentences are too lenient. These views are linked to perceptions of rising crime: held by the majority of the population despite a large actual decline over the last 15 years. It is also clear that people tend to underestimate systematically the severity of current sentencing practice. Underneath these very general views, people often express more nuanced attitudes when asked about sentencing in ways that are not affected by these misperceptions. Questions pitched at a general level tend to elicit punitive responses, but when people are presented with the actual consequences of specific cases and asked to select a suitable sentence, they select a wide range of sentences, often in line with or more lenient than current practice. People are familiar with the idea that imprisonment can be counterproductive, with prisons serving as 'schools for criminals'.

A recent public opinion survey asked about suitable penalties for cannabis possession, amongst other offences, and found marked differences by age, with younger people wanting less tough punishment than their elders for this offence. It also showed that for the first time a majority of the French supported allowing cannabis under certain conditions (maintaining the bans on minors and driving under the influence). This proportion doubled over the 2008–2012 period from 31 to 60% even though an increasing awareness of the risks of regular daily consumption was reported. Nevertheless, 78% are against the unrestricted sale of cannabis (Tovar et al., 2013).

Analysis shows that the policy reform initiatives have been limited to developments and adjustments around an affirmation of the existing regime, coupled with a call for flexibility in implementation of that regime. However, the debate on drug policy reform is persistent.

The major policy developments since the 1970s include the successive penal instructions, which amended the legal framework to maximise access to health provision for drug offenders and the introduction in 2004/2005 of cannabis outpatient clinics aimed specifically at recruiting young problem users. Lately, the government has provided the possibility for French police services to use a rapid penal measure (*transaction pénale*) for minor misdemeanours such as drug use, instead of prosecution or even other alternatives to prosecution.

Since the late 1970s there has been a significant body of reports and academic expertise addressing the French drug policy. Four consecutive reports (Pelletier, 1978, Trautmann, 1990, Henrion, 1995, Roques, 1999) have been commissioned by the government on the approach taken on drug policy and more specifically on the law of 1970. Two of them recommended decriminalisation. The Roques report opened the debate on the possible depenalisation of cannabis, described as less harmful than alcohol. Still, until the 2000s, the legal establishment constantly stressed law enforcement as a basic principle for drug policy.

Within the political parties, there have been several calls for legal initiatives to regulate the cannabis market in France, mostly advocated by the Green Party, even though some officials from the Socialist Party also went vocal on that topic. Since the 2000s, the Green Party has been making various attempts to open the debate but all of them failed. One of the most significant occurred in February 2014, when the first ever Bill proposing legal cannabis in France was proposed by Green Party senator Esther Benbassa.

In the French Socialist Party, a few initiatives were also taken to initiate a reflection upon legal changes on cannabis. In June 2011 a parliamentary report – compiled by a Socialist Party (PS) working group headed by the former Interior Minister Daniel Vaillant – recommended 'controlled legalisation' of the cultivation and consumption of cannabis. It argued that the cultivation and sale of cannabis should become a state-controlled activity, like the sale of alcohol and tobacco (Vaillant, 2011). The proposal did not gain significant support in the PS. The following year, during the 2012 presidential election campaign, French President-to-be François Hollande opposed the proposal to convert the criminal offence of cannabis use into a misdemeanour. Within the newly elected government, two government officials tried to open the debate on cannabis legislative changes in

2012 but they were immediately stopped by the Prime Minister, who stated that 'decriminalisation of cannabis is not on the agenda'.

Most recently, a parliamentary report on the evaluation of drug policy proposed to transform cannabis-use offence into a third class contravention, with a maximum fine of €450 (Le Dain and Marcangeli, 2014). One of the two rapporteurs, the Socialist MP Anne-Yvonne Le Dain, even recommended the legalisation of use in private settings for adults, and the establishment of a regulated supply of the product under the control of the State, a position close to the one taken in 2011 by former Interior Minister Vaillant. One month later, by the end of 2014, the French think tank Terra Nova, close to the Socialist Party, published the report *'Cannabis: réguler le marché pour sortir de l'impasse'* (Cannabis: Regulate the market to break the deadlock), which shattered the current policy – 'one of the worst imaginable' – and built scenarios for change, including regulation with a state monopoly – like Uruguay – with a higher price, that could have a positive fiscal impact of €1.8 billion (Ben Lakhdar et al., 2014). According to the authors, this would allow better support of people in difficulty by allocating significant resources to prevention and to ensure better control of the prevalence of use by acting on prices. This plea for the legalisation of the production, sale and use of cannabis, as part of a public monopoly, has created controversy. The most recent initiative emerged in the framework of the 2015 Health Law; the Senate approved an amendment proposing to punish the first drug use by a fine instead of imprisonment but this proposal was not included in the final draft of the law.

Conclusion

Since the early 1970s when the current legal framework was set up, and more recently since the levels of cannabis use reached their peak in the late 1990s, drug law enforcement and effectiveness have become important and highly contested topics in domestic policy discussions. Although cannabis use is illegal per se, France has one of the top prevalence rates of lifetime and recent use in Europe, especially among young people. And yet, in a rapidly changing cannabis policy landscape, with recent policy reforms in Uruguay, US States (Colorado, Washington, Alaska, Oregon and District of Columbia) and announcements in Canada (Zobel and Marthaler, 2014), legal changes have remained scarce in France, where the official appetite for drug policy reform remains limited and drug policy remains rather control-oriented. The ultimate aim is to deter drug use, which has resulted in a stricter policy than that of most other European countries. French drug law does not make a distinction between soft and hard drugs depending on harm but, in fact, cannabis use is treated severely. Policing strategies ensure that cannabis users are targeted with vigour.

In this context, the problems related to criminalising drug users, the social and economic costs of this approach, and its failure to reduce drug availability, are hardly addressed in public policy. As a result, the costs of criminalising illicit drug use continue to rise steadily.

References

BECK, F., OBRADOVIC, I., JAUFFRET-ROUSTIDE, M. and LEGLEYE, S. (2010) Regards sur les addictions des jeunes en France. *Sociologie.* 4(1). pp. 517–536.

BECK, F., RICHARD, J.-B., GUIGNARD, R., LE NEZET, O. and SPILKA, S. (2015) Les niveaux d'usage des drogues en France en 2014. *Tendances.* 99. pp. 1–8.

BEN LAKHDAR, C., KOPP, P. and PEREZ, R. (2014). *Cannabis: réguler le marché pour sortir de l'impasse.* Terra Nova.

BERGERON, H. (1999) *L'État et la toxicomanie. Histoire d'une singularité française,* Paris: PUF.

BOEKHOUT VAN SOLINGE, T. (1997) Cannabis in France. In Böllinger, L. (ed.) *Cannabis Science. From Prohibition to Human Right.* Frankfurt am Main: Peter Lang GmbH.

COUR DES COMPTES (1998) *Le dispositif de lutte contre la toxicomanie : Rapport au Président de la République suivi des réponses des administrations, collectivités et organismes intéressés.* Paris: Ed. des Journaux officiels.

EUROPEAN MONITORING CENTRE FOR DRUGS AND DRUG ADDICTION (EMCDDA) (2015) *European Drug Report. Trends and developments.* Lisbon: EMCDDA.

HENRION, R. (1995) *Rapport de la commission de réflexion sur la drogue et la toxicomanie, sous la présidence de R. Henrion, ministère des Affaires Sociales de la Santé et de la Ville.* Paris: La Documentation française.

HIBELL, B., GUTTORMSSON, U., AHLSTRÖM, S., BALAKIREVA, O., BJARNASON, T., KOKKEVI, A. and KRAUS, L. (2012) *The 2011 ESPAD Report – Substance Use Among Students in 36 European Countries.* Stockholm: CAN.

LE DAIN, A. Y. and MARCANGELI, L. (2014). *L'augmentation de l'usage de substances illicites: que fait-on ? Comité d'évaluation et de contrôle des politiques publiques.* Paris: Assemblée Nationale.

MISSION INTERMINISTERIELLE DE LUTTE CONTRE LA DROGUE ET LA TOXICOMANIE (MILDT). (2013) *Government Plan for Combating Drugs and Addictive Behaviours 2013–2017.* Paris: La Documentation française.

OBRADOVIC, I. (2012) La pénalisation de l'usage de stupéfiants en France au miroir des statistiques administratives. Enjeux et controverses. *Déviance et Société.* 36(4). pp. 441–469.

OBRADOVIC, I. (2015a) Trente ans de réponse pénale à l'usage de stupéfiants. Évolutions du traitement policier et judiciaire de l'usage de drogues illicites en France depuis les années 1980. *Tendances.* 103. pp. 1–6.

OBRADOVIC, I. (2015b) Dix ans d'activité des consultations jeunes consommateurs. *Tendances.* 101. pp. 1–8.

OFFICE CENTRAL POUR LA REPRESSION DU TRAFIC ILLICITE DES STUPEFIANTS (OCRTIS) (2015) *Tendances du trafic de stupéfiants en France. Bilan 2014.* Paris: Ministère de l'Intérieur.

PARQUET, P.-J. (1997) *Pour une politique de prévention en matière de comportements de consommation de substances psychoactives.* Vanves: CFES.

PELLETIER, M. (1978) *Rapport de la mission d'étude sur l'ensemble des problèmes de la drogue.* Paris: La Documentation française.

POUSSET, M. (2012) *Cocaïne, données essentielles.* Saint-Denis: OFDT.

ROQUES, B. (1999) *La dangerosité des drogues: rapport au secrétariat d'État à la Santé.* Paris: Odile Jacob/La Documentation française.

SPILKA, S., LE NEZET, O., BECK, F., EHLINGER, V. and GODEAU, E. (2012) Alcool, tabac et cannabis durant les années collège. *Tendances.* 80. pp. 1–6.

SPILKA, S. and LE NEZET, O. (2013) Alcool, tabac et cannabis durant les années lycée. *Tendances.* 89. pp. 1–8.

SPILKA, S., LE NEZET, O., NGANTCHA, M. and BECK, F. (2015) Les drogues à 17 ans: analyse de l'enquête ESCAPAD 2014. *Tendances*. 100. pp. 1–8.

TOVAR, M.-L., LE NEZET, O., BASTIANIC, T. (2013) Perceptions et opinions des Français sur les drogues. *Tendances*. 88. pp. 1–6.

TRAUTMANN, C. (1990) *Lutte contre la toxicomanie et le trafic des stupéfiants: rapport au Premier Ministre*. Paris: La Documentation française.

VAILLANT, D. (2011) *Légalisation contrôlée du cannabis, Rapport du Groupe de travail parlementaire de députés SRC*.

ZAFIROPOULOS, M. and PINELL, P. (1982) Drogues, déclassement et stratégies de disqualification. *Actes de la recherche en sciences sociales*. 42. pp. 61–75.

ZOBEL, F. and MARTHALER, M. (2014). *Du Río de la Plata au Lac Léman. Nouveaux développements concernant la régulation du marché du cannabis*. Lausanne: Addiction Suisse.

Chapter 7

German drug policy

Tilmann Holzer

Introduction

Is there anything interesting about German drug policy? From a legal perspective, it is all the same: every state in Europe obeys international laws such as the Single Convention and other treaties. There are some minor differences regarding punishment. Drug policy and law becomes fascinating if you introduce a timeline into the analysis. In Germany two years are milestones marking deep shifts in policy and the culture of drug regulation: 1920 and 1968. Until 1968, drug policy and narcotic law had been a very specialised, obscure part of pharmaceutical law. Drug consumption was rare, with few exceptions. The orientation of German drug policy until 1968 was unusual. In practice, it amounted to an uncompromising support for drug producing companies, especially regarding the export of drugs all over the world. Due to negligible drug consumption in Germany before 1920, special laws against narcotic drugs were deemed superfluous. Due specifically to article 295 of the Versailles Treaty, Germany adopted its first narcotic law in 1920, the *Opiumgesetz* (opium law). German drug policy in the modern sense originated after 1968 and the sudden explosion of juvenile drug consumption. German politicians reacted with a new law, the 1972 narcotic law, which is still the valid legal framework.

We will analyse this process in three steps. Firstly, we will look at the history of German drug production, policy and consumption. Subsequently, we will briefly describe the current legal framework. In a third step, we will analyse the main forces, ideas and actors in today's drug policy discourse. Finally, we will also offer some basic elements for a drug policy theory.

History of German drug policy

To begin with it will for analytical purposes be beneficial to distinguish between the drug itself, drug consumption and the legal regulation of drugs. Drug policy focuses mostly on the existing framework of narcotic laws. But the analytic separation on a timeline will offer some stimulating insights for drug policy reform, its obstacles and possible outcomes. Germany is an interesting case for

Drugs, drug production and regulation in Germany before and after international drug control

Drugs are nowadays regarded as dangerous and therefore strictly regulated under several international treaties and national law. But for a drug like morphine, this is only half of its lifespan. Morphine was discovered by Friedrich Wilhelm Sertürner in 1804, but included in a narcotic law in 1920. So for 116 years, there was no regulation at all, or as in later times, a condition that morphine could only be sold in pharmacies. No special regulations for production, trade or export existed. Similar circumstances applied for heroin and cocaine. Cocaine was first isolated by Friedrich Gaedcke in 1855 and heroin synthesised by Felix Hoffmann in 1897 for Bayer, and immediately marketed on an international scale. Methamphetamine was reinvented by Werner Dobke and Friedrich Keil in 1937 and in 1938 introduced onto the market. Ecstasy (MDMA) was first discovered by Merck chemist Anton Köllisch in 1912, but until the late 1960s, nobody recognised the psychoactive potential of the substance. Methadone was first discovered by chemists at Hoechst in 1941 but not introduced to the market until the late 1940s. Cannabis was a drug imported from Asia and Africa and traded by pharmaceutical companies, but also under no special legislation until the end of the 1920s. Codeine was discovered by French chemist Pierre Robiquet, but only the production scheme of Albert Knoll, developed in Ludwigshafen in 1886, made codeine into the most commonly used narcotic until this day. Knoll had the world monopoly for the first years, later sharing production with the pharmaceutical companies mentioned above, later still, with other European companies.

The intriguing thing about the case of Germany is that there is no other society in Europe which had been confronted as early and on as large a scale with the availability of industrially produced drugs. And until 1920 these drugs had hardly been regulated. The strictest form of regulation, the requirement of a prescription, was only introduced in 1930 with a special regulation. Until then the main condition was that the selling of these drugs take place only in pharmacies. This condition was introduced as one of the first laws of the new German Reich in 1872 and contains only one obligation: that the drugs in the annex shall only be sold in pharmacies. The original list of drugs was a wild mixture between substances like aloe or valerian root but also included opium, morphine, codeine and 'Indian hemp' (Reichsgesetzblatt, 1872, pp. 85–89, cited in Wissler, 1931, p. 137). In 1890, cocaine was added and in 1900, heroin. This law included no sanctions, no limits on the amount of drugs, nor any other conditions.

In 1911, the German government stated internally that there was no need for an international narcotic treaty 'because our laws are enough' (Instructions to the German delegation for the Hague Conference 1911, cited in Holzer, 2007, p. 99).

Why then was a specialised 'Opium law' introduced just nine years later if there was enough national regulation? The answer is that complicated political developments in South-East Asia – especially the Indian opium export to China – generated an international trade (not to mention the American (moral) opposition to this trade) including drugs besides opium from European and German production (Brook and Wakabayashi, 2000; Lowes, 1966).

On the other hand, there were the German production numbers for the above mentioned drugs: Merck in Darmstadt had produced cocaine since 1862. From the 1880–90s onwards, production took place on an industrial scale, with about five producing companies. In 1892 these German companies organised the first cocaine cartel in history. In 1892 this cartel produced 2.2 tons of cocaine and 4.5 tons in 1897. Production peaked in 1913, with 9.0 tons of cocaine, most of it for global export. We know very little about the consumption of this cocaine, but apart from anecdotal evidence like the consumption of some physicians like Sigmund Freud, most of it was not consumed in Europe. However, cocaine was available in pharmacies and could easily be ordered from companies like Merck, Boehringer or Gehe. Commercially, the most important drug was morphine, with production numbers between 2.4 tons in 1906 and 24.0 tons in 1929. Heroin production was lower, starting with 0.5 tons in 1900 and rising to a peak of 5.0 tons in 1923 (Holzer, 2007, pp. 89–96, for all above-mentioned numbers). In the nineteenth century Germany was the only source for some of these drugs. Later, there were a handful of pharmaceutical companies in Europe producing these drugs; one contemporary expert noted in 1931: 'Between two thirds and four fifths of the global heroin and cocaine production apply to Europe' (Wissler, 1931, p. 137).

The German pharmaceutical industry defined the national interest in German drug policy between the 1880s and early 1960s: protection of the drug industry on the international level and repelling restrictions for drug exports. German governments did a lot to protect this national interest and secure the production and export in drugs during the period of the opium conferences between 1909 (Shanghai), 1911 (The Hague) and 1924 (Geneva) until the Single Convention (here only the ratification process). The strong lobbying power of the pharmaceutical industry corresponded with the perception of the bureaucracy that there was a duty to protect German industry on an international level and the products primarily meant for export. If you compare the notes of the preparation meetings to the international conferences, the bureaucrats make stronger demands in their meetings than even the industry delegations in the mixed meetings.

German drug policy started, therefore, at an international level with participation in the International Opium Commission of 1909 in Shanghai, with the aim of inhibiting the opium trade between India and China, with no policy effects in Germany. Two years later, the International Opium Conference gathered in The Hague. Due to British requirements the regulation of (German) morphine and cocaine production was the main topic of debate (Taylor, 1969). To prepare these international conferences, the responsible Ministries of the Interior and the Foreign Office invited representatives of the pharmaceutical companies and agreed together on the German bargaining position. The delegation had been briefed to restrict the negotiations to opium and avoid any agreement on morphine, codeine or cocaine. Regarding cannabis the delegates should deny having instructions regarding this issue (Holzer, 2007, p. 75ff). However, Germany did not achieve its goals, and the convention draft included all major drugs besides cannabis. The German delegation then altered its strategy and introduced a new principle to the international law: the ratification of a treaty by all sovereign nations before it came into force, even if only a few nations negotiated the treaty (Lowes, 1966). The aim was to circumvent the treaty: 'In this way did narcotic control get its global approach. The Hague Convention was to be an all-or-nothing affair' (Lowes, 1966, p. 178). With this ratification clause in place Germany refused to ratify the Convention in the two following Opium Conferences of 1913 and 1914. It was not until the Treaty of Versailles, specifically article 295, that Germany was forced to ratify the Hague Convention and to pass a national Opium Law (*Opiumgesetz*) in 1920.[1]

Cunningly, the regulatory body required by this law, the Opium Agency (*Opiumstelle*) was given to an agency of the chemical industry: the Federal Working Group Chemistry (*Reichsarbeitsgemeinschaft Chemie*). Additionally, there was no narcotic policy until the 1930s outside the city of Berlin. In 1924 this unsatisfactory situation was changed and the Opium Agency was integrated into the Federal Health Agency, first as *Reichsopiumstelle* and after 1945 as *Bundesopiumstelle*, where it has remained until today.

During the two Geneva Opium Conferences in 1924 and 1925, Germany continued to do everything to protect its national drug production and industry. During the second conference, the USA tried to enact a new principle in drug control, a manufacturing ban of a drug: heroin. In Germany, heroin was still produced by several companies and only regulated by a prescription requirement. Companies required a licence for production, and most of the production was exported to the US and the Far East. Internal consumption for medical uses was around 50kg per year during the 1920s. The German government consulted several physicians and unanimously repudiated a manufacturing ban, because the drug was deemed medically necessary. Germany and most other European delegations rejected the proposal for a heroin ban, and heroin was therefore legal in Germany until 1970 and the new Narcotic Law. Another result of the 1925 conference was a new international organisation, the Permanent Central Opium Board (PCOB) and precursor of the INCB. Germany, again protecting its industry, signed the treaty with the reservation that it would only ratify the treaty if a German representative would be a member of the PCOB. After some dispute between Chamberlain and Stresemann, Germany achieved this goal in 1928 and passed the new Opium Law in 1929. This Opium Law was the main legal framework in force until 1970, with only minor changes. It also included, for the first time, cannabis. The law was accompanied by a regulation about medical use and together with the Opium Law established a detailed regulation regime,

1   *Reichsgesetzblatt* 1921, pp. 2–28.

regulating every step of handling and distributing narcotics. The difference was the 'soft' penalisation with a maximum of three years' imprisonment. However, like the first Opium law of 1920, it was enforced by international developments and conferences. From the German point of view, there was no need for a specialised narcotic law until the end of the 1960s.

Drug consumption until 1933

The interesting question is what kind of effect these quite lax (compared to contemporary regulations) laws had on drug consumption in German society. The general answer is there had been no massive drug consumption in Germany before 1968 like in many Western European countries. After the wars in 1871 and 1918, there had been reports about morphine misuse by soldiers. And in the 1920s, some cocaine misuse in cities like Berlin had been reported, but as an exotic problem of small importance.

Between 1875 and 1918, drug addiction changed from a mere vice to a disease in the medical sense. Before, the consumption of drugs and alcohol was seen as a moral problem originating in a lack of character. The conception of addiction is mostly a product of the nineteenth and early twentieth century (Acker, 2002). Alcohol was the most common, and therefore leading, drug to which the conceptualisation of a complex disease or addiction could be ascribed. The emerging science of psychiatry together with the uncoupling of addiction from church-based asylums, treatments and clinics supported this process.

Despite the first diagnoses of *Morphinismus* in 1875, it was not until the Weimar Republic that this diagnosis was accepted as a disease and addicts were treated in psychiatric hospitals. Cocaine consumption increased significantly after the publications of Sigmund Freud, the first promoter of the drug. Before Freud's publications in 1884, Merck in Darmstadt produced 122g of cocaine annually: in 1884–85 it produced 30kg, in 1886–87 257kg, and in 1896–97 831kg (Friman, 1999, p. 85).

Specialised drug counselling was first offered in Berlin during the mid-1920s, but only in Berlin. After the First World War, there had been the first reports about morphine and cocaine misuse, but no cases for cannabis, heroin or other drugs were reported. In 1917 there were ten cases of illegal drug sales, in 1920 there were 450, but mainly due to the selling of war stocks (of morphine and cocaine). However, in the 1920s Berlin especially became a place known for cocaine and morphine consumption (Hoffmann, 2011). The treatment of addicts was a new phenomenon in German psychiatry, rising from 500 cases in 1918 to 2,000 in 1928.

Drug policy in Nazi Germany

A major shift in German drug policy was seen in 1933. For the first time drug policy attracted some attention on a national level. Based on the idea of racial hygiene, the treatment, prevention and policing of drug users was reorganised (Holzer, 2007). As early as 1933, the four abstinence organisations were forced into a new institution called Reichs Work Group for Combating Narcotics (*Reichsarbeitsgemeinschaft für Rauschgiftbekämpfung*). This organisation concentrated on the treatment of drug addicts and the prevention of drug consumption, and focused on alcohol, tobacco and all illegal drugs. Several racial hygiene laws included regulations for addicts, like the possibility of forced sterilisation, prohibition of marriage or forced drug treatment for up to two years in psychiatric hospitals. In 1936 the criminal police force was centralised and later merged with the Gestapo. For the first time, there was a specialised police force combating drugs with narcotic officers in every local criminal investigation unit, the Reich Central Office for Combating Drug Offenders (*Reichszentrale zur Bekämpfung von Rauschgiftvergehen*). The Nazis also introduced the first criminal statistics for drug crimes in Germany. In spite of all the new organisations and laws, there was only a small increase in forced treatment: from 66 cases in 1934 to 77 in 1937. Altogether there were 756 addicts in forced treatment until the end of 1942, most of them in Berlin. All offences against the Opium Law increased due to more police work, but remained at a low level, for example, 1,901 offences in 1938. The confiscation of drugs for the same year was a small amount of opium, 4g of heroin, 7g of cocaine and 20g of Indian hemp. The complete prohibition of heroin was again rejected because, as the President of the Federal Health Agency put it in 1933: 'There is already enough control and regulation and "only" a medical usage of four kilogram heroin per year'. By contrast with heroin, a new drug attracted a lot of attention in Nazi Germany: Pervitin, better known as Crystal Meth today. Pervitin was introduced to the market by Temmler Pharma, Berlin. The drug spread quickly, first among the civilian population and from 1939 among the military. The Wehrmacht used Pervitin to enhance their troops' deployment. Between 1938 and 1945 there was a recorded consumption of 105 million Pervitin pills (for 1939 there are no production numbers and for other years data are missing); 62 million pills were consumed by soldiers and 36 million pills by civilians, with some for export. Due to massive civilian consumption and the racial hygiene discourse within the bureaucracy Pervitin was included in the control regime of the Opium Law in 1941, after nearly three years of virtually no legal controls. The 'soft prohibition' (prescription requirement) under the Opium Law did not change consumption rates.

The year 1945 was characterised by an odd mix of discontinuity and continuity in German drug policy. Almost all civil servants were replaced, but for the criminal police, psychiatry and prevention organisations, the personnel remained largely the same. Also, most of the laws were still valid, except for the explicitly racial hygiene laws. Due to these circumstances, the discourse in the young German republic after 1945 was determined by old Nazi 'experts' with their authoritarian and subliminally eugenic belief systems (Holzer, 2007, p. 295ff).

The calm before the storm: German drug consumption until 1968

After the Second World War the number of German drug addicts remained stable at a low level of 4,000 to 5,000 addicts. Most of them were employed in the medical field or pensioners, addicted to morphine or opioids but not heroin. Until 1967 there were no heroin confiscations, not a single gram. The number of offences against the Opium Law ranged between 88 and 189 from 1955 to 1965. In 1971 they suddenly rose to 22,521. In 1960 the police confiscated 1kg of cannabis, and more than 6,000kg in 1971. In 1968 German drug consumption, drug culture and drug policy underwent a tectonic shift. All numbers exploded; there was not a linear, but an exponential rise for consumption, confiscation, offences and penalties. And from the beginning of the 1970s, a new indicator completed the drug policy discourse: the number of drug-related deaths. In 1968 the first two drug-related deaths at state level were registered. Starting in 1973, the federal number of drug-related deaths was disclosed: starting with 103 in 1973, quickly rising to 623 in 1979 and climaxing in 1991 with 2,125. The numbers have declined to around 1,000 in recent years (Holzer, 2007, p. 367; Bundeskriminalamt, 2014). These numbers have formed and dominated drug policy discourse since 1968.

Popular drug consumption as a result of subcultural shifts

From the perspective of other European countries, Germany and its youth were still boring in the early 1960s. As a British hippy framed it at the time: 'Germany is not on the freak map' (Holzer, 2007, p. 399, footnote 1782). German youth started to listen to American and British popular music more, but consumed no mind-altering drugs. Cannabis consumption only spread from jazz and beat-clubs, mostly in combination with the attendance of members of the US armed forces. But in 1968, cannabis consumption within the youth protest movement grew rapidly. Cannabis consumption became a sign of a left-wing-protest life style. This radical change occurred between 1966 and 1968 (Holzer, 2007, pp. 368–410; Miller, 2014; Baumann, 1980).

In 1966 the Bavarian police stated in an internal report: 'Hashish simply doesn't match with European taste'. At the same time the 'Living Theatre' in Berlin dealt out a free LSD trip with every ticket: 'They were getting high, but not enough' (Julian Beck from 'Living Theatre' about his German audience, in Holzer, 2007, p. 400). Especially in 1968, a fast and dramatic political radicalisation of German youth took place. As an effect of this radicalisation process, more interaction with drug consumers from other European countries and the US, and more easily available drugs (including from young German dealers) cannabis consumption exploded. The news magazine *Der Spiegel* in 1969 entitled an article 'The Hashish Wave. Tibet is Everywhere'. This subculture institutionalised itself with a series of Woodstock-like music festivals all over Germany starting with the *Essener Song Tage* in 1968. Even a new, drug soaked, music style evolved in these times, German 'Kraut Rock'; songs were composed and played with drug consumption (especially LSD), including bands like Amon Düül, Ash Ra Tempel or Faust.

In 1971, a survey based on interviews with 4,797 high school students reported a drug use of 23% among all pupils from 7th grade to high school in Hamburg

(Senat der Freien und Hansestad Hamburg, 1971, p. 329). Of these, 82% consumed hashish, 45% amphetamines, 19% hallucinogens and 7% consumed opiates. As a result of these cultural shifts German politicians decided to reform the 1929 Opium Law.

Present legal framework

The present legal framework is composed of the Federal Narcotics Law (*Betäubungsmittelgesetz*, BtMG) and several ordinances. The basic idea of German anti-drug policy since 1971, BtMG, is that tough sentences will prevent drug dealing. So far, there is no evidence to support this assumption in Germany, but there is widespread criticism. The second basic idea is to help the 'innocent drug consumer or addict' with the concept of 'therapy instead of prison' (§35 BtMG). And there are less severe punishments for minors under age 18 or 21 (§38 and Youth Courts Law).

In the last 20 years the non-prosecution of small quantities of narcotic drugs for personal use came into practical importance, but mainly for cannabis. Important criteria for a decision of non-prosecution are the amount and type of drugs, the involvement of others, the personal history of the accused and the degree of public interest in prosecution. On a state level there are 16 different regulations – one for each state – in place, regulating the type of drug and the amount of drugs. Most states define 6g (some 10g, one 15g) of cannabis for first time offenders as the threshold, but not an obligation, for prosecution. The role of the *Länder* (States) is mainly executing the law (prosecuting, police) and in their constitutional rights they have to approve every change in legislation by the *Bundesrat* (Federal Assembly). Apart from these penal regulations, the German Federal Narcotic Law mainly regulates the legal trade of approved narcotics regulated in Schedule III.

The Narcotic Law is the result of the drug wave of 1968 and the heroin problem beginning in the early 1970s that resulted in many drug-related deaths. The new law took effect in 1971 and banned most of the known drugs in Schedule I from production, distribution and even medical use, including cannabis, LSD, and heroin. The main focus was on tough sentences for drug trading, including new minimum sentences of one year and raising maximum sentences from three to ten years. Following an increase in the severity of penalties during the 1970s and 1980s (more statutory offences, longer mandatory sentences, no decriminalisation), the Federal Narcotic Law is one of the strictest laws in Germany. There are minimum penalties of five years (§30a BtMG) for drug dealing with greater amounts of drugs. In Germany these penalties are rarely applied and only for very severe crimes, e.g. manslaughter (§212 StGB). Maximum sentences are 15 years for drug dealing, importing or even possession of larger amounts of drugs (§29a, 30, 30a BtMG). An acrimonious discussion about decriminalisation for young consumers, especially of cannabis, did not result in legal changes.

108 Tilmann Holzer

Drivers of change and conservative forces in current policy

German Drug Policy in the 1970s and 1980s was dominated by rising numbers of drug-related deaths and repressive measures culminating in the first national anti-drug strategy: the National Plan to Combat Drugs (*Nationale Rauschgiftbekämpfungsplan*) of 1990. This strategy was a mixture of total abstinence, new forms of abstinence-oriented drug therapy, drug prevention especially addressed to youths, and several new legal measures to combat the illegal drug trade and organised crime. Chancellor Helmut Kohl contributed a preface to the strategy and hosted a national anti-drug conference introducing the strategy to the public. In the ten years before this conference, the German public was confronted with rapidly increasing amounts of drug use, drug scenes in every large city and mounting criticism of government policy.

There were few measurable effects of this law enforcement approach on the number of drug offences. In fact, the number of drug offences rose from 122,240 in 1993 to 253,525 in 2013 (Bundeskriminalamt, 2001, 2013). Two-thirds of these were minor offences of consumption, most of them cannabis. If the statistics for 2013 are isolated, there were: 145,013 cannabis, 42,594 amphetamine, 16,577 miscellaneous, 14,129 cocaine, 12,064 heroine, 5,903 ecstasy and 337 LSD offences. If cannabis offences are analysed, 117,443 of the 145,013 are only minor offences (Bundeskriminalamt, 2013, p. 27). These numbers indicate that the main goal of a repressive, supply-reduction drug policy is not being achieved and mainly targets consumers. This hypothesis has been one of the dominant issues in the 20 years of heated debate after the first German drug strategy. The debate focused mainly on these issues: cannabis consumption, and heroin addiction and drug scenes in the inner cities.

Heroin addiction and the inner city drug scenes

Due to the rising numbers of heroin addicts, some of them visible in inner city drug scenes (e.g. in Frankfurt or Berlin) and the failure of repressive approaches, city councils especially and the German states searched for new and more effective approaches towards the drug problem.

After a very controversial discussion in the medical community and the public during the 1970s and 1980s and some first trials concerning the use of different substances in the 1970s (e.g. methadone in Hannover from 1973 to 1975), and systematic studies in the late 1980s (dihydrocodeine by Gorm Grimm), a federal court decision in October 1991 led to a breakthrough and opened a legal window for a regulation from the health system.[2] The Federal Committee issued the first guidelines for methadone substitution (NUB-Richtlinien).[3] In 1992 the German Narcotic Law experienced its first introduction of harm reduction reforms. AIDS

---

2   Bundesgerichtshof, 17.5.1991, 3 StR 8/91.
3   Current guidelines available from: https://www.g-ba.de/informationen/beschluesse/ 7/ [Accessed: 5 May 2016].

was one of the drivers of the acceptance of methadone substitution as a harm reduction measure.[4] Today more than 70,000 heroin addicts are treated with methadone or similar drugs. In the past 20 years the very strict rules of 1992 were changed to liberalise the substitution regime, though it is still highly regulated concerning all aspects of delivery, possession, administration, take home of the substitution drug, minimum age and duration of addiction.

Due to several side effects of methadone substitution some of the Federal States (e.g. Hamburg), some cities (most importantly, Frankfurt) and some physicians demanded the treatment of heroin addicts with pure heroin and additional psychotherapy. The city of Frankfurt made, in 1993, the first formal request for a study according to the Swiss model. The Federal Institute of Health, however, denied the request. This discussion had begun in the 1980s but it was not until the change of government in 1998, from conservative to a social democratic and Green Party coalition, that it could be put into practice. In 1999 the new government started a ten-year process to re-regulate heroin as a medical drug with the aim of treating drug addicts. In 2009 the German Bundestag changed the Narcotic Law[5] after several regulatory and medical studies, and since 2010 heroin treatment (diamorphine) is available in eight cities for 500 patients. These patients have one treatment option provided that they are older than 23 and have failed in at least two drug therapies.[6] Public health insurance pays for the heroin treatment. Parallel to this discussion in the early 1990s, the first supervised injection sites started in Hamburg and Frankfurt, legalised following a 1993 legal opinion by prosecutor Dr Körner of Frankfurt. In 2000 an amendment to the Narcotic Law legalised the situation.[7] Today there are 23 supervised injection sites in Germany.[8] Supervised injection sites are one of the reforms bringing the drug scene from public places into harm reduction facilities. Many studies have proved the benefits in both fields – reducing crime and improving the health of addicts.[9]

Cannabis reform debate

Besides heroin the main issue in the German drug policy debate for more than 40 years has been cannabis. The first drug debate in the German Bundestag in 1971 actually discussed only cannabis (and indirectly LSD) because the 'heroin wave' had not yet hit Germany, or more precisely, the German public. In the 1990s,

---

4 For the early history, see Gerlach, 2004.
5 Amendment and parliamentary debate available from: http://dipbt.bundestag.de/extrakt/ba/WP16/175/17510.html [Accessed: 5 May 2016].
6 Study results available from: http://www.heroinstudie.de/ [Accessed: 5 May 2016].
7 BT-Drucksache 14/1515, parliamentary documents available from: http://dipbt.bundestag.de/doc/gm/14/14098.pdf [Accessed: 5 May 2016].
8 List available from: http://drogenkonsumraum.net/standorte [Accessed: 5 May 2016].
9 Most studies are cited here: http://drogenkonsumraum.net/publikationen [Accessed: 5 May 2016].

together with the general movement of the drug policy debate towards a more liberal approach, the cannabis prohibition regime came under pressure from several sides. In 1994 the Federal Constitutional Court delivered a famous judgment on cannabis.[10] The court stated there is no 'right to intoxication', but in minor (i.e. individual) cases of cannabis consumption, there should be no punishment and that the German states should define a unitary amount of cannabis that would not have legal implications (*geringe Menge* or marginal amount). A 2006 legal study reported that there are still major differences in the level of prosecution for each German state (Schäfer and Paoli, 2006). In 1997 the government of the northernmost German state Schleswig-Holstein filed an application for a 'Cannabis in *Pharmacies-Model*' at the Federal Opium Agency (*Bundesopiumstelle*).[11] Customers over 16 would be allowed the purchase of pure and controlled cannabis in pharmacies. The regulatory body rejected the project. In 2011 the opposition party *Die Linke* (The Left) made a motion in the Bundestag for cannabis regulation by Cannabis Social Clubs.[12] In 2014 both opposition parties (Left and Green) made a motion for a first (!) official and independent evaluation of the German drug policy; the motion is still pending.[13] Also in 2014, the Green Party introduced the first draft law for a Cannabis Control Law, including special and licensed cannabis shops, a minimum age of 18, a maximum of 30g per person per day, three plants for home growing. The draft law required preventive and youth protection measures as well as a ban on advertising cannabis. Also required were: trained personnel in the shops, controls and regulatory standards for cannabis, control of the whole supply chain from growing to selling, regulation of import/export and wholesale, a tax of between €4 and €6 per gram of cannabis, and, finally, a driving limit of 5ng/ml active THC in whole blood. One of the two governing parties, the Social Democrats, moved in the same direction by adopting their new strategic drug policy paper 'From Repression to Regulation' in October 2015, also favouring a regulated, controlled cannabis distribution model for citizens over 18.[14] During the second half of 2015 several German cities filed applications for local cannabis shops to the federal regulatory body, most famously Berlin-Kreuzberg. The regulatory body rejected this proposal.[15]

10 Bundesverfassungsgerichts 90, 145, 9.3.1994, available from: http://www.servat.unibe.ch/dfr/bv090145.html [Accessed: 5 May 2016].
11 Application available from: http://www.drogenpolitik.org/download/sh/Antrag_SH.pdf [Accessed: 5 May 2016].
12 Motion available from: http://dipbt.bundestag.de/extrakt/ba/WP17/387/38727.html [Accessed: 5 May 2016].
13 Motion available from: http://dipbt.bundestag.de/extrakt/ba/WP18/604/60432.html [Accessed: 5 May 2016].
14 Available from: http://library.fes.de/pdf-files/iez/11582.pdf [Accessed: 5 May 2016].
15 Both application and rejection are available from: http://www.berlin.de/ba-friedrich shain-kreuzberg/politik-und-verwaltung/service-und-organisationseinheiten/qualita etsentwicklung-planung-und-koordination-des-oeffentlichen-gesundheitsdienstes/aktuel les/artikel.158549.php [Accessed: 5 May 2016].

For all these conflicts the drivers for reform had been, and still are, the affected cities or German States. Professionals with close contacts with the interested groups tend to advocate drug policy reform, and, in recent years, a growing number within psychiatric societies[16] and police unions.[17] All political parties besides the Christian Democrats are more or less in favour of drug policy reform. Even the Christian Democrats accept some changes afterwards, sometimes promoting them on a state level. But there are major concerns, within all parties, regarding youth protection, control of consumption and a general, subtle fear of possible negative outcomes of drug policy reform. In civil society more and more actors contribute to a more rational debate; some are harm reduction alliances such as Akzept e.V.[18] and Deutsche AIDS-Hilfe (German AIDS Help)[19] while others are dedicated cannabis reformers like the German Hemp Association e.V.[20] There are a growing number of professionals contributing their arguments and proposals for drug policy reform, like judge Andreas Müller who has published a book on cannabis reform (Müller, 2015), or the city of Bielefeld police chief Hubert Wimber, who founded the organisation Law Enforcement Against Prohibition[21] together with other law enforcement professionals. In addition to the official drug reports about the drug situation in Germany (Reitox report for Germany[22] and the official drug report by the federal government[23]), several NGOs now publish a yearly *Alternative Drug Report*.[24]

How can drug policy be explained? Modernity's deep unconscious fear of intoxication

There is a deficit in theorising drug policy in the legal and social sciences. Most approaches try to explain individual behaviour or aggregated data for epidemiological needs. But there is barely any approach trying to explain the century-long path of dependencies in drug policy. If you consider the almost 120 years of German drug policy, there is a need to explain why at least four (very) different political systems have applied the same approach (with different ideologies) to

16 See for example the Deutsche Gesellschaft für Suchtmedizin: http://www.dgsuchtm edizin.de/fileadmin/documents/dgs-info_extra_20150218/DGS-BtMG-Pru%CC% 88fbedarf-2015.pdf [Accessed: 5 May 2016].
17 See for example the Bund Deutscher Kriminalbeamter: https://www.bdk.de/ der-bdk/positionspapiere/drogenpolitik [Accessed: 5 May 2016].
18 http://www.akzept.org/ [Accessed: 5 May 2016].
19 http://www.aidshilfe.de/ [Accessed: 5 May 2016].
20 http://hanfverband.de/ [Accessed: 5 May 2016].
21 http://www.leap.cc/ [Accessed: 5 May 2016].
22 2015 Reitox report for Germany available from: http://www.dbdd.de/content/view/ 90/1/ [Accessed: 5 May 2016].
23 Official drug report by the federal government available from: http://www.drogenbea uftragte.de/presse/pressemitteilungen/2015-02/drogen-und-suchtbericht-2015.html [Accessed: 5 May 2016].
24 Available from: http://alternativer-drogenbericht.de/ [Accessed: 5 May 2016].

drug consumption. At the time of the Weimar Republic (especially in Berlin and only as a beginning), Nazi Germany, the German Democratic Republic and unified Germany followed more or less the same basic assumptions: drug consumption is bad for the population, it is uncontrollable and the wise leader protects the people from this vice. Exceptions are only acceptable for exceptional people like artists and musicians, or in the knowledgeable hands of doctors using drugs as medicine. But even the last exception has fallen victim to a radicalisation in drug policy discourse. Only in recent years have drugs like methadone or cannabis been legally rehabilitated as legitimate medical drugs. But recreational drug consumption is literally unthinkable. Drug policy discourse often includes the non-articulated subconscious fear of the results of mass-scale drug consumption in a given population. This fear is the *Rausch* or with some loss in significance 'intoxication'. The modern, rational society is built on the absence of intoxication; there is no place for intoxication in all modern political theory or ideology, which the German case demonstrates very well. All the different regimes in modern German history, in their ideologies, regarded drug consumption as a danger to society. Therefore a theory of drug policy should analyse the underlying discourse of *Rausch*, which emphasizes the protection of societies from the imagined total chaos of boundless intoxication and the collapse of all rational practice, especially work. The difference between a traditional and modern society is that in every traditional society some kind of drug consumption is included and enclosed by some rituals or tradition. In a modern society, there are no metaphysical needs for these rituals but there is also no space or room for such extra-rational behaviour.

Most interestingly in the history of drug law is the instrumental use, or even the absence of, the concept of addiction. In Germany in the decades before 1968 addiction was not an, or only a minor, issue. After 1968 drug consumption was regarded as the equivalent of drug addiction, even in the case of LSD for which drug addiction is not reported in the medical journals. To be clear, addiction as defined in DSM V or ICD 11 is a disease included in a medical nosography as the many troubles addicts and their relatives suffer. But not all drug consumption fulfils the criteria of addiction from an empirical point of view. And the recreational consumption of drugs and the drug policy surrounding this behaviour is the most interesting aspect of a theory of drug policy. The main discourse and its policy instruments in Germany, until the early 1990s, were dominated by a paradigm of war against the dangers of irrationality: using drug laws, the police and psychiatry as instruments of the re-rationalisation of society. Useful in these kind of analyses are the writings of Michel Foucault who describes in *Madness and Civilisation*: 'The language of psychiatry, which is a monologue of reason about madness, has been established on the basis of such a silence. I have not tried to write the history of that language, but rather the archaeology of that silence' (Foucault, 1973, p. 8). Drug policy on a normative level is the attempt to create spaces of controlled irrationality in a modern and therefore rational world. The analysts of drug policy should be wanderers between both worlds.

References

ACKER, C. (2002) *Creating the American Junkie: Addiction Research in the Classic Era of Narcotic Control.* Baltimore: Johns Hopkins University Press.

BAUMANN, B. (1980) *Wie alles anfing.* München: Rotbuch.

BROOK, T. and WAKABAYASHI, B. T. (2000) *Opium Regimes: China, Britain, and Japan, 1839–1952.* Berkeley: University of California Press.

BUNDESKRIMINALAMT (2001) *Rauschgiftjahresberichte.* Wiesbaden: BKA.

BUNDESKRIMINALAMT (2013) *Rauschgiftjahresberichte.* Wiesbaden: BKA.

BUNDESKRIMINALAMT (2014) *Rauschgiftjahresberichte.* Wiesbaden: BKA.

FOUCAULT, M. (1973) *Wahnsinn und Gesellschaft.* Frankfurt: Suhrkamp.

FRIMAN, H. R. (1999) Germany and the Transformation of Cocaine, 1860–1920. In GOOTENBERG, P. (ed.). *Cocaine. Global Histories.* London: Routledge.

GERLACH, R. (2004) Methadon im geschichtlichen Kontext: Von der Entdeckung der Substanz zur Erhaltungsbehandlung. Münster: INDRO e.V. [Online] Available from: http://www.indro-online.de/entdeckungmetha.htm [Accessed: 5 May 2016].

HOFFMANN, A. (2011) *Drogenkonsum und -kontrolle.* Wiesbaden: Verlag für Sozialwissenschaften.

HOLZER, T. (2007) Die Geburt der Drogenpolitik aus dem Geist der Rassenhygiene: Deutsche Drogenpolitik von 1933 bis 1972, PhD Dissertation. University of Mannheim, BoD.

HOLZER, T. (2002) *Globalisierte Drogenpolitik. Die protestantische Ethik und die Geschichte des Drogenverbotes.* Berlin: Verlag für Wissenschaft und Bildung.

LOWES, P. (1966) *The Genesis of International Narcotics Control.* Geneva: Droz.

MILLER, R. (2014) *Drugged: The Science and Culture Behind Psychotropic Drugs.* Oxford: Oxford University Press.

MÜLLER, A. (2015) *Kiffen und Kriminalität. Der Jugendrichter zieht Bilanz.* Freiburg: Herder.

SCHÄFER, C. and PAOLI, L. (2006) *Drogen und Strafverfolgung. Die Anwendung des § 31a BtMG und anderer Opportunitätsvorschriften auf Drogenkonsumentendelikte.* Forschung aktuell | research in brief no. 34, Freiburg i. Br.: Max Planck Institut für auslandisches und internationales Strafrecht [Online] available from: https://www.mpicc.de/de/forschung/forschungsarbeit/kriminologie/archiv/drogenkonsum.html [Accessed: 5 May 2016].

SENAT DER FREIEN UND HANSESTADT HAMBURG (1971) Drogenkonsum Hamburger Schüler. Ergebnisse einer im Auftrag der Behörde für Schule, Jugend und Berufsbildung durchgeführten Untersuchung. *Bundesgesundheitsblatt.* 22. pp. 328–332.

TAYLOR, A. (1969) *American Diplomacy and the Narcotics Traffic, 1900–1939.* Durham: Duke University Press.

WISSLER, A. (1931) *Die Opiumfrage.* Jena: Verlag von Gustav Fischer.

Chapter 8

Italian drug policy

Grazia Zuffa

The origins of drug legislation and the shift to prohibition

In Italy the first anti-drug legislation was approved in 1923, after the international convention on opium was signed in the Hague in 1912.[1] The target of the criminal law was the illegal trade of psychoactive substances, while possession and personal use were not considered crimes. The 1923 norms were included in the Penal Code enacted in 1930 under Fascism: called *Codice Rocco*, after the then-Minister for Justice, Alfredo Rocco.

Article 729 of the 1930 Penal Code provided fines (or prison sentences of short periods) for 'whoever is caught *in a public space* in a condition of serious psychic alteration for abuse of psychoactive substances'. This article follows the blueprint of the norms for alcohol which punish 'whoever is caught in a public space in a blatant drunken state' (art. 688 Cp). The rationale of the two articles is clear: neither use nor abuse of alcohol and drugs were considered crimes per se. Rather, abuse is simply an instance of socially reprehensible and scandalous conduct if it occurs in public. Nevertheless, a particularly harsh and hideous provision was introduced under the fascist regime:[2] people caught in states of intoxication were considered psychiatric patients and, therefore, could be referred for coercive treatment in psychiatric asylums (Margara, 2010; Corleone, 2010).

The shift to prohibition and punishment of general drug use took place in 1954, when a new law was approved.[3] Following the scheme provided by the 1931 Geneva International Convention, it provided harsh prison sentences (from 3 to 8 years) for possession (*detenzione*) of illicit drugs. Furthermore, coercive treatment in psychiatric asylums for drug users was confirmed. The wording of the key article in the 1954 drug law is worth noting: 'whoever purchases, offers, offers for sale (...) or *is in any way in possession* of substances scheduled in this law (...)' (art. 6). Some jurists argue that the wording was not meant to establish

---

1 Law 396/1923, signed by '*il duce*' Benito Mussolini and Minister Alfredo Rocco. Italy was among the signatories of the Hague Convention and this event is mentioned in the Italian law text.
2 Art. 153 of Single Text of Public Security, 18/6/1931, n. 773.
3 Law1041/1954.

Italian drug policy 115

possession for personal use as a crime, rather, 'possession' was related to drug trafficking and dealing, also quoted in the same article. This interpretation is based on the general principles of the Italian legal system: only conduct that harms individuals or personal property can be qualified as crimes. Psychoactive substance use does not meet those requirements and should, therefore, be a matter of personal choice or 'life style' (Margara, 2010, p. 45). From this perspective, the establishment of drug use as criminal conduct was a breach of the general framework of Italian criminal law.

Nevertheless, the Court of Cassation ruled in favour of the strictest prohibitionist interpretation of the norm, establishing any possession of drugs, personal use included, as a crime. The Court of Cassation's decision made it evident that drugs had already become a socially sensitive issue.

Such peculiar wording of the drug legislation, quoting so many different conducts in the key article, follows the blueprint of the international treaties. This is one of the reasons why it has never substantially changed in the various revisions that have since occurred (in 1975, 1990, 2006).[4] In the following decades, one of the main concerns of Italian legislators will be to find a way to distinguish among the various offences, so as to avoid an indistinct criminalisation and penalisation of all drug-related behaviours.

From the 1970s to the 1990s: the mild approach versus the moral model

Such a tough approach was soon challenged by the development of the drug problem in the 1960s and the 1970s. As drug use began to rise, particularly cannabis use among youth, the shortcomings of a legislation exclusively focused on criminal law enforcement became clear. On one hand, such heavy penalties appeared disproportionate, with no distinction between soft and hard drugs: the risk of social marginalisation resulting from the overall criminalisation of youth behaviours was a matter of public concern. On the other hand, punishment and imprisonment were seen as major obstacles to treatment for the intensive users of hard drugs, who 'were to be recognised as sick people, not guilty' (Cancrini, 1975). In July 1975, a hunger strike was launched by *Gruppo Abele*, an NGO working in the social field, led by the catholic priest Luigi Ciotti.[5] The protesters urged the government and the parliament to immediately emend the drug law in the name of 'solidarity with drug addicts'. In the same months, the radical leader

---

4   See art. 36 of the Single Convention on Narcotic Drugs (1961): 'each party shall adopt such measures as will ensure that cultivation, production (...) possession, offering, offering for sale (...) shall be punishable offences...'.

5   About 200 young people took part in the hunger strike. They built a tent in a central square of Turin (Piazza Solferino). The tent was visited by prominent personalities, among them Dario Fo (who was later awarded the Nobel Prize) and the Archbishop of Turin, Michele Pellegrino (who sent a letter to the President of the Republic in support of the protest) (*La Stampa*, 1/7/1975).

Marco Pannella took a civil disobedience initiative, smoking a joint during a press conference to advocate decriminalisation of cannabis use. Clearly, this movement was rooted in the 1970s political culture, where both individual freedom of choice and social support were seen as key (and integrated) values (Ippolito, 1989).

In December 1975, the new drug legislation was approved. The core innovation of the 1975 revision made the distinction between personal use (to be addressed by the Health System through drug-addiction services), and drug dealing and trafficking (to be tackled by the Justice and Prison systems). A further distinction was introduced between crimes related to soft drugs (cannabis, classified in Schedule II) and hard drugs (heroin, cocaine, amphetamines, classified in Schedule I), the former to be punished with milder penalties. Decriminalisation of personal use was accomplished by establishing that the possession of a 'limited amount' (*modica quantità*) of psychoactive substances was 'not punishable' (*non punibile*) (art. 80): a peculiar legislative solution, aimed at ruling possession for personal drug use out of the criminal code, though this conduct was still considered illicit behaviour. Clearly, decriminalisation as provided by the 1975 law was far from legalising drug use. Quite simply, drug use and addiction were seen as health problems. Users caught with a limited amount of substances were expected to enter treatment in the drug services (a system of drug-addiction facilities was just starting up at the time). No defined quantities were set in art. 80 of the law and in the end it was up to the judges to determine whether the limited amount of drugs would be accepted as personal use or not.

The 1975 legislation was the milestone of the mild approach to drug policies, focused on decriminalisation of personal use, with the aim of giving a more efficient response to drug addiction. Noticeably, decriminalisation of drug use included all drugs. The Italian drug reform movement has never campaigned for cannabis decriminalisation only (though cannabis regulation will subsequently be advocated by anti-prohibitionists as a distinct first step issue in the legalisation perspective).

In the following years, the controversy between mild and tough policies developed mainly around the issue of personal use, hovering between the crime and health systems.

A major prohibitionist shift occurred at the end of the 1980s, under the centre-left coalition (Socialist and Christian Democratic parties) led by the Socialist premier Bettino Craxi. The premier himself initiated the 'tough on drugs' campaign after his visit to the United States, with the aim of aligning Italian drug policies and legislation to Nancy Reagan's famous *Just Say No* campaign. He blamed the rise in heroin addiction and the spread of HIV on the 1975 drug law. In his opinion, punishing drug demand – not only supply, as in the present legislation – should be the response to the problem to reduce drug availability and stop drug addiction. The dispute focused on art. 80 (establishing possession of a limited amount of drug as not punishable): for the government, the norm became the symbol of the loathed laxity. Indeed, the controversy was mainly ideological, about the symbolic function of crime legislation and the role of the State in supporting moral values through the punishment of immoral behaviours. The hard liners argued that the 1975 law, by not providing punishment for drug use, had established it as a legitimate behaviour (Zuffa, 2000).[6] Therefore, one of the key innovations introduced by the government in the *Jervolino-Vassalli* bill was the 'manifesto norm' (specifically, art. 72) which solemnly instituted drug use as a prohibited behaviour. It was the preliminary conceptual step towards the introduction of sanctions and penalties for personal-use possession. In place of the loathed 'not punishable' and 'limited amount', the government introduced the daily average dose, i.e. the assumed average amount of substance a drug user consumed daily. The daily average dose was the threshold meant to distinguish personal use from amounts for dealing and trafficking. Personal use was punishable, but with less severe penalties.

The rise in penalties for drug dealing was considerable, ranging from 8 to 20 years of imprisonment for crimes related to substances in Schedule I, and from 1 to 6 years for substances in Schedule II (e.g. cannabis). The penalties were so harsh as to challenge the principle of proportionality in the criminal law:[7] as one magistrate noted, one might wonder whether murder was still considered by Italian legislators as the most serious of crimes (D'Elia, 1998).[8] Such a question is still relevant as penalties for dealing have never been reduced in the following revisions (rather, they were increased in 2006, as we will see later).

The complex system of administrative sanctions instituted for possession of amounts of drugs below the daily average dose is worth noting. Severe punishments were enacted, such as suspension of the driving licence and/or passport, seizure of vehicle and prohibition from leaving the town of residence. Penalties and imprisonment were provided for users not complying with the administrative sanctions. These measures were highly stigmatising, and drug users' civil rights were consistently curtailed so as to 'establish a sort of apartheid for drug users' and downgrade them to 'citizens of a lower rank' (Pepino and Sorgi, 2000, p. 7).

The *Jervolino-Vassalli* bill became law in 1990 (Law 309/90) and its effects on criminalisation soon became evident, as we can see from the official government data about incarceration. Towards the end of 1990, 7,229 citizens were in jail for drug and drug-related crimes, but by the end of June 1991 the figure had risen to 9,623. By the end of 1992 it had peaked to 14,818: a 100% increase in two years.[9] The repressive 1990 law was in force for three years until spring 1993 when a referendum abolished the key articles including the 'manifesto norm', the quantitative thresholds and penalties for personal-use possession. As a result,

6   The concept was stressed by many representatives of the government coalition, in particular by MPs Condorelli and Casoli, rapporteurs of the government bill in the Senate (Zuffa, 2000, pp. 91–92).
7   According to the principle of proportionality, punishment should be in proportion to the severity of the crime.
8   The magistrate quoted is Francesco Maisto, interviewed by Cecilia D'Elia.
9   From the 1990, 1991, 1992 Annual National Reports on Drug and Drug Addiction (collecting data from the Ministries of Justice, of Health, and the Department of Prisons Administration). See also Zuffa, 2011.

possession for personal use, though still punished with administrative sanctions, was decriminalised. In the article addressing personal use, as amended by the referendum, there was mention neither of the daily average dose nor of the previous limited amount: it was up to the judge to decide whether possession was meant for dealing or for personal use.[10] The referendum was promoted by CORA, the anti-prohibitionist association of the Radical Party, as well as many groups, MPs and other actors who had previously been engaged in the opposition to the government's bill and now endorsed the initiative.[11]

The decriminalisation of drug use prompted an International Narcotics Control Board (INCB) response: in the annual report for 1994, they claimed that the Italian Legislation was not in line with the 1961 and 1988 Conventions. The Board also sent two missions to Italy, in 1994 and 1999, reiterating the concern (INCB Report, 1995, p. 52; 2000, p. 61). The Italian government (represented by high-ranking administrators from the Ministry of Justice) argued for a different interpretation of the Conventions. Noticeably, the INCB position had no consequences at the international level and was ignored in the media and in the Italian political debate (Corleone and Zuffa, 2011, p. 15).[12]

Criminalisation versus treatment? The ambiguities of the social solidarity approach

Two main approaches have dominated drug policies during the last century: the moral and the disease models, usually believed to be alternatives to one

10 Before the referendum took place in 1993 the daily average dose had been rejected by the Constitutional Court. The Court decreed that the amount of substance in the possession of the defendant could not be considered by itself as evidence of the destination of the drugs, but only one among several criteria (Sentence 333, July 10, 1991). In 1995 (Sentence 360, July 24, 1995), the Court again argued that the amount of drugs *as well as* 'other circumstantial evidence will allow the judge to consider the aim of possession of the substances'. Among the other circumstantial evidence, judges usually considered the condition of addiction, evidence of packaging in doses, the possession of tools to weigh, etc. The magistrate Franco Maisto stated that following the referendum, 'the penal system concerning drugs has been brought back to a legality model' (2003, p. 6) because the burden of proof is on the Prosecutor who is required to gather full evidence of the crime of dealing. By contrast, in the 1990 law, the defendant was required to prove that the amount of substance above the threshold was for personal use.
11 Among them were *Gruppo Abele; Lega Italiana Lotta Aids* (LILA); *Magistratura Democratica (MD)*; and *Coordinamento Nazionale Comunità di Accoglienza* (CNCA), a consortium of about 75 groups running therapeutic communities for drug addicts and 19 groups helping AIDS patients.
12 In addition, the Italian representatives made it clear that in the Italian institutional system legislators have no limits apart from complying with the Constitution. This principle is even more compelling when the law is a result of a popular vote. In other words, even in case of a conflict, national legislation takes priority over the Conventions.

another.[13] According to the moral model, drug use is seen as deviant behaviour deserving punishment. In this perspective, drugs are a crime issue. In the disease model, drug use is seen as a preliminary to drug addiction, a disease in need of treatment; therefore, drugs are a health issue. The two models are less alternatives to each other than it may appear (Marlatt, 1996).[14] In the first instance, both focus on the harmful, addictive, chemical properties of drugs with scarce if no attention paid to environmental and social factors such as the harms of criminalisation and social marginality, and the role of poverty and stigmatisation in promoting more harmful patterns of drug use. In the moral model, the (chemical) harm of drugs is emphasised so as to justify prohibition. In the disease model, the same harmful properties of drugs are considered the causal factor of addiction. As a consequence, both have abstinence as an ultimate goal, whether in the moral or in the disease models. A full comprehension of this is crucial to understanding the differences (but also the similarities) between hard- and soft-liners in the roaring public debate which took place in Italy about the 1990 revision of the drug legislation and the 1993 referendum.

Opponents of the punitive shift gave birth to an NGO coalition, significantly called *Educare senza punire* (*Education without Punishment*). The coalition was inaugurated in spring 1989 and brought together many groups and associations (mostly Catholic) working in social services and drug-addiction facilities.[15] They campaigned for the development of welfare measures to help drug users get out of difficult psychological and social conditions by providing prevention, treatment and rehabilitation for drug addiction. They also stressed the detrimental role of punitive criminal law; penalties would have no deterring effect, instead, they would 'blame the victim' and add punishment to poverty and social marginalisation. The coalition strongly advocated a culture of social solidarity, and the importance of the role of welfare which had inspired the 1975 non-punitive drug law as well other important innovative legislations such as the legalisation of abortion (Law 194/1978) and the reform of psychiatric care (Law 180/1978).[16] But social solidarity was one of the leitmotivs of the punitive shift supporters as well. In parliamentary debate, they advocated an 'active and *militant solidarity*' in opposition to the helpless, cowardly 'pietism' and 'weak culture' of tolerance and selfish indifference. This philosophy has been termed 'authoritarian solidarity': 'a mix of public severity and social control, of paternalism and punishment for good' (Manconi, 1991, p. 28). From this perspective, the criminalisation of drug use and the threat of imprisonment for drug addicts is seen as the gateway to treatment and rehabilitation.[17]

---

13 A more in-depth analysis of the issue can be found in Zuffa, 2000.
14 For a review of the moral and disease paradigms, see also Ronconi and Zuffa, 1996; Trautmann, 2013; Zuffa, 2014.
15 The coalition included many Catholic organisations, such as ACLI, AGESCI, *Azione Cattolica* and the *Coordinamento Nazionale Comunità di Accoglienza* (CNCA).
16 From the Manifesto *Educare senza punire* (1989).
17 For the speeches of prominent representatives from the Christian Democrat as well as from the Socialist party, see Zuffa (2000, p. 98) and following.

120 Grazia Zuffa

This form of coerced or quasi-coerced rehabilitation is consistent with a particular view of addiction: drugs are supposed to take complete possession of users, who will be unable to manage their own lives. This idea of drug addiction has much in common with a traditional representation of psychiatric patients (before the change of philosophy introduced by the psychiatric reform): both the insane and the addict are deemed incompetent and incapable of caring for themselves. Accordingly, they are not entitled to the same rights as other citizens; the State has the right and the duty to limit their freedom and to segregate them: the former in asylums, the latter in prisons and/or in coerced or quasi-coerced treatment facilities.

In spite of the many differences in the concept of rehabilitation between the soft- and hard-liners, the bi-partisan emphasis on social solidarity led them to converge on developing drug addiction facilities: a network of public addiction services (SerT) was established and priority-financed in the 1990 punitive drug law. In addition, therapeutic alternatives to imprisonment were introduced for drug addicts serving prison sentences of less than four years.[18] Quasi-coercive treatment was also introduced for drug use: administrative sanctions could be suspended, if the user agreed to be referred to treatment.

The victimisation of the drug addict

Another shortcoming of the disease model is worth highlighting. In the effort to avoid punishment for drug users, the seriousness of the disease of addiction is highly emphasised; addiction is seen as a chronic, relapsing disorder. The addicts are victims of drugs: under the effect of cravings, they have no choice other than to continue using and to commit crimes (such as drug dealing and robbery) to feed their habit. Imprisonment is supposed to be an unfair response to drug use because addicts have a sort of limited responsibility for their actions and conducts. The inconveniences of victimisation have been analysed in-depth in the sociological literature (Pitch, 1989). As for the drug issue in particular, users as victims of drugs pay a high price for exemption from punishment (Ronconi and Zuffa, 1996). First of all, the limited responsibility of addicts has consequences in the treatment field; it legitimises authoritarian forms of treatment giving users limited freedom of choice, both in the decision to submit to treatment and in the choice of available treatment. Owing to the appealing social representation of helpless users, the peculiarities and shortcomings of quasi-coercive therapeutic alternatives were hardly debated. Instead, they were welcomed by the proponents of competing models. Secondly, the victimisation of addicts calls for the over-criminalisation of drug dealers, represented as hideous criminals and 'sellers of Death', in spite of

18 Therapeutic alternatives were also available to addicts with more severe sentences in the last four years of imprisonment. Remarkably, the four-year-threshold for therapeutic alternatives was more benign than the three-year-threshold for ordinary alternatives.

Italian drug policy   121

the fact that many addicts are also dealers. As a consequence, reducing penalties for dealing and trafficking has never been on the agenda of any government, not even of the proponents of mild policies. Moreover, if the disease of addiction shields addicts from punishment, what about drug users who are not addicts; are they, therefore, considered fully responsible for their behaviour? Perhaps this is the greatest ambiguity of the disease model in the Italian social-solidarity version. In an effort to defend the 1975 legislation, some soft-liners argued that the non-punitive norms were for addicts, while questioning whether cannabis or cocaine recreational users consuming drugs without the disease and misery of addiction, should be exempted from punishment (Romano, 1988).[19] In other words, the disease model does not challenge the view of drug use as an illicit behaviour. In fact, in the parliamentary debate, even the opponents of the punitive shift offered a strict moral interpretation of the non-punitive 1975 law which, in their opinion, clearly established drug use as illicit (though not punishable), and so it was to remain. In the end, the over-emphasis on the harm of addiction coexists with a moralising attitude towards drug use, and both offer support for prohibition. That is why those who support non-punishment (in the name of social solidarity) have always been reluctant to join legalisers in campaigns against prohibition, or for the legalisation and regulation of cannabis use (Corleone, 2014).

The introduction of harm reduction

The 1993 referendum victory prompted the introduction of harm reduction, which was seen as a coherent development in the mild policies towards drug use. Harm reduction was officially launched at the First Governmental Conference on Drugs and Drug Addiction just a few months after the referendum. In addition to abolishing penal sanctions for personal possession of any kind of drug, the referendum eliminated law provisions aimed at limiting methadone prescriptions. The referendum's aim was the normalisation of addiction treatment, which was to be brought back 'under the rule of Science' like any other treatment. Methadone maintenance has gained ground ever since, so as to become the treatment of choice for heroin addiction.

Since the mid-1990s, harm reduction has been mainly implemented through methadone maintenance programmes provided in public addiction services (SerT)[20] and the introduction of low-threshold facilities ranging from outreach work for needle-exchange programmes and overdose prevention, to detoxification

19 The concept was articulated by the psychiatrist Luigi Cancrini, interviewed by the journalist Cinzia Romano.
20 A larger availability of methadone maintenance programmes was crucial in the development of public addiction services (SerT). In 1993, 59,000 users (mostly heroin users) were enrolled in the existing 530 SerT, among them 16,000 in substitute treatment. About a decade later, in 2006, 168,000 drug users were enrolled in the existing 544 SerT, 104,000 of them in substitute (mainly methadone maintenance) treatment (data from the Annual National Reports on Drug and Drug Addiction).

programmes and drop-in centres targeted to marginalised problem drug users. Since the 2000s, risk reduction interventions targeted to young drug users in the night-club scenes and at rave parties have also been developed (Zuffa, 2008). Most of the low-threshold facilities have been provided by the same NGOs running drug-free programmes in therapeutic communities. A network of therapeutic communities had been built in the 1980s with the initiative of NGOs (most of them Catholic). These had a strong emphasis on abstinence as the only acceptable goal of treatment. At the time, therapeutic communities were engaged in a difficult confrontation with public addiction services offering substitute programmes. The shift made by the NGOs in the 1990s, from a drug-free philosophy to harm reduction, is impressive; the fight against the 1990 punitive shift had prompted a serious debate in many therapeutic communities, opening their eyes to the risks of a drug-free-moral rhetoric and quickening their conversion to the disease model.[21]

The particular Italian context (with such a large number of therapeutic communities) had an impact on the interpretation of a harm-reduction strategy. From the beginning harm reduction was mainly presented as a set of public-health interventions (methadone maintenance, needle exchange, etc.) *in continuity*, rather than as an alternative to, traditional drug-free programmes. As one protagonist in the harm reduction debate wrote: '*the only difference between the harm reduction strategy and what we have been doing so far* is that the user is not required to stop drug using before being enrolled into treatment. The choice is *between drug free treatment only and drug free treatment also*' (Campedelli, 1995, p. 20). Therefore, the leitmotiv was integration between harm reduction and the existing, traditional drug-free programmes. Low and high-threshold interventions were to be strictly connected, to build a complex network of drug-addiction services. Integration also meant cooperation between public and private (NGOs) services: a radical shift from the previous drug free versus methadone maintenance controversy in the 1980s. This conciliatory approach had the advantage of making harm reduction acceptable to many NGOs and public services professionals. But it had disadvantages as well. First of all, the moralising attitude towards drug use was not completely overcome. Significantly, the document on harm reduction drafted in the Second Governmental National Conference (1997) included an ethical preamble in which a rejection of drug abuse (defined as 'behaviour which is self-destructive and harmful to others') is solemnly declared. Once again, abstinence is established as 'the ultimate goal of all interventions'. As a consequence, harm reduction objectives such as stepping down to less intensive and more controlled patterns of use were seen as a last resort, for chronic (heroin) users only.

---

21 Of course, this process did not involve all therapeutic communities. The shift to harm reduction was strongly opposed by the more conservative communities which had welcomed the criminalising approach of the 1990 law; in particular, by San Patrignano, led by Vincenzo Muccioli, as shown in the debate at the First National Conference on Drugs and Drug Addiction (*Presidenza del Consiglio dei Ministri*, 1993).

Italian drug policy 123

In other words, harm reduction was evolving as a sort of ancillary strategy to traditional treatment, limiting the ability of drug services to connect with different typologies of users. For example, users of drugs other than heroin, who are not willing to quit but would rather step down to more moderate patterns of use, have scarce if no resources for their needs in the current network of Drug addiction facilities. In addition, the moralising concern has prevented the full development of harm reduction. In the above-cited ethical preamble, a clear distinction is advocated between so-called authentic harm reduction and 'those hyper-pragmatic interventions (*di un pragmatismo esasperato*) which reject the possibility of every addict achieving a drug-free life and complete rehabilitation'. The reference was to heroin-treatment trials (at the time carried out in Switzerland), as well as to drug consumption facilities. Significantly, none of the hyper-pragmatic interventions have ever seen the light in Italy.

After the referendum (1993–2006): lessons learnt from the decriminalisation experience

Decriminalisation of drug use following the 1993 referendum was in force until 2006 (and again after 2014, as we will see later). Undoubtedly, Italy has had one of the longest experiences of mild drugs legislation in the European scenario. Nevertheless, the limits of the norms as revised by the referendum soon became evident because no significant reduction in the figures of imprisonment for drug crimes was registered. As two prominent jurists noted: 'decriminalisation of drug use is not sufficient to address the problem of most marginalised addicts involved in petty crimes and in small scale drug dealing. Presently, provisions for dealing are still calibrated to large scale dealing and trafficking, resulting in over penalisation of small dealers' (Pepino and Sorgi, 2000, p. 9). Accordingly, the reform movement advocated a comprehensive revision of the drug legislation including milder penalties for drug dealing; a further reduction for minor dealing and for offering drugs not finalised to sale; and a thorough review of administrative sanctions for drug use. In addition, a full implementation of harm reduction was called for. Most of these requests found a response in a bill drafted by a special committee of experts established by the Minister for Justice at the end of the 1990s (Zuffa, 2011).[22] The experts' committee outlined a full revision of the drug legislation, drafting the *La Greca Text*. The centre-left government never presented it to the parliament. In the debate within the government coalition, the reduction of penalties provided in the bill were the main obstacle because it appeared to contradict the new 'tough on petty crime' stance. In those years, the neo-conservative

22 It was called the *La Greca* draft after the magistrate who chaired the committee, together with the Undersecretary for Justice, Franco Corleone. In addition to differentiating between penalties for small- and large-scale dealing, the text introduces an original wording in the key section (art. 73) redefining possession as 'possession aimed at delivering substances so as to make profit from them'. The new wording clearly rules drug use and all related conducts (like growing for personal use) out of the penal provisions.

124 Grazia Zuffa

'broken windows' philosophy was on the rise and came to dominate, even in the left-wing parties. Also, the abolition of administrative sanctions for drug use was a highly controversial issue, and the moderate component of the government coalition feared it would legitimise drug use.

The second punitive shift (2006–2014)

In 2002, the Centre-Right government, led by Silvio Berlusconi, launched a campaign against the milder norms introduced by the 1993 referendum. The Right spokesperson and Vice-Premier Gianfranco Fini took leadership of the issue and announced a new revision of the drug legislation. In particular, he criticised the abolition of quantitative thresholds which, in his opinion, gave judges too many discretionary powers: the thresholds were to be restored for certain punishment of any drug-related conduct, beginning with drug use itself. The key point of the *Fini-Giovanardi* bill was the upgrading of cannabis to a Schedule I drug (with hard drugs), resulting in a significant increase in penalties: cannabis crimes were to be punished with prison sentences ranging from 6 to 20 years (instead of 1 to 6 years). As for alternatives to imprisonment, they were still provided for but mainly in the form of detention in therapeutic communities. In addition, more, and harsher, administrative sanctions were to be enforced, and for longer periods: they were particularly harsh with recidivists in petty-drug-related crimes (Caputo, 2004; Grosso, 2004). The 'tough on drugs' stance has always been a traditional aspect of the Centre-Right 'tough on crime' rhetoric but the offensive against cannabis use, in particular, was a reaction to the normalisation and increasing social acceptance of its use. Cannabis use was particularly loathed as it was seen as the weak point of prohibition. The *Fini-Giovanardi* bill met strong opposition among drug-addiction stakeholders and in parliamentary debate as well. After four years of hard infighting, the government found an unconstitutional *escamotage* to have the bill approved by the Parliament during the last days of the legislature in 2006.[23] Eight years later, in 2014, the *Fini-Giovanardi* norms were abolished by the Italian Constitutional Court. As a result, the two Schedules were restored (Schedule I for hard drugs and Schedule II for cannabis) and penalties for cannabis crimes were significantly reduced.[24]

Drug policy reformers break the stalemate?

The long fight against the *Fini-Giovanardi* law helped to strengthen the drug reformers' movement. A coalition of NGOs working not only on drug policies, but also in justice and human rights, got engaged in evaluating the criminalisation impact of the 2006 law on the penal and prison systems. From 2009 to 2015, six

23 The 2006 anti-drug law was surreptitiously introduced as a single article in a law issued by decree on a totally different matter: the funding of 2006 Turin Olympics. Therefore, in 2014, the judges ruled that it did not meet the strict constitutional requirements for laws by decree.
24 Sentence n. 32/2014.

Italian drug policy 125

issues of white books on the *Fini-Giovanardi* law were released, based on official data from the Annual Reports on Drugs and Drug Addiction. The white books have been quite helpful in the campaign against the punitive law, as they showed the striking increase in rates of imprisonment for drug crimes and in the figures of incarcerated drug addicts (although the latter to a more limited extent) since 2007 (Zuffa, 2011).[25] In 2013, the European Court of Human Rights ruled that conditions in Italy's overcrowded prisons were violating the basic rights of prisoners. This had a striking impact on the political debate and on public awareness about the link between the harsh anti-drug norms and the chronic overcrowding of Italian prisons. Also, the NGOs' reform coalition had a decisive role in promoting the referral of the *Fini-Giovanardi* law to the Constitutional Court. The legitimacy of the 2006 law was first challenged by the NGO *Società della Ragione*, which released a memorandum on the issue, drafted by a group of prominent jurists.[26]

The abolition of the 2006 repressive drug legislation by the Constitutional Court gave new impulse to the reformers: in 2015, a large coalition of both left and right wing MPs was established to promote the legalization of cannabis for all purposes and in 2016 a number of NGOs drafted a citizens' initiative bill and collected the necessary signatures on it. Also, a bill for the complete decriminalization of personal use of all drugs has been introduced both at the Chamber of Deputies and at the Senate. One more important change in public attitudes is worth mentioning, on the normalisation of drug use. Illegal drug use is progressively aligning itself with legal drug (alcohol) consumption; it is becoming increasingly evident that controlled patterns of use are exhibited by many, if not most, illegal drugs users (as well as by most alcohol users). This is particularly clear for cannabis, the most widespread illegal drug (Parker et al., 1998; Blackman, 2010). This would suggest a change of paradigm in drug policies: shifting the emphasis from the harmful chemical properties of drugs to individual self-regulation abilities; from legal controls (prohibition) to informal social controls; and recognising the crucial role of cultures of use and of public health interventions in promoting moderate, less risky, patterns of use (Zinberg and Harding, 1979; Zinberg 1984; Cohen, 1999; Reinarman et al., 2004; Zuffa, 2014).

This brings a new perspective to harm reduction. The harm reduction model, aimed at decreasing the negative consequences of drug use, without necessarily reducing the consumption of drugs, is becoming the leading approach to drug policy, not only to drug addiction interventions. The drug policy reformers now have a conceptual framework for getting out of the political impasse of the disease model of addiction.

25 The sixth, and final, white book on the *Fini-Giovanardi* legislation offers an overview of 8 years of the law's implementation. The project for evaluating the drug legislation was led by *Forum Droghe* joined, over the years, by many other NGOs.

26 Following the publication of the memorandum, several judges took the initiative of suspending trials for drug crimes and called for a decision from the Constitutional Court about the legitimacy of the anti-drug legislation. A few days before the Court's decision, an appeal by 138 jurists and academics (*Certamente incostituzionale*) advocated the abolition of the 2006 legislation (Pugiotto, 2014).

References

ACLI et al., (1989) Educare senza punire. *Aspe* 7(10). pp. 16–21

BLACKMAN, S. (2010) Youth Subcultures, Normalisation and Drug Prohibition: The Politics of Contemporary Crisis and Change? *British Politics.* 5(3). pp. 337–366.

CAMPEDELLI, M. (1995) Riduzione del danno: non solo tossicodipendenza. *Animazione Sociale.* 25(89). pp. 19–26.

CANCRINI, E. (1975) Proposte e prospettive. *Sapere.* 77(785). pp. 35–37.

CAPUTO, A. (2004) Un nuovo modello punitivo per i consumatori di droghe. *Questione Giustizia.* 1. pp. 114–123.

COHEN, P. (1999) Shifting the Main Purpose of Drug Control: From Suppression to Regulation of Use. Reduction of Risks as the New Focus for Drug Policy. *The International Journal of Drug Policy.* 10(3). pp. 223–234.

CORLEONE, F. (2010) Droghe: diritti e castighi. In Corleone, F. and Margara, A. (eds.). *Lotta alla droga. I danni collaterali.* Forum Droghe, Fondazione Michelucci. Firenze: Edizioni Polistampa. pp. 13–29.

CORLEONE, F. (2014) Canapa fra diritto e salute. *Medicina delle dipendenze.* 4(15). pp. 59–65.

CORLEONE, F. and ZUFFA, G. (2011) Verso un cambio di paradigma: nel mondo, forse anche in Italia. In Transform Drug Policy Foundation. *Dopo la guerra alla droga. Un piano per la regolamentazione legale delle droghe.* Roma: Ediesse. pp. 11–21.

D'ELIA, C. (1998) Cambia forse la legge, paternalismo e cura coatta rimangono. *Fuoriluogo.* Monthly supplement to *Il Manifesto.* June. p. 6.

DIPARTIMENTO PER GLI AFFARI SOCIALI (1993) *Atti della Prima Conferenza Nazionale sulla droga.* Palermo, 24–25 June. Roma: Presidenza del Consiglio dei Ministri.

DIPARTIMENTO PER GLI AFFARI SOCIALI (1997) *Contro le droghe cura la vita.* Documenti elaborati dai gruppi di lavoro, Seconda Conferenza Nazionale sui problemi connessi con la diffusione delle sostanze stupefacenti e psicotrope e sull'alcoldipendenza. Napoli, 13–15 March. Roma: Presidenza del Consiglio dei Ministri.

GROSSO, L. (2004) L'incremento del danno. *Questione Giustizia.* 1. pp. 103–113.

INTERNATIONAL NARCOTICS CONTROL BOARD (INCB) (1995) *Report of the International Narcotics Board for 1994.* New York: United Nations.

INTERNATIONAL NARCOTICS CONTROL BOARD (INCB) (2000) *Report of the International Narcotics Board for 1999.* New York: United Nations.

IPPOLITO, F. (1989) Introduzione. In Pepino, L. (ed.). *Droga tossicodipendenza legge.* Quaderni di Questione Giustizia. Milano: Franco Angeli.

MAISTO, F. (2003) Da consumatori a spacciatori. *Fuoriluogo.* Maggio 2003. p. 6.

MANCONI, L. (ed.) (1991) *Legalizzare la droga. Una ragionevole proposta di sperimentazione.* Milano: Feltrinelli.

MARGARA, A. (2010) Il proibizionismo in Italia: lo sviluppo storico. In Corleone, F. and Margara, A. (eds.). *Lotta alla droga. I danni collaterali.* Forum Droghe, Fondazione Michelucci. Firenze: Edizioni Polistampa. pp. 31–47.

MARLATT, G. A. (1996) Harm Reduction: come as you are. *Addictive Behaviours.* 21(6). pp. 779–788.

PARKER, H., MEASHAM, F. and ALDRIDGE, J. (1998) *Illegal Leisure: The Normalisation of Adolescent Drug Use.* London: Routledge.

PEPINO, L. and SORGI, C. (2000) Introduzione. In Pepino, L. and Sorgi, C. (eds.). *Primo: non nuocere. Politiche e pratiche per la riduzione del danno.* Torino: EGA.

PITCH, T. (1989) *Responsabilità limitate. Attori, conflitti, giustizia penale.* Milano: Feltrinelli.

PUGIOTTO, A. (2014) La Fini Giovanardi a corte: un appello. *Fuoriluogo.* 5 February 2014 Available from: http://www.fuoriluogo.it/sito/home/mappamondo/europa/italia/ra ssegna_stampa/la-fini-giovanardi-a-corte-un-appello#more [Accessed: 4 May 2016].

REINARMAN, C., COHEN, P. and KAAL, H. L. (2004) The Limited Relevance of Drug Policy: Cannabis in Amsterdam and in San Francisco. *American Journal of Public Health.* 94. pp. 836–842.

ROMANO, C. (1988) No al carcere per chi si buca. *L'Unità.* October 26. p. 5.

RONCONI, S. and ZUFFA, G. (1996) La legge sulla droga fra criminalizzazione e medicalizzazione. *Democrazia e Diritto.* 1(96) pp. 181–190.

SOCIETÀ DELLA RAGIONE, FORUM DROGHE, ANTIGONE, CNCA, CGIL (2015) *Sesto Libro Bianco sulla legge sulle droghe,* I dossier di Fuoriluogo. Available from: http://formazione.fuoriluogo.it/pubblicazioni/libro-bianco [Accessed: 4 May 2016].

TRAUTMANN, F. (2013) Drug Use: Change From the Crime to the Health/Illness Paradigm. Presentation at the International Seminar 'Innovative Cocaine and Multi-drug Abuse Prevention Programme', Forum Droghe, Florence, 22–23 June 2013.

ZINBERG, N. E. and HARDING, W. M. (1979) Control and Intoxicant Use: a Theoretical and Practical Overview. Introduction. *Journal of Drug Issues.* 9. pp. 121–143.

ZINBERG, N. E. (1984) *Drug, Set and Setting.* New Haven: Yale University Press.

ZUFFA, G. (2000) *I drogati e gli altri. Le politiche di riduzione del danno.* Palermo: Sellerio editore.

ZUFFA, G. (2008) Treatment, AIDS/HIV: a 'Latin' Approach to Harm Reduction. *Drugs and Alcohol Today.* 8(3). pp. 26–30.

ZUFFA, G. (2011) How to Determine Personal Use in Drug Legislation. The 'Threshold Controversy' in the Light of the Italian Experience. *TransNational Institute-Series on Legislative Reform of Drug Policies.* 15 (August). pp. 1–12.

ZUFFA, G. (2014) Le droghe come questione penale. Verso un cambio di paradigma? *Democrazia e Diritto.* 3. pp. 119–132.

Chapter 9

Drug policy in the Netherlands

Jean-Paul C. Grund and Joost J. Breeksema[1]

Introduction

Deviating from international drug conventions since the late 1960s, the Netherlands has been simultaneously praised and criticised for its pioneering spirit, liberal attitude, tolerant drug policies and harm reduction measures. The essence of modern Dutch drug policy (DDP), its measurable successes, shortcomings and (un)intended and unanticipated consequences is a mixture of pragmatism, politics and paradox and can be traced back to the revision of the Opium Act in 1976. This paper examines the context and consequences of this legal change, intended to separate the markets for illicit substances with diverging risk profiles, exemplified by cannabis and heroin. It is structured around the parallel developments surrounding these two substances, focusing on the evolution of the coffee shop policy, the policy of tolerance and the responses to the parallel hard drug problem, as these developed from the late 1960s onwards. Whereas the 'drug problem' was initially treated as a social and medical phenomenon in the 1970s, the drug policy discourse started changing in the late 1990s, when an increasingly conservative political climate took shape in the country. Successive governments emphasised public order, safety and law enforcement, shifting the policy focus towards containing public nuisance and crime.

This chapter is based on an analysis of the available literature on five decades of DDP, complemented by interviews with key stakeholders in its recent history. Political documents, research publications and drug related data are juxtaposed with the experiences and lessons learned by key participants in DDP, framed in light of wider societal developments and the changing political climate in the country. In this chapter we describe the (recent) history of drug use in the Netherlands and the policy responses developed in response to the use of, on the one hand, cannabis and, on the other, hard drugs, such as heroin and (crack) cocaine.

---

1 Acknowledgements: GDP/OSF funding. Respondents: Eddy Engelsman and Henkjan van Vliet for helping to clarify the legal base of the Dutch drug policy. Thank you so much for all this love and support.

History and legal framework of Dutch drug policy

Mercantilism and morals

Built for the wealthy during the height of the Dutch Golden Age, the picturesque canal district fuelling Amsterdam's prospering tourist industry is also living proof of the long and economically fruitful relationship of the Dutch with psychoactive substances. Many of the beautiful canal mansions were financed by what nowadays would be labelled 'drug money'.

In the seventeenth century the *Vereenigde Oostindische Compagnie* (VOC, 1602–1799), or United Dutch East-Indies Company, secured firm control over the global opium trade and with the *Opium Regie* the Dutch monopolised opium production and trade in Asia in 1894 (Vanvugt, 1985). They also grew coca on Java (present-day Indonesia) and after 1900 the *Nederlandsche Cocaïnefabriek* (Dutch Cocaine Factory) in Amsterdam dominated the world's cocaine market (De Kort, 1995). The Dutch role in opium and cocaine production ended only early in the Second World War (Leuw and Marshall, 1994; De Kort, 1995).

The Dutch were among the first signatories of the International Opium Convention in 1912 and introduced anti-drug legislation long before any drug problem was noticeable in the country. After signing the International Opium Convention in 1919 (UNODC, 2009), import and export of cannabis were included in the 1928 Opium Act (Korf, 2002). Use, possession, cultivation and trade of cannabis were criminalised in 1953, in some cases leading to strict sentences (Korf, 2002; Blok and Kennedy, 2014). Illicit drug use was rare in the Netherlands until the late 1950s except for some limited opium use in the Chinatowns of Amsterdam and Rotterdam. Contained to marginal populations, it raised few concerns (De Kort, 1995).

Social transformation, youth culture and 'new' psychoactive substances

In the 1960s and 1970s, the Netherlands transformed from a rather closed society, organised along religious and ideological lines, to a more secular and individualised social order. The use of psychoactive drugs increased rapidly in the 1960s and Dutch law enforcement authorities initially responded forcefully (Cohen, 1975; Korf, 2002). However, enforcement and successful prosecution proved difficult as well as time consuming, without noticeable reductions in drug availability or use. This repressive approach was widely criticised, in part because those arrested were often not typical criminals but teenagers from middle- and upper-class families. In 1969, the Public Prosecutor's office shifted the focus of policing and prosecution away from cannabis *consumption* towards the *trafficking* of cannabis and of 'hard drugs,' LSD, amphetamine and opium in particular (De Kort, 1995).

After local police had refrained from enforcing drug infractions at the large scale 'Holland Pop Festival' in Rotterdam in 1970, an informal policy of tolerance gradually emerged around cannabis use and consumer transactions. Government-subsidised youth centres and pop venues became the locus of the emerging youth culture. At these centres hashish was used and sold semi-openly, largely without substantial police intervention (De Kort, 1995; Korf, 2002). In response, venue staff began tolerating discreet sales by dealers whom they trusted to only sell cannabis. The authorities were well aware of these Opium Act infractions but feared that closing youth centres would lead to cannabis dealing moving into less controllable areas of Amsterdam and expose cannabis consumers to hard drugs. This was deemed unacceptable (De Kort, 1995). Eventually these venues established a system of tolerated, trusted 'house dealers', who sold hashish and marijuana from a table in a corner or standing at the bar.

Meanwhile, the attention of the police got diverted. In 1972 heroin made its entrance in the country's counter culture, raising concerns in civil society, politics, the medical community and law enforcement alike. Heroin use increased at an unprecedented pace and soon became the leading drug of concern in the Netherlands (Grund and Blanken, 1993; De Kort, 1995), greatly influencing the debate on drug policy and becoming a driver of the decriminalisation of cannabis.

Two influential interdisciplinary government advisory committees supported the growing perception that cannabis and heroin had very different risk profiles and rejected the *conventional wisdom* (Galbraith, 1958) that use of the first would inevitably lead to the use of the other. Both the Hulsman (1971) and Baan (1972) committees emphasised the importance of 'social context' and suggested that involvement in criminal settings would encourage experimentation with other, more harmful drugs (Cohen, 1975). Both committees proposed separating subcultures or scenes involved in drugs with highly different risk profiles. Cannabis-using youngsters should not be exposed to scenes involving potentially more harmful substances, such as amphetamines or heroin. This fundamental insight would provide the justification that shaped DDP from that point onwards into the late 1990s (Cohen, 1994; MacCoun and Reuter, 2001), including the 1976 revision of the Opium Act.

The 1976 revision of the Opium Act

The 1976 revision of the Opium Act brought all substances classified in the United Nations' 1961 Single Convention on Narcotic Drugs (United Nations, 1961) under the new Opium Act, but introduced two lists of substances:

1 'substances with an unacceptable risk'; and
2 'cannabis products'.

Possession of 30 grams of cannabis or less could either be dismissed or charged as a petty offence or misdemeanour (comparable to a traffic ticket) and, importantly, would not result in a criminal record. In addition, another distinction was made between possession for personal consumption and possession with intent to distribute, formalising the 1969 Public Prosecutor's office enforcement guidelines (De Kort, 1995). This legal distinction was made to prevent the marginalisation and stigmatisation of cannabis consumers. In 1993 substances included in List III and IV of the 1971 Convention on Psychotropic Substances (United Nations, 1971) would be added to list 2 of the Opium Act, which would be renamed 'other substances' instead of 'cannabis products' (Commissie Garretsen, 2011).

The 'drug problem' was seen as a public health and social issue and became the primary responsibility of the Ministry of Health (MoH). The Ministry of Justice (MoJ) did not dispute the MoH's policy prerogative, as law enforcement was seen as *ultimum remedium* in dealing with drug use and addiction. Drug related health and public order problems were also viewed as largely local matters, in need of local responses. By 1977, shortly after the revision of the Opium Act, the Public Prosecutor's office assigned prosecuting house dealers a low priority, relegating prosecution of use and small-scale cannabis sales to the 'local triangle'.

This 'local triangle' consists of the mayor, the Public Prosecutor and the chief of police of a municipality: it is responsible for coordinating local policing efforts. Soon, the number of house dealers in youth centres sky-rocketed (De Kort, 1995). The municipalities had successfully advocated that the administrative and prosecutorial policy towards the use and small-scale sales of hashish in youth centres would be coordinated locally (Ministry of Foreign Affairs, 1983). Thus, in its formative phase, DDP was not only the responsibility of the MoH, but it was also shaped by strong local forces and priorities. As a result, the daily priorities in drug law enforcement moved from cannabis to hard drugs and to larger quantities (Ministry of Foreign Affairs, 1983). Mere possession and sales of consumer quantities of cannabis would no longer be a reason for arrest or prosecution, in particular in youth centres.

Over the years the Dutch have received international critique and (successively more) acclaim on various aspects of their drug policy. The Dutch government maintained that its policies were fully in agreement with the International Conventions and within the boundaries of Dutch law. In response to the International Narcotics Control Board (INCB), the Minister of Foreign Affairs explained the legal basis for refraining from prosecution of cannabis sales in youth centres: 'The principle of prosecutorial discretion (...) means that the Public Prosecutions Department has the discretion to decide not to bring a criminal offence case into court on grounds derived from the public interest [and] a decision not to prosecute in less serious cases' (Ministry of Foreign Affairs, 1983). The public interest is, in this case, represented by the Dutch drug policy. This principle, also known as the 'expediency principle', can be traced back to 1870 Dutch legal practice and was officially included in Dutch law in 1926 (Hart, 1994; Boekhout van Solinge, 2010). The implication is that repressive intervention is not the standard response to (minor) infractions of the law (Korf, 2002). Both the absence of enforcement of drug use and the prohibition of dealing at the Rotterdam Pop Festival in 1970 and the tacit condoning of 'house dealers' in youth venues into the 1980s (Blom, 1998) would have been impossible without the expediency principle. Eventually, it provided the legal leeway for the emergence of coffee shops (Uitermark, 2004; Meeus, 2014). Indeed, the 1976 revision of the Opium Act legally sanctioned practices of tolerance that had emerged in the previous decade, providing authorities with the power to creatively interpret the new legislation in the subsequent decades.

From youth centre to tea house to coffee shop

Meanwhile, several entrepreneurs were exploring alternative ways to supply cannabis outside of youth centres (Bruining, 2008; Meeus, 2014). The government had not anticipated these entrepreneurial initiatives. 'Coffee shops just emerged', said Eddy Engelsman, then the head of the MoH drug policy office (Eddy Engelsman, 2012, personal communication). The Dutch government reacted pragmatically and with restraint to this unanticipated consequence (Merton, 1936), applying the tolerance criteria developed for house dealers to these alternative outlets (Korf, 2002). Using off-the-record guidelines since 1978 (Blom, 1998), new guidelines for the public prosecution were officially published in 1979 (Korf, 2008), stating that police should enforce the Opium Act only if small-scale trade was publicly advertised or otherwise provocatively effected (De Kort, 1995). House dealers at youth centres, when working 'under the trust and protection' of the staff would no longer be prosecuted (Blom, 1998). These new guidelines also provided the legal leeway for the government to tolerate coffee shops (De Kort, 1995), but left it unclear under which circumstances and according to which criteria police should enforce the rules (Jansen, 1989). Some coffee shops were left in peace, while others were raided regularly (De Kort, 1995). The number of coffee shops grew steadily throughout the 1980s, but only in 1991 did the government introduce formal criteria intended to regulate these new enterprises. These were based on the informal house rules pioneered in Amsterdam and adopted by coffee shops around the country. These broadly formulated AHOJ-G criteria were enacted officially only in 1994 (*Staatscourant*, 1994) and left room for development of local policies by the 'local triangle'.

These criteria would be tightened in the following years. The minimum admission age would be set at 18 years, the maximum transaction amount was decreased from 30 to five grams per person per day and a trading stock limit of 500 grams was added (Korf, Riper and Bullington, 1999; Eerenbeemt and Visser, 1995). As of December 2000, coffee shops could no longer sell alcohol (Bieleman et al., 2008). Many of these new restrictions were in direct response to pressure from neighbouring countries, the International Narcotics Control Board (Van der Stel, 1999; Boekhout van Solinge, 2010) and certain media (Wiedemann, 1994).

The back door problem

Since the regulation of coffee shops, sales of small quantities (the front door) are exempt from prosecution. However, the cultivation of larger quantities and

Drug policy in the Netherlands   133

Table 9.1 Dutch coffee shop criteria

	a. Original 1994 'AHOJ-G' criteria (Staatscourant, 1994)
A	No Advertising: no more than (very) low profile signposting of the facility
H	No Hard drugs: these may not be sold or held on the premises
O	No Nuisance (Overlast in Dutch): including traffic and parking, loitering, littering and noise
J	No sales to under-aged customers (Jeugdigen) and no admittance of under-aged customers to coffee-shops. (Minimum age was set to 18 in 1996)
G	Transaction size is limited to 'personal use,' defined as 30 Grams per person per coffee shop per day (Transaction size was lowered to 5 grams in 1996). Since 1996, this criterion also included to the limited trade stock of coffee shops (no more than 500 grams)
	b. Criteria added in 2012 (Aanwijzing Opiumwet, 2012)
B	Coffee shops needed to be small and membership-only (Besloten) (Abolished in January 2013)
I	Coffee shops are only open to residents of the Netherlands (Ingezetenen). Introduced nationally on January 1, 2013.

supply of cannabis to (the back door of) coffee shops has been a high priority for law enforcement since 1969 (De Kort, 1995). This ambiguity is known as the 'back door problem'. Although the first Purple Government (1994–1998) hinted at a more prominent role for home-growers in the supply of coffee shops (Buruma, 2008; Boekhoorn et al., 1995), by the early 2000s small-scale home-growers were increasingly targeted by law enforcement (Belackova et al., 2015). The unanticipated consequence was a significant increase of criminal organisations' involvement in cannabis cultivation (Boekhout van Solinge, 2010). The MoH did not feel responsible for the back door, and coffee shop policy became increasingly framed in terms of 'organised crime' and public order. Coalition politics, anxiety over international critique and pressure from neighbouring countries prevented initiatives from regulating this inconsistency in the DDP until today.

And then there was heroin: From moral panic to pragmatism

Before 1972, growing opium use among native Dutch youth raised considerable concern among the authorities and combating opium trade became a policing priority. Three years later, the police dismantled the Chinese Triad responsible for the importation and distribution of opium. Within months, competing triads introduced high purity no. 4 heroin into the Amsterdam and Rotterdam drug markets. Soon after, the first street heroin markets emerged around youth centres, bars and nightlife spots in Amsterdam and Rotterdam. In the following years, heroin diffused rapidly among both middle- and working-class youth and among the first generation of Surinamese immigrants (Janssen, Swierstra and Barneveld, 1982; Grund and Blanken, 1993).

Around the independence of Suriname in 1975, the Netherlands faced an unprecedented wave of Surinamese immigrants, including many single young men. The Netherlands was in the middle of a recession that followed the first Oil Crisis in 1973 and ill-prepared to absorb the new immigrants. Many ended up on social benefits and in boarding houses with their peers and few contacts beyond, further complicating social integration. Many of these alienated youngsters ended up in the emerging consumer-level heroin market, selling and using the drug (Fabri, 1976; Janssen, Swierstra and Barneveld, 1982; Van Gelder and Sijtsma, 1988; Grund and Blanken, 1993). The street heroin scenes in the inner cities of Amsterdam and Rotterdam grew exponentially, and heroin diffused to Utrecht and other provincial cities (Janssen, Swierstra and Barneveld, 1982; Verbraeck, 1984; Korf, Mann and Van Aalderen, 1989; Korf et al., 1990; Grund et al., 1992).

The sudden boom in heroin use increasingly provoked civil anxiety, which focused on the role of the Surinamese in the bulging street markets. Feelings of lack of safety, fear, discontent and civil unrest threatened to escalate in the affected neighbourhoods by 1980 (Beets and Stengs, 1992). It was kindled also by the recession after the second Oil Crisis in 1979 as rising unemployment hit hardest these same neighbourhoods. In response the police cracked down on the street heroin markets. In the aftermath of these street sweeps, most heroin dealing gradually moved out of the city centres into working-class neighbourhoods where dealers set up shop in empty housing awaiting renovation. These so called 'house addresses' became the fulcrum of the re-emerging heroin scene (Blanken and Adriaans, 1993; Grund, 1993; Grund and Blanken, 1993). Indoor dealing became the primary mode of consumption level drug transactions in most Dutch cities far into the 1990s (Barendregt, Schenk and Vollemans, 2001; Van de Mheen and Gruter, 2004), at first attracting many new customers.

Local de facto decriminalisation of hard drugs

After local authorities realised that indoor dealing resulted in significant decreases in drug related nuisance on the streets, they decided to tolerate the house addresses. In an effort to contain nuisance, local police in Rotterdam, Arnhem and other Dutch cities quietly applied the A, O, J and G (no advertisement; nuisance; no youth inside; consumer amounts only) criteria to these hard drug 'speakeasies', ten years before the coffee shop criteria were first published in 1991 (Blanken and Adriaans, 1993; Grund, 1993; Grund and Blanken, 1993; Barendregt, Blanken and Zuidmulder, 2000; Grund and Breeksema, submitted). Amsterdam was, however, less tolerant to house addresses and the police established a team that focused exclusively on indoor dealing (Joop van Riessen, 2012, personal communication). But in several cities, the police, drug services, urban planners, and

Drug policy in the Netherlands   135

neighbourhood organisations actively collaborated with dealers and proprietors of house addresses. The city of Rotterdam went as far as actively trying to regulate the 'basements' where local law enforcement tolerated heroin and cocaine dealing, and prevention workers distributed harm reduction materials such as clean needles (Blanken and Adriaans, 1993; Barendregt, Schenk and Vollemans, 2001; Van de Mheen and Gruter, 2004; Barendregt, van der Poel and van de Mheen, 2002).

These unwritten municipal hard drug policies were seldom recorded in official documents. Elsewhere we have described that this aspect of municipal hard drug policies represented a compromise between multiple local policy priorities that, besides public health, included concern about rising unemployment, social order and, in particular, the urban renewal process (Grund and Breeksema, submitted). In condoning these off-the-record police practices, the local law enforcement authorities obviously applied the expediency principle. In doing so, they balanced at the limits of the law, considering that the 'public interest' was never clearly defined, as it was for the tolerant policy towards cannabis (Ministry of Foreign Affairs, 1983).

Pioneering harm reduction

This fundamentally different Dutch approach to policing drug use and drug markets is mirrored in the comprehensive treatment and harm reduction approach that materialised in the 1980s.

The first drug services in the Netherlands were established in the 1960s (Van den Brink, 2010) and after 1972 these mainly revolved around heroin dependence. Many different drug services saw the light of day in the 1970s, initiated by municipal health services, (new) NGOs and faith-based organisations. Most NGOs offered abstinence-based treatment, such as in- or out-patient detoxification, in-patient clinics programmes or therapeutic communities. Other NGOs and municipal services focused on providing health care, social support, income and housing. These two approaches represented the classic ideological divide between 'abstinence only' and 'addressing immediate needs', which ran through civil society, the media, local government and parliament (Blok, 2008; 2011).

Methadone detoxification was introduced in 1968 in response to opium addiction (Van den Brink, 2010) and the first methadone maintenance programmes were piloted in 1977. Five years later, methadone maintenance would be scaled up, after intense ideological debate in the media and in parliament (Blok, 2008; 2011). The final model of opioid substitution treatment (OST) represented an ideological and political compromise. With a few exceptions, OST is only provided in methadone programmes (Staatstoezicht op de Volksgezondheid, 1981). Heroin Assisted Treatment was introduced in 1996 as a scientific trial and, after a favourable evaluation, was registered as a legal medication for the treatment of 'chronic, treatment-resistant heroin-dependent patients' in 2006 (Blanken et al., 2010; Fischer et al., 2007). By 2000, the Netherlands had the highest opiate substitution treatment (OST) coverage in the EU except for

Spain (EMCDDA, 2002), with 44% of Dutch heroin consumers in substitution treatment.

Already in the early 1970s Amsterdam drop-in centres provided their clients with sterile injecting equipment (Blok, 2011). In response to a local epidemic of hepatitis B, the *Rotterdam Junkie Union* started distributing syringes on the streets in 1981. A few years later, after the first publications on HIV among people who inject drugs, Needle and Syringe Exchange Programmes (NSEP) were introduced in the Netherlands (Grund et al., 1992). In 2012 there were around 150 syringe exchange programmes across the country (EMCDDA, 2012). As early as 1974, off-the-record drug injection rooms were available in two Amsterdam drop-in centres (Blok 2008). In Rotterdam, Reverend Visser of the Saint Paul's Church established an injection room in the church basement in 1982. These activist projects laid the groundwork for the official safe consumption facilities that were opened after 1995 in most of the larger cities. In 2012 there were 37 drug consumption rooms across the country, targeting injectors, smokers and even alcohol users (Schatz and Nougier, 2012; EMCDDA, 2012).

Recent Dutch drug policy (1995–present): continuity and change

After roughly two decades without any fundamental changes in DDP, the beginning of the 1990s marked a tightening of the coffee shop regulations. Although the first Purple Government (characterised by the absence of the moral rejection of drug use by the Christian Democratic Party – CDA) took pride in the successes of the harm reduction policies of the past 25 years – low prevalence of HIV infection, injecting drug use, drug dependence and dwindling rates of initiation into hard drug use – explicit attention was also drawn towards the increasing use of crack on the streets and, in particular, the adverse side effects related to (lack of regulation of) coffee shops. The influence of criminal organisations; public nuisance; their vicinity to schools; cross-border tourism and the Netherlands' 'international reputation' were of particular concern. These worries were first expressed in the influential 1995 government policy paper, *Dutch Drug Policy: Continuity and Change*, (Kuipers, Mensink and de Zwart, 1993; Tweede Kamer, 1995; Breeksema and Grund, submitted).

Tightening tolerance and stalled reform in cannabis policy

Increasing regulation

Municipalities were further empowered to add local conditions, such as by-laws stipulating business hours and zoning criteria and minimum distance between coffee shops and schools (250 or 350 metres) (Bieleman, Goeree and Naayer, 2005). Two additional articles to the Opium Act significantly increased options for administrative enforcement, by further decentralising coffee shop policy to

Drug policy in the Netherlands   137

local authorities. The 1999 Damocles Act (article 13b) gave mayors the power to close down coffee shops (and venues selling hard drugs) using a broad set of public order and safety criteria (Bieleman et al., 2008). The 2002 Victor Act allowed mayors to close down commercial premises and residences causing a public nuisance and evict their tenants. The Act aimed to reduce the flow of foreign drug tourists, but was also used to shut down both coffee shops and house addresses. Finally, the introduction of Integrity Assessments (BIBOB[2]) aimed at preventing coffee shop permits going to proprietors with ties to criminal organisations, without the intervention of a judge.

New criteria

The end of the decade was marked by increasing concern over large, professionally organised coffee shops in the southern border provinces and increased cross-border drug trafficking. In May 2012, despite widespread protest from local governments, the national government introduced the 'weed club pass' on a pilot basis in the three southern provinces. Two new criteria were added to the national AHOJ-G criteria: **B** and **I**. Coffee shops needed to be small and membership-only (*Besloten*) and could only be frequented by residents of the Netherlands (*Ingezetenen*) (Aanwijzing Opiumwet, 2012). Nuisance from street drug sales and feelings of lack of security increased (SSC Onderzoek en Informatie, 2012). Local consumers refused to register at coffee shops, citing privacy concerns (Wouters and Korf, 2011; Nijkamp and Bieleman, 2012) and many regulars abandoned the shops, resorting to illegal markets instead (Maalsté and Hebben, 2012). Soon after its introduction, in January 2013 the **B** criterion was abolished, while implementation of the **I** criterion was delegated to municipalities (Opstelten, 2012). In practice, the mayors of the four biggest cities, as well as many other municipalities, do not enforce this new criterion (De Volkskrant, 2012).

Local versus national hegemony

As noted, the early development of drug policy in the Netherlands was driven by the initiatives and interests of the major cities to a great extent – initially drugs were a 'big city problem'. The drug policies at both levels of government often aligned but not always. Around the mid-1990s, a national trend in legislation and enforcement towards more repression started. But local authorities have by and large spoken out against repressive approaches, demanding space for local experimentation with alternative approaches and requesting the national government to take steps towards regulating the cultivation and wholesale of cannabis (Reinking, 2011; Van Steenbergen, 2014; Kas, 2014). Since the early 2000s, tension between state and municipal authorities increased. Broad coalitions for cannabis reform

---

2 BIBOB stands for 'Wet Bevordering Integriteitsbeoordelingen door het Openbaar Bestuur', (Promotion of Integrity Assessments by the Public Administration Act).

included a small parliamentary majority in 2000 (Tweede Kamer, 1999/2000); appeals from a large number of mayors of all political colours (in 1999 and 2008); a combined parliamentary-municipal initiative, the 'Manifest of Maastricht' (2005); and a 2014 manifest called 'Joint Regulation' – signed by the mayors of 54 municipalities (Depla, Everhardt and Van Gijzel, 2014) which was thwarted by a slim parliamentary majority (Tweede Kamer, 2014/2015). All subsequent governments turned down these calls, citing a study by the Asser Institute (2005), which suggested that international treaties did not leave room for experimentation (Van der Stel, Everhardt and Van Laar, 2009; Everhardt et al., 2009). Several years later, investigative journalists found out that the government had withheld a first draft of the report which stated that experiments were *not* at odds with international treaties. After changing the assignment, the subsequent version conformed to the government's position (Althuisius and Driessen, 2012; Polak, 2012, personal communication).

A final hit: crack, aging and institutionalisation

Cocaine indoors; crack on the streets

During the 1990s the tolerance for house addresses decreased notably and their closure resulted in the drug market returning to the streets. In the preceding years, cocaine smoking had penetrated into all corners of the heroin scene. As the number of house addresses dwindled, the street markets grew exponentially, drastically changing the risk environment of hard drug use once more. Without the protective environment of the house addresses and the social control it provided, people smoking cocaine in the streets became increasingly prone to its negative side effects. Crack became the driver of a reinvigorated and volatile street drug scene, characterised by ageing consumers, chaos, mental health problems and repressive policing (Grund, Adriaans and Kaplan, 1991; Blanken, Barendregt and Zuidmulder, 1999; Barendregt, Blanken and Zuidmulder, 2000).

Preoccupied with heroin, methadone maintenance treatment services initially stood empty-handed. However, first prompted by the Continuity and Change policy paper in 1995, subsequent Dutch governments invested significant resources in establishing a comprehensive and integrated harm reduction, treatment and social support system targeting people with drug problems, the homeless and chronic psychiatric patients, particularly in the past ten years. Meanwhile, the incidence of heroin and, subsequently, crack use had dwindled and those consuming these drugs were rapidly ageing.

Taming the tail of the epidemic: institutionalisation and criminal justice interventions

After 2000 the traditional street drug markets gradually disappeared. Ageing, treatment, and law enforcement may all have played a role, but the demise of street dealing is probably best explained by technological innovation. Since 2000, drug dealers and their clients were quick to adopt mobile phones, taking away the need to frequent specific areas (Barendregt, van der Poel and van de Mheen, 2006).

After 2006, simultaneous investments in sheltered housing, the integration of drug treatment, public mental health care, and services for the homeless and in criminal justice interventions (Rijk en vier grote steden, 2006) effectively resulted in the institutionalisation of an ageing population, increasingly characterised by severe drug and/or mental health problems. The criminal justice system became an increasingly important stick behind the door and the (new) Ministry of Security and Justice (MSJ) increasingly influenced the Dutch approach to hard drugs, prioritising reduction of drug-related crime and nuisance. Most street drug users now live in sheltered or supported housing where they receive welfare, medical care and tailored drug treatment or consume their drugs in on-site drug consumption rooms (Schatz, Schiffer and Kools, 2010). Those who continue to cause nuisance or engage in crime are subjected to various criminal justice interventions, including compulsory treatment and other forensic psychiatric interventions (Van Laar et al., 2015).

Discussion

Drug policy making in practice: compromise, pragmatism and restraint

Relatively early on, the overall goals of DDP were formulated in terms of public health and public order. Yet the development of drug policy in the Netherlands has largely been concerned with finding a middle ground between opposing views and building political majorities around this complex social issue. As former Prime Minister and MoJ Van Agt explained, 'there was no parliamentary majority for decriminalising the supply of cannabis or other drugs in 1976 and the Dutch government did not want to risk diplomatic or economic problems with neighbouring countries and the international community'. The compromise eventually allowed consumers safe access to cannabis in regulated retail shops but did not secure a regulated and controlled supply to these same tolerated outlets (the back door problem) and discourages home growing (Maalsté and Panhuysen, 2007; Belackova et al., 2015). Our analysis shows that municipal drug policy was equally the result of compromise with various other public policy interests.

The primary objective of DDP never was to decrease drug use, but to contain the associated social and medical problems. Former policy maker Eddy Engelsman (2012, personal communication) confirms that the goal of the Dutch government was to 'normalise' the issue and to treat it like any other health issue: 'Since we can never fully contain the problem, we can at least control the excesses'. Given the lifespan of epidemics of addictive drug use and the role of youth culture and nightlife in recreational – mostly unproblematic – drug use, the immediate effects of drug policy on prevalence are a feeble measure of the success of drug policy. 'Prevalence [of use] is almost policy resistant,' as former drug policy maker Marcel de Kort (2012, personal communication) put it eloquently. Humble expectations regarding the immediate effects of drug policy on prevalence are thus advised. Instead, we think that the effects of drug policy on drug related harms may be less dubious; more immediately manifest and, furthermore, better to measure in a society. With that in mind, from an EU or international perspective the Dutch policies have clearly paid off.

Dutch policies did not develop in a vacuum. Beyond diplomatic and economic influences, our analysis points towards the importance of unforeseen environmental contingencies and 'unanticipated consequence of purposive social action' (Merton, 1936). Indeed, coffee shops were not a bold regulatory intervention or social experiment but an unanticipated entrepreneurial response to tolerating low level sales in youth venues. They were deemed expedient because they served the public health goal by contributing to the separation of soft and hard drug markets.

Table 9.2 Outcomes of Dutch drug policy

Cannabis use is on par with the European average and the Netherlands has the lowest level of problem drug use in the EU (Van Laar and Van Ooyen-Houben, 2009) while the overall prevalence of drug use in the general population is below EU and USA averages (ECMDDA, 2012; Van Laar et al., 2014). The most recent data show that both the lifetime prevalence (26%) and recent use of cannabis (7%) in the Dutch population between 15 and 64 years (Van Laar et al., 2014) are in line with the European average (EMCDDA, 2012).

One of the principal motivations for the 1976 revised Opium Act was to prevent the stigmatisation and marginalisation of (young) drug consumers. In comparison to other European nations, arrests and convictions for use of illegal substances and possession for personal use are very low in the Netherlands (3 per 1,000 users, compared to 44 per 1,000 users in Austria) (Room et al., 2008). Arrests and criminal records for use or minor possession are extremely rare in the Netherlands.

The Netherlands is one of the countries with the lowest percentage of injecting among people who use opiates (7% of all people in treatment for heroin dependence) and per 1000 15–64 year olds (0.22) in Europe (range: 0.2 in Spain to 5.89 in Estonia) (EMCDDA, 2015).

Together with Belgium, The Netherlands has the lowest HIV incidence in Europe (EMCDDA 2011). Less than 5% of HIV infections in the Netherlands are associated with injecting drug use (Van Laar and Van Ooyen-Houben, 2009; Van den Brink, 2010; IDU Reference Group, 2010).

The low rate of drug injection and the associated lowered risks for overdose and HIV contributed to the relatively high survival rates of people involved in heroin and crack use in the Netherlands. From the late 1980s onwards, this group was rapidly aging. In 2014 81% of clients in treatment for opiate dependence were over 39 years old (Van Laar et al., 2014). In 2002 only 2% of Dutch methadone maintenance patients was under 26 years of age (IVZ, 2004). Treatment for heroin dependence increasingly has elements of geriatric care and the EMCDDA recently complimented the Netherlands for pioneering senior citizens homes for the aging group of heroin consumers (EMCDDA, 2015).

The introduction of heroin, after the Amsterdam police successfully interrupted the availability of opium in 1972, is perhaps the most powerful example of Merton's Law. Local authorities responded with repressive policing tactics of city centre drug markets, citing public order concerns in response to moral panic and civil unrest (Beets and Stengs, 1992; Kieft, 2014). This did not stop the escalation in heroin use in the 1970s (Schreuder and Broex, 1998). Along with environmental contingencies such as mass immigration and unemployment, increasingly pushing street scenes off-centre merely contributed to the diffusion of heroin into working-class neighbourhoods.

While the 1970s and 1990s were characterised by more active and repressive policing of drug markets, during the 1980s law enforcement tolerated indoor drug dealing. The restrained policing of these 'drug sanctuaries' is instrumental in explaining perhaps the key health outcome of DDP: beyond an initial outbreak in Amsterdam, the Netherlands never experienced a large-scale HIV epidemic. Unbothered by the authorities, the house addresses became the 'incubator' of a subcultural transition from injecting heroin to smoking heroin and cocaine. While heroin use continued to increase, new initiations into drug injecting rapidly declined (Grund and Blanken, 1993). Gradually, heroin use stopped being a vector in the spread of HIV. Unlike in other European countries, there were already relatively few people who injected drugs in the Netherlands during the 1980s and 1990s when HIV ravaged drug users' communities across the European continent. Early investments in harm reduction services have certainly made an important contribution to the favourable health outcomes of DDP but this unanticipated policy consequence is perhaps the most important factor in what sets the recent Dutch history of hard drugs apart from that of the rest of Europe.

After 2006, institutionalisation and criminal justice measures became the leading policy response towards the rapidly ageing population of people afflicted by chaotic drug consumption, mental health problems and homelessness. Although these criminal justice interventions contributed to overall improvements in public order, they have raised concerns about their proportionality and the human rights of those detained under these measures.

As the heroin epidemic peaked in the 1980s and the use of crack cocaine levelled off in the early 2000s, the policy focus inevitably turned to (negative aspects of) cannabis and coffee shops. Numerous measures were taken to reduce the number of coffee shops and to restrict their operating room, while leaving key negative side effects of the policy unsolved, partly because of the lack of drug policy reform in neighbouring countries. Virtually all study respondents agree that the failure to regulate the supply to coffee shops and cannabis cultivation is the source of many of the current negative side effects of the Dutch cannabis policy – from the involvement of criminal enterprise to the lack of quality control. Over the years, the influence of criminal organisations in cannabis cultivation and the supply of coffee shops have not subsided, despite enormous investments in law enforcement. At the same time, the Dutch government felt unable to regulate the back door because of alleged potential diplomatic and economic consequences. Targeting small-scale cannabis cultivation reportedly increased the influence of organised crime in cannabis cultivation (Maalsté and Panhuyzen, 2007; Belackova et al., 2015). This created a self-fulfilling prophesy for the government, by reinforcing a problem it was trying to fight: the influence of organised crime in cannabis cultivation (Boekhout van Solinge, 2010).

Conclusions

In our analysis of DDP we can roughly distinguish three periods. In the first (1960–1980), the Netherlands was first confronted with the rapid spread of several psychoactive substances in a time of social transformation; hashish and subsequently psychedelics and amphetamines in the 1960s and heroin in the 1970s. The government first tried to repress cannabis use, but arrests mostly concerned middle-class youth, fuelling protest and fervent drug policy discussions in parliament and the media. 1970, when the Rotterdam police left massive and open drug consumption and dealing undisturbed at the Rotterdam Pop festival, marks the genesis of pragmatic tolerance towards use and small transactions in cannabis. Meanwhile that attention of the public, the media and politicians was distracted by the rapidly emerging heroin epidemic (Van Brussel, 1995) and the first post-war drug panic it raised. Until 1980, repressive law enforcement was the primary policy response to heroin. The emerging drug treatment and support services were hampered by ideological battles over the goals of treatment. Coordination between these two drug policy instruments was basically absent.

The 'distinguishing years' of DDP are undoubtedly the 1980s, when the Dutch pioneered a pragmatic public health response to heroin. A wide variety of *avant la lettre* harm reduction interventions were introduced and brought to scale. Law enforcement focused on the higher levels of drug trafficking. Enforcement of local low-level drug activity became increasingly instrumental in public health and was influenced by other local public interests. Local authorities extended the expediency principle to consumer level hard drug dealing. With variations between the cities, this *détente* lasted for over 10 years. Integration of public health and law enforcement instruments are gaining policy attention, but remain rare in practice.

In the 1990s, DDP has increasingly been affected by the 'law of the handicap of a head start' (Romein, 1937). The initial head start in progressive drug policies became a burden in the long term. As the Dutch were relatively successful in dealing with their own drug problems, they became more vulnerable to those of their neighbours. Without much international support, the Netherlands struggled with drug tourism from neighbouring countries with less liberal policies. Drug tourism contributed to considerable civil unrest, focused on coffee shops in border communities and on the hard drugs markets in Rotterdam and many provincial cities. Hard drug tourism amplified the re-emerging street hard drug scenes. As politics became more populist in the 2000s, the directive force of drug policy moved from the health department to Security and Justice; public order and crime fighting became the primary drivers of drug policy – a situation that has lasted until this day.

References

AANWIJZING OPIUMWET (2012). Geldend van 01-01-2012 t/m 31-12-2012. Available from: http://wetten.overheid.nl/BWBR0030993/2012-01-01 [Accessed 20 May 2015].

ALBAYRAK, E., WEEKERS, F., VAN DER HAM, B., and LEERS, G. (2005) Manifest van Maastricht: Experiment voor het reguleren van de teelt en handel van softdrugs. Available from: http://www.hetccv.nl/binaries/content/assets/ccv/dossiers/ hennepteelt/pvdax_vvdx_dx66_manifest_van_maastricht.pdf [Accessed 20 May 2015].

ALTHUISIUS, J. and DRIESSEN, C. (2012) Ziende blind, horende doof. Het Nederlandse drugsbeleid word op valse aannames gevoerd. Dagblad *De Pers*. 28 Mar.

BARENDREGT, C., BLANKEN, P. and ZUIDMULDER, L. (2000) Drugshandel en Overlast in Rotterdam. *IVO Bulletin*. 1(2). pp. 1–23.

BARENDREGT, C., SCHENK, M., and VOLLEMANS, L. (2001) *Kwaliteitscriteria voor dealadressen – ideeën voor de regulering van drugshandel vanuit vaste locaties*. Rotterdam: Addiction Research Institute Rotterdam.

BARENDREGT, C., VAN DER POEL, A. and VAN DE MHEEN, D. (2002) *Gebruiksruimten in Rotterdam, in het perspectief van gezondheidsbevordering en overlastvermindering*. Rotterdam: Addiction Research Institute Rotterdam.

BARENDREGT, C., VAN DER POEL, A., VAN DE MHEEN, D. (2006) The Rise of the Mobile Phone in the Hard Drug Scene of Rotterdam. *Journal of Psychoactive Drugs*. 38(1), pp. 77–87.

BEETS, J, and STENGS, I. (1992) De heksen zijn nog onder ons. Junkies als belichaming van het kwaad. *Etnofoor*. 5(1/2). pp. 45–60.

BELACKOVA, V., MAALSTÉ, N., ZABRANSKY, T. and GRUND, J. P. (2015) 'Should I Buy or Should I Grow?' How Drug Policy Institutions and Drug Market Transaction Costs Shape the Decision to Self-Supply with Cannabis in the Netherlands and the Czech Republic. *International Journal of Drug Policy* 26(3). pp. 296–310.

BIELEMAN, B., GOEREE, P. and NAAYER, H. (2005) *Aantallen coffeeshops en gemeentelijk beleid 1999–2004: Coffeeshops in Nederland 2004*. Groningen: Intraval, Den Haag: WODC.

BIELEMAN, B., BEELEN, A., NIJKAMP, R. and DE BIE, E. (2008) *Coffeeshops in Nederland 2007. Aantallen coffeeshops en gemeentelijk beleid 1999–2007*. Groningen/Rotterdam: Interval.

BLANKEN, P. and ADRIAANS, N. F. P. (1993) *Echo's van een mespuntje fantasie. Een model voor lokaal drugbeleid gericht op beheersbaarheid van ongewenste neven-effecten van druggebruik onder prohibitie*. Rotterdam: Instituut Voor Verslavingsonderzoek (IVO).

BLANKEN, P., BARENDREGT, C. and ZUIDMULDER, L. (1999) The evolution of crack and basing cocaine in the Rotterdam heroin scene. *Journal of Drug Issues* 29(3). pp. 609–625.

BLANKEN, P., VAN DEN BRINK, W., HENDRIKS, V. M., HUIJSMAN, I. A., KLOUS, M. G., ROOK, E. J., WAKELIN, J. S., BARENDRECHT, C., BEIJNEN, J. H., VAN REE, J. M. (2010) Heroin-Assisted Treatment in the Netherlands: History, Findings, and International Context. *European Neuropsychopharmacology*. 2010(20). P. S105–S158.

BLOK, G. (2008) Pampering 'Needle Freaks' or Caring for Chronic Addicts? Early Debates on Harm Reduction in Amsterdam, 1972–1982. *Social History of Alcohol and Drugs*. 22(2). pp. 243–261.

BLOK, G. (2011) *Ziek of zwak. Geschiedenis van de verslavingszorg in Nederland*. Amsterdam: Nieuwezijds.

BLOK, G. and KENNEDY, J. (2014) Geef die joint eens door. Het problematische idealisme van het Nederlandse softdrugsbeleid, 1976-heden. In van Dam, P., Turpijn, J.

and Mellink, B. (eds.). *Onbehagen in de polder: Nederland in conflict sinds 1795*. Amsterdam: Amsterdam University Press.

BLOM, T. (1998) *Drugs in Het Recht, Recht Onder Druk*. Rotterdam: Kluwers.

BOEKHOORN, P., VAN DIJK, A. G., LOEF, C. J., VAN OOSTEN, R. N. J., STEINMETZ, C. H. D. (1995) *Softdrugs in Nederland. Consumptie en Handel*. Amsterdam: Van Dijk, Van Soomeren en Partners; Amsterdam: STEINMETZ advies en opleiding.

BOEKHOUT VAN SOLINGE, T. (2010) Het Nederlands drugsbeleid en de wet van de remmende voorsprong. *Nederlands Juristenblad*. 85. pp. 2579–2636.

BREEKSEMA, J. J. and GRUND, J.-P. (Submitted) 50 Years of Illicit Drug Policy in the Netherlands, part 1: Cannabis and Coffee shops, an Uneasy Compromise.

BRUINING, W. (2008) Van Coffeeshop naar Cannabisclub – van gedogen naar reguleren. Available from: http://cdn.vellance.com/speakersa/data/_backup/speakers/1395/publications/Van%20Coffeeshop%20naar%20Cannabis%20club%20beleidsver sie.pdf [Accessed 28 September 2015].

BURUMA, Y. (2008) European Integration and Harmonization. Available from: http://www.drugtext.org/Law-and-treaties/european-integration-and-harmonization.html [Accessed 20 May 2014].

COHEN, H. (1975) *Drugs, druggebruikers en drugscene*. Alphen a/d Rijn: Samsom.

COHEN, P. (1994) The Case of the Two Dutch Drug Policy Commissions: An Exercise in Harm Reduction. Paper presented at the 5th International Conference on the Reduction of Drug Related Harm, 7–11 March 1994, Addiction Research Foundation, Toronto.

COMMISSIE HULSMAN (1971) *Ruimte in het drugbeleid. Rapport van een werkgroep van de Stichting Algemeen Centraal Bureau voor de Geestelijke Volksgezondheid*. Meppel.

DEPLA, P., EVERHARDT, V. and VAN GIJZEL, R. (2014) Manifest Joint Regulation. Available from: http://www.voc-nederland.org/persberichten_pdf/LR_Manifest_Joint_regulation_31_januari_2014.pdf [Accessed: 30 November 2015].

DE VOLKSKRANT (2012) Geen gemeente lijkt de wietpas nog te willen. *De Volkskrant*. 28 September 2012.

EMCDDA (2002) *Drug Use in Prison*. Selected Issue. Available from: http://www.emcdda.europa.eu/html.cfm/index34919EN.html [Accessed 21 May 2015].

EMCDDA (2011) *Statistical bulletin 2011*. Lisbon: EMCDDA.

EMCDDA (2012) Country Overview: Netherlands. Available from: http://www.emcdda.europa.eu/publications/country-overviews/nl [Accessed 23 May 2015].

EMCDDA (2015) *European Drug Report 2015. Trends and Developments*. Luxembourg: Publications Office of the European Union.

EVERHARDT, V., WAGEN, W. VAN DER, TRAUTMANN, F., BLESS, R., KETELAARS, T. and KEIZER, B. (2009) Internationale samenwerking. In: Van Laar, M. and Van Ooyen-Houben, M. (eds.). *Evaluatie van het Nederlandse drugsbeleid*. Utrecht: Trimbos-instituut;Den Haag: WODC.

EXPERTCOMMISSIE LIJSTENSYSTEMATIEK OPIUMWET (COMMISSIE GARRETSEN) (2011) *Drugs in Lijsten. Rapport Expertcommissie Lijstensystematiek Opiumwet*. Available from: https://www.rijksoverheid.nl/binaries/rijksoverheid/documenten/rapporten/2011/06/27/rapport-drugs-in-lijsten/rapport-drugs-in-lijsten.pdf [Accessed 23 May 2015].

FABRI, M. (1976) *Het witte monster*. Rotterdam: Werkgroep voor Arbeidersliteratuur Rotterdam.

FISCHER, B., OVIEDO-JOEKES, E., BLANKEN, P., HAASEN, C., REHM, J., SCHECHTER, M.T., STRANG, J. and VAN DEN BRINK, W. (2007) Heroin-Assisted Treatment (HAT) a Decade Later: A Brief Update on Science and Politics. *Journal of Urban Health*. 84(4). pp. 552–562.

GALBRAITH, J. K. (1958) *The Affluent Society*. Boston: Houghton Mifflin Harcourt.

GRUND, J. P., ADRIAANS, N. F. and KAPLAN, C. D. (1991) Changing Cocaine Smoking Rituals in the Dutch Heroin Addict Population. *British Journal of Addiction*. 86 (4). pp. 439–448.

GRUND, J.-P., BLANKEN, P., ADRIAANS, N. F., KAPLAN, C. D., BARENDREGT, C. and MEEUWSEN, M. (1992) Reaching the Unreached: Targeting Hidden IDU Populations with Clean Needles via Known User Groups. *Journal of Psychoactive Drugs*. 24 (1). pp. 41–47.

GRUND, J.-P. C. (1993) *Drug Use as a Social Ritual: Functionality, Symbolism and Determinants of Self-regulation*. Erasmus University Rotterdam. Available from: http://repub.eur.nl/res/p ub/39132/ [Accessed 23 May 2015].

GRUND, J.-P. C. and BLANKEN, P. (1993) *From 'Chasing the Dragon' to 'Chinezen': The Diffusion of Heroin Smoking in the Netherlands*. Addiction Research Institute (IVO), Rotterdam. Available from: http://www.drugtext.org/pdf/grund02.pdf [Accessed 23 May 2015].

GRUND, J.-P. C. and BREEKSEMA, J. J. Submitted. 50 Years of Illicit Drug Policy in the Netherlands, part 2: At the Other Side of the Fence.

HART, A. C. (1994) *Openbaar ministerie en rechtshandhaving*. Arnhem/Gouda: Quint.

IDU REFERENCE GROUP (2010) *Country Data: Germany. Secretariat of the Reference Group to the UN on HIV and Injecting Drug Use*. Available from: http://www.idurefgroup.org/coun try-data-and-maps/Germany#idu [Accessed 30 November 2015].

IVZ (2004) Methadon in de verslavingszorg in Nederland (1994–2002). *LADIS bulletin* 2006 (6). Houten: Stichting IVZ.

JANSEN, A. (1989) *Cannabis in Amsterdam: een geografie van hasjiesj en marihuana*. Muiderberg: Coutinho.

JANSSEN, O., SWIERSTRA, K., and BARNEVELD, P. (1982) *Heroïnegebruikers in Nederland: een typologie van levens-stijlen*. Groningen: Criminologisch Instituut van de Rijksuniversiteit Groningen.

KAS, A. (2014) 'Geef je ons de ruimte of geef je die ruimte aan criminele netwerken?' *NRC Handelsblad*, 27 January.

KIEFT, T. (2014) Het 'Harlem' van Amsterdam. Bachelor Thesis, University of Amsterdam. Available from: http://heroineepidemie.nl/wp-content/uploads/2015/03/tom-kieft-ba chelorscriptie.pdf [Accessed 18 November 2015].

KORF, D. J., MANN, R. and AALDEREN, H. VAN. (1989) *Drugs op het platteland*. Assen/ Maastricht: Van Gorcum.

KORF, D. J., VAN AALDEREN, H., HOGENHOUT, H. P. H., SANDWIJK, J. P. (1990) *Gooise Geneugten: Legaal en illegaal drugsgebruik (in de regio)*. Amsterdam: SPCP Amsterdam.

KORF, D. J., RIPER, H. and BULLINGTON, B. (1999) Windmills in Their Minds? Drug Policy and Drug Research in The Netherlands. *Journal of Drug Issues*. 29(3). pp. 451–472.

KORF, D. J. (2002) Dutch Coffee Shops and Trends in Cannabis Use. *Addictive Behaviours*. 27(6). pp. 851–866.

KORF, D. J. (2008) An Open Front Door: The Coffee Shop Phenomenon in the Netherlands. In Rödner Snitzman, S., Olsson, B. and Room, R. (eds.). *A Cannabis Reader: Global Issues and Local Experiences*. Lisbon: EMCDDA, pp. 137–154.

DE KORT, M. (1995) *Tussen patiënt en delinquent. Geschiedenis van het Nederlandse drugsbeleid*, Hilversum: Verloren.

KUIPERS, S. B. M., MENSINK, C., and DE ZWART, W. M. (1993) *Jeugd en riskant gedrag; roken, drinken, druggebruik en gokken onder scholieren vanaf 10 jaar.* Utrecht: Nederlands Instituut voor Alcohol en Drugs (NIAD).

LEUW, E. and MARSHALL, I. H. (eds.) (1994) *Between Prohibition and Legalization: The Dutch Experiment in Drug Policy.* Amsterdam/New York: Kugler Publications.

MAALSTÉ, N. and PANHUYZEN, M. (2007) *Polderwiet. Een veelzijdig en onthullend beeld van de wietteelt in Nederland.* Baarn: De Fontein.

MAALSTÉ, N. and HEBBEN, R. J. (2012) *Gevolgen invoering wietpas Zuid Nederland.* Available from: http://www.detransparanteketen.nl/upload/files/Gevolgen%20invoering%20wietpas%20Zuid%20Nederland.pdf [Accessed 20 May 2015].

MACCOUN, R. J. and REUTER, P. (2001) *Drug War Heresies: Learning from Other Vices, Times, and Places.* Port Chester: Cambridge University Press.

MEEUS, J. (2014) Het begon met een paar simpele regels. *NRC Handelsblad.* 6 December 2014.

MERTON, R. K. (1936) The Unanticipated Consequences of Purposive Social Action. *American Sociological Review.* 1(6). p. 894.

MINISTRY OF FOREIGN AFFAIRS (1983) *Reply to Aide Mémoire of the International Narcotics Control Board of 12 November 1982 concerning the sale of cannabis preparations at 'De Kokerjuffer' youth centre in Enschede.* The Hague, 18 January 1983 (DIO/SM- 137.85/O 4).

NIJKAMP, R. and BIELEMAN, B. (2012) *Coffeeshopbezoek rotterdam voorjaar 2012.* Groningen/ Rotterdam: Intraval.

OPSTELTEN, I. W. (2012) *"Brief coffeeshopbeleid".* Brief aan de Tweede Kamer, 19 November 2012.

REINKING, D. (2011) The Dutch Cannabis Policy: an effective policy under threat. 'Cannabis: Usos, seguridad jurídica y políticas'. San Sebastian, Spain, 26 October 2011.

RIJK EN VIER GROTE STEDEN (2006) *Plan van aanpak Maatschappelijke Opvang.* 7 februari 2006. Available from: http://www.opvang.nl/site/item/plan-van-aanpak-maatschappelijke-opvang-g4 [Accessed 18 November 2015].

ROMEIN, J. (1937) *De dialectiek van de vooruitgang. Het onvoltooid verleden.* Amsterdam: Querido.

ROOM, R. et al. (2008) *Cannabis Policy: Moving Beyond Stalemate. The Global Cannabis Commission Report.* Oxford: The Beckley Foundation.

SCHATZ, E. and NOUGIER, M. (2012) *Drug Consumption Rooms: Evidence and Practice.* IDPC Briefing Paper, June 2012. Available from: http://idpc.net/publications/2012/06/idpc-briefing-paper-drug-consumption-rooms-evidence-and-practice [Accessed 20 May 2015].

SCHATZ, E., SCHIFFER, K., and KOOLS, J. P. (2010) *The Dutch Treatment and Social Support System for Drug Users: Recent Developments and the Example of Amsterdam.* IDPC Briefing Paper, January 2011. Available from: http://idpc.net/publications/2011/01/idpc-paper-dutch-drug-treatment-programme [Accessed 30 November 2015].

SCHREUDER, R. F. and BROEX, V. M. F. (eds.) (1998) *Verkenning drugsbeleid in Nederland. Feiten, opinies en scenario's.* Zoetermeer: Stichting Toekomstscenario's Gezondheidszorg.

SSC ONDERZOEK EN INFORMATIE (2012) *Monitor omvorming coffeeshops tot besloten clubs in Breda. Resultaten metingen juni 2012.* Breda: Gemeente Breda/Afdeling SSC Onderzoek en Informatie.

STAATSCOURANT (1994) Richtlijn opsporingsbeleid inzake coffeeshops. *Staatscourant,* 12 oktober 1994.

STAATSTOEZICHT OP DE VOLKSGEZONDHEID (1981). *Brief aan alle artsen in Nederland betreffende de ambulante behandeling van verslaafden aan opiummiddelen.* Leidschendam: Geneeskundige Hoofdinspectie.

T.M.C. ASSER INSTITUUT (2005) *Experimenteren met het Gedogen van de Teelt van Cannabis ten Behoeve van de Bevoorrading van Coffeeshops – Internationaal rechtelijke en Europees rechtelijke aspecten.* Available from: https://zoek.officielebekendmakingen.nl/kst-24077-175-b1.pdf [Accessed 19 July 2015].

TWEEDE KAMER (1999/2000) Kamerstukken II 1999/2000, 24 077, 75.

TWEEDE KAMER (1995) Kamerstukken II. (1995) 24 077, 3. *Nota 'Het Nederlandse drugbeleid: continuïteit en verandering'.*

TWEEDE KAMER (2014/2015) Kamerstukken II. (2014/2015) 29911, 104. *Motie van het lid Oskam.*

UITERMARK, J. (2004) The Origins and Future of the Dutch Approach Towards Drugs. *Journal of Drug Issues.* (2004). pp. 511–532.

UNITED NATIONS (1961) *The Single Convention on Narcotic Drugs, 1961.* Available from: http s://www.unodc.org/unodc/en/treaties/single-convention.html [Accessed 12 May 2015].

UNITED NATIONS (1971) *Convention on Psychotropic Substances.* Available from: http:// www.unodc.org/pdf/convention_1971_en.pdf [Accessed 12 May 2015].

UNITED NATIONS OFFICE ON DRUGS AND CRIME (UNODC) (2009) *Chronology: 100 years of drug control.* Available from: http://www.unodc.org/unodc/en/frontpage/ the-1912-hague-international-opium-convention.html [Accessed 12 May 2015].

VAN BRUSSEL, G. H. A. (1995) Drugsgebruik in Amsterdam, een 'public health' probleem. *Nederlands Tijdschrift voor de Geneeskunde.* 139. pp. 2635–2639.

VAN DE MHEEN, D. and GRUTER, P. (2004) Interventions on the Supply Side of the Local Hard Drug Market: Towards a Regulated Hard Drug Trade? The Case of the City of Rotterdam. *Journal of Drug Issues.* 34(1). pp. 145–161.

VAN DEN BRINK, W. (2010) *Opioid Dependence Treatment in the Netherlands: Current and Future Outlooks.* Amsterdam: Amsterdam Institute for Addiction Research.

VAN DEN EERENBEEMT, M. and DE VISSER, E. (1995) Thuiskwekers leveren al volop nederwiet aan koffieshops. *De Volkskrant,* 29 August 1995.

VAN DER STEL, J. (1999) *Een nieuw drugsbeleid? Voor- en nadelen van de legalisering van drugs.* Zoetermeer: Raad voor de Volksgezondheid en Zorg, Den Haag: Raad voor Maatschappelijke Ontwikkeling.

VAN DER STEL, J., EVERHARDT, V. and VAN LAAR, M. (2009) In Van Laar, M. and van Ooyen-Houben, M. (eds.). *Evaluatie van het Nederlandse drugsbeleid.* Utrecht: Trimbos-instituut, Den Haag: WODC.

VAN GELDER, P. J. and SIJTSMAJ. H. (1988) *Horse, coke en kansen: Sociale risico's enkansen onder Surinaamse en Marokkaanse harddruggebruikers in Amsterdam. Deel I Surinaamse harddruggebruikers.* Amsterdam: Instituut voor Sociale Geografie, Universiteit van Amsterdam.

VAN LAAR, M. W. and VAN OOYEN-HOUBEN, M. (eds.) (2009) *Evaluatie van het Nederlandse drugsbeleid.* Utrecht: Trimbos-instituut, Den Haag: WODC.

VAN LAAR, M. W. et al. (2014) *Nationale Drug Monitor. Jaarbericht 2013–2014.* Utrecht: Trimbos-instituut, Den Haag: WODC.

VAN LAAR, M. W. et al. (2015) *The Netherlands Drug Situation 2014.* Utrecht: Trimbos-instituut.

VAN STEENBERGEN, E. (2014) Wietclub zoekt toestemming. *NRC Handelsblad.* 12 September 2013.

VANVUGT, E. (1985) *Wettig Opium. 350 Jaar Nederlandse Opiumhandel in de Indische Archipel.* Haarlem: In de Knipscheer.

VERBRAECK, H. (1984) *Junkies: Een etnografie over oude heroinegebruikers in Utrecht.* Utrecht: Stichting WGU.

WERKGROEP VERDOVENDE MIDDELEN (COMMISSIE BAAN) (1972) *Achtergronden en risico's van druggebruik.* Den Haag.

WIEDEMANN, E. (1994) Frau Antje in den Wechseljahren. *Der Spiegel,* 9. 28 February 1994. Available from: http://www.spiegel.de/spiegel/print/d-13685150.html [Accessed 30 November 2015].

WOUTERS, M. and KORF, D. (2011) *De wietpas en het sociaal clubmodel. Meningen en verwachtingen van coffeeshop-bezoekers in Utrecht.* Amsterdam: Rozenberg Publishers.

Chapter 10

Polish drug policy[1]

Kasia Malinowska

Introduction

Poland, a post-socialist democracy with a strong interest in successful integration into the European Union and a strong Catholic tradition, currently has some of the most restrictive drug laws in Europe. Structural violence towards drug users has intensified as a result of decades of shifting drug policies and the more recent process of political and economic liberalisation.

Since 2000, with the introduction of Article 62, all drug possession, even small amounts for personal use, is considered a criminal offence. In 2011, amended Article 62a gave prosecutors and judges the option of dismissing criminal proceedings for new offenders and those with drug dependence. However, this slight shift in the law is inconsistently applied and not reflected in the actions of the police who are still indiscriminately detaining people who use drugs.

This chapter offers an assessment of the ideological foundations and implications of modern Poland's drug policies. The resulting analysis provides an account of the relationship between drug use, drug policy, the systemic disempowerment of drug users, and how all of these factors result in policies and practices that are woefully inadequate for treating those in need of care.

My methodology is to explore the complexities of drug use and drug policy making in Poland as a single, holistic case study that encompasses the contextual socio-historical conditions, as they are highly pertinent to the subject. The findings of this article are based on a review of primary and secondary sources. Primary sources include: transcripts of Polish parliamentary debates and sub-committee hearings related to drugs and AIDS; legislative amendments to the existing drug law; newspaper and media reports covering all sides of the debates about drug treatment and policy reform; and engaged listserves and portals which hosted discussions generated by electronic campaigns. My primary sources also include in-person, semi-structured interviews with key actors involved in the events

---

1   An earlier version of this chapter was prepared for 'HIV among Drug Users in Poland: The Paradoxes of an Epidemic', a dissertation submitted in partial fulfilment of the requirements for the degree of Doctor of Public Health in Columbia University's School of Public Health, 2013.

including interviews with city and national officials currently responsible for drug and HIV policy, current and past legislators engaged in health-related issues, advocates in the area of drug policy and HIV, as well as drug treatment providers.

Secondary sources include extensive historical and contemporary documentation related to HIV and drug policies including scholarly literature, 'grey' literature, international reports, as well as official documents of the National AIDS Centre, the National Drug Prevention Programme, and numerous NGOs. The internal reports of the government entities responsible for drugs and HIV, their annual reports and parliamentary records, were essential to establishing how policies were developed and implemented. They demonstrate, for example, how various officials responded to public perceptions of drug use, as well as how they assessed their progress in the provision of services, and HIV and drug prevention efforts. At the same time, I observed that some reports were highly political which can be seen when comparing the highly edited published accounts of meetings with the verbal reports of the participants. The documents of international organisations such as the United Nations Office on Drugs and Crime (UNODC), the Joint United Nations Programme on HIV/AIDS (UNAIDS), and the European Monitoring Centre for Drugs and Drug Addiction (EMCDDA), as well as professional journals, serve as important forums for the publication and discussion of standards for policy making in the areas of drugs and HIV and assessment of practice in the area of service provision. *Alkoholizm and Narkomania* is the only Polish journal in which the practice of drug treatment is discussed. The scarcity of peer-reviewed literature indigenous to Poland poses a serious limitation to any work specific to drugs and HIV in Poland. I relied on international publications for policy-related, peer-reviewed articles. Collecting and analysing publications, websites, listserves, records, and archives of non-governmental organisations (NGOs) that engage in HIV and drugs policy debates allowed me to understand their priorities and also the institutional relationships they had with each other and various other actors. This also enabled me to see how the NGOs understood the social and political context. The NGOs include the Social AIDS Committee, the Polish Drug Policy Network, MONAR, and JUMP. Modest archives consisting of a few rows of documentation shed light on the historical context in which drug use and HIV emerged in Poland.

Drug use in Poland

To say that the Second World War was violent and traumatic for Poland would be an understatement of vast proportions. The subsequent reconstruction of the devastated nation, followed by the establishment of a socialist regime, left almost no record of drug use. It is not until the late 1950s and early 1960s that there is increased mention of reliance on medications for relaxation and anxiety alleviation. There is also some suggestion that physicians were quite liberal in prescribing tranquillisers, pain medicines and benzodiazepines (Frieske and Sobierch, 1987).

The late 1960s and early 1970s brought noticeable shifts in the use of drugs. In the mid-1950s, Poland made slight gestures opening up to the West; western radio stations were no longer jammed, and western film and theatre were available to the Polish public. Historian Tom Junes wrote: 'During the 1960s, an influential conveyor of Western youth culture was rock music ... The Polish regime did not prohibit Western music, but rather passively tolerated it since it was thought that it served as a distraction and kept the younger generation from engaging in political activity' (Junes, 2015). Rock bands such as the Animals and the Rolling Stones toured Poland: 'The sheer fact that these provocative icons of western youth culture visited and played in a supposedly disciplined socialist state had a shocking impact' (Junes, 2015). Although it is difficult to pinpoint how a movement expands transnationally, one can assume that these cultural influences were, at least in part, responsible for the arrival in Poland of Western, anti-establishment social movements of the 1960s, protesting for peace, social justice and personal freedoms. The use of illicit substances, for some, became a ritual that bonded the young and freedom-seeking in an increasingly oppressive society. Additionally, since heavy alcohol use had been a serious problem, associated with violence as well as intellectual and emotional impairment, it has been suggested that illicit substances became, for youth, a way to distinguish themselves from previous generations (Fatyga and Rogala-Oblekowska, 2002). However, drug use was not exclusive to the hippie movement. Drug use, as is the case around the world, is motivated by a variety of environmental, developmental and social factors (Tatarsky, 2007; Reuter, 2010; Drucker et al., 2011). In Poland, there were several social groups whose experimentation with illicit substances was not at all inspired by ideological motives. The most common explanations for drug use were difficulties in the family, at school and efforts to avoid mandatory military service (Frieske and Sobierch, 1987).

In the absence of cannabis and LSD, at the time unattainable in the socialist block, the quest for psychoactive substances led users to pharmaceutical and chemical products. It was discovered that TRI (a stain-removing compound) caused euphoria and hallucinations when inhaled, as did various other mixtures of pharmaceuticals. As the 1970s progressed, locally grown poppy attracted the interest of those experimenting with psychoactive substances. Gradually, products derived from the more widely available poppy replaced experimentation with various chemicals and pharmaceuticals. Poppy-based products included 'milk' (*mleczko*), extracted from unripe poppy heads or 'soup' (*makiwara*) produced by cooking poppy straw and, the most potent of all, *kompot*, also known as 'Polish heroin'. Competently prepared kompot could contain up to 80% morphine. By the end of the 1970s, 90% of patients hospitalised for drug dependence were there because of their use of kompot.

In the 1970s law enforcement reports on drug use began to increase. In 1973 the police reported, for the first time, 528 cases of group drug consumption (an illicit activity under Polish law). In 1970 only eight people were reported to have distributed illicit substances; in 1973 this number went up to 539. In 1968 a total of 14 drug-related offences were reported in all of Poland; by 1973 this number had risen to 819. In the first half of the 1970s media and professional publications expressed concern over growing drug use.

In the waning years of communist rule the visibility of drug use was contingent on the leadership's explicit political goals. When the political system was showcasing Poland as a successful, socialist state, drug users were hidden in psychiatric institutions and portrayed as anomalies of a 'happy, successful society'. Later, as Western influence over Poland increased images of drug users were brought out of the shadows as proof of the decadent and decaying Western way of life. Because of the political agenda driving the level of visibility of drug use, the data from this period is inconsistent and questionable.

In the mid-1970s, there was a sharp decrease in media coverage as well as in public and professional interest in drug use. Therefore, it is difficult to understand the unfolding of the next phase of the history of drug use in Poland. The only consistent reports are from the *milicja* (the national police force), which continued to reflect an increase in drug use. Half of the 2,300 recorded drug crimes committed in 1977 were identified as 'group drug use'. The police increasingly harassed drug users, especially those who were visibly identifiable as part of the hippie culture. Their views, often aligned with, and inspired by, the freedom movement of the West, were considered unpatriotic and a threat to the socialist state. Repression of the hippie movement escalated to the point where some were considered enemies of the socialist state. In response to the crackdown, larger drug-using communities began to fracture into much smaller, harder to identify, groups. The process of kompot production, in individual apartments and for small groups, facilitated this trend. By the end of the 1970s a problem that had once been visible and openly discussed was relegated to the shadows.

It was not until the summer of 1980 with the biggest political protests in Poland since the war and the emergence of the Solidarity movement, that a wave of media interest in drug use re-emerged. In a personal interview, one advocate recalled: 'I remember the summer of 1980 – people felt defiant, free. They travelled to summer music festivals in groups and once you arrived, the smell of cooking kompot was overwhelming. The police did nothing. Only later it became clear that their lack of action was intentional. The government needed proof that things are deteriorating and that a crackdown was justified. We were just one small piece of a huge puzzle.' In 1981 alone, the first year of martial law, 300 articles on drug use were published in the popular press (Frieske and Sobierch, 1987). While the scientific community estimated that approximately 20,000 people used kompot, a number of press reports speculated that there could be anywhere between 100,000 and 500,000 users (Cekiera, 1998). The divergent estimates in the media are now attributed to internal power struggles within the socialist party. The newly elected leadership depicted drug use as proof of the failure of their predecessors (Kuźmicz et al., 2009). Growing moral panic about drugs occurred a few more times and always seemed to have a political agenda.

As Poland gained independence in 1989 and opened up to the West, so did its illicit drug market. Various imported substances slowly replaced the native kompot. Native to the region for centuries, poppy cultivation without a government permit was made illegal in 1990 and a new, morphine-free species was introduced to enable farmers to continue poppy cultivation (Curtis, 1992). Over a decade later, in 2002, the first national survey was conducted to document the prevalence of drugs. The study documented several changes in the market for drugs, the most notable being that cannabis, unavailable during the socialist regime, had now become the substance of choice. The increasing trend of cannabis use, in which lifetime prevalence increased from 5% in 1992 to over 30% in 2005, is consistent with average rates of use throughout the rest of Europe. What is less clear, and requires further analysis, are the number of opiate users. Kompot and heroin users were not included in the 2009 National Report due to the marginal prevalence of both substances. However, in the same year, 16% of people in residential treatment were documented opiate users. The situation is further complicated by the fact that 63% of people in treatment fall into the 'combined and unspecified' category and an unknown portion of them are opiate users as well. The difficulty of understanding opiate use in Poland has been a problem for decades and is often the result of various political tensions and interests.

Drug policy setting institutions and expenditures

In Poland the two most significant institutions responsible for national drug policy, treatment and prevention are the National Bureau for Drug Prevention (created in 1993) and the Council for Counteracting Drug Addiction (created in 2001). In order to democratise, introduce capitalism, and join the well-established and bureaucratically developed European Union (EU), many of Poland's policies, tools and institutions simply copied those of Western Europe. However, this was done without having gone through the discussions, tensions and debates on which the West spent decades building consensus. A prominent sociologist, Jadwiga Staniszkis, termed this phenomenon an 'institutional mix' – a process by which various inspirations for institution-building are absorbed from external sources without proper reflection and integration (Staniszkis, 2004). Historically, this process of adaptation was very familiar to the Polish administration. For 45 years, during the socialist system, Polish bureaucracy received instructions from the Soviet Union and integrated policy directives directly into its political system, national policy and public life. The current integration process with the European Union, despite all its benefits, has left little room for Poland to discover its own way and no provisions have been made to generate reflection on this process. The process of adaptation can also be misleading to the casual observer. On paper, Poland's drug policy institutions appear strikingly similar to those of its Western neighbours. They have developed and implemented a national programme for counteracting drug dependence that addresses prevention (treatment, rehabilitation, harm reduction and social reintegration); supply reduction; international cooperation; as well as research and monitoring. However, in practice, a weak state and ineffective governance results in insufficient delivery of services, superficial discourse, and limited engagement of potential partners. This process of adaptation was strongly encouraged with substantial financial and moral backing by the United States and Europe (Hardy, 2010). It was important to Poland and its neighbours that it fit smoothly into the Western hemisphere, a goal which often took precedence over internal processes and debates.

The work of harm reduction in Poland has largely been driven by, and is the domain of, non-governmental organisations. Syringe-exchange programmes were first established in 1988–1989 following detection, in 1988, of the first HIV cases among drug users. The treatment NGO, MONAR, began syringe exchanges in its counselling centres and at drug users' public gathering points. As the number of HIV infections among drug users grew, needle and syringe exchange became a higher priority for a few programmes. Over time MONAR, in Krakow and in Warsaw, came under tremendous pressure from management and its board of directors to curtail harm reduction activities, harm-reduction being at odds with MONAR's treatment priority of abstinence. Harm-reduction programmes are now few and far between in Poland. In 2013 there were 13 needle-exchange programmes in 10 cities, a decline that does not correlate with the estimated number of injecting drug users. The National Drug Prevention Bureau reports that there is no clear evidence that the number of injecting drug users is falling; the classification used in medical statistics makes it impossible to determine the actual number of injecting users (2010 National Report).

The financing of various public health initiatives has undergone significant change. Of the funding for drug prevention efforts, 70% comes from local districts. While this is often portrayed as a success of decentralisation, and progress from the centralised Soviet system, many of the sources I examined show that prevention funding at the local level is part of a general pool that includes resources allocated for building soccer fields, after-school programmes and soup kitchens. Such methods for managing public spending often do not allow for more difficult issues, such as needle exchanges, to be debated or addressed, especially in smaller, predominantly Catholic, communities.

NGOs find it difficult to be critical of the local and national government since they receive funding from one or all of the responsible government entities; in a personal interview, one NGO staffer stated: 'It is inaccurate to call us NGOs – we are at the service of the government.'

Polish drug legislation

The first drug law in Poland, *The Act on Narcotic Substances and Preparations*, was adopted on 22 June 1923. As drug problems were not viewed as an issue at the time, the act served more to bolster Poland's position internationally because it implemented the provisions of the 1912 Opium Convention (EMCDDA, 2014). In the mid-1930s physicians and psychiatrists, increasingly aware of drug use, created the Polish Committee on Narcotics and Prevention of Narcotics Use, which promoted a medical approach to the issue. After the Second World War Poland's new communist government enacted the Control of Pharmacological, Psychoactive and Other Sanitary Items. Under the new law unauthorised production, trafficking and sale of drugs remained a criminal offence punishable by imprisonment and a fine. It criminalised drug use without a prescription and public drug use with a penalty of up to one year in prison. This article of criminal law remained in effect for several decades.

The first modern legislation fully dedicated to drug-related matters was adopted on 31 January 1985, at a time when the country was negotiating various political freedoms. The 1985 Law on the Prevention of Drug Abuse put Poland in the vanguard of progressive thinking about drugs in Europe because it did not penalise drug possession for personal use. Addiction was treated like an illness requiring medical treatment. The 1985 law penalised acts contributing to drug supply – cultivation, processing, trafficking, etc. This legislative framework was in place until 1997 and was not questioned during the first years of democracy. The Polish socialist government had a somewhat hostile relationship with the United States at the time so it is possible that Polish drug policy was deliberately in opposition to policies promoted internationally by the United States. While it is difficult to support this hypothesis with evidence, it is highly plausible considering the amalgam of severely strained economic and political relations with the United States.

As Poland changed its political and economic system in 1989, legislative changes followed. It is difficult to understand how external political interests influenced this process. The United States was the most significant and respected supporter of the Polish quest for democracy and the purging of socialism. In 1992 a United States-funded report criticised Polish drug law as antiquated: 'Drug use is not a crime in Czechoslovakia, Poland, and (as of December 1991) the Russian Federation. In Poland, penalties are not necessarily imposed for possession of large quantities of drugs' (Lee, 1992). The report further states: 'Incredibly, only about 30 full-time drug enforcement police patrol the entire country...' (Lee, 1992), and then observes: 'Not surprisingly, the authorities themselves exhibit a relatively relaxed attitude toward illicit drugs... Prosecutors, judges and even police regard this crime in the same category as petty theft' (Lee, 1992). The report expressed alarm over increasing drug use in the region, and the laws and relaxed attitudes which were significantly different from the War on Drugs-style rhetoric prevalent in the United States.

If there was a difference in the Polish approach to drug policy compared to that of its Western European neighbours, it would be in the concept of drug users' rights. This debate, taking place in Western Europe, was not a part of the Polish discourse. Rather, the socialist state viewed people who used drugs as infirm and requiring the care of the state apparatus. It may be that this crucial difference in viewpoint is responsible for the ease with which drug policy shifted and drug use was criminalised only a few years later, without regard for lessons learned from previous practice. Even though the legal penalties were not focused on users, in practice many were absorbed into the criminal justice system. Since production and distribution were considered felonies and most opiate use was the homemade poppy-brew kompot, ongoing harassment by the police and the resulting criminal charges were a reality of drug users' lives. Given this policy context, high levels of discrimination against drug users, and those living with HIV in particular, are not surprising.

In 1997 Poland began the process of negotiations for accession to the European Union with a referendum in which 72% of Poles voted in favour of joining the EU (Stulik, 1998). In 1999 Poland joined the North Atlantic Treaty Organization (NATO). Drug law came under scrutiny and in April 1997 new legislation was adopted bringing with it significant changes. The 1985 law had focused on production and sales, but did not comment on possession of illicit substances. Parliamentary debate on the new act took a moralistic tone as many were concerned that the law was too permissive. The vote was almost split in half, with a small margin in favour of continued decriminalisation. Though the 1997 Drug Abuse Prevention Act made possession for personal use illegal, a compromise was reached by introducing Paragraph 48, Article 4 which suspended criminal penalties for personal use possession. Since the amount considered 'personal use' was left undefined, each case was assessed at the court's discretion. In practice, the police and the prosecutor's office avoided prosecuting petty consumers, and the courts were reluctant to punish them.

With a noticeable shift towards the political right, only three years later new legislation was proposed. In October of 2000 the non-punitive nature of the Polish drug law was rolled back when Article 62 introduced criminal charges for possession of any amount of illicit substance. Three options for punishment were instated: the first (and most favoured) was incarceration for up to three years; the second was incarceration for six months to eight years for cases involving considerable quantities of drugs; and the third was a 'privileged' penalty that included a fine, the limitation of liberty, or incarceration for up to one year in cases of 'lesser gravity' (Kuźmicz, 2010).

This change greatly increased the influence of law enforcement. Since 2000 Poland has had one of the most restrictive anti-drug laws in Europe, punishing possession of any amount of illegal substance. The police were given unfettered power to conduct body searches (even for trivial reasons) and to raid homes on suspicion of a drug offence. The number of drug users entering the criminal justice system and being charged with personal possession has risen significantly each year since 2000 and are presented in Figure 10.1.

The first study summarising the impact of the amendment of 2000 criminalising personal possession was conducted by Dr Krzysztof Krajewski, a professor of law at the prestigious Jagiellonian University in Krakow. It showed a substantive increase in arrests for drug possession. In 2000 less than 3,000 people were arrested for drug possession but by 2001 this number had more than doubled. In 2004 the number exceeded 25,000 and in 2006 it had risen to over 30,000.

In addition to showing a dramatic increase in the number of arrests for drug possession after the introduction of the 2000 law, the study pointed out that 56%

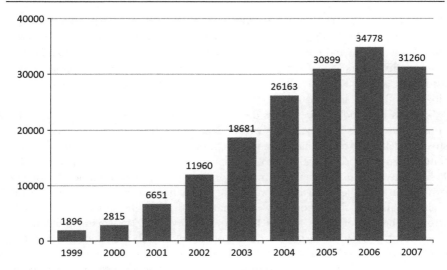

Figure 10.1 Drug possession arrests in Poland, 1999–2007
Source: Krajewski, 2009

of those possessing cannabis and 60% of those with amphetamines had less than 1 gram of the illicit substance. In less than 5% of the cases was possession more than 20 grams, an amount typically held by a dealer. Krajewski's research also showed that 60% of drug arrests were the result of routine patrols at the gathering places of young people, whereas only 20% were the result of specialised police investigations targeting drug dealers.

In the limited public discussion that immediately followed the changed drug law of 2000 two reasons were given for toughening legislation. First, it was argued that criminalising possession would help reduce drug trafficking because personal possession allowances made it more difficult for law enforcement to discern between drug dealers with small amounts of an illicit substance from personal use possession. Further, it was assumed that criminalising personal possession would be a criminal deterrent for young people. Nine years later the Institute of Public Affairs tested both of these assumptions. Almost half (48%) of surveyed police officers and 60% of prosecutors did not find criminalising personal possession to be an effective tool in apprehending drug traffickers. Similarly, as many as 66% of prosecutors, 58% of probation officers, 46% of judges, and 51% of police officers did not think that criminalising personal possession deterred potential drugs users either (Kuźmicz, 2010).

The legislative change in Poland occurred at a time when the political right was gaining strength and the future President, Lech Kaczynski, was emerging with his conservative law-and-order discourse. Tension between the ruling party and the political right rapidly gaining popularity was increasing. It appears that the left sacrificed on an issue that was less important to them to appease the increasingly powerful right. It is worth noting that Aleksander Kwaśniewski,

President of Poland from 1995 to 2005, enjoyed a strong relationship with the United States, which supported Poland's entry into NATO. Drug use, previously considered a social and medical issue, was re-framed as a problem of law and order in which drug users were viewed as criminals, social outcasts, threats to public safety, associates of the Russian Mafia and perpetrators ready to attack law-abiding citizens with HIV infected needles.

Though drug policy discussions did not use overtly religious language and the church did not visibly participate in the debate, the presence of the church was strongly felt. It greatly influenced perceptions of how illicit substances affect human dignity, and contributed to the conceptualisation of the ideal post-socialist Polish citizen as an independent, morally strong actor, responsible for his or her own destiny. In the first case, it was argued that human dignity is based on the ability to make a distinction between what is morally right and what is morally wrong. The use of drugs at best blurs this ability, and, at worst, annihilates it completely. 'Blessed sobriety' is a phrase often used by church leaders when they publicly engage in discussions of substance use. In the second instance, drug users were categorised into a larger group labelled *Homo-Sovieticus*, a term recognised in contemporary Russian psychology and popularised in Poland by one of the most significant and progressive figures in the Polish Church, Professor Tishner. Homo-Sovieticus is a person so stuck in the past and in the Soviet mentality that they are unable/unwilling to assume individual responsibility for their own existence, and remain forever dependent on the paternalistic Soviet apparatus. According to Cockerham et al. (2002), they are of a collectivist orientation and support the notion of socialist heritage. Both of these church-promoted notions were present in public debates about drug policy. As politics in Poland shifted to the right and aligned more closely with the church, the discussion over who does and does not deserve state-funded care became more dominant, as did the rhetoric of blaming the individual for their health outcomes. Having Polish citizenship was no longer sufficient qualification for state-funded public health measures or access to health care; in the new paradigm, one had to be morally deserving as well.

The process of political transformation in Poland can be divided into two periods starting from the early 1980s. The early years can be characterised as pro-democracy and liberal-leaning. There was a relatively transparent set of goals put forward by leaders with long political histories and wide recognition who were generally respected. The second phase was characterised by populist appeals that drove public debate. Paradoxically, integration with the European Union created space for a nationalistic discourse that reflected back on Poland's difficult history under German and Soviet occupation (Fundacja Batorego, 2010).

After the introduction of the punitive drug law in 2000, harm-reduction programmes began reporting problems with uptake. Drug users were reluctant to access services, concerned that this would implicate them in illegal activity. User behaviour in Poland is consistent with international literature suggesting that criminalising personal drug use deters users from seeking health services (Beyrer et al., 2010; Jelsma, 2009; Sarang et al., 2013). Fear of police intervention also circumscribed drug use networks making it harder to locate gathering points and more difficult for outreach workers to engage with these groups.

In 2005, a year after Poland joined the European Union, Health Minister Marek Balicki attempted to undo the 2000 amendment, in part out of concern for the difficulties faced by harm-reduction programmes. Minister Balicki's effort failed in parliament. In an increasingly conservative climate attempts to liberalise legislation related to personal possession of illicit substances was met with significant resistance by both conservative and liberal parties. Interestingly, most of the drug-treatment providers did not support Balicki's plea. They claimed that the 2000 amendment to the drug law had no influence on the reduced number of users seeking access to harm-reduction services and that this was purely a reflection of a decreasing number of injecting drug users (MONAR, 2009).

The police argue that criminalising possession improves police effectiveness in combating the illicit drug industry, but do not provide any hard data to support this assertion. Along with production, trafficking, distribution and transportation, the possession of illicit substances continues to be criminalised. The production, trafficking, purchase and possession of all equipment used for drug production is also illegal. In addition, liabilities are imposed on the owners and managers of various establishments to report distribution or trafficking of forbidden substances. The police remain unrestricted in their right to conduct body searches, as well as searches of a person's place of residence. The Institute of Public Affairs published an analysis of police data from 2008 showing that only 4% of drug offences were due to possession of a significant amount of an illicit substance (Kuźmicz et al., 2009). Krajewski's data has shown that lawyers have assisted 24% of defendants while 76% of defendants accepted prosecutorial plea bargains without legal assistance, having been told that pleading guilty on the spot would greatly speed the judicial process and improve their chances of a reduced sentence. However, once the defendant pleads guilty there is little opportunity later to recant their plea. For these reasons, the system is skewed to the police and judicial system, and, as a result, thousands of young people enter adulthood with criminal records.

Shaping Poland's current drug policy

It was clear that any shifts in drug policy would not be easy. In 2008, the Jagiellonian University impact study inspired then-Minister of Justice Zbigniew Cwiakalski to establish a multidisciplinary committee that would suggest changes to the drug law. Professor Krajewski was appointed to chair the committee. In mid-2009 this multidisciplinary committee presented its recommendations. Reflecting the conservative political climate in the country at the time, its suggestions for change were cautious.

A year after the Commission made its recommendations and debate began, Andrzej Czuma was appointed as the new Minister of Justice. Czuma is a lawyer who has spent a significant part of his career in the United States, and who was best known for his lobbying efforts to relax gun laws in Poland. While maintaining the view that the law needs to change, in his proposal charges against the accused would only be lifted if the detainee disclosed information about their supplier. This iteration caused significant discussion on both sides of the debate. One of the leading progressive journalists in Poland expressed concern: 'Current Polish drug law sends to prison young people caught with small amounts of drugs. It is absurd and it should be changed. The trouble with the current proposal is that it proposes to substitute one absurdity with another; the possibility of dropping the charges if a person who is caught reveals the source of the drug. Small dealers are usually part of larger underground structures. Will the state be able to ensure the safety of the people who gave out the name of a dealer?' (Żakowski, 2009).

In December 2010 draft legislation made its way to the Parliamentary Committee on Human Rights and Justice where it was attacked by the conservative party *Prawo i Sprawiedliwość* or PiS (Law and Justice), as well as the Chief Prosecutor whose office had been integral to the long negotiating process. The newspaper *Gazeta Wyborcza* suggested that the change in attitude by the prosecutor's office might be the result of internal discussions on the increased time required of prosecutors on each drug-related case (Siedlecka, 2011). The majority party, *Platforma Obywatelskam* or PO (Civic Platform), was fully represented at the next committee meeting and the draft proposal made its way out of committee and onto the list of projects awaiting parliamentary vote. The *Sejm*, Poland's lower House of Parliament, which is composed of 460 deputies elected by proportional representation, voted to adopt the new drug legislation on 1 April 2011. The Senate, or upper house, voted in favour of the legislation on 28 April, and President Komorowski signed it into law at the end of May 2011 (Harm Reduction International, 2012).

The new legislation, Article 62a, grants the prosecution and the courts discretionary authority over criminal proceedings against persons in possession of small amounts of illicit substances for personal use. The amendment, while limited in scope, may have been successful for a few reasons. First, the data showing the criminological consequences of the 2000 law was produced by a leading Polish university and embraced by the Minister of Justice (who had himself been appointed by the ruling party and had a strong relationship with the Jagiellonian University and the study's author). Around the same time, international funding was made available to a few, newly founded advocacy groups including the Polish Drug Policy Network. The PDPN established important relationships with the media, participated in parliamentary expert groups, and was generally very visible. The more liberal media covered the Polish debate, and also increased coverage of the discussion internationally in support of the Polish argument for liberalisation. A bolder amendment may not have passed the legislature. Since the proposal was originally made by the ruling party, *Platforma Obywatelska*, it stood by this very minor change during the parliamentary vote. With relatively broad support from the liberal media, it would have found itself in a complicated position if it had voted against its own proposal.

In 2014, three years later, the Helsinki Foundation for Human Rights (HFHR) released a report on the impact of Article 62a. The report found that

Polish drug policy 161

while the amendment was a step in the right direction, it has yet to be fully implemented across Poland; too few cases are dismissed using the provisions introduced in the amendment (Kubaszewski, 2014). According to the HFHR report:

> The amendments to the Act were designed to facilitate discontinuation of criminal proceedings by prosecutors just after the person carrying a minor amount of drugs is detained. In this respect, however, the Police have not changed their conduct because, according to Article 62a, it is the prosecutor and the court that may discontinue the proceedings, not the police. A person carrying drugs can therefore be detained and the premises where he/she lives can be searched without warrant, i.e. just with the "flash of the badge"... [S]uch a search without warrant is subsequently pronounced legit by the prosecution service. The idea alone of searching the perpetrators' premises based on Article 62 of the Act on Prevention of Drug Abuse, justified as the necessary inquiries as defined by Article 308 of the Code of Criminal Procedure seems to be dubious (Kubaszewski, 2014).

According to Ministry of Justice data, Article 62a was applied in 2,305 cases in 2012. However, data from the General Prosecutor's Office also show a wide variation in the application of the Article throughout the country. The Poznań region (Western Poland) saw 496 dismissals based on Article 62a, compared with 195 in the Warsaw region (the capital), and only 11 in the Rzeszów region (South Eastern Poland) (Kubaszewski, 2014). 'In light of this data,' commented Dr Adam Bodnar, HFHR's Vice President, 'we must consider whether the current shape of the Act is effective and appropriate and whether we should not contemplate introduction of a new Act which would comprehensively regulate the issues related to prevention of drug abuse' (Kubaszewski, 2014).

The history of drug policy in Poland suggests that creating policy and putting drug policy into practice occurs in a highly politicised context, and as a result, is somewhat unpredictable. The most recent policy change is consistent with the literature suggesting that evidence-based research is used by policymakers when researchers engage with them directly. It was the criminal justice study by Professor Krajewski which inspired the Ministry of Justice to take action. Also persuasive in prompting the change that led to Article 62a were numerous letters and other advocacy efforts by civil society, bolstered by various forms of support from the increasingly vocal drug-policy-reform international community and outreach from the popular and academic media.

References

BEYRER, C., MALINOWSKA-SEMPRUCH, K., KAMARULZAMAN, A., KAZATCH-KINEM., SIDIBEM. and STRATHDEE, S. (2010) Time to Act: a Call for Comprehensive Responses to HIV in People who use Drugs. *The Lancet.* 376(9740). pp. 551–563.

CEKIERA, C. (1998) *Psychoprofilaktyka uzależnień oraz terapia i resocjalizacja osób uzależnionych; metody, programy, modele, zakłady, wspólnoty*, Lublin: Towarzystwo Naukowe KUL.

COCKERHAM, W. C., SNEAD, M. C. and DEWAAL, D. F. (2002) Health Lifestyles in Russia and the Socialist Heritage. *Journal of Health and Social Behavior*. Mar; 43(1). pp. 42–55.

CURTIS, E. G. (ed.) (1992) *Poland: A Country Study*. Washington: GPO for the Library of Congress. Available from: http://countrystudies.us/poland/45.htm [Accessed: 1 July 2012].

DRUCKER, E., NEWMAN, G. R., NADELMANN, E., WODAK, A., WOLFE, D., MARSH, D. C., OSCAPELLA, E., MCNEELY, J., YA, Y., MALINOWSKA-SEMPRUCH, K. (2011) Harm Reduction: New Drug Policies and Practices. In Lowinson, P. and Ruiz, S. (eds.). *Substance Abuse: A Comprehensive Textbook*. Philadelphia: Lippincott Williams and Wilkins.

EMCDDA (2009) *National Report 2009: Poland*. Available from; http://www.emcdda.europa.eu/html.cfm/index142788EN.html [Accessed: 1 July 2012].

EMCDDA (2014) *Drug Policy Profile: Poland*. Available from: http://www.emcdda.europa.eu/publications/emcdda-papers/policy-profile-poland [Accessed: 18 June 2012].

FATYGA, B. and ROGALA-OBLEKOWSKA, J. (2002) *Style zycia mlodziezy a narkotyki; Wyniki badan empirycznych*. Warsaw: Instytut Spraw Publicznych.

FRIESKE, K. and SOBIERCH, R. (1987) *Narkomania interpretacja problemu spolecznego*. Poland: Instytut Wydawniczy Zwiazkow Zawodowych.

FUNDACJA BATOREGO (2010) *Pytania 20-lecia, 1989–2009*. Warsaw: Fundacja im. Stefana Batorego.

HARDY, J. (2010) *Nowy polski kapitalizm*. Warsaw: Instytyt Wydawniczy Ksiazka i Prasa.

HARM REDUCTION INTERNATIONAL (HRI) (2012) *Global State of Harm Reduction Report 2012*. London: Harm Reduction International.

JELSMA, M. (2009) *Legislative Innovation in Drug Policy, Latin American Initiative on Drug Policy*. Amsterdam: Transnational Institute.

JUNES, T. (2015) *Student Politics in Communist Poland: generations of consent and dissent*. Lanham, MD: The Rowman and Littlefield Publishing Group, Inc.

KRAJEWSKI, K. (2009) Drug Possession Cases in Courts in Krakow. Paper presented at Connections Conference, Krakow, March 26. Available from: http://www.connectionsproject.eu/conference2009/presentations-downloads/cat_view/26-1st-connection s-conference/38-thursday-26-march-plenary-2 [Accessed: 1 July 2012].

KUBASZEWSKI, P. (2014) *Nowelizacja ustawy o przeciwdziałaniu narkomanii w trzy lata po jej wejściu w życie – raport z praktyki stosowania*. Helsinki: Helsinki Foundation for Human Rights.

KUŹMICZ, E., MIELECKA-KUBIEŃ, Z. and WISZEJKO-WIERZBICKA, D. (2009) *Karanie za posiadanie. Artykuł 62 ustawy o przeciwdziałaniu narkomanii – koszty czas, opinie*. Warsaw: Instytut Spraw Publicznych. Available from: http://www.archiwum.isp.org.pl/publikacja/79/341/karanie-za-posiadanie-artykul-62-ustawy-o-przeciwdzialaniu-narkomanii—koszty-czas-opinie [Accessed: 1 July 2012].

KUŹMICZ, E. (2010) *Drug Policy in Poland: Time for a Change*. Warsaw: Institute for Public Affairs.

LEE, R. (1992) *Drugs in Post-Communist Societies*. Washington, D.C.: The National Council for Soviet and East European Research, pp. 5–7.

MONAR (2009). *Sprawozdanie Merytoryczne*. Available from: http://www.monar.org/czytelnia/raporty-i-sprawozdania [Accessed: 1 July 2012].

REUTER, P. (ed.) (2010) *Understanding the Demand for Illegal Drugs*. Washington, D.C.: The National Academies Press.

SARANG, A., RHODES, T. and SHEON, N. (2013) Systemic Barriers Accessing HIV Treatment Among People who Inject Drugs in Russia: A Qualitative Study. *Health Policy and Planning*. 28(7). pp. 681–691.

SIEDLECKA, E. (2011) Co z dyspensą za skręta?*Gazeta Wyborcza*, January 11, p. 4.

STANISZKIS, J. (2004) *Wladza globalizacji*. Warsaw: Wydawnictwo Naukowe Scholar.

STULIK, D. (1998) European Integration in Poland and Czech Republic. In Dornisch, D., Elvins, P. and Kania, R. (eds.) *Post-Communist Transformations*, Warsaw: IFiS Publishing. pp. 39–75.

TATARSKY, A. (2007) *Redukcja szkód w psychoterapii. Nowe podejście w leczeniu uzależnień od narkotyków i alkoholu*. Warsaw: Krajowe Biuro ds. Przeciwdziałania Narkomanii.

ŻAKOWSKI, J. (2009) Druga strona medalu. *Gazeta Wyborcza*, November 30. p. 3.

Chapter 11

Portuguese drug policy

Caitlin Hughes[1]

Introduction

On 1 July 2001 Portugal decriminalised the use, possession and acquisition of all illicit drugs. The law reform, which took place as part of a comprehensive shift towards a public-health-oriented approach to illicit drugs in Portugal, has received an unprecedented level of attention from media, advocates, policy makers and researchers across the globe. Indeed, fifteen years post-reform, Portugal continues to receive almost monthly visits from interested outsiders (Goulão, 2015). Many accounts and analyses of the reform impacts have been given (Domoslawski, Siemaszko and Człowieka, 2011; Gonçalves, Lourenço and da Silva, 2015; Greenwald, 2009; Hawkes, 2011; Hughes and Stevens, 2012; Hughes and Stevens, 2010; Laqueur, 2015; Moreira, Trigueiros and Antunes, 2007; Murkin et al., 2014; Pinto Coelho, 2010; Sapp, 2014; Vale de Andrade and Carapinha, 2010; Woods, 2011). There are instances where evidence has been misused to give either an overly glowing or overly pessimistic account of the impacts of the Portuguese drug law reform (for an overview of the two most divergent accounts and misuse of the evidence see Hughes and Stevens, 2012). Nevertheless, within these two extremes it is clear that the reform has facilitated numerous positive developments. These include reductions in problematic drug use; reductions in drug-related overdose and HIV; reductions of the burden on the criminal justice system, particularly prisons; increases in access to drug treatment and reintegration services such as employment services (Hughes and Stevens, 2012; Hughes and Stevens, 2010); and reductions in the social costs of illicit drugs (Gonçalves et al., 2015). Reflecting this, the Portuguese reform has been cited by prominent groups including the World Health Organization (2014, p. 91) as evidence of the benefits of decriminalising all illicit drugs.

This chapter supplements these analyses by exploring the policy process that led to the 2001 Portuguese drug law reform. It examines the history of the drug law and policy, the current legal framework and drivers of reform. It concludes by

1 Acknowledgements: Sincere thanks to the key informants who took part in the research. The National Drug and Alcohol Research Centre at the University of New South Wales Australia is supported by funding from the Australian Government.

Portuguese drug policy 165

examining policy implications for other nations. To assist the reader, a timeline of key events leading to the Portuguese decriminalisation of illicit drugs covering the period 1926 to 2001 is provided in Table 11.1.

History of drug law and policy

Portuguese drug law and policy largely preceded the 1980s–1990s development of a 'drug problem'. The first drug law in Portugal was adopted in 1926 (Decree 12 210) (see Table 11.1), but it had a fiscal function: the sole purpose was to regulate trade and prevent taxation fraud (Agra, 2009). Consumption became a criminal offence in 1970. In 1983 Portugal incorporated components of the 1961 and 1971 United Nations Conventions, ratified by Portugal in 1971 and 1979, respectively, and increased penalties for drug trafficking. Criminal penalties for drug use were maintained, but provisions were added whereby punishment could be dropped for dependent drug users who sought treatment. Some commentators argued that, in practice, this increased the punishment of drug users (Rodrigues Almeida, 1997).

In 1993 Portugal adopted what has remained their main law on drug trafficking: Decree-Law 15/93. The law retained criminal penalties for drug use as well as trafficking and trafficking-consumption but stated that drug use was to be sanctioned in a quasi-symbolic manner: to encourage drug dependent users to seek treatment and to avoid marginalising occasional users. The maximum penalty for use, acquisition or possession was one year imprisonment.

Early Portuguese drug policy had two main emphases: law enforcement (supply reduction) and prevention (demand reduction). Portugal introduced their first national campaign against drugs in 1987: Projecto VIDA (Life Project). This sought to prevent drug use and encourage abstinence and healthy living (Resolução do Conselho de Ministros n.º 23/87, de 21 de Abril, 1987). Early approaches used shock tactics to warn youth of the dangers of drug use (Niza, 1998). Later iterations also included treatment and reintegration (Ministro da Juventude, 1989), albeit not until 1994 and 1995, respectively (Mendes, 1994), and the treatment centres remained oriented towards drug-free living (Comissão Parlamentar de Juventude, 1992).

The end of the 1990s, however, marked a significant shift in Portuguese drug policy. In May 1999, the first Portuguese drug strategy was adopted: National Strategy in the Fight Against Drugs (Estratégia Nacional de Luta Contra a Droga – ENLCD). The ENLCD was built on eight principles, including pragmatism and humanism (Resolução do Conselho de Ministros n.o 46/99 de 26 de Maio, 1999). Pragmatism recognised the need to abandon idealist goals of a drug-free society in favour of a public-health-oriented and evidence-informed approach. Humanism recognised the inalienable human rights of all citizens, including drug users, to healthcare, housing and social services and the need to abandon approaches – including criminalisation – that curtailed such rights. The new strategy comprised thirteen elements which included decriminalisation of the

Table 11.1 Timeline of key events leading to the Portuguese decriminalisation of illicit drugs

Date	Event
1926	First drug law adopted (Decree 12 210): prohibited drug trafficking but not use as a criminal offence
1970	New drug law (Decree-Law 420/70) criminalised illicit drug use, traffic and production
1973	First addiction treatment service opened: abstinence only First anti-drug campaign: 'Drugs-madness-death'
1974	Portugal emerged from dictatorship. New Constitution (1976) emphasised human rights and proportionality
1976	Minister for Justice Almeida Santos proposed to decriminalise illicit drug use
1983	Decree-Law 430/83 came into effect: incorporated 1961 and 1971 UN Conventions. Increased penalties for use but also provided option to suspend punishment if the offender accepted treatment
1987	First National Programme to Fight Against Drugs adopted – Projecto VIDA
1993	Decree-Law 15/93 proposed quasi-symbolic sanctions for drug use
1994	Drug Addiction Treatment and Prevention Service (SPTT) created. Director – José Castanheira
1995 (Oct)	Socialist Party (PS) elected after 10 years in opposition – PM António Guterres
1995 (Nov)	Parliamentary Committee created to evaluate drug trafficking and consumption. Ran until July 1999
1996 (Sep)	Law 45/96 – increased min and max penalties for drug trafficking
1997 (Jan)	D Day – drug abuse was declared 'public enemy number one'
1997 (Jan)	European Commission reported AIDS was stabilising except in Spain, Italy and Portugal.
1997 (Mar)	João Goulão replaced José Castanheira as head of SPTT (Drug Treatment Service)
1997 (Jun)	President Sampaio held debate: 'Drugs: context and new directions'
1997 (Oct)	Parliamentary President Almeida Santos proposed to depenalise drug use. Opposed by medical field
1997 (Nov)	José Sócrates became Adjunct Minister to the Prime Minister. Appointed Drug Strategy Coordinator
1998 (Feb)	José Sócrates stated that Casal Ventoso (open air drug market in central Lisbon) had become a central and symbolic problem in Portugal
1998 (Feb)	Alexandre Rosa became National Coordinator/High Commissioner of Projecto VIDA
1998 (Feb)	Sócrates established Commission for a National Drug Strategy (CNDS). Head: Alexander Quintanilha. Key members included João Goulão, Nuno Miguel and Luís Patrício
1998 (Mar)	Reports indicated Portugal had the highest rate of TB in the EU and extreme rate of AIDS

Portuguese drug policy 167

Table 11.1 (continued)

Date	Event
1998 (May)	Detailed plan for reconversion of open air drug market Casal Ventoso approved
1998 (Jun)	First low threshold methadone programmes started in Portugal in Casal Ventoso
1998 (Oct)	CNDS completed report: recommended decriminalisation and other options
1999 (May)	National Strategy in the Fight Against Drugs (ENLCD) approved – with option to decriminalise illicit drugs
1999 (Oct)	Socialist Party re-elected. New Drugs Strategy Coordinator appointed: Vitalino Canas
1999 (Nov)	EMCDDA Annual Report: Portugal had 2nd highest incidence of AIDS
2000 (Feb)	INCB 1999 Annual Report criticised Portugal for proposal to decriminalise illicit drug use
2000 (May–Jun)	Political contestation over decriminalisation: Left Block – proposed to legalise cannabis People's Party (CDS-PP) called for a referendum on decriminalisation and Social Democratic Party (PSD) members proposed decriminalisation with CDTs Decriminalisation debated in Parliament on 21 June 2000 – requested that the President hold a public referendum (not held) CDS-PP issued a motion of censure for failure to hold referendum
2000 (Jul)	President Sampaio used open presidency to call for an end to the political games about drugs
2000 (Oct)	EMCDDA Annual Report: Portugal had highest drug-related AIDS in the EU
2000 (Sep)	INCB delegation visited Portugal to hear about new drug law reform model
2000 (Nov)	Law 30/2000 adopted – decriminalised possession and consumption of all illicit drugs
2001 (Jul)	Decriminalisation of illicit drugs commenced

acquisition, possession and use of all illicit drugs when deemed for personal use. Other strategy elements included guaranteed access to drug treatment; promotion of social reintegration (including subsidies for employers hiring drug-dependent individuals); and expanded harm reduction services (including free hepatitis B vaccinations, shelters, and pill testing programmes) (Moreira et al., 2011; Moreira et al., 2007). The strategy was supported by €160 million in funding, an implementation plan (Governo de Portugal, 2001) and new laws, including Law 30/2000 which put decriminalisation into practice.

Two further strategies have since been adopted. The most recent is the National Plan for the Reduction of Addictive Behaviours and Dependencies

2013–2020 (Serviço de Intervenção nos Comportamentos Aditivos e nas Dependências, 2013) which addresses gambling and internet addiction as well as illicit drug use, but retains similar core principles and a strong public-health approach.

Existing legal framework

The current legal framework addressing drugs in Portugal consists of three main laws: Law 30/2000, Decree-Law 15/93 and Decree Law 54/2013. Under Law 30/2000, since 1 July 2001 the use, possession and acquisition of *all* illicit drugs – including cannabis, heroin, amphetamines, cocaine and ecstasy – when deemed for personal use, are an administrative, rather than criminal, offence.

A new administrative system is used to respond to drug users: Commissions for the Dissuasion of Drug Addiction (CDTs). The CDTs are regional panels comprised of a treatment professional, social worker and lawyer. They are connected with a broader network of agencies, including drug treatment, primary care, mental health, schools, employment, social services and child protection (EMCDDA, 2015). There is one CDT for each of the 18 regions of continental Portugal and three in the autonomous archipelago of the Azores.

Since 1 July 2001 any drug user who is detected by the police (without evidence or reasonable suspicion of involvement in drug trafficking) has their drugs weighed. If their drugs are below a threshold of 10 days' worth of drugs – defined, according to Portaria 94/96, as 1 gram of heroin or MDMA, 2 grams of cocaine, and 25 grams of cannabis – the drugs are seized and they are referred to their local CDT. The CDTs conduct an interview with referred offenders to explore patterns and history of drug use (in particular to determine whether someone is an occasional or dependent user), and where relevant, mental health history, and motivation for entering drug treatment. They also assess whether there are any social issues that can addressed, such as school, employment or housing (and refer those affected to the relevant support agencies). The CDTs then decide on an appropriate ruling or sanction. They have a range of possible sanctions including warnings, community service, suspended sentence, bans on obtaining a firearms licence and fines (though not for dependent users). For dependent users the principal goal is to refer people to drug treatment services.

In practice, most offenders are deemed non-dependent and receive a suspended sentence. In 2013 the CDTs completed 7,528 rulings and the majority of rulings (70%) involved suspended sentences for non-dependent users (EMCDDA, 2015). A further 12% of rulings involved suspended sentences with a referral to treatment for dependent users, and 11% were 'punitive', of which 8% required periodic attendance at a specified site e.g. an employment service (EMCDDA, 2015).

Under Decree-Law 15/93 trafficking-consumption, trafficking, manufacturing and cultivation of illicit drugs continue to be criminal offences sanctionable with up to three years of prison (trafficking-consumption); 1–5 years of prison (minor trafficking); or 4–12 years of prison (major trafficking). Users found in possession of more than 10 daily doses can also be sanctioned for a criminal drug possession offence (of up to 1 year in prison). In practice most people convicted or imprisoned under Portuguese drug law are traffickers. In 2013 there were 1,779 individuals convicted: 79% (n=1,398) for trafficking; 1% (n=18) for trafficking-consumption and 20% (n=353) for possession (EMCDDA, 2015). Moreover, of those imprisoned in 2013, 89% were imprisoned for major drug-trafficking offences and 10% for minor drug-trafficking offences.

The final law, Decree Law 54/2013, was adopted in April 2013 to provide a framework for new psychoactive substances (NPS). This prohibits the production, export, advertisement, distribution, sale or simple dispensing of NPS which are administrative offences. Sanctions include fines of up to €45,000, or closure of premises. In line with Law 30/2000, the use and possession of NPS has been decriminalised and anyone detected is referred to a CDT.

Drivers of change

A number of different accounts have emerged about the drivers of the change with regard to Portuguese drug law and broader policy. The first account sees this as a rational response to a rapidly increasing public-health crisis – involving intravenous use of heroin, growing rates of HIV, AIDS and other infectious diseases – as well as a government decision to enact an elite commission of experts to advise on an appropriate response and fully implement their recommendations (Vale de Andrade and Carapinha, 2010). The second account sees the reform as inevitable, the result of the 'ongoing tension between the criminalisation of drug use and the desire to help drug users': two decades of debates that culminated in the end of criminalisation (Moreira et al., 2011, p. 23).

A third and final account is based on accounts and interviews with stakeholders active in and around the reform (Hughes, 2006; Van Het Loo, Van Beusekom and Kahan, 2002). This account suggests that the other two narratives belie the complexity of the reform process. From this perspective, the reform was a consequence not only of a burgeoning drug problem or history, but also a unique set of events, interactions and compromises in the years preceding reform. This is reflected in a shift in the political system, and in the actions of stakeholders driving and shaping reform. This account is provided here, and highlights six factors: long-standing Portuguese values; the burgeoning drug problem; evidence and experts; policy actors and interest groups; politics; and the international conventions and community. The analysis draws upon face-to-face interviews conducted with 26 Portuguese key informants in 2004 (6 politicians, 5 health professionals, 5 criminal-justice officials, 6 researchers, 2 non-government actors from SOMA, a drug-law-reform group, and Abraço, an NGO supporting people with HIV/AIDS) about the process of reform. Secondary analysis relies on government documents, laws, media and academic research (for full details see Hughes, 2006).

Portuguese values and the constitutional and legal system

Portugal experienced military dictatorship until 1974. Post liberation, the Portuguese Constitution placed a strong emphasis on human rights and proportionality of punishment (see Table 11.1). For example, the 1976 Constitution guaranteed human rights and freedoms, including access to health care (Assembleia da República, 1976). Further, the Portuguese legal system used criminal law as a last resort: distinguishing between criminal acts, administrative acts, and contra-ventions (Machado, 1999). Thus, Portugal had a strong emphasis on rights and a long history of dealing with minor infractions outside of criminal law (one notable exception was abortion which was illegal until 2007, due in large part to the vocal opposition of the Catholic Church).

Equally important, there was (as noted by Moreira et al., 2011, p. 23) a long history of debate and tension in Portugal between criminalisation and helping drug users. Prominent people had supported drug law reform, including the then-Minister for Justice Almeida Santos in 1976 (Poiares, 2003). From 1983 onwards the drug law was used (in rhetoric, if not in practice) in a quasi-symbolic manner for drug users. This contributed to a long-standing view in Portugal that 'decri-minalisation (of drug use) should arrive one day, that it was a better strategy and policy' (Carlos Costa – Law Enforcement Officer).

Public health and the human rights crisis

The late 1990s saw, as noted by Vale de Andrade and Carapinha (2010), a bur-geoning public-health crisis surrounding illicit drug use. While Portugal had long been a gateway for drug trafficking into Europe (Institute for Drugs and Drug Addiction, 2008), it had historically low levels of illicit drug use: only an estimated 7.8% of the population aged 15–64 had ever used an illicit drug (Balsa et al., 2004). However, the drug context changed rapidly in the 1980s with a large rise in problematic drug use (particularly intravenous heroin) and harms. Rates of infectious diseases, including HIV, AIDS, tuberculosis, and hepatitis B and C soared, creating a public health crisis. Between 1990 and 1997, the overall number of drug users with AIDS increased from 47 to 590 and peaked at 635 in 1999 (Instituto da Droga e da Toxicodependência, 2004).

At the same time, the Portuguese drug problem shifted in other important ways. Open-air drug markets emerged in Portugal, the most infamous of which was Casal Ventoso, a slum located on the outskirts of the capital city of Lisbon (Chaves, 1999; Fugas, 2001), which developed into the biggest open-air drug market in Europe (Miguel, 1997). Casal Ventoso attracted up to 5,000 drug users daily in search of drugs and had extremely high rates of infectious diseases, homelessness and social marginalisation: 60% were HIV positive (Gabinete de Apoio ao Toxicodependente, 2003), and 74% HCV positive (Valle and Coutinho, 2001). Eight hundred dependent users lived permanently in the slum. Television and newspaper coverage about illicit drugs increased during 1997 and

1998; an almost daily coverage depicted Casal Ventoso's public health and humanitarian crisis.

This confluence of changes created a clear agenda-setting opportunity to address the drug problem. As summed up by one NGO worker 'the problem could no longer be ignored' (Maria José Campos – Member of AIDS NGO). This series of events, Casal Ventoso in particular, highlighted drugs as both a health and human rights issue, and provided a symbolic and emotive focusing event to re-frame the problem. As summed up by Rodrigo Coutinho, a drug treatment professional, it 'helped to change opinion about drug addiction', leading to a paradigmatic shift in which drug users were seen as citizens who were sick, not criminals (Chaves, 1999; Fugas, 2001).

Evidence and experts

Local research into the Portuguese drug problem also increased during the 1980s and 1990s. This was important as research was previously limited. For example, the first national survey of drug use was not conducted until 2001 (Balsa et al., 2004). The new research thus provided the first academic estimates of the size and nature of the drug problem (Miguel, 1997; Ribeiro, 1999). International research, particularly from the European Monitoring Centre for Drugs and Drug Addiction (established in 1994) further contextualised the scale of the problem: it showed that preceding reform, Portugal had the highest rates of drug-related HIV and AIDS in Europe (EMCDDA, 1998, 2000).

Equally important, in the mid- to late 1990s politicians established two expert bodies on drugs with a mandate to discuss policy alternatives. The first of these, a parliamentary committee from 1995 to 1999, concluded that drug use had spread throughout the country and that there were problems in all areas of Portuguese drug policy: prevention, treatment, reintegration and supply reduction (Niza, 1998). The second expert body, the Commission for a National Drug Strategy (CNDS), ran from February to October 1998 and comprised nine experts selected by the then-Drug Strategy Coordinator José Sócrates drawn from health, law enforcement and academia. Their final report also found systemic problems in Portuguese drug policy and called for the immediate cessation of the abstinence-oriented Projecto VIDA policy. It found that the Projecto VIDA policy was too ideological, that it promoted drug-free living rather than evidence-based ways to address harms and risk factors. Moreover, in spite of reformulations of the Projecto VIDA policy (in 1994 it sought to supplement prevention with treatment) it remained too narrow and focused on prevention and supply reduction: to the neglect of harm reduction and the legal framework in which drug policy operated. The CNDS outlined a new mandate, arguing that the optimal response was to decriminalise all illicit drug consumption and possession for personal use (recommendation 3.2.6), while significantly expanding harm reduction, prevention, and social and treatment responses (Comissão para a Estratégia Nacional de Combate à Droga, 1998). Importantly, they also showed that decriminalisation was evidence-informed and feasible. The CNDS showed that in spite of the 1993 drug law's stated intent of imposing 'quasi-symbolic sanctions', criminal convictions for drug users remained common, referrals to treatment rare, and courts continued to sanction many more users than traffickers. Criminalisation was thus deemed harmful, inefficient and incompatible with a public-health response to drug use. Moreover, the CNDS showed that decriminalisation was in line with the United Nations conventions whereby member states may waive criminalisation of possession for personal use if to do so would conflict with the 'constitutional principles and the basic concepts of its legal system' (Art. 3, United Nations Convention against Illicit Traffic in Narcotic Drugs and Psychotropic Substances of 1988), in this case, Portugal's emphasis upon criminal punishment as a last resort. Research and expertise thus served to quantify the scale of the drug problem, to highlight irrevocable flaws with past policies and to provide a feasible alternative: decriminalisation of illicit drugs.

Policy actors

In the lead-up to decriminalisation three key sectors played active roles in mobilising support for reform: criminal justice officials, political lobbying groups and health professionals.

Criminal justice officials

During the 1990s, Portuguese criminal justice officials became early supporters of reform. As noted by the head of the Criminal Police, José Braz, decriminalisation was not a controversial response to drug users: 'It is a good invention for the consumers.' Police and judges took the view that the criminal law *itself* was the problem. This was for three reasons. First, criminal law on drug possession was seen as a major drain on police resources, reducing capacity to confront the real challenge of transit: drug trafficking (Polícia Judiciária, 2000). Second, the law was seen as ineffective and incapable of halting the drug trade. Of particular concern, post-introduction of Decree Law 15/93, was the growing number of drug-related offenders within Portuguese prisons contributing to prison overcrowding (Polícia Judiciária, 2000) and a 'veritable marketplace of drugs' (Council of Europe, 2001). Thirdly, after years of applying criminal measures to the issue, the majority of the sector had shifted to viewing drug use as a health and social issue. As summed up by former Drug Strategy Coordinator, Vitalino Canas: 'Police and judges were saying it was no use to arrest these people, because they were not really criminals ... They required medical help.' Moreover, from 1997 this sector (a vital voice in the debate) became more vocal in their support for reform at conferences and public forums; in one example, the 1997 Conference of the Union Association of Portuguese Judges specifically advocated for the decriminalisation of drug consumption.

Political lobbying groups

Historically, Portugal lacked drug user organisations. The first drug user group (CASO – Consumidores Associados Sobrevivem Organizados) was not established until 2007, six years post-reform. As noted by Maria José Campos, Member of Abraço (a non-government organisation supporting people with AIDS/HIV), a long-term constraint upon reform was that 'we never had the (drug user) movements that you can find in England, Netherlands or even in France'. However, throughout the 1990s, the political-lobbying groups SOMA (a drug-law reform group) and Abraço increased in size and a new National Association for the Intervention with Drug Addiction (ANIT Portugal – *Associação Nacional de Intervenientes em Toxicodependencia*) was established. These groups helped to mobilise another broad cross-section of society, advocating in particular for the rights of drug users and the need for drug-law reform.

Health professionals

The final sector playing a role in drug-law reform were health professionals. By contrast with the other sectors, Portuguese health professionals were initially reticent supporters of decriminalisation. The key cause was that the Portuguese health sector comprised two coalitions who held very different views on the optimal approach to drugs: a coalition for abstinence and a coalition for harm reduction. The Portuguese health sector had been historically dominated by the coalition for abstinence: 'partisan' psychiatrists supported an abstinence approach towards the drugs issues. This was antithetical to drug-law reform. However, a shift occurred in the years preceding reform, abstinence-oriented approaches became more unpopular (Miguel, 1997) and the harm-reduction coalition became more vocal and started to gain the ascendancy.

Three key events in the lead-up to decriminalisation favoured a shift. First, in March 1997, a long-time advocate of harm reduction, João Goulão, was appointed head of the Drug Addiction Treatment and Prevention Service (SPTT), replacing the previous, abstinence-oriented, head of SPTT. Second, harm-reduction health professionals started to advocate through the media and through political avenues against dogmatic drug-free approaches. This led to direct conflict between advocates of abstinence and harm reduction. The harm reduction counter-view was led by a number of directors of Lisbon-based drug treatment centres (João Goulão, Luís Patrício and Rodrigo Coutinho) and a clinical director, Nuno Miguel. Finally, in June 1998 the first low-threshold methadone programmes were trialled in Portugal. The majority of health professionals were opposed to methadone at that time but post-introduction, opposition decreased. This, again, spurred many vocal calls for reform. While health professionals did not often directly advocate for decriminalisation, they became very strong advocates of the need for a paradigm shift for the treatment of drug users as citizens who warranted harm reduction and treatment, not punishment.

174　Caitlin Hughes

The three sectors playing a part in drug-law reform thus had different trajectories (particularly that of the health sector), but throughout the 1990s they all increasingly mobilised support for reform.

Politics

The 1990s saw a series of marked shifts in the political system. Portuguese drug policy had previously been perceived as an issue of low political importance. The drugs issue was rarely debated in parliament (Costa, 2002). Most political interventions, including the introduction of Projecto VIDA in 1987, were largely perceived as symbolic: 'They made much noise but they made very little impact' (Rodrigo Coutinho – Health Professional). Furthermore, coordination and control of drug policy shifted between the Ministry of Justice and the Ministry of Health without apparent reason (one perceived cause was the change of successive Social Democratic governments between 1985 and 1995).

However, October 1995 marked the election of the Socialist Party and henceforth, the drugs issue became a higher priority and made it onto the political agenda. The drugs issue was included in the Socialists' election campaign (a first), and within two months of election (November 1995), the party had established a drug-specific parliamentary committee (which, as noted above, highlighted significant problems in the previous policy). As noted by Carlos Costa (Law Enforcement Officer): 'For the first time the political power felt that this was a problem'. Nonetheless, many stakeholders contended that even with the election of the Socialist Party the political mindset between 1995 and 1997 continued to favour quick fixes and incremental reform, as opposed to a comprehensive shift in drug laws and policy. Initiatives undertaken by the Socialist Party in their first years of office support this view (see Table 11.1). These included increasing penalties for drug trafficking (Law 45/96) and tinkering with (as opposed to abolishing) the Projecto VIDA policy (Decree-law 193/96).

Many stakeholders argued that while drugs had made it onto the political agenda another key challenge was confronting political dogma, including that of then-Drug Strategy Coordinator José Sócrates, about the optimal response to the drug problem. The process of confrontation was led by a number of 'policy entrepreneurs' (Kingdon, 1984) comprised of four drug treatment professionals – Nuno Miguel, João Goulão, Luís Patrício and Rodrigo Coutinho – and Socialist politician Alexandre Rosa and President Sampaio, two 'political brokers' (Sabatier and Jenkins-Smith, 1993). Public theorists argue that policy entrepreneurs – defined as advocates for particular proposals who seek out and capitalise upon opportunities for reform (Kingdon, 1984) – and policy brokers – defined as elected officials who seek to find compromise between competing coalitions (Sabatier and Jenkins-Smith, 1993) – are often critical to generating policy change and this was particularly true in this case. Drug treatment professionals were, as noted above, vocal advocates within the health sector for a harm-reduction approach and equally, if not more importantly, they also cultivated links with politicians, particularly with Socialist politician Alexandre Rosa (then National Coordinator and High Commissioner of Projecto VIDA), and mobilised support for reform within the political arena. Alexandre Rosa acknowledged: 'the Government started to open our minds, so we could face the problem, we could look at the problem in a different way'.

Drug treatment professionals had a particularly persuasive influence on this process, first and foremost because of their professional positions, but secondly, because they themselves had been forced to 'open their minds' to the true nature and scale of the drug problem in Portugal, and the failings of earlier approaches. As summed up by Alexandre Rosa: 'These people are the openers of the minds ... They opened up their own minds and willed the process of opened minds.' They were therefore able to challenge political reticence and pave the way for drug law reform.

A number of factors helped in the confrontation of political dogma and helped drive the commitment to reform. The first was Casal Ventoso, which health professionals and politicians, including the then-President, used as an instrument to draw attention to the issue. The president even held press conferences from the streets of Casal Ventoso. This helped to reinforce a criticism of systemic failings, including the government's neglect of the basic rights to healthcare of drug users. The second factor was the early attempts to 'fix' the drug problem. In February 1998, the then-Drug Strategy Coordinator José Sócrates held a discussion with health professionals, including João Goulão, where it became clear that he believed that the provision of low-threshold methadone would be the solution – the magic bullet – for the Portuguese drug problem. However, as noted by João Goulão, throughout the discussions José Sócrates was persuaded that 'this was not so simple' and that piecemeal approaches within the current paradigm would not solve the problem. This led to the establishment, that same month, of an expert commission (the CNDS) comprising Portugal's best drug experts which included three of the four drug-treatment professionals who had served as policy entrepreneurs.

This having been said, evidence-informed drug policy reform was far from a given. The political response to the CNDS report warrants special mention. The head of the CNDS, Alexander Quintanilha, was 'half expecting' that the report, including calls for decriminalisation, would 'be put in a drawer and forgotten'. That it was not done was significant. Key enabling factors were that the recommendations came from trusted experts, and that the policy options outlined (including decriminalisation) were feasible and had historical resonance. Also of note, the CNDS recommendations were widely discussed and debated within parliament, government and society. This was an unusual policy-making process in Portugal, but contributed to the strong consensus that even if the outcomes could not be predicted with 100% certainty, the new direction was a better and fairer way for Portugal to respond to the issue of drugs. This led to the implementation in full of all of the CNDS recommendations, and to a substantial investment of funds. Equally important, decriminalisation has swiftly become the flagship, and pride, of the new Portuguese drug policy.

International conventions, INCB and the international community

The CNDS recommendations for reform were carefully crafted to take into account the United Nations Conventions. For example, they noted that decriminalisation, but not legalisation, was possible. Following the adoption of the national strategy Portugal nevertheless received heated international criticism about the decision to decriminalise. First, the International Narcotics Control Board (INCB) stated in their 1999 Annual Report that the new draft law 'is not in line with the international drug control treaties, which require that drug use be limited to medical and scientific purposes and that States parties make drug possession a criminal offence' (International Narcotics Control Board, 2000, p. 56), and, second, criticism from a number of European countries (including the UK). As noted by the political lobbyist Luís Mendão, the criticism could have proved fatal to drug law reform; however, in both cases, the Portuguese ministers and president responded by showing strong defiance and leadership. They invited a delegation from the INCB to visit Portugal to hear about the proposed law (in September 2000) and, according to then-Drug Strategy Coordinator Vitalino Canas, convinced the delegation that Portugal 'respected the UN Conventions or at least a certain interpretation of the Conventions'. The subsequent INCB report dropped its criticism, noting the forthcoming legislation was 'fully in line with the international drug control treaties' (International Narcotics Control Board, 2001, p. 65). Similarly, following active involvement with the international media by members across the Portuguese political spectrum, international criticism subsided. This shows that because of the international conventions and the opposition of the international community the reform could have been prevented from occurring. That it did not further exemplifies the significant about-face that had occurred in the initially reticent political sector.

Conclusion

In summary, the Portuguese decision to decriminalise illicit drug use, as part of a new and expanded public health approach, has received considerable international attention. Most attention is focused on the impacts, outcomes and worth of the reform (Domoslawski, Siemaszko and Człowieka, 2011; Gonçalves et al., 2015; Greenwald, 2009; Hawkes, 2011; Hughes and Stevens, 2012; Hughes and Stevens, 2010; Laqueur, 2015; Moreira et al., 2007; Murkin et al., 2014; Pinto Coelho, 2010; Sapp, 2014; Vale de Andrade and Carapinha, 2010; Woods, 2011). Examining the policy process provides important insight into what made this reform possible.

Reform was driven by multiple factors, in particular: an expanding and very visible public health and human rights crisis throughout the 1990s; the rise of local and international research that could provide positive feedback and further quantify the problematic nature and increasing size of the drug problem; shifts within a political party resulting in more receptivity to address the drugs issue; long-term historical and cultural factors, namely the emphasis upon human rights and proportional punishment, as well as the long-term view that Portugal should decriminalise drugs 'one day'; and the concerted advocacy by multiple interest groups and a number of policy entrepreneurs who were willing to capitalise upon these opportunities and push for reform, through the formation of links with politicians. These links can be seen as having had a long-lasting impact because the Portuguese drug law reform was never simply about changing the law but also about providing a tool for a better health and social response.

An interesting reflection can be made, particularly in the era of evidence-informed drug policy, on the roles of evidence versus ideology and symbolism. While a key element of the process of reform were the rational arguments made about the failure of past policies, their harm, inefficiency and counter-productivity, it is also true that a large part of the process was about promotion of a new ideology and a new way of viewing drug use. Key strategies that promoted this shift were, on the one hand, the use of news media and multiple venues such as Casal Ventoso (used due to its visceral appeal to heighten concern and calls for action) and, on the other hand, the promotion of a new image of the drug user – as a citizen or sick person, not a criminal – epitomised by the call to 'fight the disease, not the addict' (Resolução do Conselho de Ministros n° 46/99 de 26 de Maio, p. 2986). Such images were highly effective and were carried by policy entrepreneurs into the political arena and into society where it helped mobilise support for drug law reform and the expanded public-health and social response towards drugs. The high level of belief in the new vision ultimately proved critical in the face of international criticism and enabled 'high defiance' by the politicians of the day. As stated by the then-Drug Strategy Coordinator: 'The fight against drugs ... must be fought not in fear of innovation but with boldness, courage and reforms to the international system' (Canas 2004).

The Portuguese reform process provides a number of lessons for other would-be reform nations. In particular, it is a reminder that evidence and expert opinion are but aspects of generating evidence-informed reform. It highlights the importance of not assuming the alignment of ideology and profession (that police will necessarily oppose drug-law reform or that health professionals will necessarily support it) and the importance of mapping out the positions of different stakeholder groups. Further, we see how national culture and values (that is, not just drug policy) influence which policy proposals may have greater (or lesser) traction. Finally, it is a reminder that multiple tools can be used by potential advocates and policy entrepreneurs to capitalise upon opportunities for evidence-informed reforms, in particular through the use of alternate venues and an awareness of different approaches to framing 'drug problems.'

References

Laws

Constitution of the Portuguese Republic (1976 April 25).
Decree 12 210, 24 August 1926.

178 Caitlin Hughes

Decree-Law 15/93, 22 January 1993.
Decree-Law 193/96, 15 October 1996.
Decree-Law 266/98, 20 August 1998.
Decree-Law 420/70, 3 September 1970.
Decree-Law 430/83, 13 December 1983.
Decree-Law 54/2013, 17 April 2013.
Law 30/2000, 29 November 2000.
Law 45/96, 3 September 1996.
Portaria 94/96, 26 March 1996.

Other

AGRA, C. (2009) Requiem pour la guerre à la drogue: L'expérimentation portugaise de décriminalisation. *Déviance et Société*. 33(1), pp. 27–49.

BALSA, C., FARINHA, T., URBANO, C. and FRANCISCO, A. (2004) *Inquérito nacional ao consumo de substancias psicoactivas na população portuguesa – 2001*. Lisbon: CEOS, Investigações Sociológicas, Faculdade de Ciências Sociais e Humanas, Universidade Nova de Lisboa.

CANAS, V. (2004). *The Portuguese National Strategy on Drugs: A Multidisciplinary Approach*. The 2004 Prague Symposium on Drug Policy, Prague.

CHAVES, M. (1999) *Casal Ventoso: Da gandaia ao narcotráfico. Marginalidade económica e dominação simbólica em Lisboa*. Lisbon: Instituto de Ciências Sociais da Universidade de Lisboa.

COMISSÃO PARA A ESTRATEGIA NACIONAL DE COMBATE A DROGA (1998) *Estratégia nacional de luta contra a droga: Relatório da comissão para a estrategia nacional de combate a droga*. Lisbon.

COMISSÃO PARLAMENTAR DE JUVENTUDE (1992) *Relatório sobre a droga*. Lisbon: Assembleia da República.

COSTA, C. (2002) *A política relativamente à droga em Portugal: Estratégia dos partidos politicos 1976/2000*. (Tese de Mestrado), ISCSP/UTL, Lisbon.

COUNCIL OF EUROPE (2001) *Report to the Portuguese Government on the Visit to Portugal Carried out by the European Committee for the Prevention of Torture and Inhuman or Degrading Treatment or Punishment (CPT) from 19 to 30 April 1999*. Strasbourg: Council of Europe.

DOMOSLAWSKI, A., SIEMASZKO, H. and CZŁOWIEKA, H. F. P. (2011) *Drug Policy in Portugal: The Benefits of Decriminalizing Drug Use. Warsaw*: Open Society Foundations. Available from: https://www.opensocietyfoundations.org/sites/default/files/drug-policy-in-portugal-english-20120814.pdf [Accessed 10/06/2016].

EMCDDA (1998) *Annual Report on the State of the Drugs Problem in the European Union 1998*. Lisbon: European Monitoring Centre for Drugs and Drug Addiction.

EMCDDA (2000) *Annual Report on the State of the Drugs Problem in the European Union 2000*. Luxembourg: Office for Official Publications of the European Communities.

EMCDDA (2015) *National Report 2014: Portugal*. Lisbon: EMCDDA.

FUGAS, C. (2001) Casal Ventoso: A desértica do plano. In Torres, N. and Ribeiro, J. P. (eds.). *A pedra e o charco: Sobre o conhecimento e intervenção nas drogas*. Almada: Íman Edições. pp. 215–242.

GABINETE DE APOIO AO TOXICODEPENDENTE (2003) *Plano integrado de prevenção da toxicodependência no bairro do Casal Ventoso: relatório 2001*. Lisbon: Gabinete de Apoio ao Toxicodependente.

GONÇALVES, R., LOURENÇO, A. and DA SILVA, S. N. (2015) A Social Cost Perspective in the Wake of the Portuguese Strategy for the Fight against Drugs. *International Journal of Drug Policy*. 26(2), pp. 199–209.

GOULÃO, J. (2015) The Current State of Development of Portuguese Drug Policy. Paper presented at the ISSDP and ESC Meeting on Portuguese Drug Policy: domestic and international perspectives, University of Porto, Porto, 2 September. Available from: http://www.issdp.org/issdpesc-working-group-on-european-drug-policy/ [Accessed 10/06/2016].

GOVERNO DE PORTUGAL (2001) *National Action Plan for Drugs and Drug Addiction: Horizon 2004*. Lisbon: Governo de Portugal.

GREENWALD, G. (2009) *Drug Decriminalization in Portugal: Lessons for Creating Fair and Successful Drug Policies*. Washington, D.C.: CATO Institute.

HAWKES, N. (2011). Highs and Lows of Drug Decriminalisation. *BMJ*. 343. *d6881*.

HUGHES, C. E. and STEVENS, A. (2010) What Can We Learn from the Portuguese Decriminalization of Illicit Drugs? *British Journal of Criminology*. 50(1), pp. 999–1022.

HUGHES, C. E., and STEVENS, A. (2012) A Resounding Success or a Disastrous Failure: Re-examining the Interpretation of Evidence on the Portuguese Decriminalisation of Illicit Drugs. *Drug and Alcohol Review*. 31(1), pp. 101–113.

HUGHES, C. E. (2006) Overcoming Obstacles to Reform? Making and Shaping Drug Policy in Contemporary Portugal and Australia. PhD Thesis, Department of Criminology, The University of Melbourne.

INSTITUTE FOR DRUGS AND DRUG ADDICTION (2008) *2008 National Report (2007 data) to the EMCDDA by the REITOX National Focal Point: Portugal: New Development, Trends and In-Depth Information on Selected Issues*. Lisbon: Institute for Drugs and Drug Addiction.

INSTITUTO DA DROGA E DA TOXICODEPENDÊNCIA *(2004) A situação do país em matéria de drogas e toxicodependências*. Lisbon: Instituto da Droga e da Toxicodependência.

INTERNATIONAL NARCOTICS CONTROL BOARD (2000) *Report of the International Narcotics Control Board for 1999*. Vienna: United Nations.

INTERNATIONAL NARCOTICS CONTROL BOARD (2001) *Report of the International Narcotics Control Board for 2000*. Vienna: United Nations.

KINGDON, J. (1984) *Agenda, Alternatives and Public Policies*. New York: Harper Collins.

LAQUEUR, H. (2015) Uses and Abuses of Drug Decriminalization in Portugal. *Law and Social Inquiry*. 40(3), pp. 746–781.

LINDBLOM, C. (1959) The 'Science' of Muddling Through. *Public Administration Review*. 19, pp. 79–88.

MACHADO, M. P. (1999) Portugal. In Dorn, N. (ed.), *Regulating European Drug Problems: Administrative Measures and Civil Law in the Control of Drug Trafficking, Nuisance and Use*. The Hague: Kluwer Law International.

MENDES, L. M. (1994) Discurso proferido por sua Excelência o Ministro Adjunto na sessão de abertura do Encontro (Re)Inserção e as Toxicodependências. Paper presented at the Projecto Vida, Lisbon, 21–23 November.

MIGUEL, N. (1997) A comunidade face à droga: o que (não) temos feito. Paper presented at the Droga: Situação e Novas Estratégias, Lisbon,19 June. Available from: http://jor gesampaio.arquivo.presidencia.pt/pt/biblioteca/outros/drogas/indice.html [Accessed 10/06/2016].

MINISTRO DA JUVENTUDE (1989) Discurso do Ministro da Juventude. Paper presented at the Ao encontro da vida no desencontro da droga, Braga,13 April.

MOREIRA, M., HUGHES, B., STORTI, C. C. and ZOBEL, F. (2011) *Drug Policy Profile: Portugal*. Lisbon: European Monitoring Centre for Drugs and Drug Addiction.

MOREIRA, M., TRIGUEIROS, F. and ANTUNES, C. (2007) The Evaluation of the Portuguese Drug Policy 1999–2004: The Process and the Impact on the New Policy. *Drugs and Alcohol Today*. 7(2), pp. 14–25.

MURKIN, G., ROLLES, S., KUSHLICK, D., POWELL, M. and STEVENS, A. (2014) *Drug Decriminalisation in Portugal: Setting the Record Straight*. London: Transform Drug Policy Foundation.

NIZA, J. (1998) *Situação e avaliação do problema da droga em Portugal: Relatório da Comissão Eventual para o Acompanhamento e Avaliação da Situação da Toxicodependência, do Consumo e do Tráfico de Droga*. Lisbon: Assembleia da República.

NUTLEY, S. M., DAVIES, H. T. and SMITH, P. C. (*2000*) *What Works? Evidence-based Policy and Practice in Public Services*. Bristol: Policy Press.

PARSONS, W. (2002) From Muddling Through to Muddling Up: Evidence-Based Policy Making and the Modernisation of British Government. *Public Policy and Administration*. 17(3), pp. 43–60.

PINTO COELHO, M. (2010) *The 'Resounding Success' of Portuguese Drug Policy: The Power of an Attractive Fallacy*. Lisbon: Associação para uma Portugal livre de drogas.

POIARES, C. A. (2003) A decriminalização do consumo de drogas: Do direito à intervenção juspsicológica. *Problemas Jurídicos da Droga e da Toxicodependência*. 8(2), pp. 29–36.

POLICÍA JUDICIÁRIA (2000). *Furto, roubo e toxicodependência*. Lisbon: Polícia Judiciária.

RESOLUÇÃO DO CONSELHO DE MINISTROS n° 46/99 de 26 de Maio (1999).

RESOLUÇÃO DO CONSELHO DE MINISTROS n° 23/87, de 21 de Abril (1987).

RIBEIRO, J. (1999) Country Report: Portugal. In Heisterkamp, S. and Hickman, M. (eds.) *European Monitoring Centre for Drugs and Drug Addiction, Pilot Project to Estimate Time Trends and Incidence of Problem Drug Use in the European Union CT.98.EP.07*. Lisbon: EMCDDA.

RODRIGUES ALMEIDA, C. (1997) Uma abordagem da politica criminal em matéria de droga. Paper presented at the Droga- Situações e Novas Estratégias, Lisbon, 19 June. Available from: http://jorgesampaio.arquivo.presidencia.pt/pt/biblioteca/outros/drogas/indice.html [Accessed 10/06/2016].

SABATIER, P. A. and JENKINS-SMITH, H. (1993) *Policy Change and Learning: An Advocacy Coalition Framework*. Boulder: Westview.

SAPP, C. E. (2014) Rehabilitate or Incarcerate: A Comparative Analysis of the United States' Sentencing Laws on Low-Level Drug Offenders and Portugal's Decriminalization of Low-Level Drug Offenses. *Cardozo Journal of International & Comparative Law*. 23(1), pp. 63–98.

SERVIÇO DE INTERVENÇÃO NOS COMPORTAMENTOS ADITIVOS E NAS DEPENDENCIAS (2013) *Plano Nacional para a Redução dos Comportamentos Aditivos e das Dependências 2013–2020*. Lisbon: Serviço de Intervenção nos Comportamentos Aditivos e nas Dependências.

UNITED NATIONS (1988) *United Nations Convention against Illicit Traffic in Narcotic Drugs and Psychotropic Substances of 1988*. Vienna: United Nations.

VALE DE ANDRADE, P. and CARAPINHA, L. (2010) Drug Decriminalisation in Portugal. *British Medical Journal*. 341, c4554.

VALLE, H. and COUTINHO, R. (2001) HIV, HCV and HBV Infection in a Group of Drug Addicts from Lisbon. Paper presented at the Meeting Surveillance of Drug-related Infectious Diseases in the European Union: Routine Data and Seroprevalence Studies, Lisbon, 29 November–1 December.

VAN HET LOO, M., VAN BEUSEKOM, I. and KAHAN, J. (2002) Decriminalization of Drug Use in Portugal: The Development of a Policy. *The Annals of the American Academy of Political and Social Science*. 582 (July), pp. 49–63.

WOODS, J. B. (2011) A Decade after Drug Decriminalization: What can the United States Learn from the Portuguese Model. *UDC/DCSL L. Rev.* 15(1). pp. 1–32.

WORLD HEALTH ORGANIZATION (2014). *Consolidated Guidelines on HIV Prevention, Diagnosis, Treatment and Care for Key Populations*. Geneva: World Health Organization.

Chapter 12

Spanish drug policy

Cristina Díaz Gómez and Emiliano Martín González

History

Legislation intended since its beginnings to protect public health

The origins of the Spanish legal framework regulating drugs goes back to the 1848 Penal Code (Articles 351–353) and to the laws and regulatory instruments which were gradually adopted during the period 1918–1928. The motive which led the state to establish certain obligations and constraints was the defence of public health, with the specific aim of protecting those it governed from the acts of 'malicious' or 'inexpert' persons (Beltrán Ballester, 1977). Notably, this dual concern underpinned intervention by the state: both the right of the administration to prohibit the preparation or sale of substances harmful to health by those unauthorised to practise this profession, and to prosecute those who, even if authorised and possessing the necessary skills, might practise such activities without complying with the formalities laid down in the respective regulations (Molina Pérez, 2011). In this way, the medical application and the utilisation of restricted substances in order to manufacture chemical products was permitted, although subject to specific regulations. Public sale in chemist's shops or drugstores of toxic substances was authorised provided that this was covered by medical prescription.

Compliance with international agreements (such as the International Opium Convention signed at The Hague on 23 January 1912) played a determining role in the development of this emerging legislation. Prominent here was the Royal Decree of 31 July 1918 regulating the sale and dispensation of toxic substances which specifically prohibited the introduction, circulation, sale and possession of opium as well as other substances such as cocaine. This law mainly provided for administrative sanctions. However, if the offender was unable to pay the fines imposed, there were provisions for custodial sentences. It is also worth noting that these provisions – in common with other laws of that period – were in addition to those set out in the 1870 Penal Code then in force, and that as well as administrative sanctions (financial penalties, suspension of professional practice, closure of premises), offenders also faced imprisonment for between one month and a day and six months.

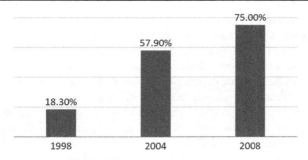

Figure 12.1 Prisons providing therapy for drug users

At the end of the 1930s, authorisation of types of use of restricted substances was extended to include the production of laboratory preparations and their use in centres for research or teaching, in addition to the purposes previously mentioned. These provisions were brought together in the Royal Decree-Law of 30 April 1928. It is noteworthy that these authorisations remain in force today. Moreover, the 1928 Law is of great importance because it laid the basis for state restriction of the distribution and sale of narcotics, in particular setting up the first public body for narcotics control (*Restricción de Estupefacientes*). This body was given the exclusive right to import and distribute restricted substances: principally opium, morphine, cocaine and foreign medications. The law also gave rise to the first statistics unit, tasked with the annual monitoring of confiscated goods and collecting data on the legal and illegal consumption of restricted substances. Another of the peculiarities of the 1928 Law was the 'official prescription form', which included the identity and other personal details of the client. In 1928, during the dictatorship of Primo de Rivera and a few years before the proclamation of the Second Republic in 1931, a new Penal Code was promulgated which distanced itself from the liberal provisions of 1870, thereby completing the anti-narcotics legislation enacted in the nineteenth century. Around this time, the expression 'toxic drugs or narcotics' (*drogas tóxicas o estupefacientes*) was used to refer to the offences of possessing and illegally trafficking drugs. The exact wording of the Spanish Penal Code as currently in force was not drafted until the introduction of the Spanish Penal Code of 1944.

The figures of the 'unwell' drug addict and the 'dangerous pre-offending subject'

In 1944 the 'Bases of National Health' (*Bases de Sanidad Nacional*) were approved (Law of 25 November 1944), which gave the state the right to impose compulsory admission of ill or unwell drug addicts for their treatment or rehabilitation. It is noteworthy that this law included this provision in its chapter regulating mental health. Similarly, Law 17 of 8 April 1967[1] which was adopted in compliance with the United Nations Convention of 1961 did not consider drug addicts to be 'delinquent' because of the sole fact of their addiction, but understood their drug dependency as causing illness. The Law consequently provided for the subjection of the drug addict to curative isolation and admission for observation or detoxification treatment and rehabilitation (Articles 25 and 29). In addition, Article 27 of the Law provides for outpatient care and the possible administration of extra-therapeutic doses of narcotics within detoxification guidelines. As regards the figure of the 'unwell drug addict' (*drogadicto-enfermo*), Law 17/1967 was intended to promote drug-related research, 'especially into substitution drugs in view to replace illicit drugs for those without side effects and new methods of detoxification and cures for those affected' (Article 26). To this end, it entrusted the unit responsible for controlling narcotics (*Servicio de Control de Estupefacientes*), which also managed the statistics unit, with new tasks in order to promote research studies and awards of grants and prizes (Article 26).

An increase in social protection mechanisms took place during these years. As the 1967 narcotics Law suggests in its explanatory statement: 'Although in Spain, the narcotics problem has not taken on the same extent and intensity with which it presents in some foreign nations, its danger prevents any standing back from the grave general concern which is produced by the confrontation between individual and social effects and those which may lead to substance abuse'. Law 16 of 4 August 1970 'on the danger and on social rehabilitation' (*Ley 16/1970 de 4 de agosto sobre peligrosidad y rehabilitación social*) inherited from the previous 'Law on idlers and vagrants' clearly reflects this phenomenon. In addition to the fact that the Spanish legal system considered drug addiction an illness, drug addicts were classified in the legislation as 'dangerous pre-offending subjects' (*sujeto peligroso pre-delictual*). In the name of social protection, the state introduced the so-called jurisdictional measures for correction and security (*medidas jurisdiccionales de corrección y de seguridad*) (Article 2, paragraphs 7.1 and 8; Article 6 paragraphs 5–6) which included isolation cures in temperance homes (*casas de templanza*), out-patient care, disqualification from driving or a ban on obtaining a driving licence, compulsory declaration of domicile or residence in a specified place in order to be subject to surveillance by the Administration and, finally, the confiscation of materials used for consumption.

---

1   The purpose of Law 17 of 8 April 1967 was to update the previous national norms of the Spanish legal system regulating drugs and narcotics, to be brought in line with the UN Convention of 1961, ratified in 1966 by the Spanish government. The previous legislation had been based on the Law of 30 April 1928 and the Law of 'Bases of National Health' of 25 November 1944, as well as international agreements enforceable at the national level. The four pillars of the preceding legal apparatus were reaffirmed in the new regulation: enforcing narcotics control from production to consumption, strengthening international cooperation, improving national coordination and developing specialised centres for drug users.

The regulation of drug consumption, possession and trafficking at the end of the 1960s

In the late 1960s the cultivation, production, manufacture and sale of narcotics was essentially regulated by Article 344 of the Penal Code and Law 17 of 8 April 1967. In line with the Royal Decree-Law of 30 April 1928, the Service of Narcotics Control (*Servicio de Control de Estupefacientes*) was responsible for providing due authorisations to professionals. Furthermore, the distribution or promotion of illicit substances included in List I of the Convention of 1961 were forbidden without specific authorisation (Article 18). Possession, use and consumption of narcotics were prohibited, except for the use of narcotics for industrial, therapeutic, educational or research purposes which continued to be permitted (Article 22). Offenders faced administrative sanctions, except where these same acts constituted a crime (Article 32). Personal consumption of illicit drugs or narcotics was considered as an administrative offence and not a crime (Article 344 of the Penal Code).

The decriminalisation of 'possession of personal use drugs' with the advent of democratic values

The promulgation of the 1978 Constitution led to the establishment of a democratic system which marked a fundamental change in Spanish penal policy and in the other legislative spheres: a key measure was the Law 'on the urgent and partial reform of the Penal Code' (*Reforma urgente y parcial del Código Penal*) of 25 June 1983. The 1983 reform introduced significant changes to Article 344 of the Penal Code which criminalised the possession and trafficking of drugs. The mere possession of illicit substances for personal use ceased to be classed as a crime; possession for the purposes of promoting, facilitating or favouring the illicit consumption of drugs alone was criminalised. At the same time, penalties were substantially reduced and differentiated according to the harmfulness of the substances. However, the concept of aggravating circumstances was introduced, including distribution of drugs to minors; within teaching, military or penal establishments; and the quantities of drugs seized. This reform of the Penal Code was generally well received by legal specialists although certain aspects came under criticism, specifically problems of interpretation, creating the danger of using preconceived assumptions against the offenders (De la Cuesta Arzamendi, 1987). Another criticism was related to the penalties fixed by the Penal Code for trafficking offences which were considered too lenient, in particular in the case of 'soft drugs'[2] (Sáez, 1989).

---

2   In 1983, trafficking offenders faced prison sentences (Article 344 of the Penal Code) from one month and a day up to six months for soft drugs (that is, 'for substances not causing serious harm to health') and from six months and a day up to six years in the case of hard drugs (those 'causing serious harm to health').

National, and above all foreign, media presented the reform as a decriminalisation of the use of drugs in Spain, although in fact the consumption of drugs had never constituted a crime within the Spanish legal system (DGPNSD, 1986). The 1988 UN Convention and the need to align national policies with international standards (Diez Ripollés, 1987) in combination with the internal pressure of the historical context of 1983–1988 (González Zorilla, 1988) gradually led to a number of counter-reforms of the Penal Code (in 1988, 1992 and 1995). These reforms led progressively to the extension of aggravating circumstances and, notably, more severe penalties for those promoting, favouring or facilitating the illegal consumption of drugs. Moreover, the laundering of capital and profits from drug trafficking became criminal behaviours at this time.

Main drivers in Spain for the counter-reforms of the 1990s

After that the progressive reform of 1983 was adopted, the Spanish drug policy was held up internationally as a bad example because of the *'permissiveness'* of its legal system (Sáez, 1989). It occurred at a turning point in Spanish history in which national authorities were intensifying efforts to integrate international organisations at the military, economic and political level. External pressure thus played a major role in the adoption of the punitive reforms that followed in the 1990s (Diez Ripollés, 1987). Public opinion was also considered as a main driver of the punitive reforms. In the mid-1980s, the problems of criminality facing citizens (drug store robberies, muggings, violence, etc.) were a major social concern in Spain (Rodríguez Cabrero, 1993). In order to address these concerns, in 1984 the Spanish Government created the position of a special prosecutor to combat drug trafficking; to strengthen the powers of the office the anti-narcotics enforcement agencies were placed under its direct command. However, the lack of effective support from the Socialist Executive led to the resignation of the special prosecutor in 1986, as noted in the media.[3] Other internal factors were social movements led by the mothers of drug addicts and by those most affected by drug addiction and the AIDS epidemic, who demanded greater control against traffickers. In fact, it should not be forgotten that although the greatest incidence of the problematic use of heroin took place in the first half of the 1980s, the greatest impact and visibility of the epidemic occurred in the second half of that decade and the beginning of the 1990s. In 1991–1992, drug-related mortality reached its peak, becoming the principal cause of death among young people in major cities and rising to the extraordinary figure of 1,700 deaths annually. New cases of AIDS diagnosed in injecting drug addicts reached its highest level in 1993–1995 (3,500 annual cases) and HIV contamination in 1995–1996 resulted in 4,300 annual deaths (De la Fuente et al., 2006).

3   See: www.elpais.com/diario/1985/07/22/portada/490831201_850215.html and www.elpais.com/diario/1985/10/09/espana/497660411_850215.html [Accessed: 11/06/2016].

Spanish drug policy 187

Development of drugs policies centred on the reduction of demand

By 1985 the Government Delegation to the National Plan on Drugs (*Delegación del Gobierno para el Plan Nacional sobre Drogas*, henceforth DGPND) was established as a government organisation under the auspices of the Ministry of Health and Consumer Affairs. The DGPND was entrusted with the preparation of the first National Anti-Drugs Plan. In the area of public health various administrations within Spain, under the direction of the National Plan on Drugs, vigorously promoted the development of harm reduction policies as programmes of treatment including methadone programmes, needle exchange programmes, prison-based programmes and also some controversial programmes such as drug consumption rooms (in Madrid and Barcelona) or the experimental heroin-assistance programme (in Andalusia). At the end of the 2000s, the Spanish state had equipped itself with an extensive, diversified network of public care resources (inpatient and outpatient services, mobile units, therapeutic communities, etc.) and specialised personnel, as reported in the evaluative Study of the Spanish Strategy for the period 2000–2008 (DGPNSD 2009). A network of social organisations with great experience had also been consolidated.

Current framework regarding drug consumption, possession and trafficking

Illicit drugs under regulation

When referring to drugs, the Spanish legal framework mainly uses the expression 'toxic drugs, narcotics or psychotropic substances' (*drogas tóxicas, estupefacientes o sustancias psicotrópicas*). Since the Spanish Constitution of 1978 came into effect, judges and courts have been legally bound to include in this category those substances designated as such in the International Conventions (Article 96, Clause 1 of the Spanish Constitution) (Beristain, 1985).

Public health as a 'legal good' protected by Spanish penal law

In Spain a special characteristic of penal policy regarding drugs is that state action is restricted to the prosecution of those who cause damage to public health (as opposed to individual health) (Córdoba Roda, 1981; Núñez Paz and Guillén López, 2008). Consequently, drug consumption has never been considered a penal offence. This legal framework is not a consequence of recent legal developments but has been the position of the state since the beginnings of state intervention in this area in the nineteenth century. Behaviours considered drug-related crimes are set out in Chapter III, Title XVII of Book II of the Penal Code under the heading 'Offences against Public Health'. In order to protect this 'legal good',[4] the Penal Code establishes a complex system of penalties and security measures.

4   The Penal Code responds thus to protect injury committed against the legally protected right of the public health, and in such a way as to be able to achieve the

Consumption and possession of drugs for personal use as an administrative offence against public safety

Spanish legislation does not provide for penal sanctions for the illicit consumption or possession of drugs for personal use. However, the legislator holds that these acts constitute a grave infringement of public safety in certain circumstances. Specifically, current administrative legislation (Organic Law 1/92 modified by Law 4/2015, on the protection of a citizen's right to security) penalises the illicit consumption and possession of drugs in public places such as streets, establishments or collective transports (Article 36.16). The conveyance of persons with the object of facilitating their access to drugs (Article 36.17) also constitutes a grave offence against public safety, as well as the acts of illicit planting and growing of drugs in places visible by the public (Article 36.18) and tolerating illegal consumption or trafficking on public premises or in public establishments (Article 36.19). The penalties fixed by the law vary between €300 and €30,050 except where these same acts constitute a crime (see below).

In the case of minors, the Law protecting public safety provides for the suspension of the penalty in cases where the offender undergoes 'treatment or cessation [therapy], if needed', or to remedial activities (Additional Provision n° 5, Law 4/2015). It is understood that some consumers of illegal substances do not have a need, from a health point of view, to undergo treatment or cessation therapy.

Behaviours considered criminal

The Spanish legal system as currently in force considers indictable any behaviours which tend to promote, favour or facilitate in any other way the illicit consumption of drugs, as well as the possession of such substances for such purposes (Article 368, Organic Law 1 of 30 March 2015, modifying Organic Law 10 of 23 November 1995, of the Penal Code[5]). The wording used is extraordinarily open and allows inclusion of a wide range of behaviours which require the existence of malicious intent including an awareness of the harmful character of the illicit substances and the will to commit an offence. Additionally, in determining whether an offence has taken place, judges must decide in cases of illicit possession of drugs whether the substances seized were intended for the owner's personal consumption or, on the contrary, destined for illegal trafficking. Case law is basically guided by two fundamental criteria:

- The fact of considering the incriminated person as a habitual drug user (Supreme Court Judgment 9056/1986 of 8 October). It is understood that possession for the purposes of trafficking may not apply when the accused

    objective of resocialisation which the Constitution assigns to its Penal Code (see the Preamble to the 1995 Penal Code).

5   Article 344 of the 1983 Penal Code.

person is a regular consumer of drugs or a drug addict when there is evidence that the drugs seized are intended for personal use.

- The quantity of the substances seized which must be considered 'insignificant' (Supreme Court Judgments 1713/2004 of 12 March and 2164/2011 of 20 April). In cases where there is well in excess of the daily dose (Supreme Court Judgments 8114/2004 of 15 December and 1957/2006 of 31 March), case law generally construes that there has been intention of trafficking. In order to determine whether a case is one of personal consumption or for trafficking, case law refers to the table[6] drawn up by the Spanish National Toxicology Institute (*Instituto Nacional de Toxicología*) setting out average daily consumption doses which estimates the normal amount held by a consumer to be a quantity equivalent to five days' average consumption (Manjón-Cabeza Olmeda, 2003).

System of penalties for drug-related crimes and case law

In order to determine the proper sentence, the current Penal Code distinguishes between drugs which cause severe damage to health and those which do not, but it does not define what is understood by each of these two categories (De la Cuesta Arzamendi, 1993). The interpretation of this rule is left to the legal specialists and to the discretion of the courts (Altava-Lavall, 1997). Case law principally refers to the harmful effects on the human body and the strong dependency to which the illicit substance may lead and understands most drugs to fall under this category (heroin, cocaine, LSD, amphetamines, MDMA, etc.) with the exception of cannabis and its derivatives (hashish, hash oil, marijuana, etc.) (Boix Reig, 1988).

The penalties fixed in the Penal Code for drug-related crimes are characterised by their severity, particularly if any of the aggravating circumstances are present. The latter depends on the personal circumstances of the individual (for example, if he or she holds a teaching or educational post, or is a civil servant or occupies a post of responsibility), on the victims' vulnerability (minors, intellectually disabled persons, etc.), and on the locations in which the offence occurs (in teaching centres, penal establishments, dependency therapy centres). Also considered to be aggravating behaviours are the use of violence, the adulteration or mixing of substances – increasing the possible damage to health – or if the quantities of drugs seized are considerable. Article 370 of the Penal Code also provides for cases of severe penalty, because they involve extremely grave behaviours: in cases where illegal substances cause severe damage to health, the penalties laid down may exceed those for homicide. Noteworthy among these behaviours are the

---

6   The report elaborated by the Spanish National Toxicology Institute provides the unit doses, the average daily consumption doses as well as the minimal psychoactive doses for 29 substances. On this basis, a short table for six substances (heroin, cocaine, hashish, marijuana, LSD and MDMA) was prepared by the Supreme Court and disseminated to the courts (*Cuadro resumen del Gabinete técnico del Tribunal Supremo*).

190 Cristina Díaz Gómez and Emiliano Martín González

Table 12.1 System of penalties for drug related offences

System of penalties for drug related offences	Substances not causing serious harm to health	Substances causing serious harm to health
Basic penalty (Article 368)	Prison sentence: 1–3 years	Prison sentence: 3–9 years
	Fine: between 1 and 2 times the value of the substance seized.	Fine: between 1 and 3 times the value of the drug seized.
Aggravated penalty (Article 369)	Prison sentence: Between 3 years and 1 day and 4 years and 6 months	Prison sentence: Between 9 years and 1 day and 13 years and 6 months
	Fine: between 1 and 4 times the value of the substance seized.	Fine: between 1 and 4 times the value of the substance seized.
Penalty for cases of extreme gravity (Article 370)	Prison sentence: Between 3 years and 1 day and 6 years and 9 months	Prison sentence: Between 9 years and 1 day and 20 years and 3 months
	Fine: between 1 and 6 times the value of the drug seized.	Fine: between 1 and 6 times the value of the drug seized.

involvement of minors or mentally disabled persons in committing these offences, when the amounts seized 'greatly exceed the obviously significant', and when ships or aircraft are used specifically to transport substances, among other aggravating circumstances.

Reduction, remission or conditional suspension of penalties for drug-related crimes

In accordance with the principle of proportionality between the penalty imposed and the injury to the protected 'legal good' (i.e. public health), the current Penal Code (Article 368) allows judges and the courts to reduce the penalty in cases where the 'fact is minor' and depending on the 'personal circumstances' of the accused (Supreme Court Judgment 298/2004 of 12 March).

Another aspect which has particular prominence in the Spanish Legal Code relates to the remission or conditional suspension of penalties imposed on delinquent drug addicts (Article 87). Suspension may be for between three and five years (with the possibility of it rising to seven years), but only providing that treatment for drug dependency is undergone, that the sentenced individual does not commit any further offence during the period laid down, and that those who undergo treatment do not drop out of it. Along these lines, those centres or services responsible for treatment are required to provide the sentencing body with information about a treatment's initiation, progress and endpoint. In addition, for definitive remission of the sentence, accreditation of drug dependency treatment and its continuation is required.

Penitentiary legislation

The General Organic Penitentiary Law 1 of 26 September 1979 obliges the Prison Administration to ensure the health of those in custody (Article 3.4), provides for social rehabilitation centres so that penal measures may be carried out (Article 11.c) and provides all establishments with a unit for the care of drug addicts (Article 37.6). It also provides for the organisation of programmes based on the principle of the therapeutic community (Article 66.1).

Controversial aspects in current policy

Until the last campaign for the general election (20 December 2015), no fundamental change to the current legal framework at national level as regards the legalisation of cannabis was on the political agenda of the two main Spanish political parties. The question of the legalisation of cannabis has, however, become more prominent in recent rallies and debates, in a social and economic context characterised by a fragmented political landscape. The debate has divided the political parties into three groups: those supporting the regulated distribution of cannabis (through the state or through cannabis associations), those open to discussion and finally, those drastically opposed. The population sector which generates social debate and controversy about cannabis and represents the 'pro-cannabis movement' is a network of consumer associations and clubs united by an appeal for the legalisation of cannabis. According to data supplied by the cannabis associations themselves, the number of clubs in Spain may be around 700, which would represent about 200,000 people.

> ### The development of Cannabis Social Clubs (CSC) under the umbrella of 'shared drug use'
>
> The first CSC, opened in 2001, set itself up as an association. Thus began the proliferation of pro-cannabis organisations which had to stick to a few legal requirements such as being registered as associations, operating on a members-only basis and being not-for-profit. Cannabis was collectively grown and distributed to registered members for their personal use.
>
> These CSCs developed under the umbrella of 'shared drug use' which is not considered an offence. However, membership has to be limited to a small group of users and the consumers should be easily identifiable (Supreme Court Judgment 216/2002 of 11 May). Additionally, cannabis use has to take place indoors (Supreme Court Judgments 210/2008 of 22 April and 761/2013 of 15 October). It should be kept in mind that drug use and possession for personal use are only prohibited in public places,[7] not in private, and that no penal sanctions for drug use or possession for

---

7   Because of the threat to public safety and peace.

personal use are provided for in Spanish law. It has to be added that the CSCs respect the law because the Penal Code is interpreted in a way that permits any behaviour prior to drug use (planting, growing, distributing, etc.) for personal use and not for trafficking purposes (Supreme Court Judgment 5435/2015 of 9 December). However, judges and the courts may also interpret that in certain cases the activity of the CSC has overstepped the limits of the philosophy of 'shared drug use' as, for example, in cases in which too many members registered exceed a 'small group' or when large amounts of money are seized and a reasonable explanation has not been provided. Judges and the courts interpret the law relying on specialist expert evidence and case law.

For years several Federations of Cannabis Associations (Eusfac, FedCac, CatFAC, Alacannabis...) have been asking the authorities to regulate the boundaries of their activity. Driven by the pressure of the pro-cannabis movement, a few Autonomous Communities have provided some legal basis and guidance (the Parliament of Navarre,[8] the Basque Parliament[9] and the Government of Catalonia[10]), although the authority over the legalisation of drugs falls under the competence of the national parliament. Some Autonomous Communities' legislation are controversial, such as the law 24/2014 of the 'Foral Autonomous Community' of Navarre which has not come into force,[11] pending a Constitutional Report.

Although the cannabis associations polarise the defence of legalisation of this substance, there undoubtedly exists a very significant social substratum which endorses this position, if silently. A significant nucleus is undoubtedly constituted by cannabis consumers themselves. According to the most recent survey published by the National Plan on Drugs (DGPNSD, 2013) 33% of Spaniards aged between 15 and 64 are in favour of legalising cannabis and, more significantly, this figure has

8   Foral Law of Navarre 24/2014 of 2 December regulating the activity of cannabis users groups in the Spanish territory of Navarre. Such a law (articles 22 and 23) provides legal coverage for the distribution of cannabis among the members of the cannabis associations.
9   Addiction-related Basque Law, approved by the Basque Government Council in December 2014. This law intends to provide a legal basis for the social cannabis clubs: a responsible shared use of cannabis among the members of a cannabis association (article 83).
10 Decision SLT/32/2015 of 15 January of the Health Department of the Government of Catalonia, providing guidance to cannabis associations and social clubs as a matter of public health. The Decision also provides an action framework intended for the municipal authorities in the territory of Catalonia. According to this regulation the association has to be non-profit, cannabis has to be grown and distributed to registered members for their own use, membership is restricted to persons 18 years of age and older, and the cannabis grown should be destined for personal use in private (for therapeutic and/or recreational purposes). The use of other illicit substances, as well as alcohol, are prohibited. Furthermore, this provision sets restrictions on locations and opening hours as well as a publicity policy.
11 Following an appeal of unconstitutionality presented by the Spanish prime minister, this regulation has been suspended, pending due constitutional review (Constitutional Court Decision 1534–2015 of 14 April 2015).

risen by 10 percentage points in the last five years. In this same survey, 9% of those surveyed declared that they had consumed cannabis in the last year.

Beyond the controversy surrounding the question of the legalisation of cannabis, it does not seem that the Spanish society today perceives drugs as a major concern. This is reflected in polling by the state-sponsored Centre for Sociological Research (*Centro de Investigaciones Sociológicas*, CIS) whose data for July 2015 is eloquent: only 0.4% of Spanish people place drugs among the main problems faced by the country and this percentage drops even further, to 0.1%, if they are asked about the problems which affect them personally. The minor impact of this subject on public opinion is also reflected in the low importance these questions are given in professional, political and institutional circles. Proof of this is the continual disappearance of public bodies specific to drugs and their distribution among other administrative structures, as well as cuts to budgets and programmes since the economic crisis began.

One definite piece of data is that since 1998 the national survey of drugs use – ESTUDES (14–18 year olds) and EDADES (15–64 year olds) – show a stabilisation or fall, depending on the substances and age ranges, in the prevalence of consumption of illegal drugs (DGPNSD, 2013). We should, however, not lose sight of the rising trend in 'risk consumption' of cannabis which is being observed in young consumers aged between 14 and 18. On the other hand, without diminishing the importance of this problematic development, it cannot be denied that young people who smoke cannabis and show no indications of risk consumption continue at present to represent the vast majority of consumption situations (83% in 2012). This trend seems in line with the increase in the number of admissions for treatment for cannabis abuse or dependency between 1996 and 2011. For thirty years in Spain drugs policies have centred on the reduction of demand, with public health in mind. These policies have made very significant progress as regards regularisation with a view to prevention and care for those affected by their use. One of the keys to this could be the containment effort directed at affected persons. Through the creation of a large public health network (which is free of charge) and the expansion of harm- and risk-reduction programmes, this guarantees universal coverage of the affected population. This has helped to reduce the public visibility of the problem, above all as regards the most problematic forms of consumption, such as those related to intravenous heroin use (DGPNSD, 2013).

References

ALTAVA-LAVALL, M. G. (1997) La tipificación del delito de narcotráfico. Su tratamiento en el nuevo Código Penal de 1995, *BIMJ*, núm. 1797, pp. 1145–1162.
BELTRÁN BALLESTER, E. (1977) El tráfico y consumo de drogas tóxicas y estupefacientes en la legislación histórica española. In Instituto de Criminología y Departamento de Derecho Penal (ed.), *Delitos contra la salud pública. Tráfico ilegal de drogas tóxicas o estupefacientes. Colección de Estudios*. Valencia: Universidad de Valencia.

BERISTAIN, A. (1985) Legislación Penal sobre el tráfico de drogas en España: Estudio jurídico-criminológico comparado. In Beristain, A. and De la Cuesta Arzamendi, J. L. (eds.) *La droga en la sociedad actual: Nuevos horizontes en criminología*. Donostia-San Sebastián: Caja de Ahorros Provicial de Guipúzcoa, pp. 101–140.

BOIX REIG, J. (1988) Delitos de riesgo general. Delitos relativos a las drogas tóxicas, estupefacientes y sustancias psicotrópicas. In Vives Antón, T. S. (ed.). *Derecho Penal (Parte especial)*. Valencia: Tirant lo Blanch, pp. 349–358.

CÓRDOBA RODA, J. (1981) El delito de tráfico de drogas. *Estudios penales y criminológicos*. 4. pp. 10–34.

DE LA CUESTA ARZAMENDI, J. L. (1987) El marco normativo de las drogas en España. *Revista General de Legislación y Jurisprudencia*. 3. pp. 367–447.

DE LA CUESTA ARZAMENDI, J. L. (1993) Características de la actual política criminal española en materia de drogas ilícitas. In Díez Ripollés, J. L. and Laurenzo Copello, P. (eds.). *La actual política criminal sobre drogas: Una perspectiva comparada*. Valencia: Tirant lo Blanch, pp. 37–82.

DE LA FUENTE, L., BRUGAL, T., DOMINGO-SALVANY, A., BRAVO, M. J., NEIRA LÉON, M. and BARRIO, G. (2006) Más de treinta años de drogas ilegales en España: Una amarga histoira con algunos consejos para el futuro. *Revista Española de Salud Pública*. 80(5). pp. 505–520.

DGPNSD (1986) *Plan nacional sobre drogas: Memoria 1986*. Madrid: Ministerio del Sanidad y Consumo.

DGPNSD (2009) *Evaluación final de la estrategia nacional sobre drogas 2000–2008*. Madrid: Ministerio de Sanidad y Política Social.

DGPNSD (2013) *Plan Nacional sobre Drogas: Memoria 2013*. Madrid: Ministerio de Sanidad, Servicios Sociales e Igualdad.

DÍEZ RIPOLLÉS, J. L. (1987) La política sobre drogas en España a la luz de las tendencias internacionales: Evolución reciente. *Anuario de derecho Penal y Ciencias Penales*. 40(2), pp. 347–400.

GONZÁLEZ ZORILLA, C. (1988) Política criminal y drogodependencias. *Comunidad y Drogas*. 3. pp. 45–57.

MAJÓN-CABEZA OLMEDA, A. (2003) Venta de cantidades mínimas de droga: insignificancia y proporcionalidad . Bien jurídico y (des)protección de menores e incapaces. *Anuario de derecho Penal y Ciencias Penales*. 56. pp. 45–112.

MOLINA PÉREZ, T. (2011) Breves notas sobre la evolución histórica de los estupefacientes en la legislación española. *Anuario Jurídico y Económico Escurialense*. 44. pp. 303–316.

NÚÑEZ PAZ, M. A. and GUILLÉN LÓPEZ, G. (2008) Moderna revisión del delito de tráfico de drogas: estudio actual del art. 368 del Código Penal. *Revista Penal*. 22. pp. 80–108.

RODRÍGUEZ CABRERO, G. (1993) Drogodependencias y exclusión social desde la reflexión sociológica. In Colegio Nacional de Doctores y Licenciados en Ciencia Política y Sociología, *Las drogodependencias: Perspectivas sociológicas actuales*. Madrid: ICNDLCPS. pp. 81–93.

SÁEZ, R. (1989) Política legislativa antidrogas: la ilusión represiva. *Jueces para la democracia*. 7. pp. 15–20.

Chapter 13

Swedish drug policy

Johan Edman

Framing the problem

During the latter half of the 1800s and the first part of the 1900s, non-acceptable ways to use drugs in Sweden were often referred to as misuse, an incorrect handling of substances that otherwise could be consumed in a correct manner. Essentially, the problem was formulated by doctors. What they saw were the various negative side effects of drug consumption and, to some extent, dependence on drugs that they had prescribed to their own patients. Thus, the drug problem was an individual problem that the doctors themselves managed; the main issues were avoiding side effects, and, to the extent possible, curing drug misuse with available medical expertise. The explanation for any problems was essentially linked to the preparations' intrinsic effects and to the particular characteristics of the patients themselves (Edman and Olsson, 2014).

An analysis of the situation in the 1920s shows that medical formulations of the drug problem prevailed (Olsson, 1994). The transformation of drug use into a serious public and social problem started with the introduction of amphetamines and similar stimulants around the time of the Second World War. Based on the very positive appreciations of the substances' medical properties among physicians, amphetamine use rapidly became popular and over the next two decades the use spread to large segments of the population. However, as amphetamine use became an important part of the criminal sub-culture, new moral connotations adhered to drug use and the phenomenon started to be depicted as a serious threat to young people. Medical assessments and concepts of disease proved ill-suited to describe and understand the process that was developing, so medical assessments of the situation faded away and alternative legal and social explanatory models began to emerge.

Towards the mid-1960s the drug problem was perceived to have reached such proportions that concerted governmental action was deemed necessary (Lindgren, 1993) and in 1968 the Swedish drug issue was institutionalised in an ambitious drug policy programme. The key elements – measures against smuggling and selling drugs, as well as treatment of drug users – can also be found in older programmes. However, these were more general efforts against the smuggling of goods, prosecution of violations against medicine and drug regulations, and the psychiatric care of some drug misusers. The 1968 drug policy programme was different: an attempt at a massive mobilisation of efforts against a drug problem that, in the 1960s, took shape as one of the most serious contemporary issues. The drug problem was no longer seen as a marginal matter for a minority of individuals; instead, it was formulated as a serious threat to society, the nation, and the youth of the nation. Legal action dealing with the manufacture, smuggling, and sale of drugs were therefore assembled in the new law. Funded by government subsidies, beds at various treatment centres were also created (Edman, 2012a).

With the exception of coercive treatment measures in the 1970s (see below), the drug problem remained mainly socially defined for the most part of the twentieth century. A contributing factor to this was the disjunction between drug users and the medical system. The drug using population predominantly consisted of young, physically and mentally relatively healthy criminals who embraced amphetamine use in a subculture. The overall description of drug use as a disease was therefore of no use. This social definition of drug abuse was later confirmed by the social legislation reform of 1982, and the political framing of the drug problem remained essentially social for the rest of the twentieth century. In the twenty-first century medical descriptions of the drug problem have become more frequent. A quest for evidence-based methods has made diagnostic manuals like DSM (Diagnostic and Statistical Manual of Mental Disorders) and ICD (International Statistical Classification of Diseases and Related Health Problems) more attractive. Neurobiological and neuropsychological research has offered new explanations for drug consumption, and a desire to connect to an international (American) vocabulary has in some areas replaced an older conceptual understanding of drug abuse with that of dependence or addiction.

It would be a mistake, though, to take the rhetorical conceptualisation of an evidence-based drug policy literally. This reframing serves a political purpose and there are indications that Swedish drug policy illustrates a shift from evidence-based policy to policy-based evidence that has been noticed by researchers of policy processes (Marmot, 2004; Weiss et al., 2008). This conceptual reframing of the drug problem in medical-diagnostic terms corresponds to a political need for measurability and the depoliticisation of a question that has proven hard to solve, and has also been driven by the possibility of getting better comparative statistics within the EU (Edman and Blomqvist, 2011; Edman, 2013a; 2013b; 2013d; Edman and Olsson 2014). The medicalisation of the drug issue must, therefore, not be taken for granted. As will be shown in the following, repressive drug control, the legal foundations for coercive treatment, and a very hesitant attitude towards harm reduction measures partly contradict this tendency.

Drug policy design

Swedish drug controls have their origins in the regulation of toxins and other harmful substances in the seventeenth century. Among these harmful substances you would, for instance, find opium. The legislation took particular aim at regulating how the substances were stored in pharmacies and how their trade should proceed. The first actual drug law was the 1923 Drug Proclamation, prompted by the fact that Sweden had joined the 1912 Opium Convention. A few years later this was replaced by the 1930 Drug Proclamation following accession to the 1925 Opium Convention. Prison sentences for trafficking, possession, manufacturing and/or selling of drugs were added as possibly punishable offences in 1933, but only in cases with aggravating circumstances. When the drug problem was reformulated into a serious social problem in the 1960s, drug-policy ambitions were dramatically altered.

A Swedish idiosyncrasy in the political stance towards the drug problem has been an unwillingness to separate hard and soft drugs. An analysis of the parliamentary debate on drugs (Edman, 2012b) only found a few proposals, in 1968, for decriminalisation of cannabis use, based partly on the argument that cannabis users shouldn't be forced to socialise with heavy drug users – i.e. that the very criminalisation of softer drugs was a stepping stone towards heavy drug use. However, this drastic and unsuccessful solution was never heard of after the establishment of the 1968 drug crime law. Rather, the drug crime law of 1968 can be seen as the beginning of political developments – still in progress – aimed at criminalising all forms of drug use.

Since the late 1960s, two clear trends in drug policy have been the extension of the area subject to regulation and the tightening of penalties. When the drug crime law was enacted the highest possible penalty for a serious drug offence was four years in prison. In 1969 this was raised to six years in prison, and in 1972 to ten years in prison. Increased penalties were motivated by the changing and deteriorating drug situation of more widespread use, an increase in serious crime and the increased internationalisation of the drug trade. Träskman (2011, p. 62) describes the swift rise in the maximum penalty as a 'Nordic carousel' in which Sweden, Norway and Finland rapidly increased maximum penalties with reference to what happened, or what was going to happen, in the other Nordic countries.

Repressive drug control was clearly strengthened at the expense of prevention and treatment during the 1980s. The criminalisation of drug use in 1988 (with the subsequent increase of penalties in 1993) is one of the more remarkable control-policy initiatives. This, and other drastic measures, are a manifestation of an ideological position in which the drug policy objective of achieving a drug-free society overshadowed other political visions (Träskman, 1995). This utopian goal was first formulated by moralistic anti-drug organisations but was soon assimilated by the political establishment. The close cooperation between NGOs, the government and other public bodies is a typical characteristic of Swedish drug policy and has contributed to the diminishment of influence from the medical establishment in the drug issue (Lenke and Olsson, 1999). An important part of the model is also, since the early 1980s, the cherished doctrine that it is primarily criminalising the actions of the individual drug user that will realise this goal (Olsson, 2011). This attitude reflects, in part, the influence of organisations such as the National

Association for a Drug-Free Society (*Riksförbundet Narkotikafritt Samhälle*), much valued, for instance, by the police, at least since the early 1980s (Kassman, 1998). It was founded by the charismatic, and influential, social medicine doctor Nils Bejerot in 1969. Bejerot, with his ideas about the contagion of the individual drug user, can be seen as something of a founding-father of restrictive Swedish drug policy (Boekhout van Solinge, 2002). Another distinctive Swedish characteristic is how extensive control policies are in comparison with other countries, especially if one takes into account that the Swedish drug problem has not been as severe as in other countries (Lenke and Olsson, 1999).

The interventionist feature of Swedish drug policy may be seen as a distinctive feature of a social-democratic type of welfare state: a counterpart to an inclusive and ambitious social policy. The patriarchal attitude towards citizens' activities has influenced several aspects of the public handling of the drug problem. This interventionist policy is associated with a repressive strategy without any evidence that aggressive drug policies have succeeded in addressing the drug issue (Tham, 1996; 2005). Since the 1970s, drug policy has also been part of the right-wing law-and-order policies; from the 1980s onwards a kind of 'tango politics' in which the Social Democrats have aligned themselves so closely to the bourgeois parties (the Liberals, the Centre Party, the Conservatives and the Christian Democrats) that voters have not been able to determine 'which party was really "leading the dance"' (Lenke and Olsson, 2002, p. 70). Since then, Swedish policy has been the result of political triangulation where representatives from all political camps agree that drugs are the worst problem of our time and consequently have to be battled with drastic measures (Edman, 2013d).

Treatment of drug users

One distinctive feature of Swedish drug policy is the absence of political disagreement on fundamental means and goals. Ever since the emergence of the drug problem in the 1960s, there has really not been any conflict between political parties on the matter. This has resulted in a dominant political description of the drug problem as an ever-deteriorating, and in many respects, growing phenomenon. On this ground different political dancers have managed to spin their own pirouettes – usually in accordance with their parties' ideological foundations. Drugs and drug consumption have often been subordinate in problematics that have fulfilled other political purposes. Worries about politically radical youth, foreign religions, or incomprehensible music have been refracted through the drug problem. In the Swedish Parliament the responsibility for the drug problem has been blamed on capitalist class oppression, Americanism and cultural superficiality. Modernity, urbanisation and industrialisation have also been criticised in the name of the drug problem.

The political consensus has made it hard to analyse the foundations of Swedish drug policy. One way to understand the indistinct basis and the evolution of this policy is to look at the voluntary state-funded treatment of drug users. In the treatment centres, and within the ruling bureaucracy, the key driver of voluntary treatment has been the ideology of the day. The Swedish drug-rehabilitation model has been abstinence but the effective treatment method has been elusive, and from the very beginning in the late 1960s, the Swedish government supported several service providers and heterogeneous treatment methods. Many treatment centres, established with the support of public funding in the 1970s, identified themselves as therapeutic communities. This was, however, a label that could be put on very different types of places and covered a variety of activities.

Maintenance treatment and other medical measures played a negligible role during the first decades. A vaguely defined social therapy dominated at treatment centres. An effective method has also played second fiddle in the choice of treatment solutions, and other values, such as rural romanticism, Swedishness, solidarity and diligence, have been extolled. Individualism, Americanism and profit-making have also been ideologically opposed in the treatment sector (Edman, 2013c). From the 1990s onwards, however, such conceptualisations have become subordinate to an overarching ideological quest to make substance abuse treatment subject to the market (Edman, 2013d). The Swedish pseudo market solution of publicly funded private entrepreneurs in the treatment field (and in several other welfare state functions) has favoured relatively cheap methods – such as twelve-step programmes – for a less demanding clientele (Edman, 2012b).

Voluntary institutional treatment has mainly been defined as an abstinence oriented and non-medical approach following the ideology of the day. Coercive treatment, on the other hand, mainly draws on a traditional Swedish conceptualisation of drug abuse as a social problem. As early as 1913, the first coercive treatment law for alcoholism contributed to an authoritative definition of the substance abuser that would carry on to our days. The alcohol problem was framed as a poverty problem that led to dependence on welfare, family neglect and insufficient employment. Since there was no successful medical remedy at hand, a law stipulating coercive treatment could not be grounded on a medical definition. The social problem definition of alcohol abuse was also reflected in the ration-book system for purchasing liquor introduced as an alternative to total prohibition at approximately the same time: alcohol was not the poison that the temperance movement described it to be and alcohol abuse was not considered a disease (Edman, 2004).

When the drug problem finally made its more public appearance in the 1960s, one of several responses was to set up treatment programmes. But by the 1960s the legislation on alcohol treatment, in which alcohol abuse was conceived as a social rather than a medical problem, was considered repressive legislation aimed at poor problem drinkers, and not a suitable model for a drug-treatment law. Instead, coercive treatment was linked to a diagnosis of the drug user as sick, which in turn required substantial work with concepts and definitions. In a clearly politically determined process, the Mental Health Legislation, the Minister of Health and Social Affairs and the Drug Rehabilitation Committee transformed drug abuse into a disease-like condition. Coercive treatment was exclusively dealt with in psychiatric institutions during the years 1969–1981 (Edman and Stenius, 2014). Criticism of the coercive treatment of both alcohol and drug abusers grew stronger during the 1970s and the need for a new treatment legislation that could address both alcohol and drug problems became evident. After years of investigatory work, new directives following the change of governments, competing proposals and a vivid public debate, it was agreed that drug abuse was a social, not a medical, problem; the coercive treatment law of 1982 did not consequently mention dependence or disease-like conditions at all (Edman, 2009; 2011). The rationale behind periods of incarceration was not any particular treatment method but the danger that drug users posed to themselves or to other persons.

The coercive treatment legislation was revised in 1989 but without challenging the drugs-as-social-problem foundations of the law. The 2004 public investigation of the coercive treatment legislation (SOU 2004:3), led by experts, did not challenge these assumptions either; the investigation neither made use of the word 'dependence' nor did it speculate about any causal mechanisms in line with this concept. The major discursive shift in the rationale for coercive treatment of drug users was the voluminous Abuse Investigation (*Missbruksutredningen*) from 2011. This public inquiry had a highly medicalised view of drug consumption and the means to solving the drug problem. The investigation relied heavily on the DSM-IV and ICD-10 and took, as a point of departure, the fact that these diagnostic manuals treated abuse and dependence as psychiatric diagnoses (Edman and Olsson, 2014). The proposed coercive psychiatric treatment was influenced by the notion that 'states of dependence are becoming ever more understandable in light of neurobiological and neuropsychological research' (SOU 2011:35, p. 317). The Abuse Investigation's proposals were, however, not implemented. Already in January 2013, the Minister responsible decided to retain a more socially oriented description of the mechanisms of abuse (SOU 2012/13:SoU18).

Coercive treatment is highly illustrative for the political conceptualisation and handling of the drug problem in Sweden. When compared to other countries, coercive treatment has clearly been an important part of Swedish substance abuse treatment (Lehto, 1994). Comparative studies have also shown that a social, non-medical, model of the drug problem has held a strong position in Sweden (Kaukonen and Stenius, 2005; Edman and Stenius, 2007). It is reasonable to see this as communicating certain ideas: the non-medical model has been an a priori for paternalistic treatment of the social consequences of abuse. Coercive treatment has been a yardstick in discussions of the principle relating to an individual's drug treatment and the extent to which this treatment could be based on consumption being described as a disease. Already when the first coercive treatment laws against alcohol abuse were enacted in the 1910s, these arguments of principle led to a dismissal of the disease model (Edman, 2004). With the exception of coercive psychiatric/drug treatment in the 1970s, it has since been difficult to anchor efforts to describe drug use as a disease. As coercive treatment programmes mainly consist in incarceration, aim at incapacitating drug users and steering drug users to further treatment, this approach has no use for the disease model.

Harm reduction programmes

Despite efforts to reformulate the drug issue in the 1970s and 2010s, drugs are still thought of as a social problem in Sweden. But the picture is ambiguous, and with Conrad and Schneider (1980), one could argue that the drugs-as-social-problem model at the institutional and treatment levels seems to co-exist with more medically oriented concepts. There is, increasingly, discussion of dependence and drug abuse as a 'disease-like' condition and new addictions – such as compulsive gambling – are, like alcohol and drug abuse, seen as biomedical addictions, even in parliamentary discussions (Edman and Berndt, 2016).

Medical treatment of drug abuse has, however, been scarce and is only slowly developing, reflecting a resistance towards a medical understanding of drug problems. True, methadone maintenance treatment (MMT) was adopted quite early. Lars Gunne, a psychiatrist at Ulleråker Hospital in Uppsala, had already launched MMT in 1966. Despite this, MMT was seen as a tightly regulated experimental method which did not have a decisive influence on Swedish drug treatment for a long time. In the 1970s, increased opiate use made MMT suddenly appear like a potential problem solver, but at the same time criticism of MMT was raised in the USA. The Swedish methadone programme was linked to the unsuccessful 1960s legal-prescription effort which increased political resistance to methadone treatment. It can be argued that the methadone resistance of the 1970s was a kind of delayed reaction against legal prescription efforts. And, as had been the case with the evolution of control policy measures, some NGOs had quite some influence over the drug-problem description when MMT was discussed; especially the National Association for Assistance to Drug Abusers (*Riksförbundet för hjälp åt läkemedelsmissbrukare*) which had a distinctively social model of the drug problem. The highest public health authority, the National Board of Health and Welfare (*Socialstyrelsen*), also took this approach to the drug problem (Johnson, 2003).

The methadone conflict grew throughout the 1970s and reached a climax around 1980. Battle lines cut through professions and political parties (Skretting and Rosenqvist, 2010). During the first half of the 1980s opinion swung in favour of MMT, due partly to positive results from the small but operational MMT programme and partly to a much-feared AIDS epidemic. The Physicians Against AIDS organisation (*Läkare mot AIDS*), formed in 1984, promoted the idea that drug abuse should be considered a disease treatable from within health care. In 1987 the National Board of Health and Welfare increased the number of places available in methadone treatment, a decision that marked the end of the most intense methadone resistance. After this, MMT cautiously expanded in the 1990s: in twenty years, from 1987 to 2007, the number of MMT patients grew from 150 to 1,200 patients (Johnson, 2007). By 2014 the number of MMT patients had grown to approximately 2,000 patients (Johnson, 2015).

In the 1990s an increase in drug-related deaths was the impetus, in several countries, to begin treating heroin users with buprenorphine (Subutex). The Swedish government and authorities initially reacted to the increase in drug use and drug-related fatalities by blaming everything from EU membership to the bad influence of 'drug liberals'. A successful research project on buprenorphine treatment did, however, promote this treatment from 1999 onwards (Johnson, 2007). Skretting and Rosenqvist (2010) describe the expansion of buprenorphine treatment during the early 2000s as a national feature; GPs had unrestricted abilities to prescribe buprenorphine from 1999–2004. In 2007 1,500 patients underwent buprenorphine treatment, and another 500 had entered the programme by 2014 (Johnson, 2015).

During the 2000s, maintenance treatment has been more widely available, partly as a consequence of lowering thresholds for participation in the programmes. In 2005 the requirement for participation in treatment was reduced from opiate abuse four years earlier to two years earlier, and in 2010 it was lowered to one year (Skretting and Rosenqvist, 2010). In a comparative perspective, maintenance treatment in Sweden can nonetheless be described as highly regulated and restrictive. It is reasonable to see it as a kind of mirror image of Swedish drug policy in general, in which the vision of a drug-free society has spilled over into the aim that drug treatment should also lead to total abstinence (Selin et al., 2015).

The Swedish drug-related mortality rate among adults (aged 15–64) remains quite high with 69.7 deaths per million in 2013, more than three times the European average of 17.2 deaths per million (EMCDDA, 2015). A possible explanation for these figures might be new patterns of drug consumption and the lack of harm-reduction measures to address these issues.

The same resistance towards the development of maintenance treatment has also characterised the development of needle-exchange programmes in Sweden from the mid-1980s onwards. The reason is similar: a vision of a drug-free society has made drug policy considerations more important than infection-control aspects. In Parliament, advocates of needle-exchange programmes have based their arguments on research only to meet successful opposition based on anecdotal arguments (Tryggvesson, 2012). However, after two decades of hard resistance, a law was passed in 2006 that allowed Sweden's 21 counties to introduce needle-exchange programmes. In 2015 needle exchange programmes were available in three counties, or six of Sweden's 290 municipalities (Johnson, 2015).

Needle-exchange programmes have become a more accepted part of Swedish drug policy but they are still viewed with suspicion and circumscribed by major restrictions. Maintenance treatment has, however, become an integral part of Swedish drug treatment since the late 1980s. Treatment itself is no longer debated but treatment regulation and patient admittance thresholds are. This development can be seen as a response to increased drug use and increased drug-related-fatalities, but also as an expression of the medicalisation of drug treatment and an increased interest in evidence-based practices in social services (Johnson, 2007).

Discussion

The history of Swedish drug policy shows that the politicisation of the drug issue has required the conceptual formulations and reformulations of the drug problem. The various conceptualisations of the problem have been influenced by leading stakeholders' claims and have altered with their relative influence. Important factors in the problem's formulation depends on which part of the problem is in focus, who the problem groups have been, and what knowledge has been available and advocated at any given time.

Many aspects of Swedish drug policy have, however, remained the same since this was formulated as a problem in the late 1960s. Certain structuring factors also date to social circumstances even older than that; this includes a prohibitionist tendency. The utopian quest for a drug-free society, which has led both to a repressive control policy and hampered harm-reduction measures, can be traced to the legacy of the influential and radical Swedish temperance movement (Lenke, 1991).

Another factor is a view of the drug problem which dates back to the framing of alcohol as a social issue, as well as a reluctance during the early 1900s to describe a problem in medical terms unless it was also possible to successfully treat it with medical methods. The framing of the drug problem as both socially caused and potentially resolvable with social measures – on a societal or individual level – has influenced the provision of treatment which is characterised by an emphasis on social therapy and a resistance to maintenance treatment. This ideological framework has also furnished the basis for paternalistic coercive treatment.

At the institutional level the drug issue is still seen as a social problem, though a reluctant acceptance of harm-reduction measures has nevertheless given it a partly medicalised character at the treatment level. Further, on a conceptual level medicalisation now characterises descriptions of drug use in vaguely defined addiction terms. This flexibility of the ideological framing of the drug problem readily lends itself to various kinds of political agendas. The drug problem has been a call to attention when MPs from different parties wish to discuss anything from consumerism and youth culture to the tax burden or the railway network in northern Sweden (Edman 2013a; 2013b). If the drug problem has not been solved in Parliament, it has been extensively used by MPs to draw attention to issues other than drug consumption. The expression 'the most dangerous drug use is the political use of drugs' (Christie and Bruun, 1985) is to some extent still true in Sweden.

References

BOEKHOUT VAN SOLINGE, T. (2002) *The Swedish Drug Control System. An In-Depth Review and Analysis*. Amsterdam: Uitgeverij Jan Mets.

CONRAD, P. and SCHNEIDER, J. W. (1980) Looking at Levels of Medicalization: A Comment on Strong's Critique of the Thesis of Medical Imperialism. *Social Science & Medicine*. 14(1). pp. 75–79.

CHRISTIE, N. and BRUUN, K. (1985) *Den gode fiende. Narkotikapolitikk i Norden*. Oslo: Univ.-forl.

204 Johan Edman

EDMAN, J. (2004) *Torken. Tvångsvården av alkoholmissbrukare i Sverige 1940–1981.* Stockholm: Almqvist and Wiksell International.

EDMAN, J. (2009) What's in a Name? Alcohol and Drug Treatment and the Politics of Confusion. *Nordic Studies on Alcohol and Drugs.* 26(4). pp. 339–353.

EDMAN, J. (2011) En sjukdom? Narkotikamissbrukarna och den politiska diagnosen 1967–1981. In Olsson, B. (ed.). *Narkotika. Om problem och politik.* Stockholm: Norstedts Juridik.

EDMAN, J. (2012a) Swedish Drug Treatment and the Political Use of Conceptual Innovation 1882–1982. *Contemporary Drug Problems.* 39(3). pp. 429–460.

EDMAN, J. (2012b) *Vård och ideologi. Narkomanvården som politiskt slagfält.* Umeå: Boréa.

EDMAN, J. (2013a) An All-Embracing Problem Description. The Swedish Drug Issue as a Political Catalyst 1982–2000. *International Journal of Drug Policy.* 24(6). pp. 558–565.

EDMAN, J. (2013b) An Ambiguous Monolith – the Swedish Drug Issue as a Political Battleground 1965–1981. *International Journal of Drug Policy.* 24(5). pp. 464–470.

EDMAN, J. (2013c) Red Cottages and Swedish Virtues: Swedish Institutional Drug Treatment as an Ideological Project 1968–1981. *Social History of Medicine.* 26(3). pp. 510–531.

EDMAN, J. (2013d) The Ideological Drug Problem. *Drugs and Alcohol Today.* 13(1). pp. 9–19.

EDMAN, J. and BERNDT, J. (2016) From Boredom to Dependence: The Medicalisation of the Swedish Gambling Problem. *Nordic Studies on Alcohol and Drugs.* 33(1). pp. 81–110.

EDMAN, J. and BLOMQVIST, J. (2011) Jakten på den verksamma vården. Kunskapssträvanden och målsättningar inom den svenska missbrukarvården under ett sekel. In: Olsson, B. (ed.). *Narkotika. Om problem och politik.* Stockholm: Norstedts Juridik.

EDMAN, J. and OLSSON, B. (2014) The Swedish Drug Problem: Conceptual Understanding and Problem Handling 1839–2001. *Nordic Studies on Alcohol and Drugs.* 31(5–6). pp. 503–526.

EDMAN, J. and STENIUS, K. (2007) From Sanatoriums to Public Injection Rooms: Actors, Ideas and Institutions in the Nordic Treatment Systems. In Edman, J. and Stenius, K. (eds.). *On the Margins. Nordic Alcohol and Drug Treatment 1885–2007.* Helsinki: NAD.

EDMAN, J. and STENIUS, K. (2014) Conceptual Carpentry as Problem Handling: The Case of Drugs and Coercive Treatment in Social Democratic Welfare Regimes. *International Journal of Drug Policy.* 25(2). pp. 320–328.

EMCDDA (2015) *Sweden Country Overview: A Summary of the National Drug Situation.* Available at: http://www.emcdda.europa.eu/countries/sweden. Last accessed 20 Oct 2015.

JOHNSON, B. (2003) *Policyspridning som översättning. Den politiska översättningen av metadonbehandling och husläkare i Sverige.* Lund: Statvetenskapliga institutionen.

JOHNSON, B. (2007) After the Storm: Developments in Maintenance Treatment Policy and Practice in Sweden 1987–2006. In Edman, J. and Stenius, K. (eds.). *On the Margins. Nordic Alcohol and Drug Treatment 1885–2007.* Helsinki: NAD.

JOHNSON, B. (2015) Harm Reduction Measures in Sweden. Unpublished.

KASSMAN, A. (1998) *Polisen och narkotikaproblemet. Från nationella aktioner mot narkotikaprofitörer till lokala insatser för att störa missbruket.* Stockholm: Almqvist and Wiksell International.

KAUKONEN, O. and STENIUS, K. (2005) Universalism under Re-construction: From Administrative Coercion to Professional Subordination of Substance Misusers. In Kildal, N. and Kuhnle, S. (eds.). *Normative Foundation of the Welfare State. The Nordic Experience.* New York: Routledge.

LEHTO, J. (1994) Involuntary Treatment of People with Substance Related Problems in the Nordic Countries. In Järvinen, M. and Skretting, A. (eds.). *Missbruk och tvångsvård.* Helsinki: NAD.

Swedish drug policy   205

LENKE, L. (1991) Dryckesmönster, nykterhetsrörelser och narkotikapolitik: en analys av samspelet mellan bruk av droger, brukets konsekvenser och formerna för deras kontroll i ett historiskt och komparativt perspektiv. *Sociologisk forskning*. 28(4). pp. 34–47.

LENKE, L. and OLSSON, B. (1999) Swedish Drug Policy in Perspective. In Derks, J., van Kalmthout, A. and Albrecht, H.-J. (eds.). *Current and Future Drug Policy Studies in Europe: Problems and Research Methods*. Freiburg: Ed. iuscrim, Max-Planck-Inst. für Ausländisches und Internat.

LENKE, L. and OLSSON, B. (2002) Swedish Drug Policy in the Twenty-First Century: A Policy Model Going Astray. *The Annals of the American Academy of Political and Social Science*. 582(7). pp. 64–79.

LINDGREN, S.-Å. (1993) *Den hotfulla njutningen. Att etablera drogbruk som samhällsproblem 1890–1970*. Stockholm/Stehag: Symposion Graduale.

MARMOT, G. (2004) Evidence Based Policy or Policy Based Evidence. *British Medical Journal*. 328(7445). pp. 906–907.

OLSSON, B. (1994) *Narkotikaproblemets bakgrund. Användning av och uppfattningar om narkotika inom svensk medicin 1839–1965*. Stockholm: CAN.

OLSSON, B. (2011) Narkotikaproblemet i Sverige: framväxt och utveckling. In Olsson, B. (ed.). *Narkotika. Om problem och politik*. Stockholm: Norstedts Juridik.

SELIN, J., PERALA, R., STENIUS, K., PARTANEN, A.ROSENQVIST, P. and ALHO, H. (2015) Opioid Substitution Treatment in Finland and other Nordic Countries: Established Treatment, Varying Practices. *Nordic Studies on Alcohol and Drugs*. 32(3). pp. 311–324.

SKRETTING, A. and ROSENQVIST, P. (2010) Shifting Focus in Substitution Treatment in the Nordic Countries. *Nordic Studies on Alcohol and Drugs*. 27(6). pp. 581–597.

SOU 2004:3, *Tvång och förändring. Rättssäkerhet, vårdens innehåll och eftervård*.

SOU 2011:35, *Bättre insatser vid missbruk och beroende*.

SoU 2012/13:18, *God kvalitet och ökad tillgänglighet inom missbruks- och beroendevården*.

THAM, H. (1996) Den svenska narkotikapolitiken – en restriktiv och framgångsrik modell? *Nordisk Alkoholtidskrift*. 13(4). pp. 179–193.

THAM, H. (2005) Swedish Drug Policy and the Vision of the Good Society. *Journal of Scandinavian Studies in Criminology and Crime Prevention*. 6(1). pp. 57–73.

TRYGGVESSON, K. (2012) 'Sprutbyte – visst bara de slutar med droger'. Svenska myndigheters och politikers hantering av rena sprutor till narkomaner. *Nordic Studies on Alcohol and Drugs*. 29(5). pp. 519–540.

TRÄSKMAN, P. O. (1995) Drakens ägg – den narkotikarelaterade brottskontrollen. In Victor, D. (eds.). *Varning för straff. Om vådan av den nyttiga straffrätten*. Stockholm: Fritze.

TRÄSKMAN, P. O. (2011) Narkotikabrotten och kontrollen av bruket av narkotika genom straffrättsliga medel. In Olsson, B. (ed.). *Narkotika. Om problem och politik*. Stockholm: Norstedts Juridik.

WEISS, C. H., MURPHY-GRAHAM, E., PETROSINO, A. and GANDHI, A. G. (2008) The Fairy Godmother and her Warts: Making the Dream of Evidence-based Policy Come True. *American Journal of Evaluation*. 29(1). pp. 29–47.

Chapter 14

Swiss drug policy

Frank Zobel

Until the mid-1980s Switzerland's drug policy was similar to those of many other European countries of that time (EMCDDA, 2011, 2013, 2014a, 2014b): born out of external influence, updated after new international agreements, strong on law enforcement but also promoting prevention and abstinence-oriented treatment. This changed over a period of ten years, the country becoming known for having a 'different' drug policy. What happened and how profound is the change?

A drug policy like any other: 1920–1975

Until the 1920s Swiss cantons[1] had their own regulations regarding the importation and exportation of substances such as opium and cocaine, and these were mostly handled like potent medicines or poisons (Hänni, 1998). Only two cantons (Geneva and Vaud) developed specific control measures in 1921 and 1922 following increases in recreational cocaine use (Hansjakob and Killias, 2012).

The first federal narcotics law was adopted in 1924. One of its main objectives was to allow Switzerland to ratify the 1912 Convention on Opium. The country was under increasing international pressure to do so as Swiss companies produced morphine and cocaine, some of which turned up in drug seizures in different parts of the world (Hänni, 1998). At the national level, interest in the topic was limited. Only the chemical and pharmaceutical industries lobbied against the ratification of the convention which, in their view, restricted freedom of trade and provided colonial powers with commercial advantages (Hänni, 1998). The new legislation created a national drug control system: from production and importation to sales, each player had to have proper authorisation. The list of controlled substances was limited, and centred mainly on opium and cocaine.

---

1   Switzerland is a confederation of 26 cantons. These have a high level of political and fiscal autonomy and are responsible, among other matters, for education, health services and police. The central State is in charge of external affairs, security and defence, border control, currency and national legislation. It can also intervene in other areas under the principles of subsidiarity and proportionality. The larger cities have their own police and social services.

The narcotics law underwent a full revision in 1951, primarily to adapt its content to international conventions adopted between the two world wars (Boggio et al., 1997). The list of controlled substances was extended – now including cannabis – and control mechanisms were improved with the creation of a national control authority and other measures. Drug dependence was also mentioned in the law, and doctors and pharmacists were allowed to direct patients to cantonal authorities if deemed useful for their relatives or society. The range of drug-related offences was extended and the level of sanctions increased, a trend which continued with each revision of the law including that of 1968 (Hänni, 1998). In 1969, the country's highest court ruled that drug use – which was not mentioned in the law – would now be considered an offence (Hansjakob and Killias, 2012).

The first large drug seizure was made in 1957, but it was not until the end of the following decade that drug use – mostly cannabis – became a public issue in Switzerland. The first available figures mention about 500 drug-law offences and 60kg of hashish seized in 1969 (Heller, 1992). Those numbers increased rapidly in the following years and, in 1972, heroin seizures and a first drug-related death were registered. This triggered another revision of the narcotics law. Again, the list of controlled substances and the variety of drug-related offences were extended, and the sanctions for offenders increased. A new offence for drug use was introduced, following the previous decision of the federal court, but with lower sanctions as well as exemptions for dependent users. In the following years, the larger cantons and cities started to create drug squads within their police forces.

Health and social measures were also mentioned in the new law as cantons were called upon to develop prevention of drug use strategies and provide treatment for dependent drug users. Treatment was abstinence-oriented and methadone prescriptions were only allowed under strict rules and surveillance (Hänni, 1998). This discouraged medical doctors from providing this type of treatment (Csete and Grob, 2012).

The building up of a drugs crisis: 1975–1985

By the time the revision was adopted in 1975, drug use had already reached a new level. Around 5,000 drug law offences and 35 drug-related deaths were registered that year; seizures included 443kg of hashish, 21kg of heroin and now, also, cocaine, with a seizure of 2kg. In 1977 a first estimate of dependent drug users in Switzerland put the number at around 4,000 (Heller, 1992).

The increase in drug use went along, as in many other countries, with the development of rebellious youth movements. These occurred a bit later in Switzerland than in neighbouring countries (Boggio et al., 1997) and, possibly, took longer to unfold. Around 1979–1980 several cities had weekly demonstrations often ending with street fights between the police and young adults (Grob, 2009). It led to the creation of autonomous youth centres where different groups, including heroin users, met and sometimes lived. In Zürich's centre, the first drug consumption room was illegally established in 1982 (Uchtenhagen, 2009). Shortly afterwards, cohabitation problems and frequent interventions by the police resulted in the closure of most autonomous centres, and drug users, who were growing in numbers, progressively returned to the streets (Grob, 2009).

By the mid-1980s Switzerland's drug problem was turning into a drugs crisis. The drug trade – now mainly heroin – was controlled by foreign groups and there was no sign that law enforcement had an impact on the supply of drugs, despite the 15,000 drug-law offences registered in 1985 (Heller, 1992). Crimes linked to drug use (pharmacy burglaries, housebreaking, etc.) increased and attempts to dissolve groups of drug users just made them move to other parts of towns (Kraushaar and Lieberherr, 1996). The number of drug-related deaths was now beyond one hundred a year, and it was estimated that 10,000 people were drug dependent (Grob, 2009).

The measures developed by the cantons following the 1975 law could not meet the size of the problem: a report from 1983 mentioned 320 beds dedicated to long-term drug treatment (Boggio et al., 1997). Also in 1985, there were 1,300 methadone treatments authorised which were not reimbursed by health insurance (Grob, 2009). Prevention activities were still dominated by information about the dangers of drugs, often provided by the police.

The Swiss Confederation and cantons were, however, quick to set up testing facilities and public health surveillance systems following the identification of HIV/AIDS. The first data, around the mid-1980s, showed that the country had a significant number of infected people and that most were injecting drug users (Uchtenhagen, 2009). As prostitution was one of the means of financing heroin use there was a now a fear that the deadly disease could spread to the general population.

The early identification of the link between the spread of HIV/AIDS and injecting drug use was key for the future of drug policy in Switzerland (Kübler, 2000). Drug users were progressively seen as vulnerable or sick people in need of help, and not just as criminals or socially deviant. This engaged the medical community and opened a window for new models of treatment. The spread of HIV/AIDS also left the advocates of the repressive and abstinence-oriented policy paradigm with little to say. Nothing in their drug policy repertoire was a short-term response to the spread of the virus (Uchtenhagen, 2009).

Drug policy change: 1985–1995

In late 1986 Zürich's drug users settled in a park located near the main train station. Local authorities left them alone there, under observation, after conceding that chasing them around the city was not a solution, either in terms of public nuisance and crime or public health (Kraushaar and Lieberherr, 1996). This place – the Platzspitz – would become known internationally as Zürich's infamous needle-park. Its existence provided a window of opportunity which led to an overhaul of the country's drug policy.

In the first half of the 1980s social workers and young doctors, mainly in the German part of Switzerland, had implemented the first low-threshold harm reduction interventions for drug users (Grob, 2009). One of the most controversial interventions was the distribution of clean syringes and needles to prevent the spread of hepatitis and later of HIV/AIDS. In 1985 the medical officer of the canton of Zürich threatened doctors and pharmacists with revocation of their licences for doing it. In response, 300 doctors signed a petition stating that they would continue their activity and they received the backing of their medical association (Uchtenhagen, 2009). A year later the cantonal parliament authorised syringe exchange.

The Contact Foundation in Bern opened in 1986 a low-threshold facility that included a small room where drug users could inject (Wietlisbach, 2014). A year later, the city's authorities adopted harm reduction measures as part of their drug policy and gave their support to the world's first supervised drug consumption facility. In Zürich the city council included harm reduction in its drug policy of 1987 (Kraushaar and Lieberherr, 1996), and in 1988 the Zipp-Aids project, carried out by the Red Cross and the university hospital, was started. It was located in the Platzspitz and in its first full year of operation provided four thousand sterile syringes and more than twenty medical consultations to drug users every day (Grob, 2009). In 1991, a private organisation named ARUD (Association for Risk Reduction in Use of Drugs) created the first low-threshold methadone clinic in the city (Uchtenhagen, 2009). Similar developments occurred in a few other cantons.

Such innovations were not made without strong political opposition – the most conservative party opposed most, if not all, harm reduction interventions – and from many cantons, particularly in the French- and Italian-speaking regions. Law enforcement resources also grew sharply and conflicts between the police and health and social workers were frequent, particularly around drug scenes and within the public debate (Boggio et al., 1997). However, because interventions and policies were decided at the local level and involved a multitude of players (including individuals and private institutions with a certain level of autonomy) there was a need for people to sit together, to confront their views, and, ultimately, to be pragmatic and to reach some basic level of coordination.

The needle parks were visited not only by local drug users but also by those coming from other cantons and from neighbouring countries. This created a disproportionate burden of health and security problems in some Swiss cities. This situation, as well as the HIV/AIDS epidemic, allowed the federal authorities to get more involved in drug policy, based on both the principle of subsidiarity and the national law on epidemics. Starting from about 1988 the Swiss Federal Office of Public Health took a progressively leading role in drug policy. It provided legal and financial support for innovative interventions in the cantons, offered local authorities opportunities to discuss their strategies, and funded epidemiological and other studies. The office also implemented innovative approaches within its HIV/AIDS prevention policy.

In 1991 the Swiss Confederation celebrated its 700th anniversary amidst pictures of the infamous needle parks in Bern, Zürich and other cities. More than 700 young drug users were now dying every year from overdoses and AIDS, and the number of dependent users was estimated to be around 30,000. Surveys showed that drug problems were also at the top of Swiss citizens' concerns (Longchamp et al., 1998). This drug crisis led the country's three main political parties to agree upon the need for a new policy in which the drug problem was seen as a public health, and not only a security, issue. Also, a survey commissioned by the federal office of public health showed that a majority of citizens supported interventions such as prescribing heroin to users or allowing them to inject in safe places (Fahrenkrug, 1997).

It was within this context that in 1991 the federal government published its first National Drug Strategy which, following the example of some cities and cantons, introduced harm reduction. The Swiss 'four pillars' policy (prevention, treatment, harm reduction and law enforcement) was born and it would officially become the country's drug policy a few years later. The metaphor of the four pillars (Savary, Hallam and Bewley-Taylor, 2009) provided a framework within which each player, from police officers to social workers, from abstinence-oriented treatment facilities to syringe-exchange programmes, could find its place. It retained prohibition as a framework for action but allowed for new approaches, including harm reduction measures and also innovative projects within other 'pillars'. The inevitable and sometimes deep-rooted value conflicts within drug policy were managed through wide financial and technical support by the federal authorities and the cantons, and by allowing players to meet and discuss at national conferences and within coordinating bodies. Here, a new drug policy language, centred on the results of scientific trials, the analysis of epidemiological surveys and police statistics, replaced the previous one based on experts' opinions and the personal experiences of former drug users.

Syringe-exchange programmes and supervised drug consumption rooms were increasingly implemented and other controversial measures, such as heroin-assisted treatment or syringe exchange in prisons, were already on the national agenda. In parallel, in 1992 and 1993, attempts were made to close the country's needle parks – notably the Platzspitz in Zürich and the Kocherpark in Bern – and to regain some control over the drug situation. It worked in Bern and in other cities, but not in Zürich where drug users, after some time, moved to an abandoned train station (Letten) which became the city's next needle park (Kraushaar and Lieberherr, 1996). It was closed in 1995, this time with a higher level of coordination and a better strategy involving both the federal government and the cantons. Drug services in Zürich had been expanded (including heroin-assisted treatment, begun in 1994) and the police were now handing drug users back to their cities and cantons of origin where authorities had committed to help them. Acquisitive crime and public nuisance declined dramatically at that time.

While the first half of the 1990s was the period of Switzerland's worst drug problems, it was also the time they progressively came back under control. In 1995 more than 15,000 drug users had accessed some type of treatment, mostly metha-done maintenance as the rules and recommendations for this type of treatment had been changed. In addition, 30 needle and syringe programmes distributed around 20,000 syringes daily with, in most large cities, at least one facility having a supervised drug consumption room (Zobel et al., 2004).

The (incomplete) institutionalisation of the new policy: 1995–2005

Switzerland is a direct democracy allowing citizens to submit laws for ballot initiatives or to request referendums over legislation adopted by the State. This is possible at three levels: municipalities, cantons and the Confederation. The first drug-policy related initiatives and referendums were held at the local level. In the early 1990s voters in Zürich, Sankt Gallen and Luzern rejected the implementation of drug consumption facilities, while in Schaffhausen they accepted it. These events created a learning process among harm reduction advocates who under-stood that they had to be more receptive to public nuisances issues, talk to local residents and respond to their fears (Kübler, 2001).

Drug policy came on the national agenda in the second half of the 1990s, providing an opportunity to publicly discuss the new four pillars policy. In 1993 and 1994 two groups had launched drug policy ballot initiatives which were going in opposite directions. The first was named 'Youth Without Drugs' and came from conservative circles. It called for harm reduction measures, including opioid maintenance treatment, to be dramatically reduced and replaced by abstinence-oriented interventions. The second initiative, coming from the other end of the political spectrum, was named 'Droleg' and called for drug legalisation and the state to develop regulated markets.

The two initiatives provided an opportunity to present and promote the new Swiss drug policy as a pragmatic middle ground between two extreme approaches. A growing coalition of professionals, including medical doctors and social workers, but also police officers and policy makers, supported the four pillars policy and were willing to promote it during public debates. This was made easier by the fact that, almost for the first time in a quarter of a century, there were now positive trends regarding the drug problems in Switzerland. What was not known at that time is that the number of new heroin users had already peaked around 1990 and had been rapidly decreasing since (Nordt and Stohler, 2006).

Both ballot initiatives were defeated in 1997 and 1998 by more than 70% of votes. The same occurred in 1999, although with a lower percentage, to a national refer-endum against the continuation of heroin-assisted treatment. The referendum had been called by advocates of an abstinence-oriented drug policy (Savary, Hallam and Bewley-Taylor, 2009). These advocates had now been defeated twice by the vote of citizens and, during the following years, drug policy decision-making powers which had been in their hands moved into the hands of those favouring or allowing harm reduction.

212 Frank Zobel

The country's drug policy had undergone a major change, supported by the citizens, but without changes to the narcotics law. A revision of that law was desired by many, not only to institutionalise harm reduction, but also to follow the recommendations of expert commissions which called for the decriminalisation of drug use and for a change in the legal status of cannabis. This led the government to submit to parliament a revision proposal which not only reflected the results of the recent votes but also called for an additional major drug policy change: the legalisation of cannabis use and the possibility of state regulation of that market.

The revision proposal entered parliament in 2001 and remained, for different reasons, on hold for three years. During that period, some cantons reduced their law enforcement efforts against the cannabis market which resulted in the presence of about 400 cannabis shops throughout the country by 2002 (Leimlehner, 2004). Switzerland also became a cannabis producer for neighbouring countries and new plant varieties referred to their Swiss origin. This unregulated market, in which some criminal organisations were involved, contributed to the lower house's refusal, in 2004, to discuss the revision proposal by a vote of 102 to 92. This was the end of the revision process and it gave the advocates of an abstinence-oriented policy a long-awaited victory. It also showed that they could still be influential.

Institutionalisation at last and the ongoing cannabis debate: 2005–present

The rejection of the revision of the law resulted in the closure of the cannabis shops. Their owners and other cannabis activists immediately started to collect signatures for another federal ballot initiative requiring the legalisation and market regulation of cannabis. They were joined by harm reduction advocates and many of those who had called for drug policy change in the 1990s and early 2000s. The required number of signatures was obtained and the vote was set for 2008.

Meanwhile, the Swiss Parliament still had to revise the narcotics law because heroin-assisted treatment had a temporary legal basis. In 2008 a revision of the law was adopted which was very similar to the one submitted to parliament in 2001, but without the part on cannabis. It was still too much for conservative groups and abstinence-oriented drug policy advocates who organised a referendum against that revision.

This resulted in Swiss citizens being called to vote, in November 2008, on both an initiative for cannabis legalisation and market regulation *and* a referendum against the revision of the law institutionalising harm reduction and heroin-assisted treatment. The cannabis initiative was rejected by 63% of voters while the revision of the narcotics law was accepted by 68% (Savary, Hallam and Bewley-Taylor, 2009). Harm reduction was now fully institutionalised and cannabis legalisation had been rejected by both the parliament and the citizens.

This was not, however, the end of the cannabis debate. In 2008 the advisory committee on drugs to the federal government published a new version of its 1999 cannabis report stating that cannabis policy was still in need of change (EKDF, 2008). The issue was raised again in the federal parliament as the number of offences was still growing without noticeable effect on the prevalence of use, but with increased judicial workloads. In 2012 an old parliamentary initiative was revived and used for a partial revision of the narcotics law which decriminalised cannabis use by adults. There is now an administrative fine of 100 Swiss Francs (about €90) for people aged 18 and older using cannabis and carrying no more than 10 grams of the drug. The law came into force in October 2013 and the first figures show that cantons have quite different ways of applying the fines. One reason for this is that the narcotics law, with its successive revisions, has now plenty of ambiguities which allow for very different interpretations and options for law enforcement.

In parallel with developments at the national level, some Swiss-German cities started to discuss the idea of experimenting with cannabis regulation at the local level. This debate continued with, in 2014, a group of representatives from all political parties except one (the most conservative) in Geneva coming up with a proposal for a trial with Cannabis Social Clubs as they exist in Spain and Belgium. Recently, a group of cities and cantons have met and are now officially working on a proposal for different cannabis production and distribution models, including within therapeutic settings, which would be scientifically evaluated. The proposal could be submitted for authorisation under the current narcotics law in late 2016 (Zobel and Marthaler, 2014).

Understanding Switzerland's drug policy change

Switzerland underwent an important drug policy change in the late 1980s and early 1990s, becoming one of the most innovative countries in this area. Still today almost half of all the patients who have access to heroin-assisted treatment in the world live in Switzerland. Another example of the depth of change are the two drug-checking projects which analyse more than 1,500 drug samples every year (Bücheli and Menzi, 2015).

As Switzerland is otherwise known for being rather conservative, one might legitimately wonder why and how this was, and still is, possible. The size of the drug problem certainly provided a window of opportunity for policy change. Youthful experimentation with drugs, at a time when heroin became largely available, and the inappropriate response of a very conservative state contributed to the nurturing of a large drug problem. The country's wealth might also have made it particularly interesting for criminal groups to engage in drug supply. The speed with which the HIV/AIDS epidemic was identified also added to the understanding of the size of the problem. Switzerland knew very early that it had an HIV epidemic among injecting drug users, possibly earlier than many other countries. The country also didn't have one drug problem but

214 Frank Zobel

many different ones, with some disproportionally large ones in cities such as Bern and Zürich.

The country's federal structure and dispersion of powers also played an important role in drug policy change. Within the comparatively small cities and cantons of Switzerland, drug policy players had to meet and discuss to find practical and pragmatic solutions to everyday problems of coexistence. Differences in the size of drug problems, but also in cultural and administrative traditions, led to multiple policies and interventions, including innovative ones. These came mostly from the German-speaking part of the country, where the role of the State tends to be less important and the one of private institutions, including NGOs, more important than in French- and Italian-speaking regions. This policy diversity among cities and cantons later provided an opportunity for the federal state to develop a common framework.

Direct democracy can provide a learning opportunity both for policy makers and citizens. The period 1997–1999, with its three national votes on drug policy, was an extraordinary period of societal debate on drug policy and the diffusion of knowledge on drugs issues. It also favoured the development of coalitions of like-minded people and showed that the 'harm reduction' coalition was now stronger than the 'abstinence' coalition. Before that, local initiatives and referendums had provided knowledge on how to handle the drug issue publicly in order to secure a majority of votes.

All these elements contributed to a significant move in the boundaries of the prohibition paradigm, with the implementation of ideas and measures considered unacceptable until then by many drug policy players nationally and internationally. Switzerland could also have been the first country to legalise cannabis and fully regulate its market, almost a decade before Uruguay and some US States decided to do it. This did not happen, however, notably because there was no public health or security crisis with cannabis which would have provided an opportunity for trying alternative models. Neither was there a strong lobbying group as nowadays exists in the US. All there was, and still is, is a societal debate on the coherence of drugs and alcohol policies and on the moderate impact and possibly high costs of law enforcement. This debate is still on-going and one might reasonably foresee that, if cannabis policy change comes to Europe, Switzerland may be among those who implement it.

Switzerland's drug policy also retains its roots in drug interdiction. More than 40,000 drug law offences and fines for cannabis use were registered in 2014, and there are other examples of a 'not so different' policy. One is the current response to new psychoactive substances (NPS). Each newly detected substance is automatically placed under control if it has no legitimate pharmaceutical or industrial use. Since 2011 about 170 new substances have been added to a new schedule and their use or possession are linked with the same criminal penalties as other illicit drugs. While, given the speed with which NPS appear, the approach of systematic interdiction is certainly pragmatic, it is also very similar to the way such an issue would have been handled in the 1970s.

Swiss drug policy 215

References

BOGGIO, Y., CESONI, M. L. and CATTACIN, S. (1997) *Apprendre à gérer: La politique suisse en matière de drogues.* Genève: Georg.

BÜCHELI, A. and MENZI, P. (2015) *Tätigkeitsbericht Safer Nightlife Schweiz 2013/2014.* Bern: INFODROG Schweizerische Koordinations- und Fachstelle Sucht.

CSETE, J. (2010) *From the Mountaintops: What the World Can Learn from Drug Policy Change in Switzerland.* Budapest: Open Society Institutes.

CSETE, J. and GROB, P. J. (2012) Switzerland, HIV and the Power of Pragmatism: Lessons for Drug Policy Development. *International Journal of Drug Policy.* 23. pp. 82–86.

EIDGENÖSSISCHE BETÄUBUNGSMITTELKOMMISSION. (1983). *Drogenbericht.* Bern: Eidgenössische Betäubungsmittelkommission.

EIDGENÖSSISCHE KOMMISSION FÜR DROGENFRAGEN (EKDF). (2008) *Cannabis 2008: Update zum Cannabisbericht 1999.* Bern: EKDF.

EISNER, M. (1999) Déterminants de la politique suisse en matière de drogue: l'exemple du programme de prescription d'héroïne. *Déviance et Société.* 23(2). p.189–204.

EMCDDA (2011) *Drug Policy Profiles: Portugal.* Available from: http://www.emcdda.europa. eu/publications/drug-policy-profiles/portugal [Accessed 25/08/2016].

EMCDDA (2013) *Drug Policy Profiles: Ireland.* Available from: http://www.emcdda.europa. eu/publications/drug-policy-profiles/Ireland [Accessed 25/08/2016].

EMCDDA (2014a) *Drug Policy Profiles: Poland.* Available from: http://www.emcdda.europa. eu/publications/emcdda-papers/policy-profile-poland [Accessed 25/08/2016].

EMCDDA (2014b) *Drug Policy Profiles: Austria.* Available from: http://www.emcdda.europa. eu/publications/emcdda-papers/policy-profile-austria [Accessed 25/08/2016].

FAHRENKRUG, H. (1997) Politique drogues illégales. In Müller, R., Meyer, M. and Gmel, G. (eds.). *Alcool, tabac et drogues illégales en Suisse de 1994 à 1996.* Lausanne: ISPA.

GROB, P. J. (2009) *Zürcher 'Needle-Park': Ein Stück Drogengeschichte und -politik 1968–2008.* Zürich: Chronos Verlag.

HÄNNI, C. (1998) *Im Spannungsfeld zwischen Arzneimittel und Rauschgift: Zur Geschichte der Betäubungsmittelgesetzgebung in der Schweiz.* Bern: SGGP/SSHP.

HANSJAKOB, T. and KILLIAS, M. (2012) Repression in der Drogenpolitik. In EidgenössischeKommissionfürDrogenfragen (ed.) *Drogenpolitik als Geselschaftspolitik: Ein Rückblick auf dreissig Jahre Schweizer Drogenpolitik.* Zürich: Seismo.

HELLER, A. (1992) Am Ziel? Chronik eines verlorenen Kampfes. *NZZ Folio* (online) April. Available from: http://folio.nzz.ch/1992/april/am-ziel [Accessed 5 November 2015].

KHAN, R. et al. (2014) Understanding Swiss Drug Policy Change and the Introduction of Heroin Maintenance Treatment. *European Addiction Research.* 20(4). pp. 200–207.

KLINGEMANN, H. (1998) Harm Reduction and Abstinence: Swiss drug policy at a time of transition. In Klingemann, H. and Hunt, G. (eds.). *Drug Treatment Systems in an International Perspective: Drugs, Demons and Delinquents.* Thousand Oaks: SAGE.

KRAUSHAAR, B. and LIEBERHERR, E. (1996) *Drogenland im Mafialand: Entwicklung, Kommentar und Materialen zur Drogensituation in der Schweiz.* Zürich: Werd Verlag.

KÜBLER, D. (2000) *Politique de la drogue dans les villes suisses entre ordre et santé: analyse des conflits de mise en oeuvre.* Paris: L'Harmattan.

KÜBLER, D. (2001) Understanding Policy Change with the Advocacy Coalition Framework: An Application to Swiss Drug Policy. *Journal of European Public Policy.* 8(4). pp. 623–641.

216   Frank Zobel

LEIMLEHNER, E. (2004) Der Cannabismarkt in der Schweiz. Strukturen, Veränderungen und Risiken. *Abhängigkeiten.* 2/2004. pp. 1–8.

LONGCHAMP, C., CATTACIN, S., WISLER, D. and EHMANN, P. (eds.) (1998) *Pragmatismus statt Polarisierung: Die Entwicklung von Einstellungen und Verhaltensweisen zur Drogenpolitik der Schweiz in den 90er Jahren.* Muri: SGGP.

NORDT, C. and STOHLER, R. (2006) Incidence of Heroin Use in Zürich, Switzerland: A Treatment Case Register Analysis. *Lancet.* 367(9525). pp. 1830–1834.

SAVARY, J. F., HALLAM, C., and BEWLEY-TAYLOR, D. (2009) *The Swiss Four Pillars Policy: An Evolution from Local Experimentation to Federal Law.* London: Beckley Foundation.

UCHTENHAGEN, A. (2009) Heroin-Assisted Treatment in Switzerland: a case study of policy change. *Addiction.* 105. pp. 29–37.

UCHTENHAGEN, A. (2011) The Role of Coalitions in Drug Policy: Some Theoretical and Observational Considerations. *Addiciones.* 23(3). pp. 183–187.

WIETLISBACH, J. (2014) *Die Geschichte des Berner Fixerstübli: Entwicklungstendenzen von Ende der 1970er Jahre bis 1994.* Bern: Universität Bern (Masterarbeit).

ZOBEL, F. et al. (2004) *Evaluation of the Confederation's Measures to Reduce Drug-Related Problems: Fourth Synthesis Report 1999–2002.* Lausanne: University Institute of Social and Prev Med.

ZOBEL, F. and SO-BARAZETTI, B. (avec la collaboration de ARNAUD, S). (2004) *La gestion de l'innovation dans le cadre du ProMeDro.* Lausanne: Institut universitaire de médecine sociale et préventive.

ZOBEL, F. and MARTHALER, M. (2014): *Du Rio de la Plata au Lac Léman: nouveaux développements concernant la régulation du marché du cannabis (2ème édition mise à jour du rapport Des Rocky Mountains aux Alpes).* Lausanne: Addiction Suisse.

Chapter 15

Drug policy in the United Kingdom

Susanne MacGregor

Introduction

The character of British drugs policy changed over the course of the twentieth century from an apparently ideal treatment-oriented 'system' – at a time when drug dependence was a relatively insignificant problem confined to white upper and middle class people – to one continuously grappling with change, multiplying numbers and types of users, substances and problems. The complex framework today is the result of an accretion of sometimes strategic and sometimes *ad hoc* responses to an apparently endemic desire to take mood- and mind-altering substances and the ingenuity shown by global and local suppliers in meeting this demand.

Twentieth-century history of drug law and policy

The 'British system' – a medico-legal alliance

Nineteenth-century discourse had viewed addiction as both a moral failing and disease. During the Second World War, emergency legislation further restricted opium. The *Dangerous Drugs Act 1920* initiated drug prohibition in Britain (Seddon, 2010). The *Rolleston Report 1926* recommended appropriate medical use of morphine and heroin in addiction treatment: prescribing to those gradually being withdrawn and maintenance for those who, 'after every effort had been made for the cure of their addiction', could not be completely withdrawn.

This became known as 'the British system', characterised by the 'majestic professional independence enjoyed by British physicians in the drug arena' (Trebach, 1982, p. 185). The policy framework was set until the 1960s when a new form of addict appeared. While earlier addicts had often been created during medical treatment, new ones were being 'turned on' through contact with other addicts: these were seen as social misfits. Drug taking began to be perceived as a social problem, prompting calls for a new response from government. But initially an interdepartmental committee of experts (the Brain Committee) in its report of 1961 concluded that no policy change was required.

Table 15.1 Timeline of major legislation and policies

EVENTS	DATE	LEGISLATION
	British system	
First World War	1916	Defence of the Realm Act Regulation 40B
	1920	Dangerous Drugs Act
	1921	Dangerous Drugs Regulations
Rolleston Committee (Ministry of Health)	1924	
Rolleston Report	1926 1928	Cannabis included in Dangerous Drugs Act implementing Geneva commitment of 1925
	New British system (the clinics)	
First report from inter departmental committee (Brain Report)	1961	
	1964	Drugs (Prevention of Misuse) Act
Second Brain report	1965	
	1967	Dangerous Drugs Act
Addicts Register	1968	
	1971	Misuse of Drugs Act
	Services expansion and harm reduction	
McClelland Report	1986	
Part one Report on HIV and AIDS from the Advisory Council on the Misuse of Drugs	1988	
Launch of NTORS	1995	
Tackling Drugs Together: A strategy for England 1995–1998	1995	
The Department of Health Task Force to Review Services for Drug Misusers	1996	
	Crime and drugs agenda	
UK Anti-Drugs Coordinator (aka the Drug Czar)	1997	

EVENTS	DATE	LEGISLATION
10-year strategy Tackling Drugs to Build a Better Britain.	1998	
NEW-ADAM Programme	1999	
	2000	DTTOs
Runciman Report	2000	
NTA established	2001	
Brixton experiment	2001	
Updated Drug Strategy	2002	
	2002	Proceeds of Crime Act
	2004	Cannabis reclassified from B to C
	2005	Drugs Act
	2006	Ketamine controlled as Class C
BBC claims of an ineffective treatment system	2008	
The Road to Recovery: a new approach tackling Scotland's drug problem	2008	
David Nutt dismissed as Chair of the ACMD	2009	
	2009	Cannabis reclassified from C to B
	Recovery agenda	
The Coalition Government drug strategy	2010	
	2010	Mephedrone controlled as a Class B drug
	2011	Police Reform and Social Responsibility Act specified substances to be placed in a 'temporary class'
NTA folded into the newly created Public Health England	2013	
	2013	Crime and Courts Act – new offence of drug driving
	2014	Khat controlled as Class C
	2015	Psychoactive Substances Act

220 Susanne MacGregor

The expansion of addiction services and public health

However, this view was challenged as the drug scene was expanding in London and the profile of users changing to one of hippies, drop-outs and students: an active black market had appeared largely through an overspill from lax medical prescribing. The *Brain Committee* was reconvened (Interdepartmental Committee on Drug Addiction, 1965). However, it still chose to interpret its terms of reference in a limited way: that is, that they were 'not being invited to survey the subject of drug addiction as a whole but rather to pay particular attention to the part played by medical practitioners in the supply of these drugs' (ibid., p. 5). The Brain Committee's *Second Report* focused on ensuring that the medical profession put its house in order and recommended tightening controls on prescribing. Prescribing heroin or cocaine would be limited to doctors granted licences from the Home Office. The medico-legal alliance thus continued (Berridge, 1999). Addiction was seen as a socially infectious condition but it would be psychiatrists who would be responsible for containing the epidemic. The *Dangerous Drugs Act 1967* established 'the clinics', based in London teaching hospitals. The *Addicts Register* began in 1968: 1,000 *new* heroin addicts were then in the clinics (from a total number of 2,782).

Under the *Drugs (Prevention of Misuse) Act 1964* and *Dangerous Drugs Act 1967* all drug offences were treated as equally serious. Cannabis and heroin possession attracted the same penalties. Pressure for reform built up as the law was deemed disproportionate and unfair. These Acts were superseded by the *Misuse of Drugs Act 1971* (MDA) which established a scale of harm. This key Act remains in force today, although over time it has had numerous amendments. Thereafter, offences involving different *classes* of drugs would attract varying penalties. The classes A, B and C were defined and the Advisory Council on the Misuse of Drugs (ACMD) was instituted as a statutory, advisory, non-departmental public body to make recommendations to government on the control of dangerous or otherwise harmful drugs, including classification and scheduling.

At first, the clinics continued Rolleston prescribing policies. But in the 1970s, London clinic doctors moved to cut down prescribing heroin: 'the emotional strain of continually dealing with addicts, combined (...) with the ingrained professional medical dislike of providing drugs for non-organic reasons, especially to deviant youth and to unproductive adults, worked to create a more intense revulsion to the needle among the London clinic staff' (Trebach, 1982, p. 192). Prescribing injectable heroin gradually gave way to methadone. HIV finally put injectables out of favour. The majority thereafter received oral methadone.

In the 1980s, with recognition of the link between injecting drug use and HIV/AIDS, policy shifted to support harm reduction. An 'epistemic community' shaped drug policy at this time, composed of addiction psychiatrists and voluntary sector workers and was supported crucially by the lead medical officer at the Department of Health (Dr Dorothy Black) together with progressive Conservative ministers, especially Norman Fowler. The ACMD was respected and led opinion, saying in a significant report that 'HIV is a greater threat to public and individual

Drug policy in the United Kingdom 221

health than drug misuse. The first goal of work with drug misusers must therefore be to prevent them from acquiring or transmitting the virus' (ACMD, 1988, p. 1). Services should be open and attractive to drug users. While abstinence remained their *ultimate* aim, needle exchanges and maintenance treatment expanded. The existence of a strong central government (led by Mrs Thatcher, herself a scientist) together with pressure from reforming social movements (allied with gay rights) allowed the move towards harm reduction to be presented as a pragmatic response of benefit to the whole society.

There was a significant shift towards greater attention to trafficking from the late 1980s, reflecting international developments. And from the early 1990s, a momentum built up to develop a more coherent and wide-ranging approach. There was 'a growing awareness that tackling drug misuse requires collaboration between a wider range of public services and the specialist voluntary and independent sectors who work with drug misusers' (Howard, Beadle and Maitland, 1994, p. ix). The numbers of notified addicts had continued to grow – reaching 37,200 in 1995 – and the amount of activity around responding to drugs had increased. *Tackling Drugs Together* (TDT) was introduced by Prime Minister (PM) John Major in 1995 as the new strategy for England, with complementary strategies in Scotland and Wales: partnership was at the core of the response. This is 'not just a job for Government – effective partnership to protect individuals and communities is the foundation of this strategy' said the PM. TDT marks the beginning of mainstreaming drugs. The drugs issue was brought into the public arena: no longer would it be a matter solely for specialists and hidden decision-makers. Families and communities were affected and should be involved in tackling it. Drugs policy began to be reframed away from the harm reduction and pragmatism that had characterised the 1980s and toward crime reduction (Duke, 2013).

Crime, drugs and a strong interventionist state

Through the late 1990s and into the first decade of the twenty-first century, discourses of 'enforcement' and 'community safety' began to dominate drugs policy and mandatory drug testing was introduced into the prison system (Duke, 2003). American practices such as coerced treatment, drug testing, and drug courts were transplanted to Britain (Duke, 2013). For New Labour, drugs treatment policy was part of an array of social policies focusing on modernisation, social exclusion and regeneration, all set within an 'evidence-based' approach.

Treatment was fundamental to the *1998 Ten Year Strategy*. The government and the Treasury had been persuaded that 'treatment works'. A cohort study (NTORS) evaluated favourably the cost-effectiveness of drug treatment (Gossop, 2003). The National Treatment Agency was set up to oversee what was a very big increase in expenditure. The treatment budget rose from £142 million in 2001/2002 to £406 million in 2009/2010. Increasing numbers of drug users entered formal treatment: 207,580 adults in 2008/9. The drugs workforce increased from 6,754 in 2002 to 10,628 in 2007.

The drug treatment field was transformed. New staff were recruited and trained. From being a relatively 'anarchic and quasi-religious movement', a more professional workforce appeared. With David Blunkett as Home Secretary (2001–2004) government policy focused on 'the most dangerous drugs, the most problematic drug users and the most deprived areas' (Updated Drug Strategy 2002). Drug Treatment and Testing Orders were introduced as was the Drugs Intervention Programme (DIP). Pressures were ratcheted up again with the *Drugs Act 2005* and quasi-compulsory treatment spread. Policy and expenditure focused on the 'problematic drug user' – which at this time for the British government meant those dependent on class A drugs (especially heroin, cocaine and crack) and persistent offenders. By 2009/2010 about 4,500 problematic drug users (PDUs) were entering treatment each month following referral from DIP.

However, while these achievements were being celebrated, criticisms of methadone maintenance resurfaced, creating a crisis in 2007. A BBC report 'revealed' that only 3% of drug users had left drug treatment free of all drugs (including methadone) in 2006/7. From then on, a clamour of voices attacked policy for focusing too much on numbers in treatment with not enough attention to the outcomes of treatment. A too-rapid expansion had increased the quantity but decreased the quality of the day-to-day services offered by drugs workers. The emphasis had been too much on simply containing the problem.

New Labour and the NTA accepted some of these points and produced a *2008 Drugs Strategy (Drugs: Protecting Families and Communities)* but there was little time to implement it as the government was ousted from power and replaced by a Conservative–Liberal Democrat Coalition in 2010.

Recovery, austerity and the lean and mean state

Following the 2008 financial crisis, government policies shifted towards austerity. Fortunately, statistics showed crime falling steadily. Now, the scapegoat was not the PDU but the 'scrounger' dependent on social assistance. Estimates suggested that 80% of PDUs (270,000 individuals) in England claimed an out-of-work benefit (Hay and Bauld, 2008).

In December 2010, the Coalition Government published its strategy, the shift in focus clear from the title, *'Reducing Demand, Restricting Supply, Building Recovery: supporting people to live a drug-free life'*. These policies included threats of removal of social assistance if individuals failed to address their drug and alcohol dependency. The Health and Social Care Act 2012 implemented in 2013 a reform of the health system and a transfer of some responsibilities to local authorities (LAs). The shake-up, while ostensibly encouraging strategic collaboration, led to a loss of institutional memory and a sense of fracture and fragmentation in services. New commissioning bodies were created. Although finances for public health and drug and alcohol services were initially ring-fenced, in future they would have to compete with other priorities for local political support in a context of dramatic cuts (40% to date) in LA budgets.

Drug policy in the United Kingdom   223

There was also growing concern around 'new' drugs. While treatment services tried to adapt to an ageing cohort of opiate users (MacGregor, 2015), among younger people new recreational drugs were appearing, posing a challenge to the old system of drugs classification.

Cannabis, NPS, recreational and performance-enhancing drugs

Through these years, there was another separate story regarding cannabis. Although in the later years of the twentieth century, there appeared to be a move towards decriminalisation, this went into reverse with the arrival of skunk. Liberalising moves had been encapsulated in the *Runciman Report* (Police Foundation, 2000). Attempts at reform included the Brixton police's cannabis experiment. The 2002 *Updated Drug Strategy* reclassified cannabis from B to C (but at the same time introduced an increased maximum penalty for class C supply of 14 years' imprisonment). Pragmatically, in 2004, policing guidelines indicated confiscation and warning as normal action on possession.

However, the government requested the ACMD to reconsider cannabis classification in the light of concerns about psychotic illness and increased supply of high-potency sinsemilla ('skunk'). In 2006 the ACMD advised retaining cannabis in class C, but despite this, in 2008 cannabis was reclassified from C to B. In 2009 an ACMD recommendation to downgrade MDMA to class B was also rejected by the Home Secretary.

Other changes to classification of particular substances also occurred: for example, in the *2005 Drugs Act* magic mushrooms were put in class A. October 2009 brought the firing of ACMD Chairman David Nutt, followed by the resignation of seven other members in protest, highlighting that expert advice was being overruled by politicians under pressure from the media and lobbying groups.

In 2010 a system of temporary bans on new 'legal highs' was introduced. This approach was overturned by the new Conservative government in 2015 (freed from the constraints of its Liberal Democrat partners) with proposals for a Bill to control a wide range of psychoactive substances not covered by the UN Drug Conventions. This new Bill further sidelined the ACMD and aroused controversy as it appeared set on prohibiting everything capable of producing a psychoactive effect, unless specifically exempted, like coffee or alcohol. A parliamentary committee commented that 'the speed at which the Government has brought forward this legislation, without any consultation on the specific detail of the Bill, has resulted in some weaknesses in the legislation being identified' (Home Affairs Committee, 2015, para. 20). Critics saw the Bill as legally flawed, scientifically problematic and potentially harmful (Stevens et al., 2015). The Act, passed in January, came into force in May 2016.[1]

---

1   The Psychoactive Substances Act makes it an offence to produce, supply, offer to supply, possess with intent to supply, possess on custodial premises, import or export psychoactive substances; that is, *any substance intended for human consumption that is capable of*

Trends in drug use

Were these shifts responses to changes in the way drugs were being used?

Over the years, since the MDA 1971, more drugs have been used by more people in more varied ways. Use became something familiar, not generally approved of, but recognised as a fact of life. Regular use was, however, only for a minority. Broadly speaking, there were two drug-using groups: one group selectively used on a recreational and largely non-problematic basis, and another (usually unemployed and socially excluded) took whatever drugs they could find in a chaotic and problematic manner (Buchanan, 2010).

The number of known Class A drug users rose dramatically over these years. From 509 in 1965 and 1,290 in 1967 to 450,000 in 1999 (the peak year) (Shapiro and Monaghan, 2014). It is now estimated that there are around 371,279 high-risk drug users in the UK (excluding Northern Ireland) equivalent to 9.16 per 1,000 population aged 15–64 (Burton et al., 2014).

After the turn of the century, drug use appeared to decline. Among young adults, annual cannabis prevalence fell from 30% in 2000 to 20% in 2009/10 (Bryan, Bono and Pudney, 2012). School surveys reported similar declines (Fuller et al., 2008; Davies et al., 2012). Use was higher in specific sub-groups such as club goers. Here, ecstasy and cocaine were popular while mephedrone fell out of favour. Chemsex became a problem among some gay men (McCall et al., 2015).

There appeared to be little symmetry between the extent to which illicit substances were used and their legal status (Shiner, 2009, p. 68). Much drug use was 'tentative, hesitant and short lived' (ibid., p. 69) with high rates of desistance and evidence of moderation. Most young adults who use illicit drugs focus on the less harmful substances. However tragic deaths continue to be regularly reported.

These patterns partly reflected trends in Europe as a whole but the UK shows some differences. In 2007, ESPAD reported that the vast majority of the students who had tried illicit drugs had used cannabis (Hibell et al., 2007, p. 13). But reported use of illicit drugs varied considerably across the countries (ibid.). The survey found that the overall trend between 2003 and 2007 in use of illicit drugs

producing a psychoactive effect. The maximum sentence will be 7 years' imprisonment. It excludes legitimate substances, such as food, alcohol, tobacco, nicotine, caffeine and medical products from the scope of the offence, as well as controlled drugs, which continue to be regulated by the Misuse of Drugs Act 1971. Seen as a success for scientific lobbying, it exempts healthcare activities and approved scientific research from the offences under the Act on the basis that persons engaged in such activities have a legitimate need to use psychoactive substances in their work. Responding to pressures relating to *public nuisance* at the local level, it includes provision for civil sanctions – prohibition notices, premises notices, prohibition orders and premises orders (breach of the two orders will be a criminal offence) – to enable the police and local authorities to respond with actions such as shutting down 'head shops'. Importantly, and likely to lead to issues around policing practice, it provides powers to *stop and search* persons, vehicles and vessels, enter and search premises in accordance with a warrant, and to seize and destroy psychoactive substances.

Drug policy in the United Kingdom 225

was downward, although a handful of countries displayed increases. Notably Ireland and the United Kingdom dropped substantially in illicit drug use when the whole period was considered (down roughly 14 percentage points) (ibid.). An example of variations across countries is shown by comparing Estonia with the UK: these were on the same prevalence level in 2007 (about 28%), but they had reached that point from opposite directions; an increase from 8% in 1995 in the case of Estonia and a decrease from 42% in that of the United Kingdom (ibid.).

Drug use in the UK does, however, remain relatively high in EU terms. The appendices to the European Drug Report 2015 show the UK well above average regarding most indicators compared to other European countries: for example, high rate of problem opioid use (7.9–8.4 per 1,000); lifetime use of cocaine 9.5 compared to 4.6 EU average; 11.1 amphetamines (EU 3.5); ecstasy 9.3 (EU 3.6); cannabis 29.9 (EU 23.3); and a high rate of drug induced deaths (44.6 per million, EU 17.3) (EMCDDA, 2015).

Max Daly concluded: 'The official statistics do show that what could be called "traditional" drug use has been in overall decline for some years, albeit with recent spikes in cocaine, ecstasy and ketamine use. However, with the advent of the newer drugs and increasing use of prescribed drugs, it would seem that the drug scene has become more complex, diverse and difficult to predict' (Daly, 2015).

A recent Crime Survey for England and Wales (CSEW) found that while use has dropped sharply over the past ten years, young adults remain those most likely to take drugs: about one in five 16–24 year olds used in the past year. The proportion of those aged 11 to 15 who reported ever having tried drugs is at a new low of 15%, down from 30% in 2003 (Office for National Statistics, 2015).

Key current concerns

Drugs continued to be viewed as a significant problem. Since 1996, CSEW has consistently estimated that around a quarter of adults perceive a problem in their local area with 'people using or dealing' (Office for National Statistics, 2015). This was despite the fact that since 2003 recorded acquisitive crime had fallen by 39% across England and Wales. The improved availability of drug treatment played a part in this. The number of individuals in contact with treatment services in England grew from 85,000 in 1998/9 to more than 220,000 in 2009/10, with use of heroin or crack predominating. The number of under 18-year-olds in the treatment population reporting a problem with a Class A drug is, however, very small. Their main problem drug is cannabis. In 2009/10 the number of young people reporting a cannabis problem was over 13,000, i.e. 87% of the total population of young people in contact with drug treatment services. This became a major issue.

Drug-related deaths also became a cause for concern. For example, recent evidence shows drug-related deaths in Scotland steadily increasing. In 2013, 448 unintentional and undetermined deaths involving controlled substances occurred there, over half of whom lived in the most deprived areas. The mean age of these individuals increased from 34.4 in 2009 to 39.1 in 2013 (Barnsdale, Gordon and McAuley, 2015). The drug most frequently found to be implicated in death in 2013 was heroin/morphine (44%), followed by methadone (42%). Prescription of methadone became controversial, particularly in Scotland.

Another continuing issue is the situation in prisons. Drugs offences contribute to the prison population (almost 13,000 prisoners, over 15% of the prison population). A majority of these involve drugs other than cannabis. More significantly, around two-thirds of those in custody are reported to be recent drug users with an estimated 40% of prisoners received into custody being problematic drug users, 40% of whom identify as people who inject drugs (Burton et al., 2014). A number of people are introduced to opiates for the first time while in prison.

In 2014–2015 the rapid increase in the availability of new psychoactive substances (such as 'Spice' and 'Black') was said to have had a severe impact in prisons, leading to debt and associated violence. Survey responses suggested the ready availability of illegal drugs in prisons (HM Chief Inspector of Prisons for England and Wales, 2015).

Explaining drug trends

How have sociologists explained these trends? 'Something like a coherent sociology of drug use began to emerge during the 1960s' (Shiner, 2009, p. 14), provoked by a seminal contribution from Jock Young (Young, 1971). The 1960s saw a rise in the number of young people and increasing affluence: drug use became part of a counter-culture. Use of drugs gave not just pleasure but also meaning and identity. Commenting on these times, Trebach attributed heroin use to the attraction and need for deviance, even defiance, in that decade (Trebach, 1982, p. 177).

Analyses of societal responses pointed to the role of the media in conveying distorted images (Cohen and Young, 1981; Murji, 1998; Coomber, Morris and Dunn, 2000; Davies, 2011). Moral panic arose because images were based on media representations and not direct familiarity.

These ideas challenged the medical notion of drug users as sick or under-socialised. However, the social psychiatric view based on a deficit model continued to dominate in the 1970s.

In the 1980s, ethnographic studies in the North of England showed how drug use had spread beyond London (Parker, Newcombe and Bakx, 1987; Pearson, Gilman and McIvor, 1987). The main interest now was in what was happening to working-class communities: new patterns of heroin use were associated with deprivation and social change, de-industrialisation, poverty and unemployment.

Explanations have highlighted socio-structural changes and the fact that de-industrialisation coincided with an increased supply of heroin as a result of the Iranian revolution. Globalisation and the rise of organised crime, exacerbated by the lifting of border controls in the free trade European Union, made trafficking easier. Ideological changes were also important: with the dominance of neo-liberalism, the state pulled back from providing a comprehensive universalist welfare state and in its place built a punitive state especially aiming at controlling those who were unable/unwilling to integrate into 'successful self-reliance' (Seddon, 2010).

With the arrival of the risk society (Beck, 1992) the ubiquitous concept of risk was increasingly used to explain drug-taking. Drug-related difficulties were seen in the epidemiological sense of 'risk factors' which correlate with patterns of use and harm. A reconfiguration of addiction as risky behaviour took place and corresponded with a new focus on lifestyle as a source of disease. Harms experienced were increasingly seen as the responsibility of the user rather than emanating from the social structure (Green, 1997). Individual behaviour change rather than social reform was the logical priority. While this linked to harm reduction policies in the 1980s, in the 1990s the significant change was to focus on negative consequences for communities and society rather than on harm to the individual (Bergeron and Reuter, 2009).

New cultures were being shaped within an expanding night-time economy, closely linked to nineties urban regeneration schemes. These created leisure zones with high concentrations of clubs and drinking venues. The use of illicit drugs was 'strongly linked to other leisure related activities and tends to form part of a distinct package based around pubs, clubs, binge drinking, drunkenness and smoking which suggests a particular commitment to hedonistic consumption and intoxication' (Shiner, 2009, p. 119). Studies of the raves of the 1990s (Ward, 2010) explained drug taking as deliberately disorderly behaviour. Crime and drug use were a form of rebellion – a 'slow riot'.

The North West Cohort Study disseminated the concept of recreational drug use – use for pleasure – rather than as a compensation for deprivation (Parker, Aldridge and Measham, 1998; Measham, Aldridge and Parker, 2000). These studies introduced the concept of *normalisation*. Exposure to, and experimentation with, illicit drugs had, it was argued, become a 'normalised' adolescent experience (Measham, Newcombe and Parker, 1994). Opponents of the normalisation thesis did not dispute that drug use patterns were changing and drug usage increasing in Britain during the 1990s. Rather, they asserted that the normalisation thesis over-stated the level of acceptability of such behaviours amongst young people and the pace and extent of changes in drug use patterns. Pearson and Shiner analysed responses in surveys conducted for the Runciman Report (2000). These showed that adults of all ages from 16 to 59 years of age consistently saw heroin, cocaine, ecstasy and amphetamine as 'very' or 'fairly' harmful. With equal consistency, however, a majority of two-thirds did not at that time (before the arrival of skunk and accounts of its links to psychosis) see cannabis as nearly so harmful (Pearson and Shiner, 2002). Pearson and Shiner concluded that the views of young people and adults in modern Britain are not what policy-makers and researchers often imagine them to be and that the data indicate that any shift towards normalisation has been much more ambiguous and contradictory than is allowed for in the existing literature.

Legal framework, sentencing and policing practices

While in a European context Britain's drug laws may appear relatively repressive in terms of the potential maximum length of imprisonment for various offences, in practice sentencing is relatively liberal: with regard to the proportions actually imprisoned for use or possession (EMCDDA, 2009, fig. 2); and even regarding the likelihood of being imprisoned for supply (ibid., fig. 3); although they are relatively repressive regarding the length of prison sentences for supply once conferred (ibid., fig. 5).

The current classification system is contained in Schedule 2 to the 1971 MDA and divides all the controlled drugs into three Classes – A, B and C. Since the Act came into force, there have been various amendments to incorporate new drugs as they have emerged or to reflect perceptions or evidence of changes in the harmfulness and/or misuse of existing and previously uncontrolled drugs.

The main principle dictating classification is that the greater the impact a drug has on individuals and society the higher the Class within which it will fall. This principle was challenged by a widely cited article from David Nutt and colleagues (Nutt et al., 2007). In 2006, a parliamentary report advised that the 'current classification system is not fit for purpose and should be replaced with a more scientifically based scale of harm, decoupled from penalties for possession and trafficking' (House of Commons Science and Technology Committee, 2006, p. 3).

Recent figures from the Office for National Statistics (ONS) record total drug offences in 2014 at 178,719: trafficking 28,021; and possession 150,698. A prison sentence is the most common outcome when found guilty at court of import/export and trafficking offences but a fine, community sentence or conditional discharge are the most common disposals for possession offences.

Having steadily risen between 2007 and 2011, the number of cannabis convictions fell by 6% during 2012 but were still far higher than in 2007 (+35%).

Table 15.2 Drugs classification system under the MDA

	A	*B*	*C*
Main drugs in each class	Powder cocaine, crack cocaine, ecstasy, LSD, magic mushrooms, heroin, methadone, methamphetamine; injectable Class B drugs (such as amphetamines)	Amphetamines, barbiturates, cannabis, codeine, mephedrone, ketamine	Anabolic steroids, minor tranquillisers, benzodiazepines, GHB/GBL, BZP, khat
Maximum penalty for possession	7 years' imprisonment plus unlimited fine	5 years' imprisonment plus unlimited fine	2 years' imprisonment plus unlimited fine
Maximum penalty for supply	Life imprisonment plus unlimited fine	14 years' imprisonment plus unlimited fine	14 years' imprisonment plus unlimited fine

The majority of drug offences were dealt with outside of a court setting (67%). Of the drug offences settled outside of court, over half were in the form of a cannabis warning (57%), followed by cautions (31%) with penalty notices for disorder accounting for 12%.

Of the 56,301 individuals sentenced at court for drug offences in England and Wales during 2013, 16% were given immediate custody. The most common sentence was a fine (37% of cases). The vast majority of those convicted of import/export offences received immediate custody (86%) with an average custodial sentence length of 67.4 months for Class A importation offences (Burton et al., 2014, table 9.4). The average length of a custodial sentence for cannabis production remained stable at around one year until 2006 but has seen a steady increase in more recent years, as a result of the increased incidence of large-scale home-grown cannabis cultivation. These statistics confirm the conclusions reached in EMCDDA 2009 regarding the UK's varying positions on a scale from liberal to repressive, when different offences and sentences are reviewed.

The *Misuse of Drugs Act 1971* provided police officers with powers to stop and search for drugs if they had reasonable suspicion that a citizen was in possession of harmful illicit substances. Over 550,000 searches for drugs took place in 2009/10 in England and Wales, but with only 7% of those resulting in arrest. In 2011 serious rioting erupted in London and other cities sparked by the shooting dead by police of a so-called 'drug dealer' Mark Duggan, setting off a wave of disorder inflamed by underlying grievances.

Coincidentally or not, a Freedom of Information Request has revealed offences relating to cannabis recorded by English and Welsh police forces – including penalty notices, cautions, charges and summons – fell by almost a third from a peak of 145,400 in 2011–2012 to 101,905 in 2014–2015 (Ramesh and Jayanetti, 2015). This has been interpreted as a silent relaxation of drugs policy in the past five years, although it could also be seen as a deliberate lifting of pressure on minority communities via the hated stop and search procedures. London Metropolitan Police recorded 40% fewer cannabis possession offences in 2014 than in 2009–2010.

The background to this is that a paradoxical result of the 2004 Cannabis Warning System was an increase in the number of searches in following years. This overtly more liberal measure allowed officers to write a warning for cannabis possession if the person had not been caught in the previous 12 months and was 18 years old or above. This allowed the officer to generate a sanctioned detection in less than an hour, a process that could take 10–12 hours with a shoplifting case. It was the speedy generation of a sanctioned detection that encouraged a dramatic rise in drug searches and increased feelings of resentment in some local areas towards the police.

Ethnographic research by Daniel Bear has shown the role of police decision-making at street level, which can be linked to racial discrimination and city riots (Bear, 2013). He reported that stop and search activity is directed at finding drugs nearly 50% of the time and across the London area the number of drugs stops had risen considerably. There is a very high rate of stop and search amongst BME populations. A key finding was that officers find drugs in the borough Bear researched less than 7% of the time they search someone for drugs.

A contrast thus appears between the concentration of policy rhetoric and action at the highest level on the 'problem drug user' and the reality that much policing effort has actually been targeted at low-level cannabis users. Recently, however, individual Police Commanders – partly due to shrinking police budgets – have chosen to reduce attention to cannabis in order to focus on greater threats to safety and security.

Drivers of continuity and change

Key features of the British case are the distinction between social attitudes and expert discourses, and their respective impact on drugs policy. Effectively mobilised evidence has at times played a part in the development of policy. The move to harm reduction and a more liberal approach to drugs was a response to HIV/ AIDS: research and evaluation studies, combined with active pressure from voluntary organisations and user groups, clinicians and scientists, found a window of opportunity in high level political and civil servant interest in the 1980s. Similarly, the special interest shown by Tony Blair in the late 1990s and 2000s assisted with treatment expansion and the drug testing approach.

A complex array and growing number of political actors have focused on the drugs issue in recent decades. Committees and advisory groups, participants in commissions, enquiries and reports, were drawn from people with interest, experience or expertise, such as lawyers, doctors, academics, journalists, police officers, and community and user groups. Similarly Parliamentary Select Committee consultations provided a forum within which stakeholders could mobilise and present their views, most recently featuring the celebrity comedian and activist Russell Brand. Popular books, pamphlets, television and radio programmes have also influenced opinion, often involving collaborations with pressure groups like Release or Transform (Rolles, 2009; Hari, 2015). Rethinking of opinion on cannabis and mental health reflected active pressure from leading psychiatrist Robin Murray. When scientists and doctors such as Murray and David Nutt have campaigned, they have been able to influence opinion and sometimes policy, not always in the same direction however.

Evidence has to compete with interests and values in the boxing ring of politics: the tension between evidence and values has been a consistent theme in drug policy formulation (Monaghan, 2014). For example, the turn to linking crime and drugs in the 1990s was not merely a device to alarm, manipulate and control from above. To a large extent, politicians were responding to pressures from below, from local newspapers, parents, residents, police and health workers regarding acquisitive crime, drugs paraphernalia and waiting lists for treatment. While the move to harm reduction in the 1980s had been driven mainly from the top, under the influence of expert doctors and advisors, the later broadening of the policy community and increase in the salience of drugs as a public issue led to shifts away from the pragmatism which had characterised the earlier periods (MacGregor, 1998). Over time there has been an increase in research, publications, policy documents and in the number of actors on the drugs stage – the landscape is now very crowded. Individuals, institutions and agencies jostle for influence.

Social attitudes may play a role in shaping policy. Attitudes to drugs have become more volatile, complex and nuanced over time. Views on the legal status of cannabis seem to have rebounded from the increasingly tolerant approach recorded by the *British Social Attitudes* surveys in the 1980s and 1990s and the Scottish Social Attitudes survey in 2001. For example, support for legalising cannabis fell from 37% in Scotland in 2001 (note that the Runciman national surveys had found 50% then in favour) to 24% in 2009 (Ormston, Bradshaw and Anderson, 2010). Attitudes towards prosecution for the possession of cannabis also hardened. Research based on data from the British Social Attitudes survey indicated that these changes reflected an increase in the perceived potency of cannabis and growing concern about its long-term health impacts. In 2009 fewer people accepted the more general statement that 'we need to accept that using illegal drugs is a normal part of some people's lives' than in 2001 (25% compared with 40%). However a more recent Ipsos MORI poll in 2013, commissioned by the campaigning group Transform, seemed to find that 53% supported cannabis legalisation (legal regulation of production and supply) or decriminalisation of possession of cannabis. Only 1 in 7 supported heavier penalties and more being spent on enforcement for cannabis offences. What is clear is that public opinion responds to events and to the way questions are asked and shows no consistent trend over time, although, in general, younger generations are becoming more liberal than their predecessors (Skinner et al., 2013).

Reports have also shaped understanding of the drugs problem and policy proposals. These mark staging posts on the drug policy road: examples include those from the ACMD, Audit Commission and House of Commons Select Committees (MacGregor, 2012).

A particularly significant report was excluded from public discussion until it came to light via a Freedom of Information Request. The Strategy Unit (set up to promote a rational and evidence-based approach to policy development in the early years of the Blair governments) considered the drugs situation (Birt, 2003). Its conclusions justified the high priority placed on drugs policy at that time and encouraged Prime Minister Tony Blair to take a personal interest and lead policy changes actively. This report was based on a thorough review of existing evidence. Presenting his findings to a high level, confidential meeting with the prime minister and ministers, using PowerPoint slides and outlining clear conclusions, John Birt persuaded the inner circle of policy-makers that all drugs have an adverse impact but that heroin and crack are the most addictive, expensive and harmful. The total harms arising from drug use were calculated at that time to amount to £24 billion a year (of which £16 billion related to crime). Few were receiving treatment. The policy shift to expansion of treatment and the target to increase the numbers engaged in treatment was a direct response to such evidence and a result of the effective mobilisation of evidence by those employed in the Strategy Unit, backed up by discrete lobbying by leading activists.

The evidence seemed to show that it was possible for demand-side policies to have an impact on the drugs problem but influencing supply was much more difficult. However, critics have argued that the evidence supporting causality between drug use and crime was exaggerated and overshadowed alternative explanations: there is a 'relationship' between the two but the issue of causality is complex and mediated by underlying socio-economic factors such as inequality, deprivation and unemployment (Stevens, 2010).

Other reports, especially those from think tanks, have tended to argue for a change of direction (Police Foundation, 2000; RSA, 2007). The right-wing think-tank the Centre for Social Justice vigorously criticised harm reduction and use of methadone under the Labour administration (Centre for Social Justice, 2007) supported by other reports (Gyngell, 2009; 2011) and has continued to campaign on the issue (Centre for Social Justice, 2014; 2015). An exception was the UK Drug Policy Commission (UKDPC) which was explicitly set up to encourage a more evidence-based policy (UKDPC, 2012). These reports were generally funded by non-governmental sources and charitable bodies.

Indicators of policy success and failure

One indicator of the success of the New Labour policies could be said to be that by 2011 the total heroin/crack population had fallen to 250,000 with about 150,000 in treatment.

Morgan assessed the effect that heroin and crack-cocaine use may have had on acquisitive crime (i.e. theft-type offences) in England and Wales from 1980 (Morgan, 2014) and concluded that the epidemic could account for at least one-half of the rise in acquisitive crime in England and Wales to 1995 and between one-quarter and one-third of the fall to 2012, as the epidemic cohort aged, received treatment, quit illicit drug use or died.

Several commentators have bemoaned the lack of overall policy evaluation in this field (Reuter and Stevens, 2007; House of Commons Committee of Public Accounts, 2010). The Home Office has now constructed a Drug Strategy Evaluation Framework. Reuter and Stevens observe that despite the increased investment in treatment, the majority of government spending on responding to illegal drugs is still devoted to enforcing drug laws. From the available data, they calculated that in the UK, as in other nations, enforcement expenditure (including police, courts and prisons) accounts for most of the total expenditure on drug policy. Taking into account the rise in the average sentence length (37 months for drug dealing in 2004), the courts handed out nearly three times as much prison time in 2004 as they did 10 years earlier. Imprisoning drug offenders for relatively substantial periods does not appear to represent a cost-effective response, Reuter and Stevens argued.

It has been claimed that Britain has one of the best treatment systems in the world but this is now under threat from austerity policies. With the reduced influence of addiction psychiatry, the decline of the 'clinics' and their replacement by large not-for-profit drugs agencies like Addaction, Turning Point and CGL (formerly CRI) – arguably offering a more integrated and wide-ranging, person-centred approach but possibly neglecting underlying medical conditions both physical and mental – the abolition of the NTA and the liquidation of the charity DrugScope, what was a consistent 'command and control' system is now threatened by cuts, de-professionalisation and fragmentation. As other issues like immigration, child sexual exploitation and terrorism assume centre stage, drugs has fallen down the list of policy priorities. Where it is given priority, it is linked to so-called welfare dependency and worklessness, opening the door to harsher policies as state expenditure is slashed (Monaghan and Wincup, 2013). Current discussions are considering whether drug and alcohol dependent people, along with those who are obese, should be required to engage with treatment if they are to receive social benefits (Black, 2015). A new Conservative Drugs Strategy is expected to make links to a concerted 'life-chances' social agenda, including policies on prisons, crime and troubled families, as well as continuing welfare reform.

Conclusion

From being a relatively simple (though often misrepresented) 'British system' – when 'little more than masterly inactivity in the face of what was an almost non-existent addiction problem' (Downes, 1977) – British drug policy has evolved into its current complex, contradictory set of arrangements. This pattern is characterised by variety: in the strategies of the different nations of the UK; in services and police operations in different localities, especially as decisions and commissioning are devolved to local authorities; and in differences between stated laws and policies and how these are implemented in practice. Changes over time, influenced by funding issues and competition from other policy priorities, are not easily captured by simple labels. At best, the current British case could be described as flexible and adaptable, even pragmatic: at worst, discretion in policing can emerge as unjust discrimination, and the ability of a patchwork of drugs services to respond adequately to need and to any future epidemic is questionable. 'Drugs' continues to provide copy for sensational media reports. But the essential features of the debate seem hardly to have moved over the last thirty years. Entrenched positions remain. Most likely in the future, the UK will continue to base its policies in the very English vice of hypocrisy – talking tough and 'sending the right messages' but in practice veering between relatively benign professional care and malign neglect or even deliberate scapegoating of unpopular groups. While existing laws and institutions often seem unfit for purpose, reform would not be a simple matter, as new substances and complex patterns of use appear and reappear, and related problems overlap with more deep-seated social issues.

References

ACMD (1988) *AIDS and Drug Misuse* Part 1. London: Advisory Council on the Misuse of Drugs.

BARNSDALE, L., GORDON, R. and MCAULEY, A. (2015) *The National Drug-Related Deaths Database (Scotland) Report: Analysis of Deaths occurring in 2013*. Edinburgh: National Services Scotland.

BEAR, D. (2013) Adapting, Acting Out, or Standing Firm: Understanding the Place of Drugs in the Policing of a London Borough. PhD The London School of Economics and Political Science.

BECK, U. (1992) *The Risk Society*. London: Sage.

BERGERON, H. and REUTER, P. (2009) Editors' Introduction: Policy Change and Policy Analysis. *International Journal of Drug Policy*. 20. pp. 455–457.

BERRIDGE, V. (1999) *Opium and the People: Opiate Use and Policy in 19th and Early 20th Century Britain*, London: Free Association.

BIRT, J. (2003) *Strategy Unit Drugs Project*. London: Strategy Unit. Unpublished.

BLACK, C. (2015) *Independent Review into the Impact on Employment Outcomes of Drug or Alcohol Addiction, and Obesity: Call for Evidence*. London: DWP.

BRYAN, M., BONO, E. D. and PUDNEY, S. (2012) *Licensing and Regulation of the Cannabis Market in England and Wales: Towards a Cost-Benefit Analysis*. Colchester, Essex: Institute for Social and Economic Research, University of Essex.

BUCHANAN, J. (2010) Drug Policy Under New Labour 1997–2010: Prolonging the War on Drugs. *Probation Journal: The Journal of Community and Criminal Justice*. 57. pp. 250–262.

BURTON, R., THOMSON, F., VISINTIN, C. and WRIGHT, C. (2014) *United Kingdom Drug Situation: Annual Report to the European Monitoring Centre for Drugs and Drug Addiction*. London: Public Health England.

CENTRE FOR SOCIAL JUSTICE (2007) *Addictions: Towards Recovery*. London: Centre for Social Justice.

CENTRE FOR SOCIAL JUSTICE (2014) *Ambitious for Recovery: Tackling Drug and Alcohol Addiction in the UK. Breakthrough Britain II*. London: Centre for Social Justice.

CENTRE FOR SOCIAL JUSTICE (2015) *No Quick Fix: Exposing the Depth of Britain's Drug and Alcohol Problem*. London: Centre for Social Justice.

COHEN, S. and YOUNG, J. (1981) *The Manufacture of News: Social Problems, Deviance and the Mass Media*. London: Sage.

COOMBER, R., MORRIS, C. and DUNN, L. (2000) How the Media do Drugs: Quality Control and the Reporting of Drug Issues in the UK Print Media. *International Journal of Drug Policy*. 11. pp .217–225.

DALY, M. (2015) *Down a Stony Road: The 2014 DrugScope Street Drug Survey*. London: DrugScope.

DAVIES, C., ENGLISH, L., STEWART, C., EDGINTON, M., MCVEIGH, J. and BELLIS, M. A. (2012) *United Kingdom Drug Situation: Annual Report to the European Monitoring Centre for Drugs and Drug Addiction (EMCDDA) 2012*. London: Department of Health.

DAVIES, N. (2011) *Flat Earth News: An Award-winning Reporter Exposes Falsehood, Distortion and Propaganda in the Global Media*. New York: Random House.

DOWNES, D. (1977) The Drug Addict as Folk Devil. In Rock, P. (ed.). *Drugs and Politics*. New Jersey: Transaction Books.

DUKE, K. (2003) *Drugs, Prisons and Policy-Making*, London: Palgrave MacMillan.

DUKE, K. (2013) From Crime to Recovery: The Reframing of British Drugs Policy? *Journal of Drug Issues*. 43. pp. 39–55.

EMCDDA (2009) *Drug Offences: Sentencing and other Outcomes*. Lisbon: EMCDDA.

EMCDDA (2015) *European Drug Report 2015*. Lisbon: EMCDDA.

FULLER, E., CLEMENS, S., JOTANGIA, D., LYNCH, S., NICHOLSON, S. and PIGOTT, S. (2008) *Drug Use, Smoking and Drinking Among Young People in England in 2007*. London: NatCen.

GOSSOP, M. (2003) The National Treatment Outcome Research Study (NTORS): 4–5 year follow-up results. *Addiction*. 98. pp. 291–303.

GREEN, J. (1997) *Risk and Misfortune: The Social Construction of Accidents*. London: Routledge.

GYNGELL, K. (2009) *The Phoney War on Drugs*. London: Centre for Policy Studies.

GYNGELL, K. (2011) *Breaking the Habit: Why the State Should Stop Dealing Drugs and Start Doing Rehab*. London: Centre for Policy Studies.

HARI, J. (2015) *Chasing the Scream: The First and Last Days of the War on Drugs*. London: Bloomsbury Publishing.

HAY, G. and BAULD, L. (2008) *Population Estimates of Problematic Drug Users in England who Access DWP Benefits: A Feasibility Study*. Department for Work and Pensions Working Paper. London: DWP.

HIBELL, B., GUTTORMSSON, U., AHLSTRÖM, S., BALAKIREVA, O., BJARNASON, T., KOKKEVI, A. and KRAUS, L. (2007) *The 2007 ESPAD Report: Substance Use Among Students in 35 European Countries*. The European School Survey Project on Alcohol and Other Drugs. Stockholm.

HM CHIEF INSPECTOR OF PRISONS FOR ENGLAND AND WALES. (2015) *Annual Report 2014–15*. London: HM Prisons.

HOME AFFAIRS COMMITTEE. (2015) *Psychoactive Substances: first report of session 2015–16*. London: House of Commons.

HOUSE OF COMMONS COMMITTEE OF PUBLIC ACCOUNTS. (2010) *Tackling Problem Drug Use*. London: House of Commons.

HOUSE OF COMMONS SCIENCE AND TECHNOLOGY COMMITTEE. (2006) *Drug Classification: Making a Hash of it?* London: UK Parliament.

HOWARD, R., BEADLE, P. and MAITLAND, J. (1994) *Across the Divide: Building Community Partnerships to Tackle Drug Misuse*. London: Department of Health.

INTERDEPARTMENTAL COMMITTEE ON DRUG ADDICTION (1965) *Drug Addiction*. London: HMSO.

MACGREGOR, S. (1998) Pragmatism or Principle? Continuity and Change in the British Approach to Treatment and Control. In Coomber, R. (ed.). *The Control of Drugs and Drug Users: Reason or Reaction?* Amsterdam: Harwood Academic Publishers.

MACGREGOR, S. (2012) Parliamentary Committees and Drug Policy Governance. In Singleton, N. (ed.). *Essays on the Governance of Drug Policy: Bringing Evidence and Analysis Together to Inform UK Drug Policy*. London: UKDPC.

MACGREGOR, S. (2015) Proposals for Policy Development: drugs. In Crome, L., Wu, L.-T., Rao, R. T. and Crome, P. (eds.). *Substance Use and Older People*. Oxford: Wiley Blackwell.

MCCALL, H., ADAMS, N., MASON, D. and WILLIS, J. (2015) What is Chemsex and Why Does it Matter? *British Medical Journal*. 3 November 2015. 351. h5790.

MEASHAM, F., ALDRIDGE, J. and PARKER, H. (2000) *Dancing on Drugs: Risk, Health and Hedonism in the British Club Scene*. London: Free Association Books.

MEASHAM, F., NEWCOMBE, R. and PARKER, H. (1994) The Normalisation of Recreational Drug Use Amongst Young People in North West England. *British Journal of Sociology*. 45(2). pp. 287–312.

MONAGHAN, M. (2014) Drug Policy Governance in the UK: Lessons From Changes to and Debates Concerning the Classification of Cannabis under the 1971 Misuse of Drugs Act. *International Journal of Drug Policy*. 25. pp. 1025–1030.

MONAGHAN, M. and WINCUP, E. (2013) Work and the Journey to Recovery: Exploring the Implications of Welfare Reform for Methadone Maintenance Clients. *International Journal of Drug Policy*. 24. pp. 81–86.

MORGAN, N. (2014) *The Heroin Epidemic of the 1980s and 1990s and its Effect on Crime Trends – Then and Now*. London: Home Office.

MURJI, K. (1998) The Agony and the Ecstasy: Drugs, Media and Morality. In Coomber, R. (ed.). *The Control of Drugs and Drug Users: Reason or Reaction*. Harwood: Prentice Hall.

NUTT, D., KING, L. A., SAULSBURY, W. and BLAKEMORE, C. (2007) Development of a Rational Scale to Assess the Harms of Drugs of Potential Misuse. *Lancet*. 369. pp. 1047–1053.

OFFICE FOR NATIONAL STATISTICS (2015) Crime in England and Wales, Year Ending December 2014. *Statistical Bulletin*. London: ONS.

ORMSTON, R., BRADSHAW, P. and ANDERSON, S. (2010) *Scottish Social Attitudes Survey 2009: Public Attitudes to Drugs and Drug Use in Scotland*. Edinburgh: Scottish Centre for Social Research (ScotCen). Available from: www.scotland.gov.uk/socialresearch. [Accessed 2 May 2016].

PARKER, H., ALDRIDGE, J. and MEASHAM, F. (1998) *Illegal Leisure*. London: Routledge.

PARKER, H., NEWCOMBE, R. and BAKX, K. (1987) The New Heroin Users: Prevalence and Characteristics in Wirral, Merseyside. *British Journal of Addiction*. 82. pp. 147–157.

PEARSON, G., GILMAN, M. and MCIVOR, S. (1987) *Young People and Heroin*. Aldershot: Gower.

PEARSON, G. and SHINER, M. (2002) Rethinking the Generation Gap: Attitudes to Illicit Drugs Among Young People and Adults. *Criminal Justice*. 2. pp. 71–86.

POLICE FOUNDATION (2000) *Drugs and the Law: Report of the Inquiry into the Misuse of Drugs Act 1971*. London: London Police Foundation.

RAMESH, R. and JAYANETTI, C. (2015). Steep fall in cannabis offences points to silent relaxation of drugs policy. *The Guardian* 19 October 2015. Available from: http://www.theguardian.com/politics/2015/oct/18/steep-fall-cannabis-possession-offences-silent-relaxation-of-drugs-policy [Accessed 2 May 2016].

REUTER, P. and STEVENS, A. (2007) *An Analysis of UK Drug Policy*. London: UKDPC.

ROLLES, S. (2009) *After the War on Drugs: Blueprint for Regulation*. London: Transform Drug Policy Foundation.

RSA (2007) *Drugs: Facing the Facts. The Report of the RSA Commission on Illegal Drugs, Communities and Public Policy*. London: RSA.

SEDDON, T. (2010) *A History of Drugs: Drugs and Freedom in the Liberal Age*. London: Routledge.

SHAPIRO, H. and MONAGHAN, G. (2014) UK Drug Scene Timeline: 1995–2014. *DrugLink*. London: DrugScope.

SHINER, M. (2009) *Drug Use and Social Change: The Distortion of History*. Houndmills: Palgrave Macmillan.

SKINNER, G., FORBES, C., DUFFY, B. and CAMERON, D. (2013) *Understanding Society: Generations*. London: Ipsos MORI.

STEVENS, A. (2010) *Drugs, Crime and Public Health: The Political Economy of Drug Policy*. London: Routledge.

STEVENS, A., FORTSON, R., MEASHAM, F. and SUMNALL, H. (2015) Legally Flawed, Scientifically Problematic, Potentially Harmful: The UK Psychoactive Substance Bill. *International Journal of Drug Policy*. 26(12). pp. 1167–1170.

TREBACH, A. S. (1982) *The Heroin Solution*. New Haven: Yale University Press.

UKDPC (2012) *A Fresh Approach to Drugs*. London: UKDPC.

WARD, J. (2010) *Flashback: Drugs and Dealing in the Golden Age of the London Rave Scene*. Cullompton: Willan Publishing.

YOUNG, J. (1971) *The Drugtakers: The Social Meaning of Drug Use*. London: MacGibbon and Kee.

Part III

Trends and prospects in European drug policies

Chapter 16

Changing paradigms in drug policies in EU Member States

From digression to convergence

Franz Trautmann

Introduction

Discussions about drug policies in EU Member States frequently point at the differences between EU Member States. The view on harm reduction still seems to be the main divide in the EU drug policy debate. While some countries put the emphasis on the reduction or elimination of drug use as the principal goal, other countries focus on the reduction of the adverse consequences of drug use as the principal goal. However, behind the sometimes strident dispute about the pros and cons of harm reduction, a different reality has developed. Different studies show that the past two decades are characterised by an increasing harmonisation of drug policies in EU Member States (Trautmann et al., 2009; Trautmann et al., 2015).

In our analysis of the developments of the drug problem and drug policy in the period between 1998 and 2007 we concluded: 'Looking into drug policy globally there is a surprising amount of agreement on the aims of drug policy and the measures to realise these aims. There is no real dissent about the essentials of supply and demand reduction. The only drug policy element which still evokes substantial opposition from some countries is harm reduction.' (Trautmann et al., 2009, p. 229).

This trend can be traced in policy documents like drug strategies and action plans: key concepts, objectives and key constituents reveal a broad consensus among EU Member States. This agreement is also reflected in the EU Drug Strategy (Trautmann et al., 2009). One shared key feature is the choice for a balanced, integrated and evidence-based approach, looking for an effective combination of supply and demand reduction measures, taking on board new approaches and addressing new challenges that have been identified in recent years (Council of the European Union, 2012). In drug laws and the implementation of policy measures one can also find this trend towards an increasingly broad consent in the EU. In all EU Member States there is strong political backing for prevention and treatment and a wider acceptance of harm reduction measures. On the demand reduction side one can also observe a reduced willingness to punish drug users, mirrored on the supply reduction side by a tougher, more punitive approach towards the production and trafficking of illicit drugs: apparently the other side of the same coin.

Approach

In this chapter the focus is on identifying and better understanding the key forces and factors behind this convergence. Three studies form the basis of the article. A point of departure is an analysis of the developments of the drugs problem and drug policy between 1998 and 2007 in a study based on a systematic data collection in 18 countries all over the world through desk research and expert interviews (Trautmann et al., 2009). The second is a Delphi study focusing on the future development of key trends in the illicit drugs market and drug policy in the EU (which we derived from the first study, exploring experts' expectations for the coming years) (Trautmann, 2013). The third is a study done in the ALICE RAP project (Addictions and Lifestyle in Contemporary Europe – Reframing Addictions Project ALICE RAP – www.alicerap.eu), an analysis of a number of current major trends in drug and gambling policy in the EU, building on the findings from the first two studies. In the case studies exploring the development of selected trends in a selected number of EU Member States, we focused on identifying important factors that influence policymaking and policy implementation using a rather eclectic approach: combining elements of Kingdon's Multiple Streams Model, and Walt and Gilson's Health Policy Triangle (Trautmann et al., 2015). Both serve as a heuristic model rather than a theory explaining the process of policymaking.

Kingdon's Multiple Streams Model

Kingdon (2003) distinguishes three separate streams in the process of policy-making: the problem stream (issues that are recognised as important problems), the policy stream (ideas or proposals for tackling the problems) and the political stream (organised political processes, different forms of consensus building and decision-making). These streams are seen as operating rather independently from one another until there is a change that causes the streams to meet, creating a 'policy window' and offering an opportunity for policy change. This model reflects the complex and dynamic character of the decision-making process. However, it is rather unspecific regarding the composition of the streams and therefore less useful for analysing and explaining specific policy decisions. The three streams are in themselves reservoirs containing very diverse elements (stakeholders, interests and expectations, barriers and facilitators, etc.). Moreover the contents of the reservoirs overlap. Therefore, as a tool it lacks the analytical sharpness and precision required for assessing and clearly identifying critical elements in developments or decisions. One can take something from every 'reservoir' which fits an idea and put together an explanation. Still, the model provides us with a useful visualisation of the policymaking process and its dynamic and unpredictable course, facilitating better understanding of its complexity. It is a helpful tool to analyse and describe in retrospective the important factors that create a window of opportunity for a policy change. In the analysis of current drug policy, it can contribute to an assessment of whether the time is ripe for policy change.

Walt and Gilson's Health Policy Triangle

In Walt and Gilson's Health Policy Triangle we find a simpler, but sharper, conceptual framework (Walt and Gilson, 1994; Walt et al., 2008). This model tries to capture the comprehensiveness of health policy analysis by focusing on the interaction between policy content ('what'), actors ('who'), context ('where' and 'when'), process ('how') and their impact on policymaking. The clear-cut separation of these elements is somewhat static and artificial, but useful for analytical purposes. It facilitates a clearer view of the different factors influencing policymaking and a better understanding of the 'force field' in which policymaking and governance take place. Although it is more specific because it unravels the knotty total into separate factors, it misses the dynamic of the Multiple Streams Model which attempts to grasp the complex multi-faceted character of drug policymaking.

With our case studies, we intend to contribute to a better understanding of the factors that shape the governance of drug policy and influence drug policy decision making. The Health Policy Triangle will be used as a heuristic to disentangle and order the factors of influence we discern between content, process, actors or stakeholders and context. We combined this somewhat static approach with elements of Kingdon's Multiple Streams Model, another heuristic that helped us to better understand the dynamic processes of drug policymaking and implementation, and the relationships between these factors of influence. Combining elements of both models enabled us to capture the complexity and dynamic of the drug policy trends we focus on to analyse and understand drug policymaking (Trautmann et al., 2015).

Three key convergence trends

In our market studies three key trends, denoting major drug policy changes, are important elements in this wider process of convergence (Reuter and Trautmann, 2009; Trautmann et al., 2013). We used the following three key trends for our analysis of drug policymaking and implementation in the EU:

- A wider acceptance of harm reduction[1]
- Decriminalisation of drug use (and possession of small quantities for personal use)[2]
- A growing interest in exploring the feasibility of regulation as an instrument to control the drug market.

---

1   Harm reduction refers to health policy measures aimed at reducing drug use health and social harms.
2   Decriminalisation is a change of the legal status of drug use. For our study we decided to use a pragmatic definition of decriminalisation, subsuming all measures that avoid criminal sanctions as a response to drug use and possession of small quantities for personal use.

In some countries these three trends emerged as separate strategies, while in others, as for instance in the Netherlands, they appeared as a package deal of drug policy change. Though they represent different realms, they are interrelated. While regulation mainly refers to alternatives to prohibition of demand and supply, decriminalisation also includes regulatory elements when defining small quantities of possession for personal use and contributes to reducing health harms related to the illicit status of drugs. As to regulation policies they contribute to reducing drug use health harms related to prohibition, e.g. dilution due to black market conditions.

Our studies show both commonalities and differences between the three trends and between the developments in different EU Member States. The changes analysed reflect a complex process of interrelated changing realities at different levels of society. We looked at changing circumstances (societal changes), changing views and value systems (paradigm shifts), changing importance of certain interests and arguments, and changing alliances of stakeholders.

Using the structure of the Health Policy Triangle we concentrated on:

- The process: convergence of drug policies in the EU
- The content: the paradigm changes
- The stakeholders: factors contributing to the influence of stakeholders
- The context: the impact of societal changes.

The process: convergence of policies

Although convergence of drug policy appears to be an overarching trend that can be observed all over the EU, the process and outcomes differ substantially between policy fields and between countries. One commonality of the three trends covered by our studies is that they started in a few countries as criticism of the inappropriateness of existing control policies. All three trends were in the early stages a primarily bottom-up driven process, which – in the case of the wider implementation of harm reduction and decriminalisation of use – later turned into a strongly top-down driven process.

Harm reduction

The wider acceptance of harm reduction is one example of convergence of policies. In the Netherlands and the UK, harm reduction services started to emerge in the 1970s as a response to the heroin epidemic. It was a reaction to the existing abstinence-oriented drug treatment services, which were seen as an inadequate response to problem drug use among young people. Starting from a marginalised position against powerful stakeholders, harm reduction gradually became recognised as an effective health measure. In the Netherlands it developed rather quickly into mainstream drug policy. It became a constituent of local and national drug policy planning, which marked the turning point from a bottom-up to a top-down driven development.

This process, which took place in the Netherlands, has repeated itself in other EU Member States like Germany, France and Spain. A similar process can also be seen on an international level. In EU drug policy, harm reduction moved in the past two decades from a seriously disputed position to a mainstream position, though there are of course substantial differences between Member States, particularly regarding differentiation of available services and coverage (Trautmann et al., 2009 and 2015).

When looking at the developments on the EU level, one can observe an analogy with a bottom-up driven process in the early years which later turned into a top-down force. It started with debates among Member States triggered by the deviant drug policy of the Netherlands. In fact, all other EU Member States (and many more countries) rejected the Dutch drug policy approach. However, in many countries there were also opponents of the traditional drug policy approach, pressing for a change towards a primarily health-oriented drug policy. They followed the developments in the Netherlands and in the UK, especially in Liverpool, with great interest. Their number had been growing gradually and included, besides workers and managers of drug services, politicians and policymakers. Through the years a growing number of countries introduced these changes. This had a major impact on the course of the drug policy discussions on the EU level. Harm reduction moved from being an isolated position to an increasingly well-accepted drug policy approach (Rhodes and Hedrich, 2010; Cook et al., 2010; MacGregor and Whiting, 2010). The acceptance of harm reduction by the European Commission was an important element in the development of a top-down force. The 2003 Recommendation of the Council of the European Union, encouraging all EU Member States to implement harm reduction measures, and the EU Drug Strategy 2005–2012 (Council of the European Union, 2003 and 2012) contributed to this top-down force.

Decriminalisation and regulation

The other two trends, decriminalisation of drug use and exploring the feasibility of regulation, developed in a comparable way. They also started as criticism of what was viewed as an inappropriate approach, in the case of decriminalisation: to penalise an individual for simply using illicit drugs. Criminalising drug users was criticised for having detrimental effects on the social and health situation of the user. This is why decriminalisation is frequently linked with harm reduction.

De facto decriminalisation of drug use was widely implemented in EU Member States. However, except for diversion schemes, it was never formally supported by EU drug policy documents. This might help to explain the differences between Member States' decriminalisation policies. Nevertheless, the broad consensus in the EU on the appropriateness of decriminalisation may have been shaped by the exchange of experiences among experts and policymakers (Trautmann et al., 2015).

Exploring the feasibility of regulation as a drug control instrument is still mainly limited to cannabis policy initiatives, in which bottom-up criticism of the prevailing prohibitionist approach is key, as the example of the coffee shop in the Netherlands shows. The formalisation of this cannabis policy in public prosecutor guidelines on how to apply drug law provisions can be seen as one example of a top-down driving force. However, the heated debates about cannabis regulation in an increasing number of EU Member States and the international exchange of experiences seem to have resulted in a broader basis for change. One can observe a cautious trend away from prohibition and towards regulation, from criminal to administrative law. Cannabis policy is the most prominent example of that move away from prohibition.

The content: changing paradigms

A helpful concept to better understand the process of convergence can be found in the work on paradigm changes by Thomas Kuhn (2012). He argues that science is based on expert consensus on how phenomena have to be explained. Science is therefore not fact-based but grounded on prevailing perceptions of facts, on a set of beliefs that are shared by a scientific community. This set of beliefs or assumptions is a paradigm that is supported by research findings. A paradigm change is therefore rooted in socio-psychological processes rather than in scientific or research facts.

This theory of paradigm change is a useful heuristic for better understanding the developments of the trends we have focused on. Translated into our field of studies, it means that the increased support of stakeholders for a new view has played a decisive role in the paradigm change. All the three convergence trends we analysed can be understood as paradigm changes, as the emergence of a new consensus among influential stakeholders on how elements of the 'drugs problem' have to be explained.

The change towards a wider acceptance of harm reduction is a change of the objective of health interventions. While fifty years ago the predominant objective of drug treatment was abstinence, today in many countries this has, at least partly, been replaced by harm reduction. The trend towards decriminalisation reflects a change of 'essence', the understanding that the use of drugs is not a crime, but a health issue. Regulation is a change in the choice of approach towards the control of currently illicit drugs, regulation rather than prohibition.

These changing views also show that a paradigm change does not necessarily mean a simple replacement of one view by another. Different paradigms can also exist side by side. The history of decriminalisation shows that the crime and health paradigm can coexist: one being more dominant than the other generally, and sometimes swapping positions (Trautmann et al., 2015).

The change from crime to health paradigm also shows that a new paradigm is not necessarily – in all respects – 'better' than the old one. It is simply a change in expert consensus on how a phenomenon is appropriately understood. Replacing the crime paradigm by the health paradigm was welcomed by many as a major step forward towards a more effective and humane approach to the drug user.

However, there is one uncomfortable issue. The dividing line between the health and the disease paradigm proves to be thin. It is only a small step from interpreting drug use as health issue to the view of drug use as disease (Trautmann et al., 2015).

The well-being paradigm

The health and, especially the disease, paradigm proved to have serious shortcomings. Not all drug use can be well understood from the perspective of the health paradigm, as for example experimental use or use for recreational or spiritual purposes. And not all forms of drug use can be understood as pathology.

A key element in the research of ALICE RAP has been to reframe the addiction concept. Its aim has been to use the input from the different disciplines involved in the project to come to a new understanding which can contribute to a more effective approach to addictions/drug use. The discussions among the researchers involved in ALICE RAP centred on the usefulness of the well-being concept for this reframing exercise. Compared with the health paradigm, well-being is a more appropriate paradigm and covers a broader spectrum than the health paradigm. It enables us to grasp the negative health and social impact of (problem) drug use – a decrease in well-being – but it also allows us to acknowledge and understand the positive effects of substance use as perceived by the user. It also is useful for understanding drug use as coping behaviour, as an attempt to deal with negative or stressful emotions, without labelling them a pathology.

Key contextual factors

In our case studies, numerous contextual factors influencing policymaking and governance were reviewed: historical, economic, political and social-cultural factors. Contextual factors have proven decisive in determining the influence of specific policy content or certain stakeholders. We found a number of contextual factors that had major impact on the drug policy changes in the past decades: the societal mood, the societal setting, and closely linked to the latter: 'uncertainties' in a changing policy environment.

Important contextual factors: societal mood, societal setting and 'uncertainties'

At different points in our case studies we came across references to what has been called by some experts the 'societal mood' as an explanation for drug policy changes. In the Netherlands the predominant conservative and restrictive mood, with a strong focus on discipline and order characteristic of the post-war reconstruction era, was the breeding ground for the protest movement, resulting in the 1970s 'mood for a change' and societal changes among which were the drug policy changes (De Kort, 1995). However, these changes were not as fundamental when compared with Slovenia and Spain. These two countries saw drastic social and political changes from a totalitarian state to a democracy (Gamella and Jiménez Rodrigo, 2004; Trautmann et al., 2007). These societal changes helped to create a policy window for drug policy changes.

In more recent years one can observe a swing back to political conservatism, a restoration trend emphasising public order and security, both by national governments and at the EU level, a change that has to do with the economic crisis. This conservative mood favours a more restrictive drug policy in general (Trautmann, 2013).

An additional factor restricting policy changes – not only in the drug policy field – might be the limited room for manoeuvre, currently, for individual EU Member States due to a more all-embracing EU integration process. In the 1970s and 1980s countries in the EU could operate more autonomously than today. During the debates about the Dutch drug policy changes in the 1970s, considerations about an EU drug policy framework hardly played a role. There was no EU drug policy framework as we know it today.

This does not mean that the absence of an EU drug policy framework only presented 'opportunities' for policy changes. It also presented threats, as the fierce opposition of various EU Member States to the changes in the Netherlands show. In the end it was EU drug policy documents like the Council recommendations on harm reduction and the EU Drugs Strategy 2005–2012 which enhanced the EU-wide introduction of harm reduction.

Some specifics: uncertainties create opportunities

The societal changes mentioned above were coupled with uncertainties. The transformations in Slovenia and Spain from a totalitarian to a democratic political system meant the breaking down of old structures and rules and the absence of well-established positions regarding new policies. This may have been particularly true for policies addressing relatively new social phenomena such as the then-emerging 'drug problem'. The societal changes in the Netherlands, Slovenia and Spain had a major impact on drug policy. In all three countries the ownership of the drug problem was not yet clearly defined. There was no consensus on a leading paradigm: was the drug issue a health, crime or social problem? There was no consensus on how to define the problem and how to deal with it. The territory was not yet divided, the allocation of certain responsibilities to specific stakeholders not yet established. These uncertainties contributed to a window of opportunity for developing the three approaches discussed in this study: harm reduction, decriminalisation and regulation (Trautmann et al., 2015).

Stakeholders

Stakeholders are the engine of drug policymaking and implementation. They drive and shape the process, define the content and respond to the (perceived) context. Our studies show that various stakeholders contributed to the course the three drug policy trends took. The actual influence of certain stakeholders on changes in policy and governance depended on various factors. One factor is the political and economic power of the involved stakeholders. Political power does not only rest on the size of a political party but also on its net of influence among other policy decision makers. Do other decision makers support the political views and beliefs behind the policy choices made? Another factor determining stakeholders' influence is the extent and vigour of support within one stakeholder group and, more importantly, within coalitions of different stakeholder groups. Broad support in one stakeholder group or in a stakeholders' coalition, representing different policy areas and interests, adds to the influence on the decision making process. In addition, variety in the scope of support seems to matter. Support from diverse stakeholder groups helps to make the difference, as the wider acceptance and implementation of harm reduction measures, for example drug consumption facilities in the Netherlands, shows. Influenced by the youth protest movement of the 1970s, these services were initially promoted by alternative health services, health authorities and other policymakers, and driven primarily by health interests. In the years following, the communities that had been affected by the 'public nuisance' caused by drug users slowly evolved, and with the media, police, and judiciary came to support these early health measures. This resulted in a broad coalition of stakeholders with a shared aim, but driven by different interests. Besides health protection there was also the interest of securing public order and the economic interests of entrepreneurs in the neighbourhoods that were running shops, restaurants and pubs. This 'joint venture' did not just mean a broader basis for changes. It also translated into an increased sense of urgency, which contributed to the vigour of stakeholders' support (Dolan et al., 2000).

Finally, timeliness is an important factor. 'Right time, right place' are decisive for allowing changes to happen. The societal mood is an important element here. It can, for instance, be doubted whether the drug policy reforms in the Netherlands of the 1970s would be possible in the current political climate.

All these factors help to create a policy window for changes. They play an important role in 'synchronising' what Kingdon described as the problem, policy and political streams. The increased consensus among different stakeholder groups also contributed to the paradigm change.

Though politicians and policymakers obviously had a decisive impact on the decision making process, we decided to focus on two other stakeholder groups because of their importance in the development of the trends we analysed: social movements, and science and research. They played a key role in challenging dominant paradigms, functioning as facilitators of change.

Science and research

Despite the highly politicised and ideologically charged character of drug policy, the influence of science has been substantial and – at least from time to time – decisive.

Scientific evidence has played an important role in quite a number of policy decisions. Still, critics referring to the rather limited impact of science on drug policy have a point. The radical change in Dutch drug policy, culminating in the 1976 drug law, may be one of the few examples of a drug policy change which in major part was guided by evidence. Politicians and policymakers consulted scientists and took on board the then-available evidence as the basis for their decisions, at a time when evidence base was not yet a prominent issue in (drug) policymaking. Science was one of the elements contributing to a window of opportunity (De Kort, 1995).

Still, generally speaking, political and ideological arguments frequently dominated policy decisions in the field of illicit drugs in many countries. This is also true for the Netherlands, where, after a promising start in the 1970s, political and ideological motives gained importance. In different countries one can find examples showing that scientific evidence is simply ignored or overruled by political and ideological agendas (Trautmann et al., 2015).

Social movements

From the 1960s onwards a (relatively) new stakeholder appears on the scene in different European countries, claiming a say in drug policy debates. Social movements, of mainly young people, emerged all over Europe, opposing the established social order, which – in the view of the protesters – was predominantly conservative and restrictive. In some countries these social movements also disputed the prohibitionist drug policies. They were an important element in the bottom-up forces pushing for new approaches, helping to initiate the trends covered in our studies.

These social movements differed substantially in each country. In the Netherlands changing drug policy was an important issue on the agenda of Provos, the most prominent group in the Dutch protest movement (De Kort, 1995). In Slovenia and Spain the political opposition were the movements behind the fundamental social and political changes and the breeding ground for drug policy changes. There were of course differences regarding the drug policy changes: in Slovenia the changes started with a focus on developing harm reduction services. The changes in Spain, with a long tradition of a strong cannabis social movement, took off with a focus on decriminalisation of use, in particular cannabis use (Gamella and Jiménez Rodrigo, 2004, Trautmann et al., 2007).

These differences show that the national social context in these three countries shaped the scope and orientation of the social movement. The social movements were definitely not the most powerful stakeholders in the drug policy changes. Still, they were clearly influential. They provided new answers to pressing questions and helped set the agenda of the drug policy debate. They were successful in claiming a place at the negotiating table because their ideas were rather quickly embraced by policymakers and politicians. They were at the right time, at the right place, with their ideas for better managing the drug use problem.

Conclusions

The question is, of course, what are the practical implications of our case studies? Are there any lessons to be learnt from these analyses? Does a better understanding of the factors that influence drug policymaking help to improve policymaking? We tried to formulate some short considerations.

The context

The context of policymaking and implementation, i.e. the historical, political, economic and social-cultural factors influencing policymaking, are given circumstances. They define the room for manoeuvre at a certain point in time. It is the context which largely determines whether the chosen aims and objectives of policy measures are realistic and achievable, and whether there are barriers or facilitators for achieving aims and objectives. Examining the context, including a risk analysis, should be an integral part of exploring drug policy alternatives.

The content

The policy content, generally laid down in a policy paper or plan, reflecting current paradigms, describes the underlying reasons for developing a specific policy, its objectives and the measures to be taken. Important factors determining the policy content are the context, and the perception of the problem that requires policy interventions.

A useful tool or format for systematically developing a policy plan is a so-called Logical Framework or LogFrame matrix, which helps to split the plan into logically linked constituents, including overall objectives, specific objectives, expected results and activities to realise the objectives and results. It describes the logic of the interventions along the line of these four constituents. It sets indicators to measure the achievements, defines the sources of information and means (which will be used to verify the indicators) and, finally, it elaborates assumptions. The latter includes a risk analysis, or – even better – a full SWOT, a systematic analysis of strengths, weaknesses, opportunities and threats of, in this case, a policy plan. A reflection on unintended consequences is also worth considering here. The feasibility of the objectives depends for a large part on contextual factors, as they determine the 'play area' of policymaking.

The process

The process of policymaking and implementation is the core of governance. Here, the concept of good governance comes in. The work of the UK Drug Policy Commission (UKDPC) provides useful guidance. A key theme in the work of UKDPC was to improve drug policymaking and implementation. It provided, among others, an excellent checklist of standards for good policymaking, covering the following areas: stakeholder engagement, clarity of overarching goals, strong leadership, coordination of policy efforts, policy design, use of evidence base, implementation, and accountability and scrutiny (Hamilton, Rubin and Singleton, 2012).

The stakeholders

From the UKDPC's definition of good governance it follows that the involvement of all relevant stakeholders is essential for effective policymaking and implementation. Therefore it should be standard procedure to identify all stakeholders that are either affected by, or have a professional interest in, a certain issue. There may be cases where this exercise will result in a rather long list. Producing a shortlist of the most important stakeholders will help.

The policy window

This brings us back to Kingdon's key heuristic for understanding policy changes: the policy window. This concept provides a convincing picture which helps us to understand the conditions for a policy change. A policy window can, of course, not be constructed. There are too many variables and stakeholders involved in it. The best one can do is try to support factors in favour of a window of opportunity. Building stakeholder coalitions and looking for win-win situations are, for example, elements facilitating a policy window.

A paradigm change reflecting a wider consensus among stakeholders can also be understood as an element of a policy window. Stakeholders' consensus plays a crucial role in all the three streams: in the problem stream, a consensus concerning the urgency of a problem; in the policy stream, a consensus on the 'solution' to the problem, i.e. a feasible and effective policy proposal; and lastly, in the political stream a majority of politicians supporting the policy proposal.

References

COOK, C., BRIDGE, J. and STIMSON, G. V. (2010) The Diffusion of Harm Reduction in Europe and Beyond. In EMCDDA (2010) *Harm Reduction: Evidence, Impacts and Challenges*. Luxembourg: Publications Office of the European Union. pp. 37–56.

COUNCIL OF THE EUROPEAN UNION (2003) *Council Recommendation of 18 June 2003 on the Prevention and Reduction of Health-related Harm Associated with Drug Dependence*. Official Journal L 165. 03/07/2003. pp. 31–33.

COUNCIL OF THE EUROPEAN UNION (2012) *EU Drugs Strategy (2013–2020)* Brussels: Council of the European Union (2012/C 402/01).

DE KORT, M. (1995) *Tussen patiënt en delinquent: Geschiedenis van het Nederlandse drugsbeleid*. Verloren: Hilversum.

DOLAN, K., KIMBER, J., FRY, C., FITZGERALD, J., MACDONALD, D. and TRAUTMANN, F. (2000) Drug Consumption Facilities in Europe and the Establishment of Supervised Injecting Centres in Australia. *Drug and Alcohol Review*. 19. pp. 337–346.

GAMELLA, J. F., JIMÉNEZ RODRIGO, M. L. (2004) A Brief History of Cannabis Policies in Spain (1968–2003). *Journal of Drug Issues*. 34. pp. 623–660.

HAMILTON, L., RUBIN, J. and SINGLETON, N. (2012) *Characteristics of Good Governance for Drug Policy: Findings From an Expert Consultation.* London: UKDPC.

KINGDON, J. (2003) *Agendas, Alternatives and Public Policies.* (2nd ed.). Boston: Little Brown.

KUHN, T. S. (2012) *The Structure of Scientific Revolutions.* Chicago: University of Chicago Press.

MACGREGOR, S. and WHITING, M. (2010) The Development of European Drug Policy and the Place of Harm Reduction within This. In EMCDDA (2010) *Harm Reduction: Evidence, Impacts and Challenges.* Luxembourg: Publications Office of the European Union. p. 59–77.

REUTER, P. and TRAUTMANN, F. (eds.) (2009) *A Report on Global Illicit Drugs Markets 1998–2007.* Brussels: European Commission.

RHODES, T. and HEDRICH, D. (2010) Harm Reduction and the Mainstream. In EMCDDA (2010) *Harm Reduction: Evidence, Impacts and Challenges.* Luxembourg: Publications Office of the European Union. p. 19–33.

TRAUTMANN, F., RODE, N., VAN GAGELDONK, A., VAN DER GOUWE, D., CROES, E., ZIDAR, R., STÖVER, H., GAŠPARIČ, M. and KONEC-JURIČIČ, N. (2007). *Evaluation of Substitution Maintenance Treatment in Slovenia: Assessing Quality and Efficiency.* Utrecht/Ljubljana: Trimbos Institute.

TRAUTMANN, F., REUTER, P., VAN GAGELDONK, A. and VAN DER GOUWE, D. (2009) The Drugs Problem and Drug Policy Developments Between 1998–2007. In Reuter, P. and Trautmann, F. (eds.). *A Report on Global Illicit Drugs Markets 1998–2007.* Brussels: European Commission.

TRAUTMANN, F. (2013) Key Trends of the Illicit Drugs Market and Drug Policy in the EU: What do Experts Anticipate for the Coming Years? In Trautmann, F., Kilmer, B. and Turnbull, P. (eds). *Further Insights into Aspects of the EU Illicit Drugs Market.* Luxembourg: Publications Office of the European Union.

TRAUTMANN, F., CROES, E., ELZINGA, E., MILHET, M., DIAZ GOMEZ, C., KOŠIR, M., ESTRADA, M., MILLER, D. and HARKINS, C. (2015) *Description and Analysis of Addiction Governance Practices – Understanding Changes in Governance Practice.* ALICE RAP Deliverable Report D14.2. Available from: http://www.alicerap.eu/resources/documents/doc_download/208-deliverable-14-2-addiction-governance-practices.html [Accessed 1 September 2015].

WALT, G. and GILSON, L. (1994). Reforming the Health Sector in Developing Countries: The Central Role of Policy Analysis. *Health Policy and Planning.* 9(4). pp. 353–370.

WALT, G., SHIFFMAN, J., SCHNEIDER, H., MURRAY, S.F., BRUGHA, R. and GILSON, L. (2008) 'Doing' Health Policy Analysis: Methodological and Conceptual Reflections and Challenges. *Health Policy and Planning.* 23. pp. 308–317.

Chapter 17

The changing face of harm reduction in Europe

Dagmar Hedrich and Alessandro Pirona

Introduction

> Harm reduction encompasses interventions, programmes and policies that seek to reduce the health, social and economic harms of drug use to individuals, communities and societies
>
> (Rhodes and Hedrich, 2010, p. 19).

Over the past three decades harm reduction has evolved from a controversial approach pursued in a few localities into one of the central pillars of public health and social policy on drugs across the European Union. This development was driven by the serious health and social consequences of increasing heroin use and drug injecting that emerged in Europe in the 1980s, in particular rising HIV/AIDS and overdose deaths, as well as crime and open drug scenes. Today, remarkable improvements can be documented in many EU Member states which have implemented comprehensive drug policies incorporating scaled-up harm-reduction programmes. Substantial progress has been made towards the elimination of new HIV infections among people who inject drugs (PWID). Across the 28-country Union with its over 505 million citizens, just 1,236 newly reported HIV cases were attributed to drug injecting in 2014. In many cities, crime and public order problems related to drug use have also diminished substantially.

However, containment of heroin-related problems and the normalisation of harm reduction have been accompanied by the rise of other challenges that demand new approaches to reducing harms related to drug use. These include changing patterns of drug use (stimulants, new psychoactive substances, performance-enhancing drugs); new drug markets and new populations at risk; new modes of distributing not only drugs but also information and responses via the internet; and the challenges presented by ageing populations of long-time drug users who benefited from the introduction of survival-oriented harm-reduction responses in the 1980s and 1990s. In addition, there are recent indications of increasing injecting and HIV risk in some previously low-prevalence countries; continuing low levels of implementation and coverage of harm-reduction services – especially

Harm reduction in Europe **255**

in vulnerable parts of Central and Eastern Europe; continuing high levels of HCV infection among PWID; and persisting, and in recent years increasing, numbers of drug-related deaths.

This chapter describes the evolution of harm reduction from the early pioneer years of the 1980s, through a period of increasing acceptance, mainstreaming and scaling up during the 1990s and early 2000s, to its consolidation and diversification in the first decade of this millennium. It concludes with a discussion of the new challenges and questions that harm-reduction policy now faces in the middle of the second decade of the millennium. This chapter gives a broad overview of developments in Europe. Details for individual countries can be found on the EMCDDA website.[1]

The pioneer years

> Early in the AIDS epidemic, there was so much we didn't know – what caused the disease, how it was spread or how to treat it. But, once scientists were able to isolate and establish a virus – HIV – as the cause of AIDS, that all began to change.
>
> For one thing, knowing what to look for allowed scientists to begin developing a test to detect HIV. Thirty years ago today – on March 2, 1985 – the U.S. Food and Drug Administration approved the first commercial HIV blood test. This was a major breakthrough. Testing meant that the blood supply could be essentially freed of HIV, and helped scientists and public health officials determine the extent of the epidemic. Testing also gave individuals the power of knowing their status, and enabled them to protect their partners, if infected.
>
> Jonathan Mermin, Director of CDC's National Center for HIV/AIDS, Viral Hepatitis, STD, and TB Prevention (*Huffington Post*, 3 February 2015).

Over the course of the 1980s levels of heroin use and drug injecting rose in many Western European countries. This, combined with fear of an HIV/AIDS epidemic, as well as concern over crime and public safety, meant that drugs became a political priority at both the national and EU level. Initially, however, the push for change arose at the local level in various major cities, for example, in Amsterdam, Frankfurt, Liverpool and Zürich. In these cities, expanding heroin markets and growing populations of PWID and open drug scenes posed serious public health and public order challenges that existing policies of drug-free treatment and repressive policing failed to contain.

The year 1990 saw two key milestones that signalled the gathering momentum of harm reduction in Europe. The first was the Conference of European Cities at the centre of the drug trade and the resulting Frankfurt declaration *European Cities on Drug Policy* (Schardt, 2001) which laid out the argument for an approach based on harm reduction addressing both public health and community safety. The

---

1   See country profiles, statistics and reports on trends and developments at http://www.em cdda.europa.eu.

second was the First International Harm Reduction Conference held in Liverpool, afterwards an annual event that was to develop into a major international forum for the discussion and promotion of harm reduction. These events did not, in themselves, lead directly to changes in policy but they did reflect the pressure that had been building up in parts of urban Europe, and they brought together local agencies, activists, policy makers and researchers from different European countries. In so doing, they provided forums for the articulation of new approaches, increased the visibility of harm reduction, and facilitated further activities such as the development of networks, alliances, projects, publications and information dissemination that would influence policy makers at both the national and European level over the coming decades.

The components that constituted the new approach included expansion of opioid substitution treatment (OST), mainly in the form of methadone maintenance, the introduction of needle and syringe programmes (NSP), and the promotion of HIV testing and counselling. Other components were the growth of easy access, low-threshold services, often organised by NGOs, that provided a combination of services including drop-in centres, information and advice, practical assistance, outreach and peer counselling, condom distribution, HIV testing and referral to treatment or other services, and sometimes advocacy and support for user groups. In a few countries, the first drug consumption rooms were introduced in the late 1980s and early 1990s where drug users could inject safely under hygienic conditions rather than in public, high-risk situations on the street.

These specific responses were underpinned by a broader philosophy based on a pragmatic, evidence-based, humanistic perspective of public health, social protection and human rights, as well as an awareness of the role of marginalisation and stigma and of risk environment in increasing drug-related harm. These responses also depended on the importance of gaining the cooperation of other key actors, including political and community leaders, law enforcement agencies, and general health and social services. While some activists argued for changes to the drug laws, including decriminalisation, most practitioners saw their priority as providing services to help or empower people to survive, to improve their health and social situation, and to enter and remain in treatment.

There was a large degree of variability in terms of the time-scale and degree of acceptance (or not) of harm reduction across Europe, including vocal opposition from drug-free constituencies. In some countries, tension arose between national authorities and progressive local authorities. In other cases, cities implementing a range of responses found themselves acting as magnets for drug users from other areas where services were sparse.

Figure 17.1 shows the year of introduction of OST and NSP in the EU, which can be seen as core interventions that reflect the adoption and diffusion of harm-reduction policies in the region. The number of countries introducing OST and NSP started to rise beginning in 1985, the year in which the HIV test became available. In the 1980s, these developments occurred almost entirely in Western

Harm reduction in Europe 257

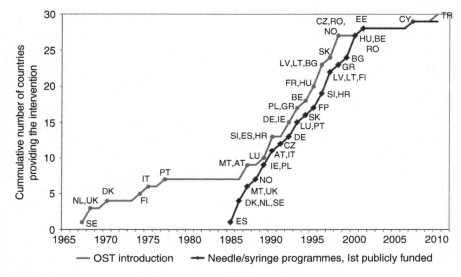

Figure 17.1 Year of introduction of OST and NSPs in EU countries
Source: EMCDDA, 2015b

Europe – countries of Central and Eastern Europe, most of them under Soviet influence until the fall of the Berlin Wall in 1989, were barely affected.

Some countries adopted harm-reduction policies quite rapidly. For example, in 1988 the UK government's Advisory Council on Drug Misuse concluded that the spread of HIV is 'a greater danger to individual and public health than drug misuse' (ACMD, 1988, p. 17) and proposed expansion of a range of community-based harm-reduction measures to prevent HIV transmission. Other early adopters included the Netherlands and Switzerland, and, to some extent, Germany, where a breakthrough was achieved following a national consensus conference on HIV/AIDS organised by a conservative health minister in 1991.

By contrast, in countries such as Bulgaria, France, Greece, Romania, or in the Baltic countries, changes in policy did not occur until well into the 1990s. Of the countries that joined the EU since 2004, only a few adopted harm-reduction measures quickly; most of them continued to emphasise high-threshold, often abstinence-oriented services (Cook, Bridge and Stimson, 2010).

At the European level, there were no formal EU competencies in the field of drug policy until the Treaty of Maastricht, which came into force in 1993, and included drug dependence under the heading of public health. This laid a foundation for an information-based and health-oriented response to the drug problem at the EU level. Before that, in 1989, the European Committee to Combat Drugs (CELAD) was established to bring together national drug policy coordinators. This committee drew up the first European plan to combat drugs, which was adopted by the European Council in Rome in December 1990 (and renewed in December 1992) as an agreed upon, though informal, basis for moving forward in this field. The plan identified the need for a coordinated, global approach addressing demand reduction, illicit trafficking, and international action, but did not specifically refer to harm reduction. Closer European cooperation on drugs as a public health issue also led, in 1993, to the establishment of the European Monitoring Centre for Drugs and Drug Addiction (EMCDDA), which became operational in 1995.

Thus, in the early years of the 1980s and early 1990s, the emergence of harm reduction was largely bottom up and European-level policies played little part. However, there were pre-existing mechanisms and networks that allowed for cross-border information exchange, including the Pompidou Group of the Council of Europe (which had provided a forum for intergovernmental cooperation on drugs since 1971), as well as seminars, networks and pilot studies funded by the European Commission which addressed drug use under the aegis of public health.

Mainstreaming and scaling up

Over the 1990s and first half of the 2000s, harm reduction steadily grew from a controversial and localised phenomenon into one of the key pillars of mainstream drug policies across the EU and in other European countries such as Switzerland and Norway (Hedrich, Pirona and Wiessing, 2008). This expansion is reflected in the increasing introduction of core harm-reduction interventions (see Figure 17.1) and their scaling up (see Figure 17.2). Growing numbers of opioid-dependent people in evidence-based treatment, together with the expansion of syringe provision, as well as the adoption of other harm-reduction activities, all point to a sea change in drug policy across much of Europe. At the same time, harm reduction became increasingly accepted in some countries in other regions, including Australia and Canada (Cook, Bridge and Stimson, 2010).

In 1993, the estimated number of clients in OST in the then-15 Member States of the EU was about 73,000 (see Figure 17.2), and by 2005 the figure for the same countries had risen to above half a million. Latest figures show that provision reached its peak in 2010–2011 with about 700,000 cases – which represents more than half of the estimated population of opioid users. Syringe-provision programmes are funded, organised and implemented in most countries at the local level, and where data are available, the expansion of syringe provision showed a similarly increasing pattern during that period.

By 2007 all but one EU Member State,[2] including those who had recently joined the EU, had adopted national drug strategies reflecting a comprehensive approach and including prevention and reduction of drug-related harm as a public health objective. Despite important differences between Member States in the level of implementation of harm-reduction interventions, the degree of

2   Except Austria, where drug strategies only exist at the provincial level, see: EMCDDA, 2014.

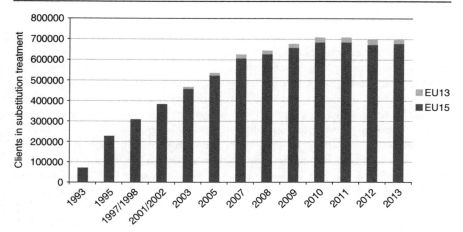

Figure 17.2 Estimated number of clients receiving opioid substitution treatment in the EU (EU15 and EU13)
Source: EMCDDA 2015b

consensus at policy level between such diverse countries with very different traditions was a remarkable achievement. A recommendation of the EU Council on harm-reduction policies and interventions (Council of the European Union, 2003), which also formed part of the EU acquis on drugs for integration of new Member States joining the EU,[3] played a significant role in this process (see below). However, a variety of factors must be taken into account in order to understand how this development and consensus came about. One key element, mentioned above, was that, especially in Western European countries, the need for action was driven by common concerns over the perceived threat to public health posed by HIV/AIDS. In some countries, though, crime and public nuisance linked to drug addiction and drug injecting were also important drivers. These shared concerns alone do not explain the direction of the shift in policy. They could also have led to more repressive approaches. The change of direction is instead due to the influence of other processes.

One of the other drivers of a pragmatic, public-health approach was the development of an accumulating evidence base, including improved evidence of effectiveness of harm-reduction interventions, in particular OST (mostly methadone maintenance at the time) and NSP. Not only did this promise a greater choice in interventions, but it also facilitated the development of a broader, more integrated 'service portfolio' of harm-reduction facilities. For example, the combination or co-location of survival-oriented services with psychosocial support of people in OST, including housing and employment support, or the addition of medical

---

3   For a timeline of policy-relevant events in Europe see MacGregor and Whiting, 2010, pp. 67–69.

services, such as wound treatments, overdose intervention trainings or infectious diseases testing. New pharmacological and technological developments (e.g. introduction of buprenorphine as medication for the maintenance treatment of opioid users, advanced onsite and offsite drug checking technologies, improved blood screening tests) and other advances in knowledge fed into this process.

However, the increased use of a growing evidence base does not entirely account for the relative rapidity with which harm reduction was adopted in many parts of Europe. Strong public health promotion in some countries, as well as active advocacy, including by drug users themselves and by their families and peers, was important. Information dissemination through media and via channels such as the annual harm reduction conference and various national and European networks, also played a crucial role in bringing the experiences and lessons learned during the early years to a wider audience of professionals and policy makers at the local and national levels. The fact that interventions such as OST also bring significant social benefits in terms of reductions in crime and illicit drug use made it easier to gain support from law enforcement agencies and political leaders.

As the 1990s progressed, EU structures and policy instruments came to play a key mediating role, bringing together the different actors and the diverse elements of the discourse on the drugs phenomenon in Europe. While European drug policy documents existed before, in 1999, for the first time, an EU drugs strategy and action plan for 2000–2004 (COREPER, 1 December 1999) introduced measurable targets on limiting infectious diseases and drug-related deaths. This was followed in 2003 by a European Council Recommendation on the prevention and reduction of drug-related harm associated with drug dependence (Council of the European Union, 2003). This defined specific interventions as part of the response and established a European consensus on principles and goals of harm reduction. Member States committed themselves to:

1   set prevention of drug dependence and reduction of related risks as a public health objective, and develop and implement comprehensive strategies accordingly;
2   substantially reduce the incidence of drug-related health damage, especially infectious diseases (HIV, hepatitis B, hepatitis C, tuberculosis) and drug-related deaths, with a number of specific services and facilities; and
3   reduce drug-related health risks by quality assurance, monitoring and evaluation.

In 2006, an evaluation report (van der Gouwe et al., 2006) showed that all Member States had policies in place which made the prevention and reduction of drug-related harm a public health objective, and that the Council Recommendation had played an important part in policy development in several new Member States. The evaluation also found that many countries had implemented a range of interventions to prevent and reduce drug-related harm, though it noted that some countries were more reserved in their commitment to harm reduction, for example Sweden and Cyprus.

The PHARE programme of assistance and training for countries of Central and Eastern Europe (CCEE), which was carried out over several years prior to the accession of the new Member States in 2004, also disseminated information about harm-reduction approaches to these countries. This played an important role in their adoption of the EU acquis.

Central to the process of establishing a coherent European approach was the role played by coordination – initially through CELAD, subsequently through the Horizontal Drugs Group in the European Council – and by information and monitoring (EMCDDA) (Estievenart, 1995). Regular European meetings, both at the level of policy makers and of technical experts, and the (joint) process of improving data collection and data comparability enabled greater weight to be given to an evidence-based approach. The tendency to seek consensus, observed across many areas of EU decision making, also facilitated a calmer, more considered approach (Edwards and Galla, 2014).

However, despite a general convergence reflected in drug policy statements and action plans, large differences in the degree of interventions remained, which can be seen in the 'two-speed Europe'. In particular, there were large differences in the regulatory frameworks, quality of implementation and levels of coverage of core harm-reduction services such as OST and NSPs, despite a near-universal adoption of harm reduction as a public health objective in the EU. The way interventions were originally conceived in some parts of Europe and the way they were implemented in others could show significant differences. For example, in several countries previously within the Soviet sphere of influence, OST was implemented in a high-threshold, tightly regulated and controlled treatment model, while in Western EU countries the current implementation and level of provision reflects a low-threshold, highly accessible treatment model, resulting in large differences in intervention coverage (see Figure 17.3).

These differences were partly due to the effect of EU enlargement, with ten new Member States joining the EU in 2004, another two in 2007, and Croatia in 2013 – each of the 13 countries had its particular drug situation and historical influences informing a response to illegal drug use. In many cases, the historical approaches of new Member States in Eastern and Northern Europe reflected a Soviet model of addiction and treatment that tended to be authoritarian, stigmatising and based on registration and compulsory treatment. This model left little space for civil society, NGOs or a human-rights-based approach to drug users. It also reflected the influence of Western advocacy groups that became active in Eastern Europe after the collapse of the Soviet Union. Some of these groups promoted drug-free oriented approaches, such as residential therapeutic communities or 12-step programmes (which originated from Alcoholics Anonymous). Other groups supported harm reduction; for example, projects funded by the Open Society Foundation, established by the investor and philanthropist George Soros to help countries make the transition from communism.

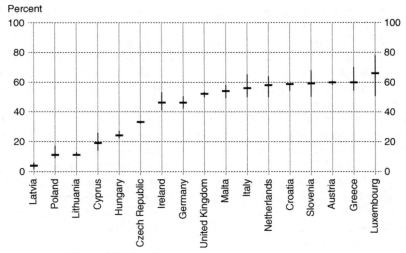

NB. Data displayed as point estimates and uncertainty intervals.

Figure 17.3 Number of problem opioid users in opioid substitution treatment as a percentage of the estimated number of problem opioid users, 2013 or most recent year available
Source: EMCDDA, 2015b

National variations in the (known or perceived) prevalence of heroin/opioid use, drug injecting, or of HIV infection among drug users meant that some countries, especially in Central Europe, may have seen harm reduction as a low priority. In Western European countries, too, there were differences in historical traditions (Cook, Bridge and Stimson, 2010), and differences in the rate and extent to which harm-reduction policies were accepted and implemented. Further, this variability did not only reflect differences between national policy makers, but also amongst health professionals, enforcement bodies, public opinion and local community leaders, among others.

Consolidation and diversification

The period from the mid-2000s to the present (2015) in Europe can be seen as a time of consolidation of harm reduction, but also as one of diversification and, at times, dissent (or, at least, perceived diminished commitment in some countries).

At the European level, the EU Drugs Strategies 2005–2012 and 2013–2020, together with their respective Drugs Action Plans 2005–2008, 2009–2012, 2013–2016,[4] built on, and consolidated, previous EU policy documents. In 2009 the

---

4 All documents accessible at: http://www.emcdda.europa.eu/policy-and-law/eu-activities.

Treaty of Lisbon substantially strengthened EU competencies in the field of public health, for example, with regards to greater complementarity between national systems and powers of initiative in co-operation with third countries and international organisations.

Thus, for the first time, the 2013–2020 EU Drugs Strategy incorporates harm reduction as a policy objective on a par with the traditional aims of reducing drug demand and supply:

> The Strategy aims to contribute to a reduction in drug demand and drug supply within the EU, as well as a reduction as regards the health and social risks and harms caused by drugs through a strategic approach that supports and complements national policies, that provides a framework for coordinated and joint actions and that forms the basis and political framework for EU external cooperation in this field. This will be achieved through an integrated, balanced and evidence-based approach.
>
> (European Union, 2012, paragraph 6).

In addition, civil society involvement, including NGO networks supported by the European Commission, and user-driven initiatives have added users' perspectives as a new dimension of input into harm-reduction implementation and policy-development in the EU. Drug use in prison has also been given increased emphasis in the strategy, to ensure that the care received by drug users in penal institutions is equivalent to that provided by health services in the community – which has been shown not to be the case (EMCDDA, 2012).

These developments are not surprising, given that harm reduction has matured and has been accepted as a regular part of a balanced and comprehensive EU drug policy, allowing for a more normative approach at the level of the EU's technical agencies. One sign of this was the production, in 2011, by EMCDDA and the European Centre for Disease Control (ECDC) of the first EU-level guidance on the prevention and control of infectious diseases among PWID (ECDC and EMCDDA, 2011). This provided for a systematic approach to assessing the public health risks of injecting drug use in Europe and enabled EU-wide HIV risk assessments to be conducted jointly by the two agencies. The significance of this will be discussed below.

At the same time, away from formal policy documents, the EU at times appears to be less homogenous regarding consensus on drug policy, and some have warned that complacency may undermine the achievements of the past two decades (Edwards and Galla, 2014). For example, policy differences have once again become more visible. This is due partly to the EU accession, in 2004, of some countries who were not fully committed to harm reduction, and also partly to disenchantment with the EU in some countries: possibly linked to the economic crisis and a general resistance to measures defined at the EU level. Consensus and continuity may also be challenged by a lack of knowledge transmission of the history and development of drug policies in Europe, and by the re-definition of health priorities under changed economic conditions. A concrete example in which this consensus was threatened is presented in Edwards and Galla (2014). Their paper discusses how the EU's Horizontal Drug Group (HDG), under the French EU Presidency in 2008, adopted a joint-EU position paper with a number of 'red lines' for the negotiations at the UN-level on the new Political Declaration of the world drug problem, to be adopted at a High Level Meeting in 2009. This joint position fully reflected existing policy as set out in the EU Drug Strategy and Action Plans. According to the authors, as negotiations proceeded Sweden and, in particular Italy, withdrew support for the term 'harm reduction'. Strong lobbying by the USA against the EU position may also have contributed to the breach in consensus.

An important factor affecting drug policy priorities today is a general perception that drugs are not the threat that they appeared to be when they came to public and political attention in the 1980s. Other issues have taken over the political agenda including international terrorism and security, the economic crisis, and most recently, immigration. Some trends in problem drug use and its consequences can be seen as encouraging this general perception. The prevalence of heroin use has broadly stabilised in many countries that had, in earlier decades, experienced epidemics, the number of new users has declined and the known user population is steadily ageing. In some countries decreasing rates of drug injecting are reported, and many countries report falling numbers of newly notified cases of HIV among PWID (EMCDDA, 2015a). Although increased use of cocaine, including crack, was seen as a serious concern in a few countries in the previous decade, rates of cocaine use also appear to be falling.

Alongside these trends, a saturation of demand for harm-reduction services has been observed in countries that have implemented high coverage. The development of highly effective antiviral treatments – which can also be used as pre-exposure prophylaxis (PrEP) to prevent infection with HIV – as well as of medications that can effectively cure hepatitis C infection, could potentially be seen as a challenge to the rationale for harm-reduction interventions. Such a conclusion may be premature, though, as modelling studies show complementary effects of harm-reduction and infectious-diseases-treatment interventions in different epidemiological scenarios (Martin et al., 2013).

Other trends contradict a conclusion that reducing drug-related harm is becoming less important. These include trends related to lifestyle choices among population groups not covered by traditional harm-reduction interventions – new and non-marginalised user groups, new synthetic drugs, changing risk behaviours, sexual risks linked to drug injecting amongst men who have sex with men (MSM), lack of transmission of safe use knowledge – as well as a possible resurgence of the heroin market in Europe and the implications for a new, younger and previously unexposed population, and changing patterns of drug injecting in some Central European countries. Other potential trends are related to the effects of the economic crisis on vulnerability, drug use and risk behaviours, as well as to investment in health and harm reduction. In 2011, for example, there were serious outbreaks of HIV among PWID in Greece and Romania. The result was that the joint contribution to new injecting-related HIV notifications from these two countries alone rose from 2.9% in 2010 to more than a third of all new injecting-related notifications in the EU in 2012 (ECDC and WHO, 2015). Risk assessments carried out by the EMCDDA and ECDC assessing coverage of core-measures recommended in the recently published EU guidance on infection prevention among PWID (ECDC and EMCDDA, 2011) revealed serious vulnerabilities in the public health capabilities of both countries. Even more worryingly, applying the criteria used in the risk assessments of Greece and Romania across Europe shows that PWID in a significant number of other countries may be at risk of HIV infection, including some previously low-HIV prevalence countries; epidemiological indicators show risks may be increasing and coverage of harm reduction interventions is inadequate (Pharris et al., 2011; Hedrich et al., 2013; EMCDDA, 2015c, p. 16).

The differences between countries in terms of implementation and coverage described above have, for the most part, continued into the second decade of this century, with the exception of Greece. Following the HIV outbreak, Greece invested in a scaling-up of opioid substitution treatment by increasing the number of clinics providing this treatment. As a result, the number of patients receiving opioid substitution treatment in the country nearly doubled in four years (2010–2013) and waiting times halved during the same period.

The success of the region as a whole in reducing HIV among PWID is challenged by economic austerity policies – resulting in a lack of investment in harm reduction as a preventive measure – especially in countries where HIV levels among this group are still low.

Challenges for the future

Remarkable progress has been made in EU Member States through the implementation of comprehensive, scaled-up harm-reduction programmes, including very significant progress towards the elimination of new transmission of HIV infections among PWID in many countries. In 2014 the number of reported new HIV infections linked to injecting drug use decreased to an all-time-low of 1,236 across the 28 EU countries (ECDC and WHO, 2015). Some might think that effective medications to treat HIV/AIDS and hepatitis C infections erode the ground on which (traditional) harm reduction stands, and at the same time, the target opioid-injecting population may be gradually diminishing. Others point not only to the persistently high levels of HCV and new outbreaks of HIV, but also to new patterns of drug use, and continuing drug injecting and risk behaviours in a variety of populations.

So, what will the policy priorities for harm reduction in Europe be in the near and distant future? In the previous two decades, Europe has been an example of 'best practices' for what can be achieved in the prevention of HIV infections among PWID. One new challenge might be to become a best practice example for the eradication of hepatitis C (HCV) infections among this group. Another challenge might be to focus more attention on reducing drug-related deaths, especially arising from opioid overdoses.

Unfinished business

While the search for new challenges may seem necessary to maintain the momentum for the consolidation and development of harm reduction, from a public health point of view, there is an equally important need to deal with issues that constitute unfinished business from the past two to three decades. Very important differences remain regarding the coverage of measures to prevent HIV and hepatitis C. Despite overall increases in the coverage of HIV-prevention measures and reductions in injecting-related HIV notifications in the EU, the most recent regional risk assessment (EMCDDA, 2015c) alerts us to existing HIV risks in around one third of Member States. The assessment points out substantial disparities in commitment to the implementation of comprehensive harm-reduction interventions, and the vulnerability of some low-prevalence but high-risk countries. Much remains to be achieved in several countries in terms of the delivery of HIV and especially HCV treatment (e.g. Papatheodoridis et al., 2016).

Other worrying issues are trends in drug-injecting including possible increases in heroin availability; new populations of heroin/opioid users; heavy stimulant use (amphetamines, methamphetamines, cocaine); and high risk sexual behaviour among some groups of non-marginalised stimulant users (e.g. MSM). Over the past decade, new psychoactive substances (sometimes labelled new synthetic drugs) have also attracted a lot of attention; new chemical variations are continually appearing on the market, with little information on what they are and on what their effects and risks are. Reliable identification of new drugs, as well as of their real risks, poses a considerable challenge for harm-reduction interventions such as pill testing at music venues.

While rates of HIV infection among PWID have diminished in Europe, and new treatments offer the possibility of containing and reducing other drug-related infections, the number of drug-related deaths (especially drug overdoses) remains high. A large majority of fatal overdoses are opioid-related. A few countries have opened supervised drug-consumption rooms in locations with high levels of street drug use and overdoses, but these have not sufficiently reduced overdose rates across the community as a whole. There is a need for the implementation of more extensive overdose-prevention programmes, in particular, take-home naloxone. Naloxone is a safe and effective antidote to opioid overdose that is widely used in hospital emergency departments. The challenge is to make naloxone available in community situations where opioid overdoses are likely to occur, and to teach users, those close to them (friends, families), and other likely first responders how to reverse suspected overdoses (Strang and MacDonald, 2016).

Another area where harm reduction is confronted with longstanding unfinished business are prisons. A much higher proportion of drug users are found in prison than in the general population, while treatment facilities and harm-reduction services generally lag well behind those provided in the community. Drug use in prison can take place in particularly risky conditions, and the risk of overdose immediately following release from prison is very high. There remains an urgent need to improve treatment and harm reduction in these settings, and to especially improve the management of transition between community and prison.

An ageing population of problem drug users

The consequences of its past successes have possibly created one of the major future challenges for European harm reduction and drug services in general: the ageing of a large cohort of problem drug users. Those who started injecting heroin in the midst of the heroin epidemics of the 1980s and 1990s constitute the largest group of those now reaching an advanced age, as evidenced by the latest EMCDDA data. Thus, the proportion of opioid clients entering treatment aged 40 or older has increased from one in five (19%) in 2006 to 40% of all opioid users entering treatment in 2014, while over the same period the proportion of over 40-year-olds among drug-related deaths increased from one third to almost half of all deaths (EMCDDA, 2015b). The ageing cohorts of current or former opioid injectors are characterised by a history of poor health, bad living conditions, intensive tobacco and alcohol use, and by a deterioration of the immune system making them susceptible to a range of chronic health problems. Additionally, in most countries high prevalence levels of HCV infection – between 40% and 80% – are found among this group: as many infections occurred decades ago there is a high likelihood of liver disease. Lack of access to treatment for infections may further exacerbate health problems and add to existing social conditions, such as long-term unemployment, unstable housing and limited social interaction with same-aged peers. Thus, problem drug users may need a level of care corresponding to that required by non-substance using elderly people much earlier in their lives.

The demographic changes are rarely accounted for in national drug policies or intervention guidelines. For example, patients above 40 will soon represent the large majority of people in opioid substitution treatment; however, very few of the existing clinical guidelines on opioid substitution treatment address age-related metabolic changes in the brain, liver and other important organs. Age-specific guidelines and recommendations for clinicians serving OST clients which address choices in substitution medications, drug interactions, dosage, modes of administration, take-home dosages and pain treatment are, however, missing in most countries. In order to halt the trend of drug-related deaths among ageing drug users, the training of drug treatment staff in chronic disease management and geriatric care needs to be enhanced.

The internet: paradigm change for drug responses?

The internet and the use of smartphones has had a significant impact on Europeans' everyday lives and this is also reflected in the drugs phenomenon. While the internet has created new ways to supply and purchase drugs, whether on the surface web or on the dark web, it has also significantly increased and facilitated the access of drug users to health-related information regarding drug consumption.

Through an infinite number of specialised drug-related websites, social media, internet forums and dedicated smartphone applications, a vast range of drug-related information is accessible to everyone at any time. One of the resulting major challenges for the user is determining the accuracy, value and reliability of the information. Contrary to the physical world, harm reduction on the internet is predominantly led by peers; health professionals have been relatively slow in embracing these new technologies and establishing themselves as a point of reference. In the absence of appropriately delivered services, other actors have filled the void. Various web-based forums have become the go-to place for harm-reduction advice, despite concerns about the quality of the information provided (Thanki and Frederick, 2016).

New smartphone applications that allow location-based mobile social computing via GPS facilitate opportunities for encounters. Concerns have been raised over accelerated diffusion of high-risk behaviour patterns, such as stimulant injection among MSM, through the ease by which contacts can be established via mobile dating apps such as Grindr. While targeted sexual-health and harm-reduction interventions, including pre-exposure prophylaxis (PrEP) with anti-HIV drugs, address the prevention needs of gay men combining psychoactive substances with sex, it is important to address stigma and improve the availability of MSM-competent drugs services to reduce risks for this vulnerable group. As users may not proactively seek harm-reduction information, outreach activities, including virtual outreach, are needed. In this respect, the main challenges faced by harm-reduction professionals operating in virtual environments are to gain the trust and interest of users, and also app developers who are highly resistant to associating their business with drugs requesting high fees to promote health advice on their applications, or simply ban any health promotion (ECDC, 2015).

However, the wide reach of the internet provides significant opportunities for harm reduction and offers considerable potential for public health gains in terms of health promotion, alerting users of immediate and long-term risks, and in generating relevant data on help- and information-seeking behaviour.

Conclusion

Much has been achieved in terms of establishing harm reduction as a major dimension of drug policy and in terms of achieving the goals of reducing harm. However, as the drug situation changes constantly, new challenges emerge, and important old challenges remain.

Globally, the EU has been a leader regarding pragmatic, evidence-based, responses to drug use, but the recent economic recession, as well as complacency about the need for harm reduction – both in some areas where harm reduction has achieved good coverage, as well as in those parts of the EU where HIV is not widespread among drug users – may put this 'regional' success at risk. Changing policy priorities, rising concern about issues such as terrorism and immigration, as well a lack of collective memory among policy makers linked to changing governments all combine to underscore concerns (see Edwards and Galla, 2014).

There is a need, now, to galvanise harm-reduction policies across Europe, particularly in the countries most affected by economic and social hardship since the 2008 crisis, and to redirect the debate towards meeting new challenges.

References

ADVISORY COUNCIL ON THE MISUSE OF DRUGS (ACDM) (1988) *AIDS and Drug Misuse, Part 1*. London: HMSO.

BOURNE, A., REID, D., HICKSON, F., TORRES-RUEDA, S. and WEATHER-BURN, P. (2015) Illicit Drug Use in Sexual Settings ('Chemsex') and HIV/STI Transmission Risk Behaviour Among Gay Men in South London: Findings from a Qualitative Study. *BMJ Sex Transm Infect 2015*; Dec; 91(8). pp. 564–568.

COOK, C., BRIDGE, J. and STIMSON, G. V. (2010) The Diffusion of Harm Reduction in Europe and Beyond. In Rhodes, T. and Hedrich, D. (eds.). *Harm Reduction: Evidence, Impacts and Challenges*. EMCDDA Scientific Monograph Series No. 10. Luxembourg: Publications Office of the European Union. pp. 37–56. Available from: http://www.emcdda.europa. eu/publications/monographs/harm-reduction [Accessed: 18 December 2015].

COREPER (1999) *European Union Drugs Strategy (2000–2004)*. CORDROGUE 64 Rev.3. Available from: http://www.emcdda.europa.eu/html.cfm/index2005EN.html [Accessed: 18 December 2015].

COUNCIL OF THE EUROPEAN UNION (2003) *Council Recommendation of 18 June 2003 on the Prevention and Reduction of Health-Related Harm Associated with Drug Dependence*. OJ L 165, 3. 7. 2003, p. 31–33. Available at: http://eur-lex.europa.eu/legal-content/EN/TXT/?uri=CELEX:32003H0488. [Accessed: 18 December 2015].

EDWARDS, C. and GALLA, M. (2014) Governance in EU Illicit Drugs policy. *International Journal of Drug Policy*. 25(5). pp. 942–947.

ESTIEVENART, G. (ed.) (1995) *Policies and Strategies to Combat Drugs in Europe*. Dordrecht: Kluwer Academic Publishers.

EUROPEAN CENTRE FOR DISEASE PREVENTION AND CONTROL/WHO REGIONAL OFFICE FOR EUROPE (2015) *HIV/AIDS Surveillance in Europe 2014*. Stockholm: European Centre for Disease prevention and Control. Available from: http://ecdc.europa.eu/en/publications/_layouts/forms/Publication_DispForm.aspx?List=4f55a d51-4aed-4d32-b960-af70113dbb90&ID=1408 [Accessed: 18 December 2015].

EUROPEAN CENTRE FOR DISEASE PREVENTION AND CONTROL (2015) *Understanding the Impact of Smart Phone Applications on MSM Sexual Health and STI/HIV Prevention in Europe*. Stockholm: European Centre for Disease Prevention and Control. Available from: http://ecdc.europa.eu/en/publications/Publications/impact-smartp hone-applications-sti-hiv-prevention-among-men-who-have-sex-with-men.pdf. [Accessed 18 December 2015].

EUROPEAN CENTRE FOR DISEASE PREVENTION AND CONTROL/EUROPEAN MONITORING CENTRE FOR DRUGS AND DRUG ADDICTION (2011) *Guidance: Prevention and Control of Infectious Diseases Among People who Inject Drugs*. Stockholm: European

Centre for Disease prevention and Control. Available from: http://www.emcdda.europa.eu/publications/ecdc-emcdda-guidance [Accessed: 18 December 2015].

EUROPEAN MONITORING CENTRE FOR DRUGS AND DRUG ADDICTION (2012) *Prisons and Drugs in Europe: The Problem and Responses*. Luxembourg: Publications Office of the European Union. Available at: http://www.emcdda.europa.eu/publications/selected-issues/prison. [Accessed: 18 December 2015].

EUROPEAN MONITORING CENTRE FOR DRUGS AND DRUG ADDICTION (2014) *Drug Policy Profile: Austria*. Luxembourg: Publications Office of the European Union. Available at: http://www.emcdda.europa.eu/publications/emcdda-papers/policy-profile-austria. [Accessed: 18 December 2015].

EUROPEAN MONITORING CENTRE FOR DRUGS AND DRUG ADDICTION (2015a) *European Drug Report – Trends and Developments 2015*. Luxembourg: Publications Office of the European Union. Available at: http://www.emcdda.europa.eu/publications/edr/trends-developments/2015. [Accessed: 18 December 2015].

EUROPEAN MONITORING CENTRE FOR DRUGS AND DRUG ADDICTION (2015b) *European Drug Report – Data and Statistics – Statistical bulletin 2015*. Available at: http://www.emcdda.europa.eu/data/stats2015 [Accessed: 18 December 2015].

EUROPEAN MONITORING CENTRE FOR DRUGS AND DRUG ADDICTION (2015c), *Drug-Related Infectious Diseases in Europe: Update from the EMCDDA Expert Network. Rapid Communication*. Luxembourg: Publications Office of the European Union. Annex 2: Risk assessment – supplementary table. Indicators of HIV notification trend, HIV and HCV prevalence estimates, transmission risk and prevention coverage in 30 European countries, p. 16. Available at: http://www.emcdda.europa.eu/publications/rapid/2015/drug-related-infectious-diseases-in-europe [Accessed: 18 December 2015]. A more detailed version of the table with full notes and references is available at: http://www.emcdda.europa.eu/attachements.cfm/att_240346_EN_UPDATED%20HIV-risk-assessment-Supplementary-Table_for%20consultation.docx.

EUROPEAN UNION (2012), EU Drugs Strategy (2013–2020). *Official Journal of the European Union* 2012/C 402/01. English Edition. Volume 55, 29 December 2012.

HEDRICH, D., PIRONA, A. and WIESSING, L. (2008) From Margin to Mainstream: The Evolution of Harm Reduction Responses to Problem Drug Use in Europe. *Drugs: Education, Prevention and Policy*. 15(6). pp. 503–517.

HEDRICH, D., KALAMARA, E., SFETCU, O., PHARRIS, A., NOOR, A., WIESSING, L., HOPE, V. and VAN DE LAAR, M. (2013) Human Immunodeficiency Virus Among People who Inject Drugs: Is Risk Increasing in Europe? *Euro Surveillance* 18(48). p.20648. Available from: http://www.eurosurveillance.org/ViewArticle.aspx?ArticleId=20648 [Accessed: 18 December 2015].

MACGREGOR, S. and WHITING, M. (2010) The Development of European Drug Policy and the Place of Harm Reduction Within This. In Rhodes, T. and Hedrich, D. (eds.). *Harm Reduction: Evidence, Impacts and Challenges*. EMCDDA Scientific Monograph Series No. 10. Luxembourg: Publications Office of the European Union. pp. 59–77. Available from: http://www.emcdda.europa.eu/publications/monographs/harm-reduction [Accessed: 18 December 2015].

MARTIN, N. K., HICKMAN, M., HUTCHINSON, S. J., GOLDBERG, D. J. and VICKERMAN, P. (2013) Combination Interventions to Prevent HCV Transmission Among People Who Inject Drugs: Modeling the Impact of Antiviral Treatment, Needle and Syringe Programs, and Opiate Substitution Therapy. *Clin Infect Dis.*; 57 Suppl 2: S39–S45.

MERMIN, J. (2015) *The HIV Test at 30: More Essential Than Ever. Huffington Post* 3 February 2015 [Online]. Available from: http://www.huffingtonpost.com/dr-jonathan-mermin/the-hiv-test-at-30-more-e_b_6771718.html. [Accessed: 18 December 2015].

PAPATHEODORIDIS, G., THOMAS, H. C., GOLNA, C., BERNARDI, M. et al. (2016) Addressing Barriers to the Prevention, Diagnosis and Treatment of Hepatitis B and C in the Face of Persisting Fiscal Constraints in Europe: Report From a High Level Conference. *Journal of Viral Hepatitis*, 23(S1), February 2016. pp. 1–12.

PHARRIS, A., WIESSING, L., SFETCU, O., HEDRICH, D., BOTESCU, A., FOTIOU, A., NIKOLOPOULOS, G., MALLIORI, M., SALMINEN, M., SUK, J., GRIFFITHS, P. and VAN DE LAAR, M. (2011) Human Immunodeficiency Virus in Injecting Drug Users in Europe Following a Reported Increase of Cases in Greece and Romania, 2011. *Euro Surveillance*. 16(48). Available from: http://www.eurosurveillance.org/ViewArticle.aspx?ArticleId=20032. [Accessed: 18 December 2015].

RHODES, T. and HEDRICH, D. (2010) Harm Reduction and the Mainstream. In Rhodes, T. and Hedrich, D. (eds) *Harm Reduction: Evidence, Impacts and Challenges*. EMCDDA Scientific Monograph Series No. 10. Luxembourg: Publications Office of the European Union. pp. 19–33. Available from: http://www.emcdda.europa.eu/publications/monographs/harm-reduction. [Accessed: 18 December 2015].

SCHARDT, S. (ed.) (2001) *European Cities on Drug Policy. Co-operation and Community Consensus – The Multi-Agency Approach to Effective Local Drug Policies*. Frankfurt: The European Cities on Drug Policy. Available at: http://www.realitaeten-bureau.de/documents/commcoop ECDP_002.pdf. [Accessed: 18 December 2015].

STRANG, J. and MACDONALD, R. (eds.) (2016). *The Prevention of Opioid Overdose Deaths Through Take-Home Naloxone*. EMCDDA Insights Series no. 20. Luxembourg: Publications Office of the European Union. Available at: http://www.emcdda.europa.eu/publications/insights/naloxone

THANKI, D. and FREDERICK, B. (2016) Social Media and Drug Markets. In: European Monitoring Centre for Drugs and Drug Addiction (2015), *The Internet and Drug Markets*. EMCDDA Insights Series. Luxembourg: Publications Office of the European Union.

VAN DER GOUWE, D., GALLA, M., VAN GAGELDONK, A., CROES, E., ENGELHARDT, J., VAN LAAR, M. and BUSTER, M. (2006), *Prevention and Reduction of Health-Related Harm Associated with Drug Dependence. An Inventory of Policies, Evidence and Practices in the EU Relevant to the Implementation of the Council Recommendation of 18 June 2003. Synthesis Report*. Utrecht: Trimbos Institute. Available at: http://www.drugsandalcohol.ie/6247/1/Trimbos_AF0699_-HRI_Rapport2.pdf. [Accessed: 18 December 2015].

Chapter 18

Legal responses to drug possession in Europe
From crime to public health

Brendan Hughes

Introduction

International legislation to control the production and supply of harmful psychoactive drugs started with the International Opium Convention of 1912, but the first significant treaty to explicitly mention protecting or improving the health of drug users was the United Nations Single Convention on Narcotic Drugs of 1961, which established the modern international legal framework for drug control. It opens with the Parties declaring themselves to be 'Concerned with the health and welfare of mankind', and Article 38 clearly instructed Parties to 'give special attention to the provision of facilities for the medical treatment, care and rehabilitation of drug addicts'. Nevertheless, Article 36(1), much as its predecessors did, requested that drug possession and distribution be a punishable offence, with serious offences liable to adequate punishment such as imprisonment. Given that international treaties are usually only concerned with cross-border offences, the term 'possession' was generally assumed to refer to possession for the purpose of supply (United Nations, 1998).

This focus on deterrence and punishment was strengthened by the UN Convention against Illicit Traffic 1988, which specifically asks each state party to establish possession for personal use as a criminal offence (subject to its constitutional principles and the basic concepts of its legal system – a 'safeguard clause' that effectively reduces an obligation to a request). This followed from the idea that enforcing a reduction in drug demand would assist efforts to reduce drug supply. In 2009 the UNODC reported that 'Drug possession and sale are illegal in most countries of the world, and, as a result, the drug problem was long seen as primarily a criminal justice issue' (UNODC, 2009, p. 166).

Less attention has been paid to Article 36.1(b) inserted by the 1972 protocol to the 1961 Convention (echoed in the 1971 UN Convention on Psychotropic Substances), which states that 'when abusers of drugs have committed such offences, the Parties may provide (...) as an alternative to conviction or punishment (...) that such abusers shall undergo measures of treatment, education, after-care, rehabilitation and social reintegration'. While much focus has been on the 1988 convention's requirement to establish personal possession as a criminal offence,

Legal responses to drug possession   273

the convention also widened the scope of the application of rehabilitative alternatives to punishment (in Article 3.4 (b–d)). This permitted such rehabilitative alternatives as options for drug offenders in general, whether drug abusers or not, including those who commit minor supply offences. These need not be exclusively delivered by courts: 'bridges between the criminal justice system and the treatment system might also be envisaged at other stages of the criminal process, including the prosecution stage' (United Nations, 1998, para. 3.108).

Thus, the international legal framework describes a system whereby unauthorised possession for personal use, and even for minor supply, may be a criminal or a non-criminal offence, with the state response being punitive or rehabilitative (or both), delivered by courts, prosecutors, police or even the health system.

Reducing the criminal justice approach

In Europe, the UN conventions have been implemented in different ways. Possession for personal use of any illicit drug may be a criminal offence, a non-criminal offence, or either, depending on the drug involved. And, since the European Monitoring Centre for Drugs and Drug Addiction (EMCDDA) started monitoring drug laws in the late 1990s, it is possible to see a contraction in the criminal justice approach, as European countries reduce the penalties for use-related drug offences.

There have been many changes, but in summary they take four main forms:

1   Changes in laws to reduce the maximum prison sentence, as in Finland, Greece, and the Czech Republic;
2   Changes in laws to remove the prison sentences for minor offences, as in Belgium and Slovenia;
3   Changes in laws to be able to simply close a minor case, such as those developed in Austria and introduced in Poland – the EMCDDA calls this 'depenalisation' (removing the penalty) – and
4   Changes in laws to modify the status of the offence from criminal to non-criminal (which then also removes the prison sentence), as in Portugal, Luxembourg, Croatia and, most recently, Malta. The EMCDDA calls this change in status 'decriminalisation'. It is still an offence, but not a criminal offence.

Many of the countries that have altered their penalties for possession have used a combination of these types of change, complicating any concise analysis. Also, the changes may apply to all drugs, to certain categories of drugs where the category determines the penalty, or to individual named drugs (notably, cannabis).

Changing the legal status of the offence is perhaps the most significant step for legislators, and this has happened in Portugal, Luxembourg, Croatia and Malta. In Portugal the law of July 2001 decriminalised possession of all drugs for personal use. This reduced the maximum punishment for possession of small amounts of drugs from three months' imprisonment to an administrative fine given by the new Commissions for Dissuasion of Drug Abuse, which prioritised health solutions over punitive sanctions. In Luxembourg, in May 2001, personal possession of cannabis was newly established as a separate offence with a lesser punishment, incurring only a fine for the first offence without aggravating circumstances. At the same time, maximum penalties for personal possession of all drugs other than cannabis were reduced from three years in prison to six months. In Croatia the new Criminal Code in force from January 2013 removed the criminal offence of possession of drugs for personal use, leaving it as an administrative offence punished by a fine. In Malta, in April 2015, a similar change took place with the 'Drug Dependence (Treatment not Imprisonment) Act', which also established the Drug Offenders Rehabilitation Board that may take various measures to help the recidivist offender recover from dependence.

Moves towards 'decriminalisation' were also made in Estonia, Belgium and Slovenia. In Estonia, before September 2002, a second administrative offence of drug possession within 12 months of the first was a criminal offence punishable by up to three years' imprisonment. The new Penal Code deleted this so a second offence is like the first, and considered a misdemeanour punishable by fine or administrative detention for up to 30 days. A change similar to that of Luxembourg took place in May 2003 in Belgium. The possession of a small amount of cannabis for personal use, without aggravating circumstances, was previously punishable by up to five years in prison, but it now attracts the lowest prosecution priority resulting in a police fine. In Slovenia the Misdemeanours Act of January 2005 removed prison penalties for all misdemeanours, one of which is possession of drugs for personal use. In this way, the maximum penalty was reduced from 30 days in prison, or five days for a small quantity, to a fine.

Without changing the legal status of the offence, six countries made changes to the way different drugs are categorised, with the category determining the penalty. In Romania the law of 2004 divided substances into high-risk and risk categories. The penalty for high-risk substances continued to be two to five years' imprisonment, while substances in the risk category are now subject to a lower penalty of six months to two years' imprisonment. In Bulgaria the 2006 Criminal Code introduced specific penalties for offences not related to distribution, namely one to six years' imprisonment for high-risk drugs (down from 10–15 years) and up to five years for risk drugs (down from three to six years); it also specified that minor offences could be punished with a fine. In the Czech Republic, from January 2010, the new Penal Code applied a lower maximum punishment for cannabis (one year in prison) than for other drugs (unchanged at two years) for personal possession of a quantity 'greater than small'. Conversely, at the end of 2006, Italy removed the differences in penalties between illicit drugs, while increasing the maximum duration of administrative sanctions, such as withdrawal of driving licence to one year for any illicit drug. In February 2014, however, the process by which this law was passed was declared invalid by the Constitutional Court, and a subsequent law established new penalties similar to the pre-2006 scale. In the

United Kingdom cannabis was reclassified from Class B to Class C in 2004, lowering maximum penalties for personal possession from five to two years' imprisonment; national police guidelines were issued not to arrest, but to give an informal warning, if there are not aggravating circumstances. In January 2009 cannabis was reclassified from Class C to Class B. This raised maximum penalties to five years' imprisonment once again, but revised national police guidelines continued to advise an informal warning for a first offence.

A third group of countries changed the penalties for personal possession without addressing legal status or relative harms. Penalties for personal possession for all drugs were simply changed in five countries, and effectively also in Slovakia, by redefining the offence. In Finland, in 2001, an amendment to the Penal Code reduced the maximum penalty for a minor narcotics offence from two years in prison to six months, allowing the prosecutor to deal with the majority of cases with a fine. In Greece, in 2003, the maximum penalty for use or possession of small amounts for personal use by a non-dependent user was reduced from five years to one year in prison, and the offence will not be entered in the criminal record if there is no re-offending for five years. Another change in Greece, in 2013, further reduced the maximum prison sentence to five months. In Denmark a guideline for prosecutors of May 2004 set out that the normal response for minor drug possession offences should be a fine, not a warning, and in 2007 this was established in the law. In France a 2007 law widened the range of possible judicial options to include a 'drug awareness course' aimed at occasional drug users and juveniles. The cost of the course is to be paid by the offender. In 2005 a change of the Slovak Criminal Code widened the definition of 'possession for personal use' from one to three doses of any illicit substance, while leaving the maximum punishment unchanged. Two new penalties can also be given to those offenders: monitored home imprisonment for up to one year, or community service of 40 to 300 hours. The change also introduced the new offence of 'possession of a larger amount for personal use', defined as up to ten doses and punishable by up to five years in prison. Previously, this would have been a trafficking offence punishable by two to eight years in prison. In Poland, in 2011, the drug law was amended to give prosecutors and judges an option to discontinue the prosecution of offenders found with small amounts of drugs for personal use, if there is a low risk of harm. In Hungary, in 2013, consumption itself was added to the offences in the new Criminal Code, attracting the same maximum penalty as personal possession (two years in prison).

Motives for change are complex and vary from country to country. For example, laws have been changed to facilitate access to treatment (Portugal, Malta), to simplify punishment (Belgium, Finland, United Kingdom in 2004, Poland), to harmonise misdemeanour penalties (Estonia, Slovenia) and to indicate levels of harm (Bulgaria, Czech Republic, France, Italy, Luxembourg, Romania, United Kingdom in 2009).

In terms of an overall European trend in penalties for personal possession of drugs it could be said that, with some exceptions, maximum penalties have been

The public health approach

The public health approach in the field of drugs is also embodied in the United Nations drug conventions, in particular in the option of giving 'alternatives to punishment', measures such as 'treatment, education, aftercare, rehabilitation and social reintegration'.

These options have been established in the Conventions since 1971, but unfortunately they seem to have a low profile. It did not help that, from about 1990 onwards, the policy discussion on 'alternatives to conviction or punishment', which were rehabilitative responses, largely metamorphosed into one on 'alternatives to prison'. In Europe the EU Action Plan on Drugs 2000–04, 2005–08 and 2009–12 all focused on the development and use of 'alternatives to imprisonment' as components of treatment objectives. With this term the emphasis on public health was only implied, not stated, so it was sometimes interpreted as no more than punishment outside prison. The latest EU Action Plan on Drugs 2013–16 (Action 21) better reflects the original wording of the conventions, encouraging provision of 'alternatives to coercive sanctions (such as education, treatment, rehabilitation, aftercare and social reintegration) for drug-using offenders'.

While 'alternatives to conviction or punishment' emphasises the aim of the policy response, 'alternatives to prison' emphasises the setting. Despite the two terms appearing to be used almost interchangeably, they are quite distinct. The term 'punishment' has been defined as 'the intentional infliction of pain or of something unpleasant' (by an authority, for breaking rules) (Peters, 1966, chapter 10), a measure with a retributive aim. Imprisonment has retribution as a key purpose but there are many lesser penalties that are also punitive. The United Nations Standard Minimum Rules for Non-custodial Measures (the Tokyo Rules) establish what such punishments (sanctions) may be: verbal sanctions such as admonition, reprimand and warning; conditional discharge; status penalties; economic sanctions and monetary penalties such as fines and day-fines; suspended or deferred sentence; and community service order. While these penalties may be given as alternatives to conviction or prison – and are frequently given to drug law offenders in Europe (EMCDDA, 2009) – they are conceptually distinct from 'measures such as education, rehabilitation or social reintegration (…) as well as (…) treatment and aftercare'.

However, the distinction is not always clear. Prison and many of the other punishments may also have a rehabilitative element, while a direction to treatment or counselling may retain some punitive element, such as the acquisition of a criminal record, some monitoring of behaviour or a fine. There is essentially a continuum of practice from a main focus on punishment with or without some rehabilitative services, to an emphasis on rehabilitation which may be supported by some degree of coercion. For simplicity we talk of alternatives to punishment and focus on that part of the spectrum that gives greater emphasis to rehabilitative measures, which will usually be oriented towards treatment or post-treatment interventions for problem drug users, or towards education for non-problem users.

From 2000 onwards, we see in Europe the development of mechanisms to increase the diversion of problem users towards treatment, from the different stages of the criminal justice system:[1] the police, the prosecutor, and the court.

In Portugal, the UK and Malta, the public health approach starts already with the police action. In Portugal, since 2001, all drug users stopped by the police, whether they appear to be experimental users or dependent ones, will be sent to a 'Commission for the Dissuasion of Drug Abuse' (CDT), established in each of Portugal's 18 districts. Distinct from drug courts, the CDTs are under the auspices of the Ministry of Health, and are multidisciplinary panels composed of a lawyer, a doctor and a social worker who meet the offender around a table, rather than a judge in a courtroom. Sanctioning by fine (the maximum possible punishment) is an available option for non-addicts, but the institutional philosophy means it is not the main objective in this phase. Following the case assessment, the CDT hears the offender and rules on the offence with the aim of treating any addiction and rehabilitating the person using the most appropriate interventions. The CDT is authorised to suspend the proceedings or execute a punitive sentence, as it considers appropriate.

In the UK, the arrest referral scheme has been established in the United Kingdom (England and Wales) at a national level since 2002, where it is not an alternative to prosecution or due process but a technique for engaging with users. Arrest referral is a partnership initiative between police and local drug services that uses the point of arrest within custody suites at police stations as an opportunity for an independent drugs worker to assess drug users and refer them to drug treatment services, if appropriate. Its principal focus was to reduce drug-related crime by engaging with problematic drug users and moving them into appropriate treatment and support. National funding has been discontinued since April 2013, but most police force areas continue to fund criminal justice intervention teams to proactively engage drug-misusing offenders following arrest. Arrest referral was piloted in Dublin, Ireland, for juveniles in 2003 and for adults in 2012. It was also piloted in Malta in 2005, though this had a low take-up and was eventually adapted to a new system in 2015.

In Malta, in 2015, the new 'Drug Dependence (Treatment not Imprisonment) Act' entered into force. Previously, personal possession would be subject to a fine or imprisonment by the Magistrate's Court, but now personal possession of (defined) small amounts may result in an administrative fine by the Commissioner for Justice. A repeat offender will appear before the new Drug Offenders Rehabilitation Board, which is chaired by a retired judge or magistrate and has three

---

1 The term 'criminal justice system' is used for simplicity, but refers also to non-criminal (civil, administrative) systems for sanctioning minor drug use or possession that are used in some countries.

members appointed by the Ministers of Home Affairs, Social Policy and Health, respectively. The Board may take various measures to help the offender recover from dependence. Also, the Magistrate's Court, supported by the Board, may decide to assume the functions of a Drugs Court in defined cases (e.g. dependent offender, some drug-related crimes) and to refer the offender to the Board. The Board will, in turn, manage the offender for up to 18 months in recovery from dependence. After this the case may be closed, or, accordingly, the prosecution continued.

At the prosecution stage, the prosecution may be suspended subject to completion of a treatment course or similar. In France, Spain, Italy, Luxembourg and Romania this is only legally possible for personal possession offences, whereas in Belgium, Greece, Latvia, the Netherlands, Austria and Poland the option is also available to problem drug users who have committed other offences that might be connected with drug use. In Romania this possibility was introduced by the new drug law in 2004. In France a 'drugs awareness course' was established as an option in 2007 to ensure that the prosecutor or judge has a constructive and proportionate response to occasional, non-problem users, rather than dismissal or criminal conviction. As the offender pays the cost of the course, often around €250, this may be interpreted as a combination of rehabilitative and punitive measures. In Spain, the administrative sanction for drug use can be suspended if the offender applies to a treatment service as agreed, while users in Italy will be interviewed by the prefecture and then may be sent to a local public drug addiction services unit to complete a rehabilitation programme. Before 2006 the offender in Italy could start a rehabilitation programme as an alternative to the administrative penalty, but under Law 49/2006 the administrative penalty is applied before any offer of a rehabilitation programme. In Poland, since 2011, it is obligatory for the prosecutor and judge to assess the offender's drug use, and there is no longer a requirement that suspension of prosecution for treatment is only applicable to a user without a criminal record.

The courts, similar to the prosecutors in the above countries, also have powers of suspension. That power is exclusive to the courts in the Czech Republic, Denmark and Hungary. In Hungary, the new Criminal Code of 2003 established alternatives to punishment for drug users seeking treatment and included several instances where lower penalties could be given for drug addicts, but changes in 2013 reduced these options considerably. If the trial is not suspended, the next step in the criminal justice system is sentencing. In addition to several of those countries already mentioned, the sentence may be suspended in Germany, Slovakia, and now Estonia, where an amendment to the Penal Code from 2011 allows substitution of a prison sentence of six months to two years with treatment, if the original offence was caused by addiction. It is also possible to sentence to rehabilitative measures in Croatia, Sweden, the UK and Norway. In the Netherlands the Act on Penal Placement of Addicts in a Penitentiary Treatment Institution was introduced in 2001, where recidivist substance users causing serious nuisance were admitted into a penitentiary institution with treatment facilities for one to two years. This became the Act on Placement in an Institution for Prolific Offenders (not exclusively for drug addicts) in 2004.

If diversion operates at the sentencing stage, it will take valuable resources to process the offender to that stage. If diversion is possible earlier, perhaps by the prosecutor, it will reduce court backlogs and improve the efficiency of justice. Gradual simplification of the procedure can be seen in Austria. Before 2008, prosecution for personal possession of a 'small quantity' could be suspended following a health report from the local authority, though this report was not required for minor cannabis offences. The 2007 amendment to the main drug law made two small but significant changes. Firstly, the imprecise 'small quantity' criterion was deleted, allowing suspension of prosecution for any personal use offence up to the legally defined threshold quantity. Secondly, the health report was no longer required in cases involving cannabis, psychotropic substances or mushrooms (and lower penalty ranges were introduced for drug-dependent offenders). In 2016 the law was adjusted again, this time to allow police officers who suspect a minor drug offence committed for personal use to report the incident directly to the health authorities and not to the judicial authorities. This is aimed at enabling a faster response by the health authorities in cases of drug misuse, and helps concentrate the resources of the public prosecutors on more severe drug offences.

From criminal justice to public health: the different journeys

Drug control was always based on the principle of protection of public health, and the increased pressure of criminal law on drug users was intended as a deterrent to reduce consumption. However, even though it is widely agreed that the general deterrent of criminal punishment has no consistent effect on consumption levels of illicit drugs (MacCoun, 1993; EMCDDA, 2011a, p. 45), drug use (together with its associated problems) continues to be considered by many as a criminal justice issue. There are concerns about moving too far away from punitive sentencing. It is often assumed that greater deviation from general deterrent approaches will 'send the wrong message': that drug use is acceptable.

A few countries have had difficulty implementing their legal provisions on rehabilitative measures, in some cases because of difficulties relating to perceptions of leniency towards criminals. In Cyprus law 57 of 1992 on 'the care and treatment of addicts' remained unimplemented in 2013, due in part to what have been referred to as 'anachronistic and non-viable stipulations' (Cyprus Monitoring Centre for Drugs and Drug Addiction, 2009). Initial support in Norway for a system similar to the Portuguese model, proposed by the Stoltenberg Commission in 2010, weakened as the decriminalisation aspect became too controversial to implement. In Romania the possibility of referral of a drug user to treatment with eventual suspension of the proceedings, established by the drug control law of 2004, was dependent on a new Criminal Code only passed in 2009, and a new Criminal Procedural Code that had not yet been passed by 2012. The new

Criminal Code of February 2014 finally removed the need for the Criminal Procedural Code. When laws are passed, they are not always implemented on the ground. In Finland, the Prosecutor General published guidelines in 2006 encouraging prosecutors to waive charges for drug users seeking treatment (notably accepting that treatment, and thus a waiver, may be required several times to break an addiction). However, it has been reported that drug users usually receive fines rather than waivers, and the available statistics show that barely 8% of those waivers were the result of referral to treatment. In Malta an arrest referral scheme was piloted in 2005, but in the first five months only 15 out of 212 people arrested for possession were referred to drug agencies by the police and the scheme fell into disuse.

To protect against this, rehabilitative measures may be accompanied by strict eligibility and procedural conditions, and a cut-off level where only those diagnosed as sufficiently 'sick' are treated, while those who are not sick are punished. This is seen, for example, in the relatively high cost charged to offenders participating in the drugs awareness course in France, and the move in Italy of offering a rehabilitation programme only after the sanction has been completed, which reduces the incentive for this option. For this reason, the numbers opting for rehabilitation fell from over 10,000 per year before the change to less than 300 in 2012. Meanwhile, the criterion of strictly limiting provision of treatment to first offenders with no criminal record effectively made that alternative non-viable in Poland. A study in 2008, looking at 300 cases over three years and using interviews with prosecutors, users and prisoners, concluded that this option was rarely implemented. While 95 offenders were diagnosed as problematic users, only 9 had no previous convictions, and ultimately not one of the 300 cases was suspended based on Article 72 (Serednicki, 2009). As a result, the requirement of not having a previous conviction was abolished in 2011, and the prosecutor and judge are now obliged to collect information on the offender's drug use, rather than, as previously, simply having the option to do so.

Some difficulties in implementation of the measures appear to stem from an attempt at compromise between the two aims of treatment and punishment. This can pervade the entire policy cycle, from design, through implementation, to evaluation. One solution to this dichotomy may be to focus firmly on treatment and education, minimising punishment – an option suggested in the UN conventions since 1971. It is the reason why the model implemented in Portugal, where the whole administration addressing the needs of drug users is in the healthcare sphere – with several rehabilitative measures available – has been described as a consistent and coherent policy (EMCDDA, 2011b). In addition, as described earlier, a number of other countries appear to be moving towards the gradual implementation of similar systems, recognising that first contact with the non-problem user is an opportunity for (indicated) prevention in order to address future levels of problem drug use. In December 2015 the President of the INCB referred to the Portuguese approach as 'a model of best practices' for respecting the Conventions, putting health and welfare in the centre, applying a balanced

Legal responses to drug possession 281

approach and respecting principles of proportionality and human rights (Sipp, 2015, p. 14).

New psychoactive substances and new responses?

Recent years have witnessed a proliferation of new psychoactive substances becoming available in Europe. This is illustrated in the rise of notifications of new substances to the EU Early Warning System, from just 14 in 2005 to 101 in 2014. Some of these substances will find their way onto the market, packaged and promoted as 'natural' or 'legal' products, in specialised physical and online shops. Yet national legal systems were not developed to face such a phenomenon. As criminal law has to be specific when defining an offence, this generally means that the drug law must clearly list all substances under its control. The traditional response to the discovery of a new 'drug', established at a time when such a discovery was a relatively rare event, was to assess the risk to public health and add it to the national list of controlled substances. The process of updating the law can be time consuming; some countries require criminal laws to be agreed to by parliament, which may take more than a year. However, the speed with which new drugs appear means that, as soon as one new psychoactive substance is identified by the authorities and controlled, a replacement is already on the shelves. The major policy challenge has been to address the combination of the diversity of new substances and the speed with which they appear. Some of the substances are so new that, at least initially, there is very limited evidence of public health risk – the risks being the primary justification for punitive control measures. This potentially weakens the credibility of control systems.

At the national level, the new drugs phenomenon has provoked a range of innovative legal responses geared towards controlling the open sale of these substances. These include rapid interventions that have been put in place to allow countries time to design other responses or to fill the gap before drug law control can be enacted. Broadly speaking, three types of response can be delineated, differentiated largely by the speed with which they can be implemented. These responses are not necessarily mutually exclusive; some countries have initiated more than one response, either simultaneously or consecutively.

Firstly, a number of European countries have successfully used consumer safety or medicine laws which are based on harmonised EU definitions and were operational in, and available to, all Member States. Consumer safety laws addressed inadequate labelling to remove products from sale. As the harmonised EU definition of a medicinal product (one modifying physiological functions by pharmacological action) appeared not to require such a product to have therapeutic properties, at least eight countries used medicine laws to quickly control supply of new drugs. However, in July 2014, the European Court of Justice ruled that this was not a correct interpretation of the harmonised EU definition, curtailing systematic use of this control method. These approaches penalise suppliers but not users.

282 Brendan Hughes

Secondly, countries have modified or extended existing drug legislation. In order to accelerate legal processes, some countries have introduced temporary control regimes, allowing time for a more detailed assessment of the risk to public health and for permanent control. For example, temporary control procedures were enacted in the United Kingdom in 2011; in Hungary in 2012; and in Latvia and Slovakia in 2013. At the end of 2014, Finland extended its Narcotics Act to also cover 'psychoactive substances banned from the consumer market' listed in a new Government Decree following a risk assessment: unauthorised supply was punishable by up to a year in prison as an offence endangering health and safety. In the majority of these cases, actions are driven by the need to protect public health, yet the legislation does not foresee penalties for users (penalties were subsequently added in Latvia and Hungary).

Thirdly, new laws have been designed and passed to manage unauthorised distribution of psychoactive substances, as has occurred in Ireland, Austria, Portugal, Romania, the United Kingdom, and Sweden. In the first five countries, a psychoactive substance is defined as one that stimulates or depresses the central nervous system, which in Ireland, Austria, Portugal and Romania is associated with dependency, hallucinations or disturbances in motor function or behaviour; in the United Kingdom it is one that 'affects' the person's mental functioning or emotional state. Prison penalties are possible for supply-related offences in Ireland, Austria, Romania and the UK; the Portuguese penalties provide for heavy administrative fines. In Sweden a 2011 law gave administrative power to police and customs to confiscate certain harmful intoxicating substances, with no other penalty; prosecutors may then order their destruction. None of these laws foresee penalties for users – though users found with named psychoactive substances in Portugal will be sent to the (health-oriented) CDTs for assessment.

Therefore, although there is no agreement across Europe as a whole on any one particular way in which to respond to the new drugs threat, two longer-term trends are nevertheless identifiable. First, there appears to be a general move towards the use of the threat of prison to deter suppliers. Second, it seems that countries are choosing not to use criminal sanctions – or in several cases, any sanctions – for those possessing a new substance for personal use.

Discussion

Legislation addressing drug possession is intended to protect public health. For many years the international legislation only required criminal penalties for unauthorised drug supply, but this was supplemented in 1988 by the request for criminal penalties of personal use possession offences in order to reduce drug demand. Requests in the international law to provide alternatives to punishment were somehow rephrased as providing alternatives to prison, concentrating only on the setting of the response rather than its aim. Drug law was seen as primarily punitive.

More recently however, several European countries have taken steps to reduce the levels of punishment for use-related offences set out in their legislation. This

Legal responses to drug possession 283

can take the form of reducing or removing prison penalties, or even decriminalising and depenalising such offences when they are somehow considered minor or are not accompanied by aggravating circumstances.

A reduction in the punitive sanction for personal possession offences, such as decriminalisation, does not, by itself, strengthen the public health response. The *Handbook of Basic Principles and Promising Practices on Alternatives to Imprisonment* (UNODC, 2007) observes that the caseload of the criminal justice system may be reduced with policy alternatives to conviction (decriminalisation) and alternatives to punishment (diversion). There is evidence to show an increase in the latter, based on limited, but promising, evidence that rehabilitative responses are more successful than the criminal justice approach at reducing recidivism and encouraging treatment uptake. But this trend does not seem to be so definite. While there are signs that countries wish to treat drug users as a health problem more than a criminal problem, changes in the legislation are often partial, leaving the legal framework as a whole looking somewhat inconsistent; the offender will be stopped by the police, and will probably be processed by the prosecutor and, in several cases, the court. Only at that point will the offender likely be offered some form of diversion to a rehabilitative measure, while still under the ultimate supervision of the Ministry of Justice ensuring the measure is completed to judicial satisfaction. Failure usually implies that a criminal prosecution will be restarted. All countries in Europe have such options, but they are circumscribed by eligibility limits and other conditions that suggest, in policy terms, that the criminal justice response is still the dominant one. Only in Portugal has the entire system been reworked and put under the auspices of the Ministry of Health as part of a coherent and consistent policy. Initially it met with great resistance but has now been described as a model of best practice.

Separately, the phenomenal rise of diverse new psychoactive substances has precipitated a trend in adapting or developing new legislation around Europe that often omits to consider the user. It will be interesting to observe how this trend develops, and whether there will be any convergence in the penal attitudes to users of the 'old' and the 'new' substances – and, if so, in which direction.

References

CYPRUS MONITORING CENTRE FOR DRUGS AND DRUG ADDICTION (2009) *2009 National Report to the EMCDDA*. Available from: http://www.emcdda.europa.eu/system/files/publications/609/CY-NR2009_310993.pdf [Accessed: 9/6/2016].

EMCDDA. (2009) *Drug Offences: Sentencing and Other Outcomes*. Available from: http://www.emcdda.europa.eu/publications/selected-issues/sentencing-statistics [Accessed: 9/6/2016].

EMCDDA. (2011a) *Annual Report 2011: The State of the Drugs Problem in Europe*. Available from: http://www.emcdda.europa.eu/publications/annual-report/2011 [Accessed: 9/6/2016].

EMCDDA. (2011b) *Drug Policy Profiles – Portugal*. Available from: http://www.emcdda.europa.eu/publications/drug-policy-profiles/portugal [Accessed: 9/6/2016].

EMCDDA. (2015) *Alternatives to Punishment for Drug-using Offenders*. Available from: http://www.emcdda.europa.eu/publications/emcdda-papers/alternatives-to-prison [Accessed: 9/6/2016].

EMCDDA. (2015) *New Psychoactive Substances in Europe – Innovative Legal Responses*. Available from: http://www.emcdda.europa.eu/publications/ad-hoc-publication/new-psychoactive-substances-europe-innovative-legal-responses [Accessed: 9/6/2016].

MACCOUN, R. J. (1993) Drugs and the Law: A Psychological Analysis of Drug Prohibition. *Psychological Bulletin*, 113(3), pp. 497–512.

PETERS, R. S. (1966) *Ethics and Education*. London: George Allen and Unwin.

SEREDNICKI, L. (2009) *Art. 72 Ustawy o przeciwdziałaniu narkomanii jako alternatywa wobec kary pozbawienia wolności. Serwis Informacyjny Narkomania, n.47 (3/2009)*. Available from: http://sin.praesterno.pl/numer/47 [Accessed: 9/6/2016].

SIPP, W. (2015) *The Portuguese Approach and the International Drug Control Conventions*. Available from: https://www.unodc.org/documents/ungass2016//CND_Preparations/Reconvened58/Portugal_side_event_December_2015_INCB.pdf [Accessed: 9/6/2016].

UNITED NATIONS (1998) *Commentary on the United Nations Convention Against Illicit Traffic in Narcotic Drugs and Psychotropic Substances 1988*. New York: United Nations.

UNODC (2007) *Handbook of Basic Principles and Promising Practices on Alternatives to Imprisonment*. New York: United Nations.

UNODC (2009) *World Drug Report 2009*. New York: United Nations.

Chapter 19

Cannabis social clubs in Europe

Prospects and limits

Tom Decorte and Mafalda Pardal

Introduction

A cannabis social club is a legally constituted non-profit association of cannabis consumers. Cannabis social clubs collectively cultivate cannabis plants for adult members to meet personal consumption needs so that they do not have to turn to the black market (Barriuso, 2005, 2011; Room et al., 2010). Spanish cannabis activists established the first known cannabis associations in the early nineties, and in the first decade of the twenty-first century the number of cannabis social clubs continued to increase, with the model spreading throughout Spain. The Spanish model was soon introduced by activists to other European countries, in particular Belgium, the United Kingdom, and also in France (Bewley-Taylor, Blickman and Jelsma, 2014). In Uruguay cannabis social clubs are now allowed under the new cannabis law approved in December 2013 (Montanes, 2014).

'Cannabis social clubs' (CSCs) can be found in many countries and the model is now a frequent subject in the international debate about drug policy reform, but the label often covers very different empirical realities. Many questions remain unanswered. In this chapter we aim to provide a description of the different contexts in which cannabis social clubs operate, and the various practices these clubs seem to have adopted. In the next section we present an overview of cannabis social clubs and their practices in Spain, Belgium, in other European countries, and elsewhere in the world. In the subsequent section, we discuss the different legal frameworks in which the CSC model has been established, and, as a result of this variation, the uncertain legal status of the model. Although the debate on cannabis policy has often been polarised around either total prohibition or legalisation, such positions tend to draw on oversimplifications and do not capture very well the range of options available (MacCoun and Reuter, 2011). The cannabis social club model is one of the possible middle ground options, on a continuum between the extreme options of full prohibition and commercialisation – a discussion that we introduce in the following section. Finally, in the last section we discuss the prospects and limits of the CSC model, based on the sparse literature and limited empirical data available. We formulate several questions that could be addressed in future research.

CSCs in Europe and elsewhere: different contexts and practices

Spain: the birthplace of the first CSCs

The cannabis social club movement began to emerge in Barcelona in 1993 when the *Asociación Ramón Santos de Estudios Sobre el Cannabis* (ARSEC) decided to test the judicial limits with regards to (personal) cultivation of cannabis in Spain. ARSEC asked the public prosecutor if it would be considered a crime to grow cannabis for a group of adult users (Barriuso, 2011; Martinez, 2015). Based on the response that, in principle, this was not criminal behaviour, ARSEC engaged in a cultivation experiment which attracted media attention (Martinez, 2015; Pares and Bouso, 2015). The crop was confiscated, but a lower court acquitted those involved. Subsequently the case was taken to the Supreme Court, which ruled cannabis cultivation as dangerous *per se* and therefore punishable (Kilmer et al., 2013; Martinez, 2015; Pares and Bouso, 2015). Despite the outcome of this judicial procedure, the experiment was a reference for other activists, and in the following years other associations were created.

Recent accounts suggest that there may be 400–600 CSCs currently active in the country, in particular in the Basque Country and Catalonia (Bewley-Taylor et al., 2014; Blickman, 2014; Kilmer et al., 2013; Marks, 2015; Martinez, 2015; Transform, 2015). As with all other associations and organisations in Spain, cannabis social clubs are listed in a registry of associations, and in some cases founding members are subject to background checks (Transform, 2013, 2015). Generally, the CSCs draft a collective agreement of their cultivation plans (Barriuso, 2011; Blickman, 2014; Martinez, 2015). The quantity of cannabis to be cultivated is based on the number of expected members and predicted levels of consumption (Barriuso, 2011, 2012; Transform, 2013, 2015). Distribution takes place at the clubs' premises, where members may also be able to consume within designated areas. Daily personal allowances of, on average, 2–3 grams per person are set as a way of encouraging what are described as 'responsible' levels of use and limiting the quantity of cannabis taken away for consumption off-site (and possibly diverted to the illicit market) (Apfel, 2014; Barriuso, 2011, 2012; Transform, 2013, 2015). The clubs may contribute to employees' social security, pay tax, corporate income tax, and in some cases VAT on the cannabis products supplied (Barriuso, 2011).

Recently, a more commercial type of club has appeared, especially in Barcelona, which functions similarly to a Dutch coffee shop, with a closed-membership policy (Bewley-Taylor et al., 2014). These clubs are rapidly increasing as cannabis entrepreneurs perceive opportunities in a potentially regulated industry or the possibility of considerable profit in a semi-legal cannabis market. Some clubs have reportedly now admitted thousands of members, including foreigners (Bewley-Taylor et al., 2014). To meet demand these clubs rely on cannabis acquired from the illicit market or from professional growers (Bewley-Taylor et al., 2014; Blickman, 2014; Pares and Bouso, 2015).

Many clubs operate under a voluntary code of practice established by the Spanish *Federation of Cannabis Associations* (FAC) (Federacion de Asociaciones Cannabicas, 2014) or by the *European Coalition for Just and Effective Drug Policies* (ENCOD) (ENCOD, 2011). These codes have no legal standing: many clubs comply with their guidelines, but some clearly do not. In clubs that are run on a not-for-profit basis all revenue generated is reinvested back into the running of the club.

Belgium: CSCs show similarities and differences with the Spanish clubs

Directly inspired by the Spanish cannabis social club movement, Belgian activists have sought to explore a legal grey zone in Belgian drug laws (see below) arguing that if one is allowed to cultivate one female plant for personal use, then one should be able to do this collectively, given a lack of aggravating circumstances or public nuisance. The first Belgian cannabis social club – *Trekt Uw Plant* (TUP) – was established in 2006. In April 2013 a subdivision of TUP, with members drawn mainly from the northeast province of Limburg, became an independent cannabis social club: the *Mambo Social Club* (officially located in the city of Hasselt). Both clubs organised workshops to inform other cannabis activists about the CSC model, and to help them set up their own clubs. Very soon three cannabis clubs were established in the French speaking community of Belgium: *Ma Weed Perso* (in the city of Liège; established in July 2013), *WeedOut* (Andenne; established in September 2013) and *Sativa* (Namur; established in November 2013) (Decorte, 2014). Meanwhile, two new cannabis social clubs, especially oriented towards medicinal users have been established: '*The Herb Club*' and the '*Medicinal Cannabis Club*' (MCC).

Elsewhere we have described in detail the formal organisation of cannabis social clubs in Belgium (Decorte, 2015). Here we only point to some of the main characteristics of the clubs active circa 2014. Membership is granted only if individuals sign a membership form confirming that they were cannabis users prior to joining the CSC, that they are aware of the Belgian drug law, and that they are signing up voluntarily. Members must reside in Belgium and/or have Belgian nationality. All clubs apply a minimum age limit, but this varies across clubs (18 or 21 years old). The organisation of cannabis production shows considerable differences between clubs. Some clubs grow all the plants *synchronously* and distribute their total cannabis harvest among their members, e.g. every three months. Other clubs grow plants *asynchronously* in order to provide their members with smaller amounts more frequently. Some clubs require growers – often called 'plant caretakers' – to be regular members of the club; others do not. Several clubs reported negative experiences with growers, either because individuals did not adhere to the clubs' standards, or because the growers were profit-oriented. Distribution is usually done at a rented location, at 'exchange fairs', which tend to be held between every six weeks and every three months. In most clubs members can pick up cannabis only at the exchange fairs; there is no constant availability of cannabis. Most clubs apply maximum consumption limits for members, but the differences between clubs are considerable: 10 grams per month in one club compared with 30 grams per month in another.[1] Some CSCs opt to keep a very low profile, but most CSCs have explicitly tried to make contact with local authorities (police, public prosecutor, the mayor or local policymakers) (Decorte, 2015).

Other European countries

In many countries, 'cannabis social clubs' can be easily found with a simple internet search, but it is usually unclear whether these are only groups of cannabis activists, or whether these 'clubs' are also producing and distributing cannabis among their members. In the United Kingdom, the *United Kingdom Cannabis Social Clubs* (UKCSC) unites more than 70 'cannabis social clubs' (United Kingdom Cannabis Social Clubs, 2012). In France, the *'Cannabis Social Clubs Français'* (CSCF) was a federation of French CSCs, but it was dissolved by a court decision in June 2013. Another association, *'Les amis du CSCF'* ('The friends of CSCF') is supposedly still in operation, and there are accounts of underground cannabis clubs cultivating and distributing cannabis. In Slovenia, there seem to be at least a few cannabis social clubs (Maribor, Ljubljana) that actively produce(d) and distribute(d) cannabis among their members. There are also some accounts of what seem to have been medical cannabis social clubs in other countries, such as *Die Grüne Blume* in Switzerland, and *LaPiantiamo* in Italy. However, it is not clear whether they are currently still active and if they engage in the production and distribution of cannabis to their members (Decorte, 2015).

The Dutch city of Utrecht has asked for an exemption from Dutch drug laws that would allow it to establish a closed-membership CSC but it is not clear whether and how this pilot project will be implemented (Transform, 2013; X, 2014). In addition, a new CSC was established in Amsterdam in 2014, *The Tree of Life*. According to information made available by the club, the minimum age to join the CSC is set at 21 years old (The Tree of Life, 2014).[2] The club only admits residents in the Netherlands, and candidates undergo an intake interview in which their use patterns are discussed (The Tree of Life, 2014). Members can receive up to 5 grams of cannabis per day (but a different limit may apply to medical users) (The Tree of Life, 2014). The CSC imposes a membership fee of €25, as well as an annual contribution fee of €50 (The Tree of Life, 2014). In addition, members are expected to contribute towards production costs based on the estimated levels of use (as discussed during the application stage) (The Tree of Life, 2014).

While we find references to CSCs in several European countries, detailed information describing how the model has been implemented in those settings is either very limited or not available. Empirical research is thus needed to shed light onto how those clubs are organised and how they function on a day-to-day basis.

---

1   The clubs may apply different thresholds in the case of users with medical needs.
2   Or 18 years old for medical users with a doctor's note.

CSCs elsewhere in the world

The new Uruguayan legislation (Law 19.172) allows cannabis production by collectives (Bewley-Taylor et al., 2014). The CSCs may admit between 15 and 45 members and are allowed to supply up to 480 grams of cannabis per member on an annual basis (Kilmer et al., 2013; Montanes, 2014). Membership in such clubs is possible for Uruguayan citizens (aged 18 or above) or permanent residents of the country (Albrecht, 2014; Pardo, 2014).

Elsewhere in Latin America, informal clubs have appeared in Argentina, Colombia and Chile, exploiting *de facto* decriminalisation regimes, favourable court rulings and some degree of tolerance by the authorities (Bewley-Taylor et al., 2014). It should also be noted that several studies on domestic cannabis cultivation have repeatedly shown that even in an illegal context users and growers can be part of informal networks or subcultures of skilled growers in which expertise, materials, cannabis and cannabis plants are exchanged or shared frequently. Although they are not formally organised as CSCs, they can be seen as co-operatives of cannabis producers (Decorte, 2010b; Potter, 2010).

Unclear legal status of the CSCs

As outlined above, the CSC model has been established in different contexts and is thus also being developed within different legal frameworks. In what follows, we distinguish clubs in a legally regulated model (Uruguay) and clubs operating in ambivalent (and often still prohibitionist) frameworks (e.g. Spain and Belgium). Finally we discuss the international legal status of the CSC model.

Regulated clubs in Uruguay

Uruguay is the only jurisdiction that formally allows and regulates the functioning of CSCs. According to that country's new legislation (Law 19.172), approved at the end of 2013, CSCs (*'clubes de membresia'*) are one of the regulated models for the supply of cannabis.[3] As mentioned above, the new legislation lays down the total number of members the clubs may admit as well as the quantities of cannabis that may be distributed among them (Albrecht, 2014; Kilmer et al., 2013; Montanes, 2014). An interesting feature introduced by Uruguayan legislation relates to registration: the members have to complete a specific registration process (Montanes, 2014; Queirolo, Boidi and Cruz, 2015a). A governmental body, the *'Instituto de Regulación y Control de Cannabis'* (IRCCA) oversees the implementation of the relevant regulations with regards to the functioning of the clubs as well as the national register of cannabis users and clubs (Kilmer et al., 2013; Montanes, 2014; Pardo, 2014). The clubs first have to register as not-for-profit organisations with the

---

3   The Uruguayan Law 19.172 foresees also the possibility of home cultivation (up to six female plants), as well as the sale of cannabis from authorised pharmacies (to a maximum of 40 grams per month) (Albrecht, 2014; Kilmer et al., 2013).

Ministry of Education and Culture, and, upon approval, then need to complete a second registration with the IRCCA (Queirolo, Boidi and Cruz, 2015a; 2015b). At this stage, the clubs have to provide information regarding the identification of the club and other basic data (e.g., address, contact details, opening hours, personal data of the club founding members), a cultivation and distribution plan, the appointment of a technical manager, and the club's bylaws, *inter alia*. According to the applicable regulation the clubs have to maintain an area exclusively for cultivation which should be secured and monitored (Queirolo et al., 2015a; 2015b). No advertisement or outside signs are authorised (Queirolo et al., 2015a; 2015b).

Ambivalent legal frameworks (Spain and Belgium)

The existing CSCs in Europe have been operating at the margins of current legislation in their jurisdictions as, in the absence of formal regulation applicable to the model, they have sought to exploit grey legal zones and/or decriminalisation policies in those contexts.

In Spain, the CSCs (now numbering in the hundreds) active in the country have tested the limits of domestic law and court jurisprudence, drawing on the *de facto* decriminalisation of possession and cultivation of cannabis (in a private space) for personal use (Bewley-Taylor et al., 2014; Kilmer et al., 2013; Room et al., 2010). A previous doctrine of 'shared consumption' applied to cocaine and heroin users which tolerated the joint purchase and sharing of those drugs for compassionate reasons (i.e., with no associated profit) may have been an important reference for those involved in the grassroots movement that led to the appearance of the first collective cultivation in 1993 by the ARSEC (Barriuso, 2011; Pares and Bouso, 2015; Martinez, 2015). Two comprehensive legal analyses by distinguished Spanish academics have also outlined a general framework within which such collectives may operate in compatibility with the current domestic legislation and case law (Diez and Munoz, 2013; Munoz and Soto, 2000). Their recommendations have not gone amiss and many CSCs have sought to adapt their internal structure and functioning to the criteria identified by those authors (Arana and Montanes, 2011; Barriuso, 2011; 2012). For example, the clubs report restricting access to regular users of cannabis only, and supply quantities consistent with personal usage only, etc. Nevertheless, the activities of the clubs have often been censured by the public authorities and despite some favourable court rulings,[4] this remains an area characterised by legal uncertainty with limited prospects for the introduction of national legislation regulating the model – recent discussions and regulatory efforts at the regional and local level[5] have been

---

4   We are aware that at the time of writing a recent decision by the Spanish Supreme Court may have taken a different standpoint on the compatibility of the activities of the clubs with Spanish legislation.

5   For example, in Navarre, a legislative piece regulating cannabis user collectives was approved in 2014 (*Ley Foral Reguladora de los Colectivos de Usuarios de Cannabis en Navarra, 24/2014 de 2 de Diciembre*) but its implementation has since been suspended by the

challenged by the central government (Casals and Marks, 2015; Kilmer et al., 2013; Pares and Bouso, 2015; Martinez, 2015).

The CSCs active in Belgium have to some extent faced similar difficulties. In Belgium cannabis production and possession is not allowed by national law and is therefore considered a criminal offence for which a fine or prison sentence can be given. However, a 2005 joint guideline issued by the Minister of Justice and the College of Public Prosecutors set out that the lowest prosecution priority was to be given to the possession of cannabis for personal use. This corresponds to the possession of quantities not exceeding 3 grams or 1 cultivated (female) cannabis plant, without aggravating circumstances[6] or disturbance of the public order[7] (Decorte, 2014, 2015; Kilmer et al., 2013).

The first Belgian CSC, *Trekt Uw Plant* (TUP), established in 2006 following the issuance of those guidelines, argued for an extension of the tolerated threshold of one cultivated cannabis plant per user to a collective context. However, that interpretation has not necessarily been confirmed by the law enforcement and judicial authorities as some of the Belgian clubs have since faced court procedures. While TUP has been charged with criminal procedures on two occasions,[8] the net result of those cases was that while (collective) cannabis production is neither allowed nor regulated under Belgian law, TUP was, in fact, able to grow cannabis without significant law-enforcement interference. At the time of writing, several other clubs (e.g., *Mambo Social Club* and *Ma Weed Perso*) have been raided by the police and are involved in criminal procedures. It is unclear how courts will rule in these cases, but some clubs (*Ma Weed Perso, WeedOut* and *Sativa*) seem to have suspended their activities, at least temporarily.

The international legal status of CSCs

At the international level, there does not seem to be a definitive assessment as to the legal status of the model and its compatibility with the relevant UN drug

    Spanish Constitutional Court, and the central government has argued that that regional parliament does not have the competency to legislate in that area (EFE, 2015; Pares and Bouso, 2015).

6   Such as the presence of minors, if committed in the context of a criminal organisation, if causing harm or resulting in the death of another individual.

7   I.e., the possession of cannabis in a prison or youth protection institute, the possession of cannabis in an educational institution or in its surrounding area, the possession of cannabis in a public place, or when accessible to the public.

8   In 2006, TUP members were charged with possession of cannabis with the aggravating circumstance of participation in a criminal organisation. While the defendants were initially condemned for the former and acquitted for the latter by a local court, the Court of Appeal could not pass judgment in 2008 as by then the criminal prosecution had become time-barred (Decorte, 2014, 2015; Kilmer et al., 2013). In a second court case, TUP faced charges related to the encouragement of drug use, following two public demonstrations by the club in 2008. This procedure resulted in the acquittal of the defendants (Decorte, 2014, 2015).

conventions.[9] Despite the so-called room for manoeuvre or latitude of the drug conventions, it seems uncontroversial to allow that the establishment of a legally regulated market for the supply (i.e., production and distribution) of cannabis for non-medical and non-scientific purposes would be in clear contravention of the UN Conventions (Bewley-Taylor et al., 2014; Bewley-Taylor and Jelsma, 2012; Kempen and Fedorova, 2014). The International Narcotics Control Board (INCB) has supported this view by expressing serious concerns about the passage of new legislation in Uruguay (Pardal, 2016). There are other cases where the interpretation of international provisions is perhaps less clear-cut, for example, the Dutch coffee shop model – given that it rests upon an expediency principle. With regard to the CSC model, the core question relates to whether the production and supply of cannabis by the CSCs can be understood within the sphere of activities for personal use (i.e., cultivation, possession and use for personal consumption) – which would fall under the less strict regime of article 3 paragraph 2 of the 1988 Convention against Illicit Traffic in Narcotic Drugs and Psychotropic Substances (Bewley-Taylor et al., 2014; Kempen and Fedorova, 2014). In a recent analysis by Kempen and Fedorova (2014), the authors discuss two different lines of interpretation with regard to this matter. On the one hand, it can be argued that CSCs facilitate the consumption of cannabis and that the production of cannabis in that context cannot be equated with cultivation for personal use, as one does not indeed produce his/her own plant, and the cannabis is shared among the members. On the other hand, it can also be argued that production by CSCs would correspond to the total cumulative production of each individual member (e.g., when the clubs are operating on a one-plant-per-member basis), and consumption occurs within a closed circle so there is no diversion to third parties and there are no commercial goals. In any case, even assuming that the activities of the CSCs can be interpreted in light of article 3 paragraph 2 of the 1988 convention, the authors conclude that while waiving prosecution of the members of the clubs could be admissible, the introduction of legislation regulating the cultivation and distribution of cannabis by CSCs would be at odds with the UN conventions (Kempen and Fedorova, 2014). Uruguay remains the only jurisdiction to have taken that step, but the INCB has not specifically commented on the regulated CSC model to date, and thus the UN stance on this matter remains unclear (Pardal, 2016).

CSCs as an alternative model for supply

While the debate on cannabis policy has often been polarised around either total prohibition or commercialization, such positions tend to draw on an oversimplification of what 'legalisation' and 'prohibition' entails and do not reflect the range of options available (Caulkins et al., 2015a; Caulkins et al., 2015b; MacCoun,

---

9   We refer here to the 1961 Single Convention on Narcotic Drugs, the 1971 Convention on Psychotropic Substances, and to the 1988 Convention against Illicit Traffic in Narcotic Drugs and Psychotropic Substances.

Reuter and Schelling, 1996; MacCoun and Reuter, 2011; Transform, 2013). In fact, the introduction of a regime of legalisation may take different forms (and have different outcomes), depending on the choices around the specific regulatory design being adopted. The potential (legal) models for the supply of cannabis will thus be shaped by various decisions about the specific activities to be prohibited or allowed, to whom the regime is applicable (i.e., adults, licence holders, patients, etc.), and other technical aspects such as where and how production and/or distribution can take place (i.e., home growing, licence system, commercial production, etc.), or the form, price, quantity and potency of the substance that can be produced and/or distributed, among many others (Caulkins et al., 2015a; Caulkins et al., 2012; Kilmer, 2014; Kilmer et al., 2013; MacCoun and Reuter, 2001; MacCoun et al., 1996).

As a result, a very diverse spectrum of policies may emerge, ranging from a model in which adults only grow cannabis for domestic consumption, to a model where the government issues a number of profit or non-profit licences to organisations supplying cannabis, to the more commonly discussed standard commercial model (e.g., as implemented in Colorado and Washington State). Building up such regulatory models is a complex task, though, and the design and technical aspects of the model will have an important impact on the effects of its implementation (Caulkins et al., 2012; Kilmer, 2014). The need to allow for a degree of flexibility so that adjustments can be made as knowledge about the benefits and risks of a given model develops should thus be emphasised (Caulkins et al., 2015b; Kilmer, 2014).

Caulkins et al. (2015a) identified and compared twelve broad supply models which could be alternatives to the current status quo prohibition regime. In this study, two policy options are introduced as commonly discussed models: a form of prohibition with decreased sanctions (for example, this may involve decriminalisation of possession or reduced fines – a policy explored in several contexts), and a standard commercial model. This last is mainly characterised by the fact that production and distribution of cannabis are left to the competitive free market – albeit subject to specific regulations. This has been the case in Colorado and Washington State since 2014 (Kilmer, 2014; Pardo, 2014). Alternatively, two other 'extreme options' are also discussed, although these are arguably less likely to be pursued: retaining the prohibitory regime and increasing the associated sanctions and removing the prohibition altogether treating the cannabis market like any other general commerce (i.e., without creating any particular regulatory framework specific to this market). There are also a range of middle-ground options, including 'locally controlled retail sales' in line with the so-called Dutch coffee-shop model, which relies on non-enforcement against retail selling and possession (drawing on an expediency principle) in certain conditions (Korf, 2011; MacCoun, 2013; MacCoun and Reuter, 2001, 2011; Room et al., 2010). Domestic cultivation or a 'grow-your-own' model which allows users to cultivate their own cannabis has also been formally accepted, or at least tolerated, in several jurisdictions including Southern and Western Australia (Australia), and Alaska

(US) (MacCoun, 2013; MacCoun and Reuter, 2011). The introduction of a government monopoly with direct control over the supply of cannabis or the allocation of that role to a public authority are other possible avenues – with a view to reducing the involvement of for-profit firms in the market. Other middle-ground options might be based on a licence-system granted only to non-profit organisations, or to a restricted number of for profit-firms.

The CSC model is also seen as as one of the possible middle-ground options. It has the potential of weakening an important part of the illegal market by offering the prospect of a stable supply for (regular) cannabis users, while avoiding the diversion of cannabis back to the illegal market (as the quantities distributed within the CSCs are relatively small and destined for personal use) (Caulkins et al., 2015a, Caulkins et al., 2015b; MacCoun, 2013). The implementation of this model would nevertheless require continued efforts by the government to curb the remaining illegal sectors of the cannabis market. It is also worth noting that by comparison to other policy options the CSC model is, in theory, perhaps less prone to some of the risks associated with large-scale supply such as stronger marketing approaches and further incentives to harmful consumption (Caulkins et al., 2015a; Caulkins et al., 2015b; MacCoun, 2013). The CSC model also lends itself more easily to the implementation of quality control and labelling processes which can be an important factor in protecting public health. Further research is needed, though, to better understand the potential and actual impacts of this model.

Cannabis social clubs: prospects and limits

An important issue in policy discussions on prohibition versus legalisation of cannabis relates to whether it is possible to move a meaningful distance along the spectrum towards legalisation without crossing over to full commercial availability (Decorte, 2010a; Kilmer et al., 2013). When it comes to the middle ground between cannabis prohibition and commercial legalisation, several models have been suggested (Bewley-Taylor et al., 2014). The CSC model is a very interesting one that deserves academic and political attention.

Generally, cannabis social clubs are not profit-driven; they only distribute cannabis to their registered members who must be regular users before they become members. Clubs may apply maximum consumption limits, and financial profit can be reinvested in the association. Some clubs are only open to national residents, reducing the risk of drug tourism. While several CSCs in Barcelona are known to recruit tourists, many other Spanish and Belgian clubs claim this practice would run counter to the basic principles of the model.

In an open legal market dominated by multinational companies (as is the case with alcohol, tobacco and caffeine), consumers are often reduced to a passive role, where their only possible option is to buy or not buy. In a black market this is even more true, since consumers have no control over the production process and consequently over the quality, potency or price of the substances (Decorte, 2010b). CSCs have fairly direct control over the varieties that are grown, the growing techniques used, and (to some extent) the quality and potency of the cannabis distributed via the club. Depending on the level of democracy within the club, members may participate in the decision-making process regarding all these aspects. As clubs become larger, though, and in the absence of regulation there is a certain risk of CSCs morphing into marketing enterprises (cf. developments in Spain, see Bewley-Taylor et al., 2014), with fewer personal relationships with members and less democratic decision-making procedures.

A regulated and generalised system of CSCs could have several economic advantages (Bewley-Taylor et al., 2014). Regulating the CSC model could make it possible to create direct jobs (e.g., employees responsible for cannabis production as well as organisational and administrative tasks). Legal employment would also generate more social-security contributions. Furthermore, CSCs might indirectly generate activity in economic sectors which provide services, equipment, and supplies to the clubs (e.g. fertilisers, cultivation material, greenhouses, transport, legal consultancy). Part of the capital currently spent buying cannabis on the black market would end up in other expenses taxed by the state generating additional VAT income. Finally, regulating the CSC model could help reduce public expenditure on policing and sentencing those involved in this segment of the cannabis market. Furthermore, the CSC model may help to reduce some of the problems associated with the illegal market: the increase of THC content, and the adulteration or contamination of cannabis would be countered through the introduction of clear thresholds and through monitoring; systemic violence and street dealing could also decrease with the establishment of a regulated CSC model. Cannabis activists claim that CSCs are already playing an important role in the prevention and early detection of problematic cannabis use with the referral of problem users to treatment and prevention centres. In a regulated framework, collaboration between treatment centres and CSCs could be structurally improved.

In the context of regulatory absence, a threat to the CSC model is the emergence of 'shadow clubs': both Spain and Belgium have seen the emergence of individuals or groups who deliberately use a CSC's name and outward appearance as a front for a criminal enterprise to produce and sell cannabis (Bewley-Taylor et al., 2014).

Finally, in the absence of legal protection, some clubs are more afraid of systemic violence from criminals than of police intervention (Decorte, 2015): there is anecdotal evidence of theft of plants or the full harvest, and intimidation by local dealers. As CSCs become a more important competitor to other cannabis suppliers, the incidents of violence may increase.

In the current ambivalent legal context (in Spain and in Belgium), an important weakness of the cannabis social clubs is their unstable or transient nature. The differences in terms of house rules, structures and organisation is also noteworthy. Clubs can be very small (as few as 15 members) or very large (up to several thousand members), and they apply varying age and consumption limits. Depending on their size and other factors, cannabis production and distribution in clubs are organised differently. Within clubs and among clubs, lively discussions are held about house rules, membership criteria, organisation goals, and the most appropriate media strategies and actions to achieve them. These discussions sometimes result in conflicts and competition, and may contribute to a sense of distrust in the general population and to negative media attention. At the same time, the diversity of CSCs offers cannabis users some freedom to organise their practice as best fits their circumstances.

Most clubs serve a small number of 'medical users', and they often apply less stringent rules (e.g. no maximum consumption limit) for members who can present a medical statement confirming that they are suffering from an illness for which cannabis use is recommended. In the absence of solid collaboration and information exchange between CSCs and medical specialists it remains an open question whether it is a good idea for clubs to provide both medical and recreational cannabis.

Concluding reflections

'Cannabis social clubs' are found in many countries but the label often covers very different empirical realities. Clearly, there is a pressing need for more detailed empirical research on how cannabis social clubs in different countries are organised and structured, how they function on a day-to-day basis, and the different societal and political responses to emerging CSCs. Many questions remain unanswered and require in-depth research. These issues include: what are the socio-demographic characteristics of social club members? Why do they join a cannabis social club, and why are other cannabis users reluctant to apply for membership? What kind of cannabis consumption patterns did the members exhibit before becoming members, and how does club membership affect personal consumption patterns? Where did members acquire cannabis prior to membership, and do members still buy cannabis through other supply channels? Regarding the organisation of the clubs, other unanswered questions are: what is the background and (criminal) career of staff members and growers? Which cultivation techniques do clubs apply, and are these cultivation procedures a sufficient guarantee for quality and potency control?

An important question relevant for academics and policymakers relates to whether and how the weaknesses of, and threats to, the CSC model could be converted into strengths and opportunities through governmental regulation to ensure best practice. Government regulation could offer CSCs legal protection and provide a framework for quality control, safe and reliable cannabis production, transport, and distribution (Barriuso, 2012). Regulation could also shape favourable conditions for improving transparency and professionalising cannabis production in the CSCs, and it would allow for the standardisation of structures and internal organisation. The implementation of clear norms and sanctions could thus contribute to the stability of the model and prevent CSCs from morphing into profit-driven organisations. In the latter scenario, a number of aspects would require careful consideration: setting membership and production limits, defining production and distribution procedures, price controls, taxation design, strength/potency controls, and advertisement and packaging requirements. Finally, an existing or new institution could be given responsibility for the implementation, monitoring and enforcement of the various aspects of regulation applicable to the clubs.

Alternatively, if the authorities choose to criminalise the CSC model, the CSCs may sooner or later slip under the radar. In the current circumstances, as the CSC phenomenon grows, maintaining self-regulation and adherence to non-profit principles becomes difficult without additional formal controls (Transform, 2013). Indeed, if the relevant authorities do decide to refrain from action, the model may develop in a way similar to the Spanish (or at least, the Catalonian) version of the last few years, in the emergence of large, commercial clubs.

At the same time, the views and reactions of the clubs and of cannabis users in general[10] may potentially have an impact on the success of a regulated model of cannabis clubs. The CSC model is also based on the premise that cannabis users must register as members. Experiences in the Netherlands (where the obligation to formally register as a member to a coffeeshop – the so-called B-criterion – was introduced on May 1, 2012, but dropped again in November 2012 after fierce opposition from coffee shop owners, cannabis users and local mayors) and in Uruguay (where cannabis clubs and members are legally required to register) seem to suggest that cannabis users may be reluctant to register officially as cannabis users, especially if there is some degree of distrust towards the authorities (Queirolo et al., 2015a, 2015b).

References

ALBRECHT, L. (2014) Uruguay's Drug Policy Reform: At the Cutting Edge of Alternative Policy. *Journal of Peace and Conflict Studies*. 1(1). pp. 39–49.

APFEL, F. (2014) *Cannabis – From Prohibition to Regulation. 'When the music changes so does the dance'*. ALICE RAP Policy Paper Series, Policy Brief 5.

ARANA, X. and MONTAÑÉS, V. (2011) Cannabis Cultivation in Spain – The Case of Cannabis Social Clubs. In Decorte, T., Potter, G. R. and Bouchard, M. (eds.), *World Wide Weed: Global Trends in Cannabis Cultivation and its Control*. Surrey: Ashgate.

BARRIUSO, M. (2005) Propuesta de modelo legal para el cannabis en el estado español. *Revista del Instituto Vasco de Criminologia*. 19. pp. 151–167.

BARRIUSO, M. (2011) Cannabis Social Clubs in Spain: A Normalizing Alternative Underway. *Transnational Institute Series on Legislative Reform of Drug Policies*. 9. pp. 1–8.

BARRIUSO, M. (2012) Ni prohibición ni mercantilización: buscando el equilibrio en la regulación legal del cannabis. In LAMARCA: *Cannabis: usos, seguridad jurídica y políticas* Victoria-Gasteiz: Ararteko. pp. 167–181.

BEWLEY-TAYLOR, D., BLICKMAN, T. and JELSMA, M. (2014) *The Rise and Decline of Cannabis Prohibition. The History of Cannabis in the UN Drug Control System and*

10 For instance, the clubs' openness to professionalising their protocols and internal organisation and to the acceptance of legal restrictions and sanctions.

Options for Reform. Amsterdam: Transnational Institute and Global Drug Policy Observatory.

BEWLEY-TAYLOR, D. and JELSMA, M. (2012) The UN Drug Control Conventions. The Limits of Latitude. *Transnational Institute Series on Legislative Reform of Drug Policies.* 18. pp. 1–24.

BLICKMAN, T. (2014). Cannabis Policy Reform in Europe: Bottom Up Rather than Top Down. *Transnational Institute Series on Legislative Reform of Drug Policies.* 28. pp. 1–24.

CASALS, O. and MARKS, A. (2015) *Proceso de regulación de clubes sociales de cannabis en Catalunya.* Observatorio Civil de Drogas.

CAULKINS, J. P., KILMER, B., KLEIMAN, M. A. R., MACCOUN, R. J., MIDGETTE, G., OGLESBY, P., et al. (2015a) *Considering Marijuana Legalization: Insights for Vermont and Other Jurisdictions.* Santa Monica: RAND Corporation.

CAULKINS, J. P., KILMER, B., KLEIMAN, M. A. R., MACCOUN, R. J., MIDGETTE, G., OGLESBY, P., et al. (2015b) *Options and Issues Regarding Marijuana Legalization.* Santa Monica: RAND Corporation.

CAULKINS, J. P., KILMER, B., MACCOUN, R. J., PACULA, R. L. and REUTER, P. (2012) Design Considerations for Legalizing Cannabis: Lessons Inspired by Analysis of California's Proposition 19. *Addiction.* 107(5). pp. 865–871.

DECORTE, T. (2010a) The Case of Small-scale Cannabis Cultivation. *International Journal of Drug Policy.* 21(4). pp. 271–275.

DECORTE, T. (2010b) Small Scale Domestic Cannabis Cultivation: An Anonymous Web Survey among 659 Cultivators in Belgium. *Contemporary Drug Problems.* 37(2). pp. 341–370.

DECORTE, T. (2014) De Belgische 'Cannabis Social Clubs': middenweg tussen zwarte markt en commerciele beschikbaarheid? *Panopticon.* 35(6). pp. 520–537.

DECORTE, T. (2015) Cannabis Social Clubs in Belgium: Organizational Strengths and Weaknesses, and Threats to the Model. *International Journal of Drug Policy.* 26. pp. 122–130.

DÍEZ, J. L. and MUNOZ, J. (2013) La licitud de la autoorganización del consumo de drogas. *Libertas: Revista de la Fundación Internacional de Ciencias Penales.* 1. pp. 111–154.

EFE. (2015) El Constitucional suspende la ley foral que regula los clubes de cannabis, pero los promotores de la ILP la 'defenderán'. *Noticias de Navarra.* [Online] 15 April 2015. Available from: http://www.noticiasdenavarra.com. [Accessed 25 August 2015].

ENCOD. (2011) *Code of Conduct for European Cannabis Social Clubs.* [Online] Available from: http://www.encod.org/info/CODE-OF-CONDUCT-FOR-EUROPEAN.html [Accessed: 14 August 2015].

FEDERACIÓN DE ASOCIACIONES CANNÁBICAS. (2014) *Código de Buenas Prácticas.* [Online] Available from: http://www.fac.cc/csc/ [Accessed: 10 September 2015].

KEMPEN, P. H. van and FEDOROVA, M. (2014) *Internationaal recht en cannabis. Een beoordeling op basis van VN-drugsverdragen en EU-drugsregelgeving van gemeentelijke en buitenlandse opvattingen pro regulering van cannabisteelt voor recreatief gebruik.* Deventer: Kluwer.

KILMER, B. (2014) Policy Designs for Cannabis Legalization: Starting with the Eight Ps. *American Journal of Drug and Alcohol Abuse.* 40(4). pp. 259–261.

KILMER, B., KRUITHOF, K., PARDAL, M., CAULKINS, J. P. and RUBIN, J. (2013) *Multinational Overview of Cannabis Production Regimes.* Santa Monica: RAND Corporation.

KORF, D. (2011) Marihuana Behind and Beyond Coffee Shops. In Decorte, T., Potter, G. and Bouchard, M. (eds.). *World Wide Weed. Global Trends in Cannabis Cultivation and its Control.* Surrey: Ashgate Publishing Company.

MACCOUN, R. (2013) The Paths Not (Yet) Taken: Lower Risk Alternatives to Full-market Legalization of Cannabis. In Tate, K., Taylor, J. L. and Sawyer, M. Q. (eds.). *Something's in the Air: Race, Crime, and the Legalization of Marijuana.* New York: Routledge.

MACCOUN, R. and REUTER, P. (2001) *Drug War Heresies: Learning from Other Vices, Times & Places.* New York: Cambridge University Press.

MACCOUN, R. J. and REUTER, P. (2011) Assessing Drug Prohibition and its Alternatives: A Guide for Agnostics. *Annual Review of Law and Social Science.* 7. pp. 61–78.

MACCOUN, R., REUTER, P., and SCHELLING, T. (1996) Assessing Alternative Drug Control Regimes. *Journal of Policy Analysis and Management.* 15(3). pp. 330–352.

MARKS, A. (2015) *The Legal and Socio-political Landscape for Cannabis Social Clubs in Spain.* Observatorio Civil de Drogas. [Online] Available from: http://www.law.qmul.ac.uk/docs/staff/department/148791.pdf [Accessed: 29 August 2016].

MARTÍNEZ, D. P. (2015) Clubs sociales de cannabis: normalización, neoliberalismo, oportunidades políticas y prohibicionismo [EN translated version: Cannabis Social Clubs: Normalisation, Neoliberalism, Political Opportunities and Prohibition]. *CLIVATGE.* 3. pp. 92–112.

MONTAÑÉS, V. (2014) *Rompiendo el hielo: la regulación del cannabis en Paises Bajos, Colorado y Uruguay.* San Sebastian: Fundación Renovatio.

MUÑOZ, J. and SOTO, S. (2000) Uso terapéutico del cannabis y creación de establecimientos para su adquisición y consumo: viabilidad legal. *Boletín Criminológico.* 47. pp. 1–4.

PARDO, B. (2014) Cannabis Policy Reforms in the Americas: A Comparative Analysis of Colorado, Washington, and Uruguay. *International Journal of Drug Policy.* 25. pp. 727–735.

PARDAL, M. (2016). Cannabis social clubs in Belgium: growing in a legal haze? In J. de Maillard, A. Groenmeyer, P. Ponsaers, J. Shapland, & F. Viannello (Eds.), Crime and order, criminal justice experiences and desistance (Vol. 4, pp. 13–30). Antwerpen: Maklu.

PARÉS, O. and BOUSO, J. C. (2015) *Cannabis Social Clubs. Innovation Born of Necessity: Pioneering Drug Policy in Catalonia.* New York: Open Society Foundations.

POTTER, G. (2010) *Weed, Need and Greed: A Study of Domestic Cannabis Production.* London: Free Association Books.

QUEIROLO, R., BOIDI, F. and CRUZ, J. M. (2015a) Cannabis Clubs in Uruguay: Presentation of the Study and Preliminary Findings. *(Unpublished) Paper* presented at the 9th ISSDP Annual Conference, 20–22 May 2015, Ghent (Belgium).

QUEIROLO, R., BOIDI, M. F. and CRUZ, J. M. (2015b) Cannabis Clubs in Uruguay: The Challenges of Regulation. *(Unpublished) Paper* presented at the 9th ISSDP Annual Conference, 20–22 May 2015, Ghent (Belgium).

ROOM, R., FISCHER, B., HALL, W., LENTON, S. and REUTER, P. (2010) *Cannabis Policy: Moving Beyond Stalemate.* New York: Oxford University Press.

THE TREE OF LIFE. (2014) Huishoudelijk reglement [Online]. Available from: https://www.treeoflifeamsterdam.club/share/fckfiles/file/HR2016.pdf [Accessed: 29 March 2016].

TRANSFORM. (2013) *How to Regulate Cannabis: A Practical Guide.* Transform Drug Policy Foundation. [Online] Available from: http://www.tdpf.org.uk/resources/publications [Accessed: 29 March 2016].

TRANSFORM (2015). *Cannabis Social Clubs in Spain: Legalisation Without Commercialisation.* Transform Drug Policy Foundation [Online] Available from: http://www.tdpf.org.uk/resources/publications [Accessed: 29 March 2016].

UNITED KINGDOM CANNABIS SOCIAL CLUBS. (2012) Who are the UK Cannabis Social Clubs? [Online] Available from: http://ukcsc.co.uk/our-story/ [Accessed: 28 September 2015].

X. (2014) Utrecht zet plannen wietclub door, ondanks nieuw 'nee'. *AD.nl.* [Online] 17 December. Available from: http://www.ad.nl [Accessed 15 January 2015].

Index

12-step programmes 261

abortion 119, 170
Abraço 173
abstinence 5, 108; as goal of treatment 122
abstinence-based approach: Portugal 173; Switzerland 211
abstinence-based treatments 135, 207
ACMD *see* Advisory Committee on the Misuse of Drugs
acquisitive crime 210, 225, 230, 232
Act on Penal Placement of Addicts in a Penitentiary Treatment Institution 2001 278–9
Addaction 233
addiction 112; *see also* drug addiction
addiction psychiatry 220, 233
Addicts Register 220
Advisory Committee on the Misuse of Drugs (ACMD) 220, 223, 231
AFSJ *see* area of freedom, security and justice
agencies 40–1, 43–4, 47
agricultural production 3
AHOJ-G criteria 132, 150
Akzept e.V 111
alcohol 1, 34
alcoholism 199–201, 203
ALICE RAP project 242, 247
amphetamine: attitudes to 227; in France 88; in Germany 108; in Sweden 195–6
Amsterdam 129, 130, 132–4, 136, 141, 288; *see also* cannabis social clubs
Amsterdam Treaty 30
anti-drinking measures 34
anti-drug trafficking policies 16–17
anti-prohibition movement 62

antiviral treatments 264
area of freedom, security and justice (AFSJ) 20, 21
Argentina 286
ARSEC *see* Asociación Ramón Santos de Estudios Sobre el Cannabis
ARUD *see* Association for Risk Reduction in Use of Drugs
Asociación Ramón Santos de Estudios Sobre el Cannabis (ARSEC) 286, 287
Association for Risk Reduction in Use of Drugs (ARUD) 209
austerity 222–3, 233
Australia 256
Austria 273; new psychoactive substances (NPS) 282; public health approach 278, 279
'authoritarian solidarity' 119
awareness 69, 95, 96, 125; *see also* drug awareness training courses

'back door problem' 132–3
balanced approach 15, 20, 22–4
Balicki, Marek 159
Baltic countries 255
Barcelona 286, 294
Bayer 101
Bear, Daniel 229–30
Bejerot, Nils 198
Belgium 3, 59–71, 273, 274, 278, 287–8, 291; *see also* cannabis social clubs
benzodiazepines 150
Berlusconi, Silvio 124
Bern 209, 210, 214
best practice 33, 36, 265, 280, 283, 296
Birt, John 231
Black, Dorothy 220

Index   301

black markets 24, 74, 220, 244, 285, 294–5
Blair, Tony 230, 231
Blunkett, David 222
BME population 230
Boehringer 102
border controls 19, 226
Brain Committee 220
Brand, Russell 230
British Social Attitudes survey 231
Bulgaria 255, 274
buprenorphine 80, 201–2, 260

Canada 97, 256
Canas, Vitalino 176
cannabis 1, 27–8; attitudes to 227; 'back door problem' 132–3; Brixton police's experiment 223; classification of 223; criminal sanctions for consumers 64–6; decriminalisation 66–7, 94–7; growing 95, 96, 133, 141–2, 192; high-risk users 94; in Czech Republic 87; in Denmark 75; in France 87–8, 92–7; in Germany 103, 106–11; in Italy 116, 121, 124, 125; in Poland 153, 157; in Spain 87, 191–3; in Sweden 197; in Switzerland 207, 212–13; in the Netherlands 129–31, 136–9, 142; in the United Kingdom 220, 223–5, 228–31, 275; legalisation of 96, 191–3, 212, 214, 231, 292–3; policy reform 110–11; possession of 66–8, 130–1, 229; public health-oriented approach 94; public monopoly 97; relaxation of policy on 33; rethinking of opinion on 230; 'risk consumption' 193; small-scale sales 131–3; views on legal status 231; see also cannabis social clubs (CSCs)
Cannabis Abuse Screening Test (CAST) 87
Cannabis Day March 94
cannabis outpatient clinics 96
cannabis-related treatment 87–8, 93
cannabis shops 110, 212
cannabis social clubs (CSCs) 28, 95, 110, 285–97; as alternative model for supply 292–4; in Belgium 287–8; in Spain 191–2, 286–7; in Uruguay 286–7; legal status 286–9
Cannabis Warning System 229
Casal Ventoso 170–1, 175, 177
CASO 173
CAST see Cannabis Abuse Screening Test
Catania Report 34

causal beliefs 19
CDTs see Commissions for the Dissuasion of Drug Addiction
CELAD see European Committee to Combat Drugs
Centre for Social Justice 232
cgl 233
chemsex 224
Chile 286
Christian Democrats, Germany 111
chronic morphinism 73
Ciotti, Luigi 115
CIRC 94–5
cities 35; see also city riots
citizen participation 35
city riots 229
Civil Liberties, Justice and Home Affairs (LIBE) 23
civil servants 41
civil society 41, 94, 95, 111, 261
Class A drug users 224
classes of drugs 220, 228
club goers 224
CNDS see Commission for a National Drug Strategy
coca 1
cocaine: and acquisitive crime 232; attitudes to 227; cartels 102; crack 128, 138, 141, 222, 231–2, 264; discovery 101; in France 88; in Germany 101, 102, 103, 104, 108; in Spain 182; in Switzerland 206; international drug policy 2; in the Netherlands 129, 135, 138; in the United Kingdom 220, 224, 225; trends in using 264
codeine 101, 103
CODRO see Common Foreign and Security Policy Council Working Group on Drugs
coercion 41
coercive treatment 199–201
coffee 1
coffee shops 132–3, 136–7, 140, 141, 297
cognitive autonomisation 49–51
'cognitive Europeanisation' 41, 42, 44, 52
cognitive resources 53
'cognitive technologies' 40
Colombia 286
Commission for a National Drug Strategy (CNDS) 170–1, 175–6
Commissions for the Dissuasion of Drug Addiction (CDTs) 168

302 Index

Committee of Permanent Representatives to the European Union (COREPER) 21
Common Foreign and Security Policy Council Working Group on Drugs (CODRO) 30
community safety 221
co-morbidity 80
condoms 89
Conservative–Liberal Democrat Coalition 222
Constitutional Court 66
consumer safety laws 281
Convention against Illicit Traffic in Narcotic Drugs and Psychotropic Substances 1988 3, 29, 91, 272
Convention on Psychotropic Substances 1971 3, 29, 47, 131, 272
Copenhagen 74–5, 79, 80
CORA 117
COREPER *see* Committee of Permanent Representatives to the European Union
correctional punishment 66
COSI *see* Standing Committee on Operational Cooperation on Internal
Council for Counteracting Drug Addiction
Council of Europe 3, 45, 255
Council of the European Union 21
counter-culture 226
Coutinho, Rodrigo 174
crack cocaine 128, 138, 141, 222, 231–2, 264
Craxi, Bettino 116
crime: acquisitive 210, 225, 230, 232; and crack-cocaine 232; and drugs, 230, 232; and heroin 232; cross-border 23; organized 23, 228; youth 76; *see also* drug-related crimes
Crime Survey for England and Wales (CSEW) 225
criminal activities 74
criminal drug laws 70
criminalisation: and security issues 63–8; model 70; of drug consumption 27, 60, 63; of drug possession 17, 60, 62–3, 65, 158–9; of drug use 59, 62–8, 92–3, 197–8; of drug users 80–2; *see also* decriminalisation
criminality 61, 68
criminal justice approach 70
criminal justice interventions 138–9, 141, 277
criminal justice officials 172

criminal justice system 6, 63–4, 69–70, 75, 88, 91–3, 139, 156, 273, 277–8, 283
criminal policy directives 64–5
criminal preventive barriers 81
Croatia 273, 274, 278
cross-border crime 23
crystal meth 105; *see also* Pervitin
CSCs *see* cannabis social clubs
CSEW *see* Crime Survey for England and Wales 225
cultural habitus 5
Customs Mutual Assistance Group (MAG) 17, 18
customs union 28
Customs Working Party 21
Cwiakalski, Zbigniew 159
cybercrime 23
Cyprus 279
Czech Republic 273, 274, 278
Czuma, Andrzej 159

Damocles Act 1999 137
Dangerous Drugs Act 1920 217
Dangerous Drugs Act 1967 220
decision-making process 242
decriminalisation 6, 28; and prosecution policy 64–5; as convergence trend 243, 245–6; in Belgium 63–8; in Portugal 28, 34, 164, 165, 167, 172–3, 175–6; in Spain 185; limited 70; of cannabis 66–7, 94–7; of drug possession 67–8, 185, 273; of drug use 6, 28, 77; of drugs for personal use 116, 118, 123–4; of hard drugs 134–5; safety and security discourse 63–8
de-industrialisation 226
delinquency: drug-related 70; juvenile 61; urban 63
Delphi study 242
Denmark 4, 5, 73–84; cannabis 75; criminalisation of drug users 80–2; drug offences 77; drug possession 275, 278; drug treatment 77–80; harm reduction 78–9, 82–3; heroin 75; Law on Euphoriant Substances 1955 74–7, 83; medicalisation of drug treatment 79–80; policy in 73–4, 76–8
deprivation 226, 227, 232
detoxification 184
Deutsche AIDS-Hilfe 111
deviancy 77
deviant drug users 83–4

Index 303

deviant groups 1
DG Home *see* Directorate General Migration and Home Affairs
DG Justice *see* Directorate General Justice and Consumers
Diagnostic and Statistical Manual of Mental Disorders (DSM) 196; DSM IV 200; DSM V 112
DIP *see* Drugs Intervention Programme
Directorate General Justice and Consumers 15, 21, 22
Directorate General Migration and Home Affairs 14–15, 21, 22
discretion, public prosecutors 67–8, 92
disease model 118–21
dissemination 41
diversity 4–5, 7, 34, 35
Dobke, Werner 101
driving 91
Droleg initiative 211
drop-in centres 256
drug abuse 69; and deviancy 77; as criminological problem 74–5; as disease 199–201; as social problem 74–5, 77, 199, 200
Drug Abuse Prevention Act 1997 156
drug acquisition 92
drug addiction: approach to 64; as illness 183–4; treatment of 5; views on 120
Drug Addiction Treatment and Prevention Service (SPTT) 173
drug addicts: as 'pre-offending subjects' 183; incarceration of 125; treatment of 105; victimisation of 120–1
drug awareness training courses 91, 93, 275, 278, 280
drug consumers 82, 106
drug consumption: and public safety 188; approach to 69; average daily doses 189; criminalisation 27, 63; decriminalisation 69–70; in Belgium 59–63, 70; in Spain 183–4, 188–9; recreational 112, 227; repression of 63–7; *see also* drug consumption rooms; injection centres
drug consumption rooms 139, 209, 210, 211, 256, 266; in Denmark 79, 82, 83; in Spain 187; *see also* drug injection rooms; injection centres
drug control policy 77
drug counselling 104
drug dealers 74–5, 157; and technological innovation 139; over-criminalisation of

120–1; targeting 80, 157; *see also* drug distributors; house dealers
drug demand, reducing 77
drug dependence 13, 93, 149, 151, 153, 207, 217, 255, 257
Drug Dependence (Treatment and Imprisonment) Act 2015 274, 277
drug distributors 74, 77; *see also* drug dealers
'drug epidemic' 3
drug-free oriented approaches 261
drug-injecting, trends in 264
drug injection rooms 136, 209; *see also* drug consumption rooms
drug interdiction 214
drug markets 133, 135, 138, 141, 170
drug misuse 74–6, 195, 221, 255, 279
drug offences: decriminalisation 28; in Denmark 77; in Germany 108; in Poland 159; in the United Kingdom 220, 228–9; severe 279; use-related 273
drug policy: convergence 5–8, 16, 40–1, 242–4; defined 14; international cooperation 17; *see also* drug policy-making; policy integration
Drug Policy Alliance 48
drug policy-making: content 251; context 251; key convergence trends 243–4; process 251–2; stakeholders 248–50, 283; *see also* drug policy
drug possession 272–83; and public safety 188–9; as criminal justice issue 272–3; criminalisation 17, 62–3, 65, 158–9; decriminalisation 185, 273; depenalisation 273; for personal use 6, 156, 185, 188–9, 275–6, 278; in France 92, 275, 278, 280; in Poland 149, 155–9, 273, 275, 278; in Portugal 168, 169, 172, 176, 273–5; in Spain 183–4, 188–9; legal status 6; partial decriminalisation 67–8; penalties 117, 228, 273–6, 278, 283; public health approach 276–9; quantity issues 19, 274, 279; reducing the criminal justice approach 273–6
drug precursors 20
drug production 69
drug purity 23
drug-related crimes 4, 36, 124, 139; Italy 117; penalties 189–90; Spain 189–90; Switzerland 208
drug-related deaths 79, 225, 265, 266

304 Index

drug-related health damage 4
drug-related incidents 68
drug-related money laundering 91
drug-related mortality 186, 202
drugs: and crime 230, 232; as a regulatory concept 1; classification 220, 228; demand reduction 34, 187; glorification of 88; high-risk 274; incitement to consume 62; performance-enhancing 223; recreational 223, 227; relation between demand and supply 22; social attitudes to 230; supply reduction 2, 20, 22–4, 34; testing 91; tourism 68, 142; trends in use 224–7; *see also* drug trafficking; drug treatment; drug use; drug users
Drugs Act 2005 222, 223
Drugs Intervention Programme (DIP) 222
Drugs (Prevention of Misuse) Act 1964 220
DrugScope 233
Drugs Strategy (Drugs: Protecting Families and Communities) 2008 222
drug trafficking 4, 20, 21, 31; Belgium 60; control of 31; criminalisation of 60; development of policy integration 31–2; Framework Decisions 32; France 91, 92; penalties for 20, 31, 76; Portugal 165, 170, 172, 174; Spain 183–5, 188–9; Trevi Group 17; United Kingdom 221
drug treatment 5, 6, 62; abstinence-oriented 122, 135, 207; cannabis-related 87–8, 93; coercive 199–201; compulsory 139; drug-free 78; evidence-based 80; experiments in 77–8; forced 105; 'graduated goals' 79; heroin-assisted 79, 80, 82–3, 109, 135–6, 210, 211, 213; high-threshold model 261; in Denmark 77–80; individualisation 93; institutional 199; in Sweden 198–200; in the United Kingdom 221–2; juvenile delinquents 78; low-threshold model 261; maintenance 199; medicalisation of 79–80; psychiatric 200; quasi-coercive 120; sociological theories 77; Soviet model 261; voluntary 77, 93, 198–200; *see also* detoxification; social therapy
Drug Treatment and Testing Orders 222
drug use: accidents linked to 70; as a 'normal social problem' 75–6; as morally offensive behaviour 82; by young people 75–6; criminalisation 59,

62–8, 92–3, 197–8; decriminalisation 6, 28; injecting 89, 154; legal status 6; normalisation of 81, 125; sociology of 226; surveys 192–3
drug users: ageing population 78–9, 267; and legal system 60; and urban decline 63–4; co-morbidity among 80; distinguished from drug distributors 77; sick and deviant 83–4; small-time 92; stigmatisation 68, 70
DSM *see* Diagnostic and Statistical Manual of Mental Disorders
dual drug control policy 77
Duggan, Mark 229

Eastern Europe 261
ECDC *see* European Centre for Disease Control
ECJ *see* European Court of Justice
economic crisis 263–4
economic indicators 45
economic integration 28
ecstasy: attitudes to 227; discovery 101; in France 88; in Germany 101, 108; in the United Kingdom 224, 225; *see also* MDMA
EDADES 193
EDU *see* European Drugs Unit
Educare senza punire 119
Edwards, Carel 15–16
EEAS *see* European External Action Service
EEC *see* European Economic Community
EMCDDA *see* European Monitoring Centre for Drugs and Drug Addiction
ENCOD *see* European Coalition for Just and Effective Drug Policies
Engelsman, Eddy 139
England 221, 225, 226, 229, 232
ENLCD *see* National Strategy in the Fight Against Drugs
epidemiological indicators 45, 48, 50, 52–3
epidemiology 45, 47, 48
epistemic communities 18–20, 24, 220
ESPAD *see* European School Survey Project on Alcohol and other Drugs
Estonia 225, 274, 278
ESTUDES 193
ethnic minorities 1
EU Action Plans on Drugs 13, 30, 33, 34, 35, 276

Index 305

EU Drugs Strategies 13, 33, 34, 262; *EU Drugs Strategy 2005–2012* 16, 22, 24; *EU Drugs Strategy 2013–2020* 14–15, 262
EU Early Warning System 281
EU Justice and Home Affairs (JHA) 19
euphomaniac register 75
'Eurocrimes' 21
European Agenda on Security 23, 24
European Anti-Drugs Strategy 35
European Centre for Disease Control (ECDC) 263
European Cities on Drug Policy 255
European Coalition for Just and Effective Drug Policies (ENCOD) 35, 287
European Commission 21; role in drugs strategy 14–15
European Committee to Combat Drugs (CELAD) 3, 17–18, 30, 255, 261
European Communities (EC) 3
European Council 3–4, 13; in Rome 1990 30, 255
European Court of Human Rights 125
European Court of Justice (ECJ) 21; on new drugs 281
European drug policies: diversity 4–5, 7, 34, 35; historical context 1–2
European Drug Report 2015
European Drugs Unit (EDU) 30
European Economic Community (EEC) 17
European External Action Service (EEAS) 21
European Monitoring Centre for Drugs and Drug Addiction (EMCDDA) 4, 14, 21, 23, 30, 33, 35, 36, 42–54, 170, 229, 255, 257–8, 263–4; independence of 43–6; providing expertise 46–51, 53; setting up 44
European Parliament 21, 33; Committee on Civil Liberties, Justice and Home Affairs 51
European School Survey Project on Alcohol and other Drugs (ESPAD) 50n17, 224
European Union (EU): and policy integration 28–9; drug policy 3–4, 14–24; harm reduction measures 6; role of expertise 16–24
Europol 21, 30
evidence: policy-based 196; versus ideology and symbolism 177
evidence-based approach 80, 165, 175, 177, 195, 221, 261
expediency principle 131, 142

expert investigation, standards 46–7
expertise 16–24, 46–51
experts 41, 170–1

Federal Health Agency 103, 105
Federal Working Group Chemistry 103
Fini, Gianfranco 124
Finland 273, 275, 280; alcohol policy 34; new psychoactive substances (NPS) 282
First International Harm Reduction Conference 256
Foucault, Michel 112
Fowler, Norman 220
Framework Decisions 30, 36; as form of 'hard harmonisation' 31–2; drug trafficking 32; new psychoactive substances (NPS) 32
framing mechanisms 41
France 3, 87–97, 255; amphetamine 88; and international drug policy 2; cannabis 87–8, 92–7, 288; cocaine 88; criminalisation of drug use 92–3; drug law enforcement 91–3; drug possession 92, 275, 278, 280; drug trafficking 91, 92; harm reduction 89; heroin 88; history of drug law 88–9; legal regime 90–1; national drug strategies 89–90; policy 93–7
Frankfurt 109
Freedom of Information Request 229, 231
freedom of speech 49
free movement 18, 19
Freud, Sigmund 104

Gaedcke, Friedrich 101
Galla, Maurice 15–16
gay men 224, 268; *see also* men who have sex with men (MSM)
Gehe 102
German Hemp Association e.V 111
Germany 3, 100–12, 255, 278; amphetamine 108; cannabis 103, 106–11; cocaine 101–4, 108; drug consumption until 1933; drug consumption until 1968 105–6; drug offences 108; drug policy 2, 104–12; Federal Narcotic Law (BtMG) 107, 109; harm reduction 108; heroin 101–3, 105–9; legal framework 107; National Plan to Combat Drugs 108; opium laws 103–4; popular drug consumption 106–7

306 Index

Ghent 69
Gilson, L. 243
globalisation 226
Götz, Wolfgang 13, 23
Goulão, João 173–5
governance, multi-level 34–6
Greece 255, 264–5, 273, 272, 278
Green Party: France 96; Germany 110
Gruppo Abele 115
guidelines 31, 36

Haas, Peter 18
hallucinogenic mushrooms 88; *see also*
  magic mushrooms
Handbook of Basic Principles and Promising
  Practices on Alternatives to Imprisonment 283
harm reduction 9, 254–67; and the
  internet 267–8; as a convergence trend
  243–5; as a European approach 15–16;
  cannabis 27–8; consolidation 262–5;
  diversification 262–5; European Union's
  policy approach 6, 33–4; in Denmark
  78–9, 82–3; in France 89; in Germany
  108; in Italy 121–3, 125, 262; in Poland
  154, 158–9; in Portugal 173; in Sweden
  201–2, 264; in Switzerland 209, 211–12,
  214, 255–6; in the Netherlands 135–6,
  142, 244–5, 255; in the United
  Kingdom 244–5; low-threshold 209;
  principles and goals 260
hashish 107, 130, 131, 207
HDG *see* Horizontal Drugs Group
health: damage to 189; of those in custody
  189; policy 5, 7, 41, 63, 69–70, 243;
  risks 70
Health and Social Care Act 2012 222
health-oriented interventions 94
Health Policy Triangle 243
health-related harm 13
Helsinki Foundation for Human Rights
  (HFHR) 160
hepatitis B 136, 167, 170
hepatitis C 89, 170, 264, 265
heroin: ageing population of users 267; and
  drug-related deaths 225; attitudes to
  227; controlled distribution 6; discovery
  101; epidemic 23, 141, 142, 248, 267; in
  Denmark 75; in France 88; in Germany
  101–3, 105–9; in Poland 153; in
  Switzerland 207, 208, 210; in the
  Netherlands 130, 133–6, 138, 141; in
  the United Kingdom 217, 220, 226;

treatment 109; trends in using 264; *see
  also* heroin-assisted treatment
heroin-assisted treatment 79, 80, 82–3,
  135–6, 210, 211, 213
HFHR *see* Helsinki Foundation for Human
  Rights
high-risk drugs 274
hippie culture 151, 152
HIV/AIDS 5, 23, 43, 79, 89, 108, 136,
  141, 150, 154, 170, 170, 173, 201,
  208–10, 213, 220, 254–7, 262–5; among
  drug users; 69; risk assessments 263;
  testing 256
Hoechst 102
Hoffmann, Felix 101
Hollande, François 96
home imprisonment 275
homelessness 141, 170
Homo Sovieticus 157–8
horizontal circulation 41
Horizontal Drugs Group (HDG) 21–2, 30,
  261, 261; and EMCDDA 51
Horizontal Working Party on Drugs 21
'house addresses' 134–5, 138
house dealers 131–2
human dignity 158
humanism 165
human rights 141, 170–1
Hungary 275, 278, 282
hypodermic morphine 73

ICD *see* International Statistical
  Classification of Diseases and Related
  Health Problems
ideology 177
IDPC *see* International Drug Policy
  Consortium
immigrants 64
immigration 141
incarceration 68, 70; preventive 68;
  rates 61
INCB *see* International Narcotics Control
  Board
information: collecting 44–5, 47–8;
  producing 41–2, 48, 49; providers 51;
  reliability and legitimacy 53; role of
  40–1
injecting drug use 89, 154
injecting equipment 136
injection centres 6, 109
injections 73, 89, 109; supervised sites 6,
  109; *see also* drug consumption rooms;

Index 307

drug injecting; drug injection rooms; injection centres
institutionalisation 138–9, 141, 211–13
'institutional mix' 153
Instituto de Regulación y Control de Cannabis (IRCCA) 286–7
Integrity Assessments (BIBOB) 137
Interdepartmental Mission for the Fight Against Drugs and Drug Addiction (MILDT) 90
interest groups 41
Interministerial Conference on Drugs (25 January 2010) 69; Joint Declaration 69–70
internal borders 18, 19
international cooperation 17
international drug policy 2–3, 29; innovative strategies 34–5
International Drug Policy Consortium (IDPC) 95
International Labour Office 51
International Narcotics Control Board (INCB) 83, 118, 131, 176
International Opium Commission 1909 (Shanghai) 29, 102
International Opium Conference 1911 (Hague) 59, 102
International Opium Convention 1912 (Hague) 2, 59–60, 182
International Statistical Classification of Diseases and Related Health Problems (ICD) 196; ICD-10 200; ICD-11 112
internet 267–8
intoxication 112
Ipsos MORI poll 231
Iranian revolution 226
IRCCA see Instituto de Regulación y Control de Cannabis
Ireland 225, 277, 282
irrationality 112
isolation cures 184
Italy 3, 114–25; cannabis 116, 121, 124, 125, 288; decriminalisation of personal use 116, 118, 123–4; drug possession 278; *Fini-Giovanardi* bill 124–5; harm reduction 121–3, 125, 261–2; *Jervolino-Vassalli* bill 117; *La Greca Text* 123; origins of drug legislation 114–15; prohibitionist approach 116–18, 121; reformers' movement 124–5; social solidarity approach 119–20; victimisation of drug addicts 120–1

juvenile delinquency 61, 78

Keil, Friedrich 101
Kingdon, J. 242, 249, 252
Knoll, Albert 101
know-how 51
knowledge: control over 19; policy-relevant 18, 24; producing 41–2; reliability and legitimacy 53; role of 40–1
knowledge-based networks 18
Kohl, Helmut 108
Köllisch, Anton 101
kompot 151, 152, 156
Kopp, Pierre 94
Kort, Marcel de 139
Krajewski, Krzysztof 156–7, 159, 161
'Kraut Rock' 106
Kuhn, Thomas 246

laissez-faire economics 1
Latin America 286
Latvia 278, 282
Law Enforcement Against Prohibition 111
law enforcement experts 17
Law on the Prevention of Drug Abuse 1985 155
League of Nations 2
Le Dain, Anne-Yvonne 97
'legal good', 187, 190
'legal highs' 223
legal warnings 91
leisure zones 228
LIBE see Civil Liberties, Justice and Home Affairs
lifestyle choices 264
Lisbon Treaty 30, 263
local authorities 222
'local triangle' 131
Logical Framework 251
London 220; riots 229
London Metropolitan Police 229
low-threshold harm reduction 208
low-threshold methadone 175, 208
LSD 88, 106–9, 112
Luxembourg 3, 273, 274, 278

Maastricht Treaty 30, 255
Macao 2
Madness and Civilisation 112
MAG see Customs Mutual Assistance Group
magic mushrooms 223; *see also* hallucinogenic mushrooms

308 Index

maintenance treatment 199, 202 *see also*
  methadone maintenance treatment
  (MMT)
Major, John 221
Malta 273, 274, 277, 280
Mambo Social Club 287, 291
markets: black 24, 74, 220, 244, 282,
  294–5; drug 133, 135, 138, 141, 170;
  separation of 27
MDA *see* Misuse of Drugs Act 1971
MDMA 88, 223; *see also* ecstasy
medicalisation 196
medicinal products 281
memoranda 31
Mendão, Luis 176
mental deficiency 73
mental health problems 141
mental illness 73
men who have sex with men (MSM) 264,
  266–8; *see also* gay men
mephedrone 32, 224
Merc, 101, 102, 104
methadone: and drug-related deaths 225;
  detoxification 135; discovery 101; in
  Germany 101, 108; in the United
  Kingdom 232; low-threshold 175, 208;
  oral 220; prescriptions for 225;
  substitution 108–9; *see also* methadone
  maintenance programmes
methadone maintenance programmes: in
  Denmark 78–80; in Italy 121, 122; in
  Portugal 173; in Sweden 201; in
  Switzerland 208, 211; in the
  Netherlands 135; in the United
  Kingdom 222; *see also* methadone
methamphetamine 101
Miguel, Nuno 173
MILDT *see* Interdepartmental Mission for
  the Fight Against Drugs and Drug
  Addiction
mind-altering substances 1
minimum penalties: for illicit drug
  trafficking 20, 31, 35; in control of
  NPS 35
minority communities 229
Misdemeanours Act 2005 274
Misuse of Drugs Act 1971 (MDA) 220,
  228, 229
Mitterrand, François 17, 43–4
mobile dating apps 268
MONAR 154
money laundering 20, 91

moral model 118–19
morphine 2: and drug-related deaths 225;
  discovery 101; hypodermic 73; in
  Denmark 73–4; in Germany 101–4; in
  the United Kingdom 217; misuse 73
Morphinismus 104
mortality 186, 202
MSM *see* men who have sex with men
Müller, Andreas 111
multidisciplinary thinking 20
multi-level governance 34–6
multi-level participation 35
Multiple Streams Model 242
Murray, Robin 230

naloxone 266
National Association for a Drug-Free
  Society 197–8
National Association for Assistance to Drug
  Abusers 201
National Association for the Intervention
  with Drug Addiction (ANIT) 173
National Bureau for Drug Prevention
  153, 154
national drug policy: and EU policy 16;
  autonomy 13; variations in approach 20
national penalties 32
national policies 4–5; alcohol 34;
  harmonisation of 28–9, 241
National Strategy in the Fight Against
  Drugs (ENLCD) 164
Nazi Germany 104–5
Nederlandsche Cocaïnefabriek 129
needle and syringe programmes (NSPs)
  136, 256, 256, 257; *see also* syringe-
  exchange programmes; syringe provision
  programmes
needle parks 208–9
needles: providing 208; distribution 69;
  exchange programmes 33, 69, 89, 202;
  see also needle and syringe programmes
  (NSPs); syringe-exchange programmes;
  syringe provision programmes
neo-liberalism 227
Netherlands 3, 33, 128–42, 247–50; 1999;
  2002 Victor Act 137; and international
  drug policy 2; cannabis 129–31, 136–9,
  142, 288; cocaine 129, 135, 138; coffee
  shops 132–3, 136–7, 140, 141, 297;
  decriminalisation of hard drugs 134–5;
  harm reduction 135–6, 142, 244–5, 255;
  heroin 130, 133–6, 138, 141; history

and legal framework of drug policy 129–36; normalising drug problem 27–8; public health approach 278; recent policy 136–9
networks, of knowledge-based experts 18
New Labour 222, 232
new psychoactive substances (NPS) 266, 281–3; Framework Decision 32; in Portugal 169; in prisons 225; in the United Kingdom 223; minimum penalties 35; policy development 31–2; risk assessment and control of 14, 21, 214
NGOs *see* non-governmental organizations
night-time economy 227
non-drug using environments 77
non-governmental organizations 35, 47, 256, 261; in Belgium 69; in Italy 119, 122, 124–5; in Poland 150, 154; in Portugal 170, 173; in Sweden 197, 201; in Switzerland 214; in the Netherlands 135
nonmedical drug use 1
Nordic Council 76
Nordic Council of Ministers 76
Nordic countries 34, 76
normalisation 27–8, 69, 81, 227
North West Cohort Study 227
Norway: harm reduction 256; penalties for drug trafficking 76; public health approach 278, 279
NPS *see* new psychoactive substances
NSPs *see* needle and syringe programmes
NTA 222
'nuisance policy' 68
Nutt, David 223, 228, 230

Office for National Statistics (ONS) 228
ONS *see* Office for National Statistics
open borders 20
Open Society Foundation 48, 261
opiates 1
opioid substitution treatment (OST) 89, 135, 256, 256–8, 262, 265
opium: global trade 129; government monopolies in colonies 2; in Germany 102–3; in Switzerland 206; in the Netherlands 129, 133, 135; in the United Kingdom 217; international drug policy 2
Opium Act 1928 129, 141–2; 1976 revision 130–2

Opium Agency 103
Opium Protocol 1953 3
Opium Regie 129
organised crime 228
OST *see* opioid substitution treatment
out-of-work benefits 222
out-patient care 184
overdose deaths 23, 266

Pannella, Marco 115
paradigm changes 246–7
Patricio, Luis 173
PCOB *see* Permanent Control Opium Board
PDUs *see* problematic drugs users
peer counselling 256
penalties: aggravating circumstances 189; for drug dealing 117; for drug possession 117, 228, 273–6, 278, 283; for drug-related crimes 189–90; maximum 30, 31, 165, 197, 223, 274–5; minimum 20, 35, 107; national 32
people who inject drugs (PWID) 254–5, 263–5
performance-enhancing drugs 223
Permanent Control Opium Board (PCOB) 103
persuasion 41
Pervitin 105; *see also* Crystal Meth
PHARE programme 261
Physicians Against AIDS 201
pill testing programmes 167
Poland 149–61; cannabis 153, 157; current policy 159–61; drug legislation 154–9; drug offences 159; drug policy-setting institutions 153–4; drug possession 149, 155, 156–9, 273, 275, 278; drug treatment 280; drug use 150–3; harm reduction 154, 158–9; heroin 153
police sanctions 66
police searches 229–30
police unions 111
policy-based evidence 196
policy brokers 173
policy entrepreneurs 173–4
policy integration: and EU 28–36; 'hard harmonisation', 31–3, 36; multi-level governance 34–6; pathways to 31–6; 'soft convergence' 31, 33–4, 36
policy-making: process 242; policy window 252
policy-relevant knowledge 18, 24

310 Index

Polish Drug Policy Network (PDPN) 150, 160
Pompidou, Georges 3
Pompidou Group 3, 45, 255
poppy-based products 151
poppy cultivation 153
Portugal 164–77; and international drug policy 2; Commission for a National Drug Strategy (CNDS) 170–1; Commissions for the Dissuasion of Drug Addiction (CDTs) 168, 277 282; decriminalisation 28, 34; drivers of reform 169–76; drug possession 168, 169, 172, 176, 273–5; drug trafficking 165, 170, 172, 173; drug use 170; evidence and experts 171–2; harm reduction 173; history of drug law and policy 165–8; legal framework 168–9; National Plan for the Reduction of Addictive Behaviours and Dependencies 2013–2020 167–8; National Strategy in the Fight Against Drugs (ENLCD) 165; new psychoactive substances (NPS) 282; policy actors 172–3; Projecto VIDA 165, 171, 173, 175
poverty 119, 226
power, and control over knowledge and information 19
pragmatic policy initiatives 27
pragmatism 165
pre-exposure prophylaxis (PrEP) 264, 268
prescription 14, 101, 103, 155; frauds 74; regulations 73; requirement 101, 105
prevention campaigns 6
prevention programmes 89
preventive incarceration 68
prisons: and drug offences 225; NPS substances in 225; overcrowding 125, 172; see also imprisonment; incarceration
problematic drugs users (PDUs) 222, 230
prohibition 22; principle 15; prioritised over harm reduction 81
prohibitionist approach 2, 7, 29; in Italy 116–18, 121
Projecto VIDA 165, 171, 174, 175
proportionality, principle of 117, 170, 190
prosecution: alternatives to 96; policy 64–5
prostitution 61, 75
Provos 250
psychiatric asylums 114
psychiatric institutions 200
psychiatric societies 111

psychoactive substances 1
Psychoactive Substances Act 2016 (UK) 223
psychotherapy 109
psychotic illness 223
public addiction services (SerT) 120–2
public decision-makers 41
public health 21, 170–1; as 'legal good' 187; EU competencies 263; in the United Kingdom 220–21; protection 34, 182–3; see also public health-oriented approach
public health-oriented approach 6, 9, 165, 256; and drug possession 276–9; in Belgium 59–60, 69
public nuisance 65–8, 70
public order 141
public prosecutors 64, 65, 67; discretion 67–8, 92
public safety 67, 188–9
punishment, application of 69

quantitative thresholds 124
Quintanilha, Alexander 175

racial discrimination 229
racial hygiene 104–5
RAND Corporation 22, 24
raves 227
Reagan, Nancy 116
recreational drugs 223, 227
Red Cross 208
Reducing Demand, Restricting Supply, Building Recovery 222
referendums 211, 212
regulation 243
rehabilitation 69, 119–20; programmes 278, 280
Reich Central Office for Combating Drug Offenders 105
Reichs Work Group for Combating Narcotics 105
REITOX network 30, 45, 111
Release 230
resolutions 31
risk assessment 14, 21
risk behaviours 264, 265
risk reduction 69, 70; instruments 5, 6
risk society 227
roadside drug testing 91
Robiquet, Pierre 101
Rolleston Report 1926 217

Index   311

Romania 255, 264–5, 274, 278, 279, 282
Rosa, Alexandre 174, 175
Rotterdam 129, 133–5, 142
Runciman Report (2000) 223, 227

Santos, Alemida 170
Schengen agreement 18
Schengen Information System (SIS)
    database 18
school surveys 224
scientific evidence 249–50
Scotland 221, 225–6, 231
Scottish Social Attitudes survey 231
SEA *see* Single European Act
Second World War 2
security issues 63–8
security threats 24, 43
Senlis Council 48
SerT *see* public addiction sevices
Sertürner, Friedrich Wilhelm 101
Service of Narcotics Control 183
sexual health 268
Single Convention on Narcotic Drugs
    1961 3, 29, 61, 75, 100, 102,
    130, 272
single currency 28
Single European Act (SEA) 1986 16
single market 28
sinsemilla 223
skunk 223
Slovakia 275, 278, 282
Slovenia 248, 250, 273, 274, 288
smartphones 267–8
social assistance 222
social attitudes 230
social benefits 233
social change 226
social context 130
social control 61
social decline 63–4
Social Democrats: Germany 110;
    Sweden 198
'social' drug policy 77
social exclusion 79
social-health measures 64
social integration 28
socialisation 41, 54
Socialist Party; France 96, 97; Portugal 174
social learning 41
social marginalisation 115, 119, 170
social movements 5, 89, 151, 186,
    221, 250–1

social order 61, 129, 135, 250
social policy 77, 81, 84, 198, 254; and
    integration 28, 29, 35; dual-track 84;
    national 28, 29; principle of
    subsidiarity 29
social protection mechanisms 184
social rehabilitation 183, 191
social solidarity approach 119–20
social therapy 199, 203
social vulnerability 64
social workers 77, 78, 168, 208–10
Società della Ragione 125
societal maladaptation 76
societal mood 247–8
societal settings 247–8
Sócrates, José 170, 174, 175
'soft law' practices 31
SOMA 173
Soros, George 48, 261
Soviet model 261
Spain 182–93, 248, 250; cannabis 87,
    191–3, 286–7, 287–8; cocaine 182;
    counter-reforms 186; current policy
    187–93; drug possession 183–4, 187–8;
    drug trafficking 183–4, 188–9;
    Government Delegation to the National
    Plan on Drugs (DGPNSD) 186, 192;
    penitentiary legislation 191; public
    health approach 278
Spanish Federation of Cannabis
    Associations (FAC) 287
Spanish National Toxicology Institute 188
SPTT *see* Drug Addiction Treatment and
    Prevention Service
Standing Committee on Operational
    Cooperation on Internal Security
    (COSI) 21–3
stigmatisation 70, 119
Stoltenberg Commission 279
stop and search activity 229–30
subcultures 76, 77, 83–4, 106, 130, 196
subsidiarity 4, 29, 30, 32, 35, 208
substitution treatment 33, 34, 69
supervised injection sites 6, 109
Surinamese immigrants 134
Sweden 27–8, 33–4, 195–203, 278;
    alcohol policy 34; amphetamine 104–5;
    cannabis 197; drug policy design 196–8;
    drug trafficking 76; drug treatment
    198–9; harm reduction 201–2, 261–2;
    mental health legislation 199; new
    psychoactive substances (NPS) 282; zero

312 Index

tolerance policy 4, 5; Swiss Federal Office of Public Health 208
Switzerland 206–14; and international drug policy 2; cannabis 207, 212–13, 288; cocaine 206; 'four pillars' policy 210; harm reduction 208, 211–12, 214, 255–6; heroin 207, 208, 210; policy 206–13
symbolism 177
synthetic narcotics 2–3
Synthetic Narcotics Protocol 1948 3
syringe exchange programmes: Poland 154; Switzerland 209–211; *see also* needle and syringe programmes (NSPs); syringe provision programmes
syringe provision programmes 256; *see also* needle and syringe programmes (NSPs); syringe-exchange programmes

Tackling Drugs Together (TDT) 221
TDT *see* Tackling Drugs Together
Temmler Pharma 105
temperance homes 184
Terra Nova 97
TEU *see* Treaty on European Union
TFEU *see* Treaty on the Functioning of the European Union
therapeutic communities 122, 191, 199, 261–2
therapeutic treatment 69
think tanks 232
tobacco 1
Tokyo Rules *see* United Nations Standard Minimum Rules for Non-custodial Measures
tolerance 70
total institutions, critique of 78
toxins 196
transborder regions 68
Transform 230
Transnational Institute 48
transnational organized crime 23
Treaty of Amsterdam 1997 18, 20
Treaty on European Union (TEU) 13, 18
Treaty on the Functioning of the European Union (TFEU) 20, 21
Trekt Uw Plant (TUP) 287, 291
Trevi Group 17–19
Triads 133
TRI 151
tuberculosis 170
TUP *see* Trekt Uw Plant

Turkey 34
Turning Point 233

UKCSC *see* United Kingdom Cannabis Social clubs
UKDPC *see* UK Drug Policy Commission
UK Drug Policy Commission (UKDPC) 232, 251, 252
uncertainties 248
UN Drug Conventions 15
unemployment 141, 226
Union of the Danish Chiefs of Police 81
United Kingdom 3, 217–33; *1998 Ten Year Strategy* 221; addiction services 220–21; 'British system' 217; cannabis 220, 223–5, 228–31, 275, 288; cocaine 220, 224, 225; drivers of continuity and change 230–2; drug offences 220, 228–9; drug possession 275; drug trafficking 221; drug treatment 221–2; harm reduction 244–5; heroin 217, 220, 226; interventionist state 221–2; legal framework 228–30; new psychoactive substances (NPS) 282; policing practices, 228–30; policy 2, 217–23, 232–3; public health 220–21, 277; sentencing 228–30; trends in drug use 224–7
United Kingdom Cannabis Social Clubs (UKCSC) 288
United Nations 2; Special Session of the General Assembly 7
United Nations Standard Minimum Rules for Non-custodial Measures (Tokyo Rules) 276
United States 2, 97, 155
urban decline 63–4
urban delinquency 63
urban regeneration schemes 227
Uruguay 97; cannabis social clubs (CSCs) 286–7
Utrecht 288

Vaillant, Daniel 96, 97
Vereenigde Oostindische Compagnie (VOC) 129
Victor Act 2002 137

Wales 221, 225, 229, 232
Walt, G. 243
Wehrmacht 105
welfare: role of 119; reform 233; *see also* welfare-dependency; welfare state

welfare dependency 233
welfare state: replacement with
  punitive state 227; social-democratic
  type 198
well-being paradigm 247
Wimber, Hubert 111
World Health Organization (WHO) 164

young people 64, 130; attitudes to drugs
  227; criminal preventive barriers 81;
  decriminalisation of drug use 77; drug
  use 75–6, 224–6; from socially
  disadvantaged background 76; from
  upper middle classes 76; normalisation
of drug usage 81, 227; treatment of drug
  abusers 77–8
Young, Jock 226
youth centres 131–2
youth crime 76
youth culture 88, 130
youth movements 207
youth protest movement 106
youth rebellion 75
'Youth Without Drugs' initiative 211

zero-tolerance strategy 79, 80–4
Zipp-Aids project 209
Zürich 208–10, 214